After God – The Normative Power of the Will from the Nietzschean Perspective

Dia-Logos

Schriften zu Philosophie und Sozialwissenschaften
Studies in Philosophy and Social Sciences

Bd. /vol. 24

PETER LANG
EDITION

Marta Soniewicka

After God – The Normative Power of the Will from the Nietzschean Perspective

PETER LANG
EDITION

Bibliographic Information published by the Deutsche Nationalbibliothek
The Deutsche Nationalbibliothek lists this publication in the Deutsche Nationalbibliografie; detailed bibliographic data is available in the internet at http://dnb.d-nb.de.

Library of Congress Cataloging-in-Publication Data
Names: Soniewicka, Marta, author.
Title: After God - the normative power of the will from the Nietzschean perspective / Marta Soniewicka.
Description: New York : Peter Lang, 2017. | Series: Dia-logos, ISSN 1619-005X ; Vol. 24 | Includes bibliographical references.
Identifiers: LCCN 2017038352 | ISBN 9783631716403
Subjects: LCSH: Nietzsche, Friedrich Wilhelm, 1844-1900.
Classification: LCC B3317 .S61685 2017 | DDC 193--dc23 LC record available at https://lccn.loc.gov/2017038352

This publication was financially supported by the Jagiellonian University.

Translated by Aeddan Shaw

ISSN 1619-005X
ISBN 978-3-631-71640-3 (Print)
ISBN 978-3-631-73562-6 (E-PDF)
E-ISBN 978-3-631-73563-3 (EPUB)
E-ISBN 978-3-631-73564-0 (MOBI)
DOI 10.3726/b11875

Peter Lang – Frankfurt am Main · Berlin · Bruxelles · New York · Oxford · Warszawa · Wien

This publication has been peer reviewed.

www.peterlang.com

To the memory of my beloved Father

Table of Contents

Abbreviations

All original works by Friedrich Nietzsche listed below in: Nietzsche, F. 2009. Digital critical edition of the complete works and letters. Based on the critical text by G. Colli, and M. Montinari. Berlin, New York: de Gruyter 1967-. Ed. P. D'Iorio. http://www.nietzschesource.org/texts/eKGWB.

AC – Nietzsche, F. 1888. Der Antichrist. Fluch auf das Christenthum, Autorisierte Schriften. English edition: Nietzsche, F. 2005. The Anti-Christ (trans: Norman, J.). Cambridge: Cambridge University Press.

BVN – Nietzsche, F. 1851–1889. Briefe. English edition: Nietzsche, F. 1996. Selected Letters of Friedrich Nietzsche (trans: Middleton, Ch.). Indianapolis, Cambridge: Hackett Publishing Company.

CV – Nietzsche, F. 1872. Fünf *Vorrede*n zu fünf ungeschriebenen Büchern, Nachgelassene Schriften.

DD – Nietzsche, F. 1888. Dionysos-Dithyramben, Autorisierte Schriften.

DS – Nietzsche, F. 1873. Unzeitgemässe Betrachtungen – Erstes Stück: David Strauss der Bekenner und der Schriftsteller. English edition: Nietzsche, F. 2007. Untimely Meditations. Book 1 (trans: Hollingdale, R.J.). Cambridge: Cambridge University Press.

DW – Nietzsche, F. 1870. Die dionysische Weltanschauung, Nachgelassene Schriften.

EH – Nietzsche, F. 1888. Ecce homo. Wie man wird, was man ist, Autorisierte Schriften. English edition: Nietzsche, F. 2005. Ecce Homo (trans: Norman, J.). Cambridge: Cambridge University Press.

FW – Nietzsche, F. 1887. Die fröhliche Wissenschaft (la gaya scienza), neue Ausgabe mit einem Anhange: Lieder des Prinzen Vogelfrei. English edition: Nietzsche, F. 2001. The Gay Science. With a Prelude in German Rhymes and an Appendix of Songs (trans: Nauckhoff, H., poems trans: del Caro, A.). Cambridge: Cambridge University Press.

GD – Nietzsche, F. 1889. Götzen-Dämmerung oder Wie man mit dem Hammer philosophiert. English edition: Nietzsche, F. 2005. Twilight of the Idols (trans: Norman, J.). Cambridge: Cambridge University Press.

GM – Nietzsche, F. 1887. Zur Genealogie der Moral. Eine Streitschrift. English edition: Nietzsche, F. 2007. On The Genealogy of Morality (trans: Diethe, C.). Cambridge: Cambridge University Press.

GT – Nietzsche, F. 1878. Die Geburt der Tragödie. Oder Griechenthum und Pessimismus, neue Ausgabe mit dem Versuch einer Selbstkritik. English edition: Nietzsche, F. 2007. The Birth of Tragedy and Other Writings (trans: Speirs, R). Cambridge: Cambridge University Press.

HL – Nietzsche, F. 1874. Unzeitgemässe Betrachtungen – Zweites Stück: Vom Nutzen und Nachtheil der Historie für das Leben. English edition: Nietzsche, F. 2007. Untimely Meditations. Book 2 (trans: Hollingdale, R.J.). Cambridge: Cambridge University Press.

JGB – Nietzsche, F. 1886. Jenseits von Gut und Böse. Vorspiel einer Philosophie der Zukunft. English edition: Nietzsche, F. 2002. Beyond Good and Evil. Prelude to a Philosophy of the Future (trans: Norman, J.). Cambridge: Cambridge University Press.

M – Nietzsche, F. 1887. Morgenröthe. Gedanken über die moralische Vorurtheile, neue Ausgabe mit einer einführenden *Vorrede*. English edition: Nietzsche, F. 2005. Daybreak. Thoughts on the prejudices of morality (trans: Hollingdale, R.J.). Cambridge: Cambridge University Press.

MAI – Nietzsche, F. 1886. Menschliches, Allzumenschliches. Ein Buch für freie Geister, Erster Band, Neue Ausgabe mit einer einführenden *Vorrede*. English edition: Nietzsche, F. 2000. Human, All Too Human I (trans: Handwerk, G.). The Complete Works of Friedrich Nietzsche, vol. 2. Stanford: Stanford University Press.

MAII – Nietzsche, F. 1886. Menschliches, Allzumenschliches. Ein Buch für freie Geister, Zweiter Band, Neue Ausgabe mit einer einführenden *Vorrede*. English edition: Nietzsche, F. 2013. Human, All Too Human II (trans: Handwerk, G.). The Complete Works of Friedrich Nietzsche, vol. 4. Stanford: Stanford University Press.

NF – Nietzsche, F. 2009. Nachgelassene Fragmente 1869–1888. Digitale Kritische Gesamtausgabe Werke und Briefe von Friedrich Nietzsche auf der Grundlage der "Kritischen Gesamtausgabe Werke" (eKGWB)

NW – Nietzsche, F. 1889. Nietzsche contra Wagner. Aktenstücke eines Psychologen, Privatdrück.

PHG – Nietzsche, F. 1873. Die Philosophie im tragischen Zeitalter der Griechen, Nachgelassene Schriften. English edition: Nietzsche, F. 1911. Philosophy During the Tragic Age of the Greeks. In The Complete Works of Friedrich Nietzsche. Vol. Two Early Greek Philosophy (trans. Mügge, M.A.). New York: The Macmillan Company.

SE – Nietzsche, F. 1874. Unzeitgemässe Betrachtungen – Drittes Stück: Schopenhauer als Erzieher. English edition: Nietzsche, F. 2007. Untimely Meditations. Book 3 (trans: Hollingdale, R.J.). Cambridge: Cambridge University Press.

VM – Nietzsche, F. 1886. Vermischte Meinungen und Sprüche. Menschliches Allzumenschliches II. English edition: Nietzsche, F. 2013. Human, All Too Human II (trans: Handwerk, G.). The Complete Works of Friedrich Nietzsche, vol. 4. Stanford: Stanford University Press.

WA – Nietzsche, F. 1888. Der Fall der Wagner. Ein Musikanten-Problem. English edition: Nietzsche, F. 2005. The Case of Wagner: A Musician's Problem (trans: Norman, J.). Cambridge: Cambridge University Press.

WB – Nietzsche, F. 1876. Unzeitgemässe Betrachtungen – Viertes Stück: Richard Wagner in Bayreuth. English edition: Nietzsche, F. 2007. Untimely Meditations. Book 4 (trans: Hollingdale, R.J.). Cambridge: Cambridge University Press.

WL – Nietzsche, F. 1873. Über Wahrheit und Lüge im aussermoralischen Sinne, Nachgelassene Schriften. English edition: Nietzsche, F. 1911. On Truth and Falsity in Their Ultramoral Sense. In The Complete Works of Friedrich Nietzsche. Vol. Two Early Greek Philosophy (trans. Mügge, M.A.). New York: The Macmillan Company.

WS – Nietzsche, F. 1886. Der Wanderer und Sein Schatten. Menschliches Allzumenschliches II. English edition: Nietzsche, F. 2013. Human, All Too Human II (trans: Handwerk, G.). The Complete Works of Friedrich Nietzsche, vol. 4. Stanford: Stanford University Press.

ZA – Nietzsche, F. 1883–1885. Also sprach Zarathustra. Ein Buch für Alle und Keinen. English edition: Nietzsche, F. 2006. Thus Spoke Zarathustra. A Book for All and None (trans: del Caro, A.). Cambridge: Cambridge University Press.

Acknowledgments

This work is a translation of a modified version of my thesis on the subject of Nietzsche which was published in Polish in 2016. Professor Jacek Filek, of the Institute of Philosophy of the Jagiellonian University, inspired me to take up the study of Nietzsche when I took part in his seminar, a group which undertook the considerable task of reading *Thus Spoke Zarathustra* line by line. I would like to thank Professor Filek for teaching us to 'read well, slowly, deeply, looking cautiously before and aft, with reservations, with doors left open, with delicate eyes and fingers.' I would also like to thank the reviewers of the Polish version of this work: Professor Elżbieta Paczkowska-Łagowska, who I would like to thank not only for her kindness towards my work but also for the hard-to-overestimate effect she had on me during the time I spent studying philosophy at the Jagiellonian University, and Professor Paweł Pieniążek for his valuable critique. I would also like to thank Professor Robert Audi for his invaluable help and the many philosophical discussions we had and for which I am very grateful. I thank Professor Reiner Schmidt for his inspirational lecture on the German spirit. I would also like to thank all of my friends and colleagues for the discussions which allowed me to develop many of the thoughts to be found in this book.

A special thank you and debt of gratitude is extended to Professor Jerzy Stelmach, head of the Department of the Philosophy of Law and Legal Ethics of the Jagiellonian University, for his years of academic guidance, tremendous support in my ventures and for creating the welcoming conditions necessary for development in the team coordinated by him. The publication costs of the book were covered by a research grant for young researchers awarded by the Faculty of Law and Administration to a group headed by Dr Łukasz Kurek in 2015. I would also like to thank Professor Piotr Juchacz and Professor Karolina Cern, for their help in publishing this work abroad; as well as Dr Aeddan Shaw for his tremendous and excellent translation work. Unless otherwise indicated, all English citations and references included in the book were prepared with the use of existing translations by myself.

I am grateful to my family, since thanks to them 'I become who I am and who I must become.' I completed the Polish version of this book on the 20th anniversary of the death of my father – Igor Soniewicki – and it is to his memory that I dedicate this effort.

Krakow, September 2016

Introduction

A philosophy filled with spirit communicates some of this even to its opponents
Friedrich Nietzsche[1]

Tackling the philosophy of Friedrich Nietzsche is a challenge in many respects, with the difficulty paradoxically being the wealth of the available material. It is not only that he is one of the most widely known thinkers or the most closely examined but also that his words have more than once aroused the most extreme emotions and have been found to hold many secrets. Readers have access to the whole gamut of his collected works of philosophy, first drafts, manuscripts, the whole wealth of his correspondence as well as the numerous portraits and biographies available. We know what he read, what he wore, who he met and talked to, what he listened to, what he ate and where he travelled. Much of his thought has been picked over by commentators, such as the unremarkable, oft-overlooked sentence noted by Nietzsche one autumnal day in 1881 'I have forgotten my umbrella' (NF-1881,12[62]),[2] to which Jacques Derrida subsequently devoted an entire chapter of one of his books (Derrida 1981). Faced with such a wealth of material, one must learn the difficult art of selection, particularly in regard to the choice of literature. If one wanted to read everything which has been written about Nietzsche, they would probably be unable to write anything on the topic themselves. Nietzsche himself was right when he wrote the following to a friend at the beginning of his academic career:

> [O]ur whole way of working is quite horrible. The hundred books on the table in front of me are so many tongs which pinch out the nerve of independent thought (A letter to Carl von Gersdorff of April 6, 1867, Nietzsche 1996, 22).

When starting out on the way to researching the philosophy of Nietzsche, it is necessary to carefully select the thinkers that one wishes to focus on, especially as the differences in their interpretations are so significant. Those intellectually indebted to Nietzsche include such diverse thinkers as the father of psychoanalysis, Sigmund Freud; the sociologists Max Weber and Georg Simmel; the creator

---

1 A paraphrase of Nietzsche's quotation (MAII,VM-160, Nietzsche 2013, 66).
2 I follow the Colli-Montinari manuscript numeration given after the abbreviation of the German title of Nietzsche's work (see Nietzsche 2009). I add a reference to an exact edition of a particular work, followed by the page number only in the case of quotations.

of the philosophy of life, Henri Bergson; the existentialist Albert Camus; those engaged in the philosophy of values such as Max Scheler and Nicolai Hartmann; postmodernists such as Jacques Derrida, Michel Foucault and Gilles Deleuze; the pragmatist Richard Rorty; the head of the English analytical tradition, Bernard Williams and many others. The literature devoted to Nietzsche falls into two broad categories: those analysing his philosophy and those utilizing it. One may include in the former all of the theoretical and academic works where the authors have tried to delve deeper into the works of Nietzsche, patiently chewing over his words (Za-IV-*Mensch*). Many of these works provide a precise analysis of his philosophy. The second category includes authors in which his philosophical words have found the kind of fertile soil which has been quick to bear fruit – in other words, those for whom his philosophy has become part of their own philosophy. The problem with the former is that that they can 'grind' the thoughts of the philosopher too finely and thus reduce it to 'white dust' (Za-II-*Gelehrte*) which may disappear between our fingers as we seek to grasp it. The issue with the latter is that once rooted in their own thoughts, the philosophy of Nietzsche is hard to dig out and discern. One of the best examples which combined both approaches would be the original analysis conducted by Martin Heidegger, who in the process 'was able to reconstruct Nietzsche for himself', as Hans Georg Gadamer emphasised (Gadamer 2003, 124). Such was the intention of Heidegger, who himself admitted that 'every interpretation must not only take things from the text but must also, without forcing the matter, be able quietly to give something of its own, something of its *own* concerns' (Heidegger 1991b, 191).

Three periods are usually delineated in the work of Nietzsche: his aesthetic period (idealistic), his positivist phase and his prophetic (metaphysical) one (Löwith 1997). There is a temptation to take the philosophy from one of these periods and use it in one's own work or at least use the available texts selectively, choosing the aspects which best suit our own needs, something which Nietzsche himself specifically warned against (MAII,VM-137).[3] The life work of a philosopher constitutes a whole and it is exactly as such that it will be treated in this book. It is only this kind of reading which can allow his philosophy to be shown in full, without reducing it to the critical elements that this philosopher is most frequently identified with. Aside from the critical elements which are focused around his theory of being (things in themselves), the theory of knowledge (truth) and the theory

3 'The worst readers are those who behave like plundering soldiers: they take the few things they can use, leave the rest dirty and disordered, and slander the whole' (Nietzsche 2013, 60).

of values (Christian morality), which are the subject of the first part of this work, Nietzsche offered a remarkably important but frequently overlooked positive program in his philosophy. It is based on a number of fundamental conceptions which will form the body of the second part of the work, namely: the will to power, the *Übermensch*,[4] the bestowing virtue and the notion of the eternal recurrence.

Another problem frequently associated with researching the work of Nietzsche is the unique style of the author. He is an anti-systemic philosopher, who resists analytical categorization; he is also anti-theoretical – it is a philosophy of life that escapes the academic mindset. It is neither justified to claim that it is a philosophy devoid of meaning nor that any serious attempt to utilise his philosophy must also have an anti-theoretical basis (Williams 2006). In his scepticism of philosophical systems of the type created by Kant or Hegel, Nietzsche was a faithful pupil of Arthur Schopenhauer, who wrote:

> A *system of thoughts* must always have an architectonic coherence, i.e. a coherence in which one part always supports another without the second supporting the first, so the foundation stone will ultimately support all the parts without itself being supported by any of them, and the summit will be supported without itself supporting anything (Schopenhauer 2010, 5).

One can also find a healthy scepticism of such architectonic works in Søren Kierkegaard, who wryly stated that '[t]he philosopher of systems is, as a man, like someone who builds a castle, but lives next door in a shanty. Such a fantastical being does not himself live within what he thinks' (Kierkegaard in Jaspers 1955, 25). Nietzsche was unable to play a role in any academic discipline or make a home for himself in any philosophical system primarily because he himself did not want it since his own temperament forbade it – an eternal desire to question and pursue, an all-consuming curiosity which led him on constantly towards new problems.

For Nietzsche, *philosophy was life*, deeply rooted in his existence and his experience (FW-*Vorrede*-1). In this respect he was a follower of the philosophers of antiquity:

> The Stoics, for instance, declared explicitly that philosophy, for them, was an 'exercise.' In their view, philosophy did not consist in teaching an abstract theory – much less in the exegesis of texts – but rather in the art of living. It is a concrete attitude and determinate lifestyle, which engages the whole existence. The philosophical act is not situated merely on the cognitive level, but on that of the self and of being. It is a progress which causes us to *be* more fully (Hadot 1999, 82–83).

---

4 In the English translations of Nietzsche, one can find different notions used to give the meaning of *Übermensch*, such as 'superman' or 'overman', none of which is precise enough, thus I will retain the original term in my further considerations.

Thus, Nietzsche claimed that it is only worth reading that which is written in blood, (Za-I-*Lesen*), and to talk about the things that one has personally overcome:

> One should speak only where one is not permitted to keep silent; and speak only of what one has overcome – everything else is chatter, 'literature,' lack of breeding. My writings speak *only* of my overcomings: 'I' am in them along with everything that was inimical to me, *ego ipsissimus*, in fact, if a prouder expression is allowed, *ego ipsissimum* (MAII-*Vorrede*-1, Nietzsche 2013, 3).[5]

Nietzsche feared that he would not be understood by those who had not experienced something similar (FW-*Vorrede*-1), since in his view one only has access to that which has been encountered and overcome (EH-*Bücher*-1).[6] As he put it, '[o]ne hears only those questions to which one is able to find an answer' (FW-196, Nietzsche 2001, 140). In his opinion, the most important creation of a philosopher is his own life and his works are a secondary product since every philosopher is first of all a philosopher for oneself and only then for other people (NF-1873,29[205]; NF-1874,34[37]). In his letter to Lou Salomé of September 16, 1882 he admits that, when he was lecturing in Basel, he himself learned that you can disprove a philosophical system, 'but you cannot disapprove the person behind it' (Nietzsche 1996, 192).[7] For him, philosophy is not only about works but also the interpretation of them, something which should be noted as an indication of how to read his works. Good advice was furnished in this regard by Karl Jaspers when he wrote that '[t]o understand a thinker means to understand his deepest motives', following the threads of his statements allows us to reach their essence and to understand the problems posed by them in their fullest sense (Jaspers 1961, 48). Nietzsche claimed that even one's physical state, including the illnesses one suffers from, has a powerful impact on one's philosophy (FW-*Vorrede*-3). One

---

5 This is reminiscent of the famous quotation by Ludwig Wittgenstein, 'what we cannot talk about we must pass over in silence' (Wittgenstein 2002, 3).

6 Nietzsche's Zarathustra frequently repeats, paraphrasing the Holy Gospel, '[h]e who has ears to hear, let him hear!' (e.g. Za-III-*Gesicht*-1, Nietzsche 2006a, 125). Similar thoughts can be found in the Preface to *Tractatus Logico-Philosophicus*, '[p]erhaps this book will be understood only by someone who has himself already had the thoughts that are expressed in it – or at least similar thoughts' (Wittgenstein 2002, 3).

7 This way of thinking is familiar to Witold Gombrowicz, who claims, '[w]e forget that man does not exist only to convince another man. He exists in order to win, to win to his side, to seduce, charm, possess. Truth is not a matter of arguments. It is only a matter of attraction, that is, a pulling toward. Truth does not make itself real in an abstract contest of ideas, but in a collision of persons' (Gombrowicz 2012, 89).

should not underestimate this fact, especially as the philosopher himself lost his wits and fell into a ten-year lethargy which ended only with his death.

Nietzsche's largely aphoristic style is a consequence of the anti-systematic nature of his philosophy.[8] It calls for a special kind of interpretation, often harder than is the case with traditional texts, as the author himself emphasised (Za-*Vorrede*-8). As Hanna Buczyńska-Garewicz notes, 'the essence of the aphorism is its conceptual independence: it is not reliant on premises, nor does it lead to conclusions, it speaks for itself' (Buczyńska-Garewicz 2013 (trans. A. Shaw), 11). Nietzsche treated his own aphorisms like the Riddle of the Sphinx, as something to be decoded and guessed (Za-*Vorrede*-8; NF-1885–37[35]). They are the result of the most intimate and intricate debates and discussions which the author had enjoyed for years before; they express thoughts which were deeply rooted in both his heart and mind (NF-1885–37[35]), joining his personal experiences with the feelings that were their source. Nietzsche regarded himself as the master of this form of philosophy:

> I am the first German to have mastered the aphorism; and aphorisms are the forms of 'eternity'; my ambition is to say in ten sentences what other people say in a book, – what other people do not *say* in a book... (GD-*Streifzuege*-51, Nietzsche 2005b, 223).

The author also had a love of utilising an 'army of metaphors', which he used instead of propositions together with images and intuitions instead of arguments, as a result 'making his thoughts "dance"' (Buczyńska-Garewicz 2013 (trans. A. Shaw), 15). The metaphor of dance is important in the context of Nietzsche's thought since he wanted thinking to be light, joyful, personal and, above all, all encompassing, able to express that which could not be said directly.[9] The flow-

---

8 The aphoristic style was utilised by Nietzsche for the first time when he wrote *Human, All Too Human* (1878–1879), developed in *The Wanderer and His Shadow* (1880), and reaching its final form in *Daybreak* (1881). It is primarily a literary style, used previously by many writers such as La Rochefoucauld, Chamfort, Montaigne, Leopardi and Lichtenberg, writers who he particularly prized. The difference lies in the fact that Nietzsche created and conveyed his whole philosophical message in this style and his thoughts are not separate, detached from each other remarks. Wittgenstein adopted a similar style, writing his most important philosophical works in paragraphs and numbering his theses.

9 Nietzsche's Zarathustra says, '[o]nly in the dance do I know how to speak the parables of the highest things – and now my highest parable remained unspoken in my limbs! My highest hope remained unspoken and unredeemed!' (Za-II-*Grablied*, Nietzsche 2006a, 87). This emphasis on the importance of dance is connected to the idea of ancient mysticism which fascinated Nietzsche, where 'dance joined the Gods and

ing pen of the philosopher and his linguistic talent placed him, in the opinion of Gadamer, alongside Heine as the greatest German stylist (Gadamer 2003). Thomas Mann expressed a similar opinion, regarding Nietzsche as an essayist of the highest calibre (Mann 1959). This style does not lend itself, however, to unequivocal interpretations and, since one may find thousands of aphorisms in the work of Nietzsche, each may mean exactly what one wants them to mean, as Karl Löwith noted so aptly (Löwith 1969). Thus, in order to avoid the temptation to falsify his philosophy by placing his thoughts out of context among my own argumentation (cf. Colli 1994),[10] I intend to quote Nietzsche's statements that are crucial to the problem to be analysed prior to my further deliberations. Less important quotations which will constitute confirmations or completions of the analysis conducted will be supplied in the footnotes.

When interpreting, it is vital to follow the recommendations of the author himself, who urged us to 'read well, that is to say, to read slowly, deeply, looking cautiously before and aft, with reservations, with doors left open, with delicate eyes and fingers' (M-*Vorrede*-5, Nietzsche 2005a, 5). Indispensable in this regard is the advice that, in order to understand a philosopher, one must first want to listen to them, assume that they are right and try to think with them (cf. Colli 1994; Jaspers 1961).[11]

Another difficulty in interpreting the work of Nietzsche are the numerous aporias which are encountered in his works. As Giorgio Colli remarked, 'Nietzsche said everything and everything against that' (Colli 1994 (trans. A. Shaw), 143). These contradictions are not simply accidental but rather a particular expression of a way of philosophizing which allows the author to show the limits of rational thought and to defy reason. A deep sense of these contradictions which one cannot resolve with force but should rather accept is clearly expressed, albeit in a different context, by Ryszard Przybylski:

> [D]uring the triumph of rationalist thought we learned that contradictions are the curse of mankind. (…) They irritate reason. Human thought became used to anti-thesis and antimony but always strove to avoid them, either by only choosing one of the values

---

humans on the same level of existence' (Kerényi 1997 (trans. A. Shaw), 27). In this regard, Nietzsche wrote that he only believed in a God that could dance (Za-I-*Lesen*); the motif of dance also occurs many times in *Thus Spoke Zarathustra*.

10 Nietzsche emphasizes, '*[c]are in citation* (…). Every word, every idea wants to live only among *its own society*: that is the moral of a select style' (MAII,WS-111, Nietzsche 2013, 203–204).

11 Nietzsche complains, in Zarathustra's words, that 'they talk about me, but no one thinks – about me!' (Za-III-*Tugend*-2, Nietzsche 2006a, 134).

> available or one of the claims which was correct for healthy reasoning, or by paradoxically making them agree (*coincidentia oppositorum*), which – in turn – pleased all manner of mystics (…). Contradiction has a deeper sense when we see it in its own setting which so unsettles reason. Resolving antimony means that we deprive it of that deeper sense and weaken its experience. One should adopt and accept antimonies and go beyond the realm of logic. Escaping into antithesis is a curse. In essence, truth is born from experiencing two contradictory values (Przybylski 1993 (trans. A. Shaw), 31).

Nietzsche required his readers to be confronted by antimony and issues which are not to be solved in just one way – they are there to allow us to grasp, albeit intuitively, something which is not understandable. Hannah Arendt correctly gauged that Nietzsche belongs to the group of philosophers utilising the thought-experiment, somewhat rare literary style (Arendt 1981b).[12] Instead of using rational arguments, he often utilises provocations and stylistic tricks which are intended to work on the reader's emotions since his aim was to make the reader not only read his thoughts but to experience them as well. In the Preface to *On the Genealogy of Morality*[13] he states this expressly, '[w]ith regard to my *Zarathustra*, for example, I do not acknowledge anyone as an expert on it if he has not, at some time, been both profoundly wounded and profoundly delighted by it' (GM-*Vorrede*-8, Nietzsche 2007a, 9). He deliberately provokes, formulating his thoughts in such a way that they sound like crimes or mere foolishness to unadjusted ears and he claims that his works are dangerous for lesser souls and a challenge to the higher types (JGB-30). As a result of their extreme thought experiments, the works of Nietzsche have been termed the 'school of suspicion'[14] (as well as contempt and insolence), something noted by the philosopher himself in the Preface to *Human, All Too Human* (MAI-*Vorrede*-1). Nevertheless, he was the continuator of the modern project of philosophy which had weighed up and deliberated over all of the certainties of human reasoning since Descartes, leaving behind only 'rainbow-bridge of concepts' (NF-1885,41[4]). It may still be seen that '[t]he so-called paradoxes of an author at which a reader takes offense often stand not in the author's book at all, but in the reader's head', as Nietzsche

---

12 Nietzsche himself describes his philosophy as experimental (NF-1888,16[32]).

13 I use the translation of the title of *Zur Genealogie der Moral* which is more accurate than the frequently quoted *On the Genealogy of Morals* since Nietzsche meant Christian *morality* (in singular) in his work.

14 The term 'the masters of suspicion', used with reference to Nietzsche, Freud and Marx, was popularised by Paul Ricœur, who – undoubtedly referring to Nietzsche's own words – regarded the three as the masters of hermeneutics, using suspicion as a philosophical method (Ricœur 1974).

wrote (MAI-185, Nietzsche 2000, 133). Paraphrasing Kierkegaard, one may thus come to the conclusion that the works of Nietzsche are of the kind which act as a mirror – everyone can see themselves within them (Jaspers 1955).[15] It seems that Jaspers was justified in claiming that the effect of the philosophy of Nietzsche is 'to enchant and then to disappoint, to seize and then to leave one standing unsatisfied as if hands and heart remained empty' (Jaspers 1955, 46). The intention of the philosopher is to find within us that which is true for us.

The philosophy of Nietzsche, based on his own personal experiences, created in an aphoristic and paradoxical style, using thought experiments, contradictions and provocation, is not so much a study of a particular field but rather a school for brave and critical thinking akin to the Socratic method. In Nietzsche's opinion, thoughts and values are born out of necessity, like a tree bears fruit without regard for whether anyone finds them to be tasty, '[b]ut of what concern is that to the trees? And of what concern is it to *us* philosophers?' (GM-*Vorrede*-2, Nietzsche 2007a, 4). Because of these unique features, it is a dangerous philosophy and that is why young people were warned against reading certain works of the philosopher.[16] He himself warned them by writing that they should not regard his writings as directions but rather as questions to consider which must be defended against exceptions and counter claims. He added that he was not a genius, that intelligence had not fallen upon him like manna from heaven, and that he did not have any insight into what lies within certain phenomena (NF-1876,23[156]). Nietzsche did not want to be read verbatim, to 'be believed', and thus he not only created art but the reading of his works is also a form of art, as Thomas Mann emphasised (Mann 1959).

The greatest misunderstanding which has sprung up around the philosophy of Nietzsche has its source in the attempts to uncover in his thoughts a 'redemptive formula', as Stanisław Brzozowski mockingly puts it:

> Nietzscheanism! It is as funny as abstract Marxism. (…) Nietzsche taught how to live, be and create life, work on one's own issues. The individual creative act cannot be a doctrine (Brzozowski 2012 (trans. A. Shaw), 42).

---

15 Remarkable in this context are the words of Zarathustra, who looked at himself in the mirror in a dream, 'when I looked into the mirror I cried out, and my heart was shaken; for I did not see myself there, but a devil's grimace and scornful laughter' (Za-II-*Kind*, Nietzsche 2006a, 63).

16 Hans-Georg Gadamer heard such cautionary words from his father when he was sixteen, a result of which was of course that he read the forbidden works immediately (*Thus Spoke Zarathustra* and *Beyond Good and Evil*), resulting in his longstanding dislike of the author (Gadamer 2003).

Nietzsche's philosophy has found many followers, against the wishes of the philosopher himself as expressed through the mouth of Zarathustra (Za-I-*Tugend*-3; Za-III-*Vorübergehen*). As Löwith notes, Nietzsche was separated from his 'followers' by a tremendous chasm (Löwith 1969). He belongs to a group of philosophers that one cannot follow, either in terms of style or content, without seeming ridiculous. One may also not accord oneself privileged access or insight into his philosophy, which was the personal experience of the author himself; rather, Nietzsche's philosophy should be treated as a source of inspiration for the interpretation of the problems posed therein. Despite many of the misunderstandings surrounding the reading of Nietzsche, his philosophy does not need to be defended as he noted in a letter to Carl Fuchs, '[i]t is not necessary at all – not even desirable – that you should argue in my favor; on the contrary, a dose of curiosity, as in the presence of a foreign plant, with an ironic resistance, could seem to me an incomparably more intelligent attitude' (BVN-1888,1075, Nietzsche 1996, 305).[17]

I intend to treat the intellectual achievements of Nietzsche with the requisite respect and to look at their most important aspects with curiosity in this work. To this end I do not have to agree with his philosophy. As he himself said in words which may be regarded as a motto for my approach here, '[a] book filled with spirit communicates some of this even to its opponents' (MAII,VM-160, Nietzsche 2013, 66). Despite my own personal rejection of the vision of the world proposed by Nietzsche, I intend to do justice to his remarkable insight, to his courage visible in the questions that he posed and to his profound exploration of the greatest philosophical aporias of our age.

17 A Letter to Carl Fuchs of July 29, 1888.

Part I.
The ontological and epistemological assumptions of Nietzsche's philosophy

Chapter 1. The meaning of the 'death of God' and its ontological consequences

the greatest events
in man's life
are the birth and death
of God (...)
life without god is possible
life without god is impossible
Tadeusz Różewicz[18]

The claim concerning the 'death of God' is one of the best-known of Nietzsche's thoughts, arguably the key to his philosophy. In this brief sentence, as Heidegger notes, one can see the entirety of Nietzsche's reflections on metaphysics (Heidegger 2002). The interpretation of these few words comprises an excellent entry point for my further considerations. The famous formulation of 'God is dead' (*Gott ist todt*) is to be found in a number of places in Nietzsche's works. Nietzsche first writes the words in his notebook in the autumn of 1881 (NF-1881,12[77]; NF-1881,14[25]; NF-1881,14[26]). The most famous fragment regarding the 'death of God', however, is to be found in the work published a year later, *The Gay Science*:

> Haven't you heard of that madman who in the bright morning lit a lantern and ran around the marketplace crying incessantly, 'I'm looking for God! I'm looking for God!' Since many of those who did not believe in God were standing around together just then, he caused great laughter. (...) 'Where is God?' he cried; 'I'll tell you! *We have killed him* – you and I! We are all his murderers. But how did we do this? How were we able to drink up the sea? Who gave us the sponge to wipe away the entire horizon? What were we doing when we unchained this earth from its sun? Where is it moving now? Where are we moving to? Away from all suns? Are we not continually falling? And backwards, sidewards, forwards, in all directions? Is there still an up and a down? Aren't we straying as though through an infinite nothing? Isn't empty space breathing at us? (...) The holiest and the mightiest thing the world has ever possessed has bled to death under our knives: who will wipe this blood from us? (...) Is the magnitude of this deed not too great for us? Do we not ourselves have to become gods merely to appear worthy of it? There was never a greater deed – and whoever is born after us will on account of this deed belong to a higher history than all history up to now!' (...) [O]n the same day the madman forced his way into several churches and there started singing his *requiem aeternam deo*. Led out and called to account, he is said always to have replied nothing

18 From the poem entitled *Without* (Różewicz 2008, 254).

but, 'What then are these churches now if not the tombs and sepulchres of God?'" (FW-125, Nietzsche 2001, 119–120).

The greatest recent event – that 'God is dead'; that the belief in the Christian God has become unbelievable[19] – is already starting to cast its first shadow over Europe. (...) [F]or many people's power of comprehension, the event is itself far too great, distant, and out of the way even for its tidings to be thought of as having arrived yet. Even less may one suppose many to know at all *what* this event really means – and, now that this faith has been undermined, how much must collapse because it was built on this faith, leaned on it, had grown into it – for example, our entire European morality. This long, dense succession of demolition, destruction, downfall, upheaval that now stands ahead: who would guess enough of it today to play the teacher and herald of this monstrous logic of horror, the prophet of deep darkness and the eclipse of the sun the like of which has probably never before existed on earth? (...) [W]e philosophers and 'free spirits' feel illuminated by a new dawn; our heart overflows with gratitude, amazement, forebodings, expectation – finally the horizon seems clear again, set out to face any danger; (...) the sea, *our* sea, lies open again; maybe there has never been such an 'open sea'. (FW-343, Nietzsche 2001, 199).[20]

An analysis of the above extracts begins with the formulation 'God is dead'. The utterance of the madman from the abovementioned paragraph, is different from that of the fool in Psalm 14, who in his heart claims 'there is no God' (Ps 14,1)[21] since, after all, the claim that God is dead rests on the notion that God must earlier have lived (see Kaufmann 1968; Heidegger 2002). In the cited fragment, the accusation is made that God has not merely died as much as *he has been killed* and it is exactly this unimaginable act which arouses such emotions. It gives a completely new sense to the death of God, which is not only a fact but becomes in Nietzsche an *act* (De Lubac 1998). Nietzsche attributes the 'death of God' to people; one of the factors contributing to the murder is that people wanted to remove the omniscient witness capable of seeing all of their iniquities (NF-1883,22[1]).[22] In the fourth part of *Thus Spoke Zarathustra*, the figure of 'the ugliest man' (*der hässlichste Mensch*)[23] emerges as the

---

19 Nietzsche's play on words: *un-glaub-würdig* means that belief has become unworthy of belief.

20 This paragraph is to be found in the fifth part of the book, added by Nietzsche to the second edition in 1887 (after *Also Spoke Zarathustra* had been published).

21 All scripture quotations are taken from *The Holy Bible*. King James Version, New York Bible Society since 1809, printed in Great Britain.

22 Cf. FW-*Vorrede*-4; NW-*Epilog*-2 (Nietzsche refers to an anecdote about a girl who is surprised that God is everywhere and thinks that it amounts to unprecedented spying).

23 The word *hässlich* stems from the term *Hass* (hate) and was originally used in relation to someone full of hate as well as to someone deserving hatred (Grimm 1971, Bd. 10, 556–558, entry 'häszlich'). The paradox of this person is that out of hatred for himself

killer of God (Za-IV-*Mensch*). From the mouth of Zarathustra comes the philosophical thought that God killed himself with human hands (NF-1881,12[157]; NF-1882,1[75]), the main reason and cause being his love for people (Za-II-*Mitleidige*; NF-1882,4[200]; NF-1883,12[1]; NF-1883,13[19]). Nietzsche equates God's perfect love for people with pity; pity kills since one who pities suffers at the suffering of others and therefore becomes a kind of victim. Nietzsche terms pity for people to be God's hell and also his crucifixion (Za-*Vorrede*-3). The transformation of the God of the Old Testament as a severe father into the merciful God of the New Testament, who gives up his own son as a sacrifice for humankind, is an incalculable contradiction for Nietzsche (FW-140) as well as the main cause of his demise.

In the opinion of Eric Voegelin, Nietzsche 'probed the motivations and he suffered under the fate that made him participate in the assassination. But he neither planned it nor committed it' (Voegelin 1975, 166). In order to cope with this, Nietzsche tries to turn this lament for the loss of God into a joyful awareness of a consciously made act of choice (NF-1881,12[77]). However, for this to be true, one must first understand the act. Thus, it is worth asking after Paul Ricœur, '[w]hich god is dead?' (Ricœur 1974, 445). For Nietzsche, it is the Christian God (NF-1885,34[5]), or, to be more precise, the 'moral God' (NF-1886,5[71]) and the metaphysical God (Heidegger 1991a; Heidegger 1977). In the criticism of the dead faith of Christianity made by Nietzsche, one may discern two main aspects: 1) references to an *archaic-naïve structure of the world* which is simply unbelievable; and 2) the unmasking of a *Christian vision of the world deprived of faith in the transcendence* which itself is baseless without this faith.

I. Unbelievable belief

Starting with the *unbelievable belief*, one may understand it as harmful when it stems from the need of: a) retribution; b) consolation; c) explanation. Faith based on the idea of retribution, where God punishes for evil (visiting illness, bad luck and disaster on people and ultimately by creating hell) and rewards good (bestowing luck, health, offspring and happiness upon them and by making heaven) is, as Ricœur notes, an archaic form of religious feeling (Ricœur 1974). It may provide us with a sense of security but it is remarkably superficial (Za-II-*Tugendhafte*). This archaic form of religious feeling based on 'the fear of punishment and the desire for protection' was questioned in the Old Testament, where the true yet tragic faith of Job is juxtaposed with the blind faith of his friends (Ricœur 1974,

he killed God, who was a perfect compensation for human imperfection, and ends up hating himself even more.

455). The relationship between faith and redemption may be understood in the same manner as Saint Thomas Aquinas explained the Aristotelian relationship of the virtues to the good life (MacIntyre 2007; cf. Eckhart 2009, sermon 13b). Faith is an internal resource whose goal is redemption, meaning that one may not understand redemption without faith or achieve it with the aid of any other means. A life rich in faith is thus not only good in terms that it guarantees the achievement of a goal but is itself a reward for the believer. Those who expect rewards from God for their good conduct are charged by Meister Eckhart as those who seek to 'barter with our Lord' and thus err since true faith, just like love, does not demand anything in return but is itself a gift (Eckhart 2009, sermon 6, 67).

Faith in God, sheltering us from reality, is also an archaic form of religious feeling. Seeking consolation in God (M-90) stems from a spiritual weakness on the part of humans and is a form of anaesthetic according to Nietzsche (Za-I-*Lehrstuehle*). Nietzsche also accuses Christianity of selling people a harmful lie (NF-1880,6[403]), the result of *ressentiment*[24] felt by the weak who seek consolation in the idea that they will be rewarded for their earthly miseries in the afterlife, something which I will return to in the third chapter. The naïve form of Christianity, which sees in the afterlife an escape from the world of today, is defined by him as 'Platonism for the "people"' (JGB-*Vorrede*). Yet it is worth adding that also Christian thinkers refuse to treat religion as a substitute for reality and prosperity or as a source of comfort, holding that this would interfere with true faith (Weil 2002).

Nietzsche mocks the idea of faith based on needs, which reduces God to a 'stopgap' (*Lückenbüsser*)[25] to human frailty and weakness, as well as ignorance. The debate between science and religion is often based on exactly such an approach, where the idea of God as a useful hypothetical explanation of natural processes was gradually discredited by science.[26] This same reasoning is used against treat-

---

24 The French word *ressentiment*, used by Nietzsche, has a broader meaning than the English word 'resentment'; 'it possesses a peculiar strong nuance of a lingering hate that our English word (…) does not always carry', as Andrew Tallon explains (Tallon in Scheler 1994, 5). Thus, I will use the word *ressentiment* in all the contexts in which I refer to the meaning of the word as given by Nietzsche.

25 In direct translation this word means 'replacement', 'surrogate' but, at the same time, it is also a play on words as it contains the word *Büsser*, meaning penitent. According to Nietzsche, God may not atone for people's spiritual shortcomings, an idea connected with his claim that Jesus may not take the sin of mankind upon himself.

26 In the famous anecdote about a conversation between Laplace and Napoleon concerning the best model for the movement of planets, Laplace is to have said that God was a superfluous hypothesis in his model. A similar thesis is present in the work of other scientists such as Stephen Hawking and Richard Dawkins, who hold that the

ing God as a cognitive crutch, defined by theologians as the 'God-of-the-gaps' argument (*Lückenbüßer-Gott*) and regarded as false.[27] The German theologian, Dietrich Bonhoeffer, noted in a letter to Eberhard Bethge that religious people often talk about God when they perceive human capabilities as having failed; they call upon God to help 'either for the so-called solving of insoluble problems or as support in human failure – always, that is to say, helping out human weakness or on the borders of human existence' (Bonhoeffer 1959, 124). The need to rely on God decreases in proportion to the increase of human knowledge until we finally understand that God becomes somehow redundant or relegated to the sidelines of people's lives. At the same time, as Bonhoeffer writes, '[one] should like to speak of God not on the borders of life but at its centre' (Bonhoeffer 1959, 124).

It is hard to escape the impression that the interpretation of Christianity portrayed by Nietzsche presents but a caricature of God; he is attacking the sociology of Christianity, not religion, as Henri de Lubac notes (De Lubac 1998).[28] In this respect, Ricœur regards this critique as having done Christianity a favour as it effectively cleansed it, leaving it open for true faith to emerge, beyond reproach and control (Ricœur 1974, 440).[29] In the opinion of the French philosopher, Nietzsche wanted to return to the Judaeo-Christian roots of faith which had been perverted and only partially assimilated. Nietzsche, according to Jaspers, is opposing Christianity out of Christian motivations based on his own experience (Jaspers 1961). In this regard, Nietzsche is in agreement with thinkers such as Kierkegaard in sharply criticizing all forms of simplified Christianity which amount to mere tomfoolery in no way reminiscent of the Gospels (Kierkegaard 1944). It is thus nothing strange that Nietzsche-Zarathustra is called 'the most pious of all those who do not believe in God', whose piety and excessive honesty no longer let him believe (Za-IV-*Dienst,* Nietzsche 2006a, 210–211). His criticism of Christianity

---

argument for the nonexistence of a God is that an idea of a Being who had engineered the natural order is not necessary for a scientific explanation of the universe.

27 In nature and its laws there may not be any loopholes or gaps for the existence of God to be acknowledged (see Ratzsch 2013). The term *Lückenbüsser* was used in relation to God by Carl Friedrich von Weizsäcker in a book devoted to the image of the world presented by physics (1943), and which was referred to by Bonhoeffer. It is difficult, however, to say whether Weizsäcker was inspired by reading *Thus Spoke Zarathustra*.

28 Nietzsche's relationship with Christianity is ambivalent, with derision and admiration in equal measure for the teachings of Christ, on the one hand, and a hostile opposition to its contemporary interpretations which warp it, on the other.

29 It is worth adding that true faith can take the form of a naïve total trust in God, typical of children; it can be the most precious kind of faith that the aforementioned critique does not refer to (cf. Mt 18, 2–3).

stems from the passion that he felt for its subject matter. One may thus see in this attitude a desire to be set free of any knowledge and considerations of God, stemming from the deepest faith, something that Meister Eckhart expressed in the words, 'I pray to God to make me free of God' (Eckhart 2009, sermon 87, 424).[30]

The question arises, however, of whether Nietzsche ever accepted the possibility of honest and deep faith in his times or whether the only alternative to the inadequate and archaic form of faith was nihilism? He is certainly surprised by faith (Za-*Vorrede*-2) and is afraid of taking faith away from believers as 'they go on with their dream in the midst of a world that is waking' (De Lubac 1998, 50); he also thinks it is a very rare, private form of existence (NF-1887,10[135]).[31] As Nietzsche himself mentions in his notes, he knew real Christians and accorded them utmost respect – he also gave himself the right to combat Christianity because he himself had been raised in a spiritual house and manner (NF-1888,24[1](6)). He puts forward the thesis that the logical development of an authentic Christian is his or her overcoming of Christianity. God must die in order to give birth to the *Übermensch* – in order to foster human full autonomy and self-responsibility. This notion would be developed in the thoughts of other philosophers such as Max Scheler, in which a person appears terribly lonely and absolutely reliant on oneself - taking full responsibility for their existence and for the world (Scheler 1991).

Nietzsche's problem is that his attempt to move beyond a criticism of the forms of faith failed as Ricœur writes:

> His aggression against Christianity remains caught up in the attitude of resentment; the rebel is not, and cannot be, at the same level as the prophet. Nietzsche's major work remains an accusation of accusation and hence falls short of a pure affirmation of life (Ricœur 1974, 447).

His radical rejection of this form of faith drew a creative energy to his philosophy and, by placing himself in opposition to Christianity, he could never become the true pagan, as Löwith claims (Löwith 1957).

---

30 Nietzsche invokes this quotation in *The Gay Science* (FW-292).

31 A similar thought can be found in the works of Kierkegaard, who asked, 'I wonder if anyone in my generation is able to make the movements of faith?' (Kierkegaard 1983, 34); he means the kind of faith which is the greatest passion as was the faith of Abraham. The attitude of Nietzsche towards men of faith reminds one of the words of Gombrowicz, 'I look at Simone Weil and my question is not: does God exist? I look at her with amazement and say: how, by means of what magic, has this woman been able to arrange herself internally so that she is able to cope with what devastates me? (…) A heroic existence such as Simone Weil's seems to be from another planet, a pole opposite from mine (…) antithesis of my desertion' (Gombrowicz 2012, 212).

II. The moral-metaphysical structure of the world

1. The loss of the feeling of transcendence

The second of the problems mentioned above as the axis of the considerations of the 'death of God' is the critique of a moral and metaphysical structure of the world deeply rooted in Christianity, which loses its justification without faith in transcendence. Even talking about the 'death of God' in a culture which has arisen from Christian tradition and in which Calvary plays such a crucial role may seem paradoxical. Referring to the words of Christian mystics and theologians, one may say that the death of God is essential in order for God to be born in man again.[32] The central point of Christianity is after all not death but rather *resurrection,* the victory over death and sin and the rebirth of man in God. One should note, however, that Nietzsche speaks through the mouths of the madman and Zarathustra to people who *do not believe*, ending with the shameful death on the cross. When one rejects faith in resurrection, which Nietzsche regards as a lie and invention of Saint Paul (AC-42), one is left with only death and the challenge of an empty universe,[33] something which de Lubac defined as 'the drama of atheist humanism' (De Lubac 1998).[34] This is not methodological atheism, which emerged much earlier and was strengthened by the Enlightenment, driven by the principle that one should practice science as if God did not exist (*Est deus non daretur*); it is rather a substantive atheism, based on the tragic emptiness and meaninglessness of a universe deprived of feelings of transcendence.

---

32 'God dies in order to live in thee', as it was expressed by Angelus Silesius (Angelus Silesius in De Lubac 1998, 47).

33 This brings to mind the experience of Fyodor Dostoyevsky who was deeply moved by the image of the dead Christ painted by Hans Holbein the Younger. Nietzsche may also have seen the image while working as a professor of ancient philology at the university in Basel. The hero of *The Idiot* personally recounts the experience of Dostoevsky, claiming that 'a man's faith might be ruined by looking at that picture' under the influence of the naturalism of the image which shows in all of its terrible splendour the death and loneliness of Christ (Dostoyevsky 2011, 398 and 808–810). It is unlikely that Nietzsche read the book as its German translation only came out in 1889 and thus he would only have been able to read the French edition.

34 The dead God of existentialism is in opposition to the Judaeo-Christian faith in 'a living God' (Ps 36,10; Pr 13,14; Is 12,3; Jn 4,10, Jn 1,33; Jn 3,5; Jn 7,37; Ro 14,9; 2 Cor 5,15; Re 1,18). Simone Weil points out that 'the errors of our time come from Christianity without the supernatural. Secularization is the cause – and primarily humanism' (Weil 2002, 115).

The problem of the loss of the feeling of transcendence first arose in German literature long before Nietzsche.[35] In 1796 Jean Paul, a German Romantic poet, wrote a piece entitled *Rede des toten Christus vom Weltgebäude herab, dass kein Gott sei (Speech of the Dead Christ down from the Universe That There is No God).*[36] It produced a seismic shift in European literature, presenting in this short piece an apocalyptic vision of a universe in which the world of the dead deprived of God-the Father becomes nothing more than 'the vast sepulchre of the Universe', 'mute inanimate Nothing', governed by chance and 'chill eternal Necessity' (Jean Paul 1992, 182). The man who realizes that his 'little life is Nature's sigh, or but its echo' (Jean Paul 1992, 182), does not recognize the earth. The piece ends with one awakening from a terrible dream, after which the narrator weeps for joy since he is still among the living and may yet believe in God. As revealed by the foreword, the author regarded *Speech of the Dead Christ* as a piece written as a *warning* against a loss of faith in God.[37] Jean Paul, whom Nietzsche called 'a misfortune in a dressing gown' (MAII,WS-99), expressed in his piece faith which is a kind of consolation and, as mentioned above, such faith becomes unbelievable.

The motif of the 'death of God' also featured in the work of Heinrich Heine, who Nietzsche particularly savoured for his 'divine malice' (EH-*Klug*-4).[38] The poet teases that nothing could help the old God, Yahweh – neither ruling the

---

35 The 'death of God' also appeared in a number of other famous philosophical works of the era, including philosophy of Hegel, albeit in a different context to Nietzsche. Hegel talked about the necessity of the death of an abstract God in order to give birth to a concrete God; he frequently wrote about the 'death of God' in, for example, his earlier works such as *Glauben und Wissen* or *Phänomenologie des Geistes* (see Heidegger 2002; De Lubac 1998).

36 The poem was featured in a novel by Jean Paul entitled *Siebenkäs*. It must have exerted a strong effect on Nietzsche, who would return to similar apocalyptic images in his works towards the end of his life, where, just like in Jean Paul, one can find a snake, an endless universe, its accidental nature connected together with its inevitability, creation devoid of its creator and a man who is his own father, etc.

37 The result that this piece had was, however, the opposite, perhaps best exemplified in its French translation by Madame de Staël in the book entitled *De l'Allemagne* (1808–1810). Here only half of the work was presented (the text ends with the words, 'the whole immeasurable fabric of the universe sank past us'), without the waking scene and the call to faith, which alone, according to the poet, can bring consolation (Janion 2001).

38 Nietzsche admired both Heine and Wagner as 'the two biggest fraudsters [*Betrüger*]' in the history of the 'European spirit' that had endowed Europe by Germany (NF-1888–16[41], Nietzsche 2012b, 174).

world from the capital in Rome, nor being a loving father, a friend of the people or a philanthropist – despite all these he still died, and the sound of the bells that people rang signified that the last rites were being accorded to God (Heine 1835).[39] In the interpreted fragment of *The Gay Science,* Nietzsche depicts a Christianity deprived of its original transcendence, where the church is a place of empty rituals, nothing more than the 'grave of God'.[40] It is a diagnosis of a historical-cultural fact (M-96)[41] that the idea of God lost its vitality at the moment it ceased to be fuelled by faith. The main problem is not the existence of God but rather human *inability to believe* in God, even if he did exist (NF-1888,15[44]). As Albert Camus noted, Nietzsche did not kill God but rather found him dying in the spirit of the times (Camus 1980).

The 'Madman' (*der tolle Mensch*) announces something obvious to people, something which is underlined by the metaphor 'in the bright morning lit a lantern'. The German adjective *toll* has many meanings: on the one hand it may mean 'crazy', and on the other 'wonderful', 'beautiful' or 'noble'. In the first case the word means being devoid of reason (which one may connect with Nietzsche's own rejection of speculative philosophy in religion), behaving in a manner which is strange (*wahnsinnig*), but also angry (*wütend*), indomitable (*unbändig*), full of passion (*leidenschaftlich*), and finally clownish (*närrisch*), hilarious (*ausgelassen*), and also whimsical (*wunderlich*) (Grimm 1971, Bd. 21, 631–637, entry 'toll'). The semantic depth to this adjective shows us that madness is connected with many other attributes which are prized by Nietzsche, a fact which I will return to later. As Heidegger noted, it is not only important what the 'madman' says but also *how he speaks* (Heidegger 2002). In reading the text one may think that, contrary to the accepted opinion, he is not announcing the 'death of God' but rather *looking for God,* and looking for God *aloud* and this is what makes him mad. It is reminiscent of the Old Testament prophets whom God inspired to call back those people who had turned away from their faith.[42] However, looking for God whilst at the same time claiming that he has died may only lead to fear, the same kind that is aroused by staring into the depths of an abyss (Ger. *Ab-grund*), or a groundless

39 Cf. Nietzsche, who says 'Christianity, as the evening chimes of the *good* antiquity' (MAII,VM-224, Nietzsche 2013, 97).

40 In a similar manner to Heine, Nietzsche refers to 'inverted Christianity', in which God needs man and his faith (cf. NF-1881,14[14]; NF-1881,15[4]).

41 Nietzsche writes in fragment 96 of *The Dawn* about the 10–20 million atheists in the world in his time, who would later become a powerful force in Europe.

42 'Cry aloud, spare not, lift up thy voice like a trumpet and shew my people their transgression, and the house of Jacob their sins' (Is 58,1).

(Ger. *grund-los*) empty shell of our own soul. 'Unchaining this earth from its sun' is another Copernican revolution with similar consequences for the way in which the modern world sees nature and the universe. It robs the earth of the object around which it orbits. In other words, what disappears together with God is the regularity of the functioning of the world as well as earlier cognitive criteria (NF-1885,39[15]). Nietzsche depicts this vision of a human being suspended in a vacuum, falling in all directions. The loss of God is like the loss of a fatherland (NF-1884,28[64]). The contemporary world has become 'disenchanted', deprived of its metaphysical antecedents. The position presented by Nietzsche may be defined as complete atheism, which is not the same as indifference towards faith for, as Fyodor Dostoyevsky notes, '[t]he absolute atheist stands on the next to last rung of the ladder of perfect faith (whether or not he takes the next step); but the indifferent man has no faith whatever, except for an evil fear' (Dostoyevsky 1999, 457). Nietzsche, when discussing free souls, has in mind those who have learnt to tread a fine line with a lightness of step, (Za-*Vorrede*-6), who will be able to live with uncertainty and dance above their own abyss (FW-347).

The 'death of God' requires courage to make one's own life meaningful (Za-I-*Verbrecher*). Nietzsche picks at those who are happy with themselves, who represent modernity and think of themselves as being above religion, even though in reality they are meaningless pawns in the service of an idea (JGB-58).[43] The people to whom 'madman' speaks are those who have not realised the significance of the 'death of God' and the far-reaching consequences it has for Western civilization, which is based on a metaphysical structure ultimately stemming from the idea of God (AC-38).[44] The empty space left behind by transcendence is replaced by ideals which are worthless without God's promise, e.g. the authority of God is to be replaced with that of Reason and the eternal happiness of redemption – with the earthly happiness of the majority (Heidegger 2002; cf. Taylor 2001). Nietzsche has in mind here all of the post-Christian philosophical doctrines (such as humanism, Marxism, materialism, liberalism, utilitarianism) which took certain ethical aspects from Christianity and have come to dominate a secular Europe. This phenomenon has been termed 'Christian homeopathy' and moralism (NF-

---

43 '[H]ow much naiveté – admirable, childish, boundlessly foolish naiveté – lies in the scholar's belief in his own superiority, in the good conscience he has of his tolerance, in the clueless, simple certainty with which he instinctively treats the religious man as an inferior, lesser type, something that he himself has grown out of, away from, and *above*, – he, who is himself a presumptuous little dwarf and rabble-man, a brisk and busy brain – and handiworker of "ideas," of "modern ideas"!' (Nietzsche 2002, 53).

44 'Everyone knows this: *and yet everything goes on as before*' (Nietzsche 2005b, 34).

1888,14[45]). These relics are nothing more than 'swamps or stagnant pools' which remain after 'the waters of religion' have ebbed away, as Nietzsche says (SE-4, Nietzsche 2007c, 148). Yet there are some waters in which no spirit can be found (NF-1888,14[45]), as he claims alluding to the book of *Genesis* (Gen 1,2), there are only spectres haunting Europe, just like that of the approaching totalitarianism. The courage stemming from the acceptance of the 'death of God' denotes an abandonment of the present religious shallows and sailing out into a new, open sea.[45]

When writing about the 'death of God' Nietzsche deliberately uses the language of religion (cf. Kaufmann 1968), and not of philosophy. He respects the fundamental difference between *knowledge*, stemming from reason and termed 'the wisdom of the wise', and *faith*.[46] He understands that speculative philosophy is not in any position to replace religion and all of the attempts to do so since Descartes have been fruitless. In this respect, he is attacking German philosophy, accusing it of trying to justify Christianity, attempting to reanimate a religion without faith (Löwith 1987).[47] He calls German philosophers 'subpriests' (NF-1888,15[71]; GD-*Streifzeuge*-47), 'theologians and fathers of the church' (NF-1884,26[8]; NF-1884,26[412]), and German philosophy as 'insidious theology' (AC-10), adding that it had been created by the 'pupils of Protestant preachers', undoubtedly an ironic aside since he himself came from preaching families, on both sides;[48] furthermore, he had been a would-be theologian himself. He thinks that the philosopher, aspiring to be the highest

---

45 Sea travel, sometimes linked to the voyages of Columbus, often features metaphorically in the work of Nietzsche as a synonym for thought, cognition and creation (see in particular M-575; the poem *Novus Columbus*, NF-1882,1[101]).

46 St Paul distinguishes between the wisdom of this world and the wisdom based on faith (1 Cor 1,17–25). The notion of an inconceivable God requires the wisdom of faith and not of understanding, cf. motto to *Hyperion* (Hölderlin 1990; see Ratzinger 2004). It is similar in this respect to the thought of Kierkegaard, who claimed that faith in God is the highest achievement of human capabilities, something that not everyone can experience, but with the difference that there is no point in trying to go further (Kierkegaard 1983).

47 One should not, therefore, be surprised by the claim of Jacob Taubes that the fundamental lack of understanding of the Bible amongst contemporary students of philosophy means that they are unable to correctly interpret the works of Hegel, Nietzsche, Kant, etc. (Taubes 1993). A similar tendency can be found in the early Greek philosophy which stemmed from religion, and despite abandoning the old gods, it remained religion itself, as Werner Jaeger claims (Jaeger 1948).

48 Nietzsche's paternal grandfather, Friedrich August Ludwig Nietzsche, was a Protestant scholar, who affirmed 'the everlasting survival of Christianity' in one of his works (Mann 1959).

authority, is the natural successor to the priest – and a more developed one at that, utilising the same resources (NF-1888,14[189]).

Even though Nietzsche himself claims that the idea of God may no longer be either the foundation or even a reference point in philosophy, he himself puts it at the heart of his considerations, seeing himself as both the whistle-blower and the crowning glory of philosophy of the priestly type. He objects strongly to German idealism, prophetically warning of the signs of its fall. If 'Goethe created German literature worthy of the world stage, Hegel gave the world the same kind of philosophy', as Löwith wrote (Löwith 1969 (trans. A. Shaw), 17), then in Nietzsche the revolutionary turning point, which the German spirit brought to the world, found its ultimate peak.

When trying to interpret the thoughts of Nietzsche, one may come to the conclusion that the ultimate source of the downfall of the metaphysical structure that the Platonic-Christian perspective ascribes to the world may be found within the structure itself. In antiquity, there was a clear break between the mythical world and that of reason (based on *Logos* and striving for the truth). Nietzsche devoted his first philosophical publication to this issue, presenting the dualistic approach to the world which can be found in the tension between the worlds of tragedy (the Dionysian) and of beautiful appearances (the Apollonian), which was overcome by reason (Socratism). As Joseph Ratzinger notes, Christianity (just like Judaism) chose the way of *Logos* during antiquity and, as a result, did not fall together with the demythologisation of the pagan world (Ratzinger 2004). This choice indicates that religion lays claims to objectively existing truth. At the same time, Christianity transforms the 'God of the philosophers', which means the idea of transcendence referring to itself, into 'a God of faith', which is the God of Abraham, Isaac and Jacob. It is a crucial distinction between philosophy, seeking truth via rational cognition, and the Christian religion, which accepts that truth is something incarnate. This came to pass as a result of the collision of two very different civilizations – those of Athens and Jerusalem. Thus, when faith in the living God began to fade in Nietzsche's times, it left behind only an abstract notion which leads to an idolatry of reason.

In order to better understand the critique of the providential order of the world carried out by Nietzsche, it is worth turning to the aspects of religion delineated by C. S. Lewis (Lewis 2009). The first is the experience of the incomprehensible vastness of the universe, one which arouses feelings of fear and awe and which Lewis terms *the experience of the Numinous.*[49] This experience is looking into the

49 This experience was beautifully captured by Pascal, '[t]he eternal silence of these infinite spaces terrifies me' (Pascal 1999, 233, 73). In the opinion of Ronald Dworkin,

abyss, which Nietzsche also did, and considering the possibility of 'a God "beyond good and evil"' (NF-1886,5[71], Nietzsche 2006b, 118). The second element is the experience of good and evil which one may call *the moral experience*. Both of these featured in the first religions, often independent of one another – if a divine power were discovered in the vastness of the universe, it would not be identified with morality, especially as the very existence of the universe, with all its cruelty, waste and injustice, seemed to defy morality. The third aspect manifests itself when religion begins to be associated with morality (e.g. in Judaism) and God – with the good. Finally, the fourth element which Christianity contains is the appearance of a personal God in history, a point to which I will return. Christianity did not form a new ethical code but it rather gave an extra dimension to the existing traditional morality present in Judaism, which in turn was not very different from the fundamental moral values of other peoples (Lewis 2001). Nietzsche had to have been aware of this fact, as is evidenced by his remarks on the role of customs in the behaviour of people. Despite the interpretational abuses in his analysis of the genealogy of Christian morality, Nietzsche is particularly accurate in his diagnosis of the connection between morality and religion. The significance of this connection is fundamental, since religion is a complete system of thought; its connection with the experience of good and evil makes good and evil categories independent of people and belonging to the world. Thus, the universe begins to be seen as purposeful, equipped with sense, in which good and evil exist and very existence is subject to moral valuation. Therefore, when Nietzsche writes of overcoming the 'moral God', he has in mind the human consciousness which came about as a result of the joining together of religious and moral experience, the fruit of which was the whole of Western metaphysics, accepting the existence of objective truth, absolute values, including the special and absolute value of humanity as well as the purpose and sense of existence (NF-1886,5[71]).

The notion of purpose in relation to the universe is based on conceptual categories which in turn refer to created things (Lewis 2001). If we claim that the universe was not created, we also cannot claim that it is either purposeful or purposeless; the universe just is, it simply exists. In nature there are no means, no objectives, no purpose (in the sense of final goals), there is only *becoming* which cannot be separated into means and goals (NF-1880,6[151]; NF-1887,9[73]). Nietzsche delineates four periods in humanity (NF-1871,14[29]): in the first this be-

this experience is a religious experience that does not require faith in God; one may, in his opinion, be led to adopt an axiological position towards the universe which appreciated beauty, symmetry, the law, values and which may be called 'religious atheism' or 'religion without God' (Dworkin 2013).

coming awakened curiosity (Ionic philosophy); in the second, it was considered to be a problem (metaphysics); in the third, the objective of becoming arose (theology); in the fourth, reason and cognition became more important and philosophy became both imperative and aggressive, forcing the problem of becoming into the background (dialectic). The contemporary philosophy criticized by Nietzsche was to be found in the fourth period, the dialectic, dominated by rational cognition (which resulted in the rise of rationalist ethics). This stage began in antiquity with Socrates (GD-*Sokrates*). Nietzsche thinks that our morality had been shaped by the metaphysical needs of people to have purpose and a sense of existence, and the idea of ultimate purpose had been transformed into absolute obligations or values (NF-1883,7[57]). The assumption that humanity represents the purpose of the universe is the pinnacle of vanity, because a human being does not mean anything in the ocean of becoming and fading. Humanity is the goal of the existence of the universe in the same way that an ant may be the cause of the existence of a forest, as Nietzsche writes (MAII,WS-14).

It is worth adding here, however, that for all that Ancient Greece regarded humanity as the objective of nature, it was Christianity which equated the *redemption* of people as the goal of divine providence, as Nietzsche remarks (NF-1886–7[4]), and the divine plan depended on the manifestation of love. The idolatry of humanity as the centre of the universe and the measure of all things is not characteristic of Christianity, therefore, but rather of modern humanism.[50] Modern humanism, for Nietzsche, is a kind of prejudice but he sees its source in religion. It operates on universal metaphysical foundations such as equality, freedom, human dignity, just like the idea that humanity was created for a higher purpose, but here omitting the role of the Creator. When humans took up the power to reduce the chains that bound them, 'God' became 'far too extreme a hypothesis' (NF-1886,5[71], Nietzsche 2006b, 117).

Thus, Nietzsche's critique is not only focused on morality but also on the entire metaphysical inheritance in which it is rooted in contemporary thought. Christianity is something greater than a collection of moral principles – it is a way of being in the world, where religious faith becomes something like deciding to adopt a certain frame of reference in which to live our lives. For those who do not believe, analysing Christian moral imperatives without reference to their transcendental source is like trying to understand the movements of a dancer without hearing the music which guides them or trying to describe the actions of

50 The notion of 'humanism' was used for the first time by a Bavarian school teacher and friend of Hegel in 1808 (Snell 1953).

a swimmer without referring to the water in which they are swimming.[51] Morality which is rooted in faith is intended to engage and integrate the whole of a person, not just their intellect, feelings or will. The acceptance of Christian morality without its transcendental aspect is something unjustified: the 'death of God' must therefore lead to a revolutionary change in human consciousness that requires the creation of a new frame of reference for evaluations which do not exist in the world but which are human interpretations of the world (GD-*Streifzuege*-5).[52] The philosophical fragments described above provide us with a profound insight into the significance of Nietzsche's 'death of God' for Western spirituality, an effect of which is the exposure of the falsehood and emptiness on which the moral and cultural structure of the present is based.[53]

2. The abolition of the dualism between the apparent world and the real

Platonic-Christian metaphysics is interpreted by Nietzsche from the perspective of Western idealism. This metaphysical structure is founded on the distinction between the sensuous world and the supersensuous world, which is the long-lasting, harmful error:

> HOW THE 'TRUE WORLD' FINALLY BECAME A FABLE
>
> *The history of an error*
>
> 1. The true world attainable for a man who is wise, pious, virtuous, – he lives in it, *he is it*. (Oldest form of the idea, relatively coherent, simple, convincing. Paraphrase of the proposition 'I, Plato, *am* the truth.')

---

51 The metaphor of the swimmer was used by Bergson in relation to researching religion (Bergson 1963).

52 'When you give up Christian faith, you pull the rug out from under your right to Christian morality as well. This is *anything* but obvious: you have to keep driving this point home (…). Christianity is a system, a carefully considered, *integrated* view of things. If you break off a main tenet, the belief in God, you smash the whole system along with it: you lose your grip on anything necessary. (…) When the English really believe that they "intuitively" know all by themselves what is good and what is evil; and when, as a result, they think that they do not need Christianity to guarantee morality any more, this is itself just the result of the domination of the Christian value judgment and an expression of the *strength* and *depth* of this domination' (Nietzsche 2005b, 194).

53 Nietzsche's words capture this venture particularly well, '[h]ere is a hero who has done nothing more than to shake a tree as soon as the fruit was ripe. Does that seem to you too little? Then look first at the tree that he has shaken' (MAII,WS-347, Nietzsche 2013, 291).

2. The true world, unattainable for now, but promised to the man who is wise, pious, virtuous ('to the sinner who repents'). (Progress of the idea: it gets trickier, more subtle, less comprehensible, –*it becomes female*, it becomes Christian…)
3. The true world, unattainable, unprovable, unpromisable, but the very thought of it a consolation, an obligation, an imperative. (Basically the old sun but through fog and scepticism; the idea become elusive, pale, Nordic, Königsbergian.)
4. The true world – unattainable? At any rate, unattained. And as unattained also *unknown*. Consequently not consoling, redeeming, obligating either: how could we have obligations to something unknown?… (Gray morning. First yawn of reason. Cockcrow of positivism.)
5. The 'true world' – an idea that is of no further use, not even as an obligation, – now an obsolete, superfluous idea, *consequently* a refuted idea: let's get rid of it! (Bright day; breakfast; return of *bon sens* and cheerfulness; Plato blushes in shame; pandemonium of all free spirits.)
6. The true world is gone: which world is left? The illusory one, perhaps? …But no! *we got rid of the illusory world along with the true one!* (Noon; moment of shortest shadow; end of longest error; high point of humanity; INCIPIT ZARATHUSTRA.) (GD-*Fabel*, Nietzsche 2005b, 171).

The history of an error aptly summarises Nietzsche's relationship with works of metaphysics, which themselves represent the history of post-Socratic European thought, falling in his scheme into six symbolic epochs. The first of these was the *epoch of Platonic philosophy*, which initiated the disintegration of the human world into the true world (*wahre Welt*) and the apparent one (*scheinbare Welt*). The true world is supersensuous, in opposition to the worthless world of the senses; it is a world of ideas which we may reach by means of reason and it is accessible to the wise, who, identifying with these ideas, become their personification (see Plato 1980; cf. Heidegger 1991a).

The second epoch is *Christianity*, which equates the true world (eternal) with the kingdom of God (*sacrum*) and the apparent world with the worldly – temporal and sinful (*profanum*). The notion of the 'kingdom of God' should not be understood in terms of an earthly kingdom, as it is not situated anywhere in historical-political space.[54] It manifests itself not as a promised land at a fixed point in time

54 The Christian idea of the divine kingdom is a transformation of an idea stemming from Judaism, whereby the promise of the advent of the Messiah, who was to set the chosen people free, was often understood in a historic-political sense. The Christian vision goes beyond temporal categories (Mk 1,15; Mt 12,28; Lk 17,20–21; Jn 18,36). There are many different interpretations of the kingdom of God, including: the idealistic (the kingdom of God is in the heart of everyone); Christological (the kingdom of God is Jesus Christ); eschatological (the coming of the kingdom of God is the moment of redemption); secular (the kingdom of God is a historical goal: it will bring eternal

but rather as a kind of spiritual experience which humanity may enjoy, something which Nietzsche highlights (AC-34).[55] In such an idealistic interpretation, the true world becomes an inner reality, which is a kind of progress for it, given the more substantial perversity of thought. The metaphysical foundation of truth attains here its highest point of development, Jesus – understood as a symbolic facticity – is the truth and the life (cf. Jn 14,6; AC-34). The utilisation in this context of the term 'women' (*Weib*) for striving for the truth is a reference to part two of Goethe's *Faust*, where the eternal femininity (*das Ewig-Weibliche*) personifies the divine creation and immortality, which both lifts people up and keeps them grounded at the same time.[56] This Faustian trace reveals the specific interpretation of Christianity, made by Nietzsche from the perspective of the German idealism, which the philosopher tried to overcome in himself. Christianity in such an interpretation becomes 'Platonism for the "people"' (JGB-*Vorrede*), where the desire to escape into the other world is shared by all the believers. It is worth stressing that, by reducing Christianity to a kind of neo-platonic doctrine, Nietzsche rejects the essence of Christianity which is the dogma of the Incarnation of Christ, the idea of communion between a human being and God or the idea of the resurrection of the body and the soul (cf. AC-34). Thus, the condemnation of sensuality and the desire for the other world being the hidden desire for death, which Nietzsche accurately identifies as harmful for life, recalls rather the Manichean heresy (which had been opposed by Christianity) than Christianity itself.[57]

---

peace and justice). This last interpretation is characteristic of the post-Christian doctrine which features in the philosophy of both Hegel and Kant. On the subject of the complexity of the teaching of divine kingdom see Ratzinger 2008.

55 'The "kingdom of heaven" is a state of the heart; (…) it is an experience of the heart; it is everywhere and it is nowhere' (Nietzsche 2005b, 32).

56 Goethe sought that which was eternally creative (*das ewig Schöpferische*) and identified it with the divine mothers who were visited by Faust (Goethe 1972). In this respect, Nietzsche termed European idealism as a kind of feminism (M-*Vorrede*-4). In one of the poems added to the second edition of *The Gay Science*, Nietzsche perverts the words of Goethe, identifying the divine (*das Ewig-Weibliche*) and the desire to be everlasting (*das Unvergängliche*) as a poetic subterfuge which he unmasks as foolery (*das Ewig-Närrische*); the world keeps on turning and, instead of lifting man up, it makes him join in its games where being (*Sein*) is confused with appearance (*Schein*), cf. Nietzsche 2001, 249.

57 It was elucidated by Denis de Rougemont in his insightful analysis of the myth of love in the Western culture, '[t]his what the Holy Gospel calls "death" is the beginning of a new life just here on the earth. This is not an escape of the soul beyond the world,

The third epoch is represented by the *philosophy of Kant*, in which the true world (things in themselves – *Dinge an sich*)[58] becomes unattainable, impossible to prove,[59] or promise; it becomes something purely conceptual, at the same time compelling and comforting, whose symbol is the categorical imperative. The philosophy of Kant exerted a tremendous influence upon European philosophy. Hölderlin emphasised the significance of Kant for German philosophy by saying, 'Kant is the Moses of our nation who led us out of Egyptian chains and into the free desert of his speculation and which has led Law to the holy mount' (Hölderlin 1921 (trans. A. Shaw), 381). The poet regarded the speculative philosophy of Kant as a unique source of comfort and worry at the same time, as he expressed in a letter to his brother, '[a]gain I escape to Kant, as I always do when I don't like myself' (Hölderlin 1921 (trans. A. Shaw), 241). The revolutionary significance of Kant was that he performed a 'Copernican Turn' in ethics, placing the source of morality within a human being and setting it free of an external authority, which may be best expressed in the words '*the starry sky above me and the moral law within me*' (Kant 2002a, 203). The notion of God is no longer the philosophical justification of morality but rather the opposite – it is moral law, through which freedom manifests itself, permits the possibility of God (Kant 2002a), thus causing Nietzsche to label Kant an 'underhanded Christian' (GD-*Vernunft*-6). He mockingly claims that it was in this era that the final fall of God took place when he became 'a thing in itself' (AC-17). It does not avoid the dualism of the true and the apparent worlds but rather transfers the dualism to the heart of human life, separating the phenomenal 'I' (senses) from the noumenal 'I' (reason). At this stage an ontological dualism emerges which depends on the separation of Is (*Sein*) and Ought (*Sollen*), something which Christianity had not known and which had a powerful influence on the rationalist, post-Enlightenment moral philosophy (see Hume 1960).

The fourth epoch, *positivism,* is where the real world becomes not only unattainable but *unattained.* The only accessible world is the empirical one. For Nietzsche, this is the moment where we awake from our dream of a better, more comforting or compelling world and abandon it. The cockcrow symbolises awakening from a dream of the real world and entering into a new era – hence the

---

but rather a comeback of the soul in its highest strength into the heart of the world!' (De Rougemont 1968 (trans. A. Shaw), 55).

58 For Nietzsche, 'the thing in itself is worth a Homeric laugh' and is completely empty, devoid of meaning (MAI-16, Nietzsche 2000, 27–28).

59 Nietzsche refers here to the proof of the existence of God conducted by Kant (Kant 2000).

title of one of his works, *Daybreak*. This piece belongs to the positivist stage of Nietzsche's philosophy; while remaining a follower (carrier – Ger. *Träger*) of idealism (NF-1877,22[37]), he regards positivism as a necessary aspect of philosophy. However, he does not stop here and overcoming positivism he reaches *perspectivisim* (NF-1887,7[60]), a point I will return to in the next chapter. Positivism offers two paths – either to continue and to radicalise the ontological dualism we are faced with (separating the world of ought from the empirical world) or to move towards ontological monism, which would mean reducing all spiritual phenomena (including normativity and values) to the physical world. The second solution is a radical form of naturalism which Nietzsche has in mind when he mentions positivism here, which will be further developed in the next section of this chapter.

In the epoch of free spirits (*freie Geiste*)[60] the idea of the 'true world' was rejected as being worthless, which would have the effect, in the opinion of Nietzsche, of making its creator, Plato, ashamed. As it had been unmasked as a false idea, the term 'true world' was presented here in quotation marks. The rejection of this term is on a par with that of the 'death of God'; in both cases, a claim is made for the nonexistence of the supersensuous world, which has lost its power and no longer responds to us, as Heidegger notes (Heidegger 2002). This absence leads to a 'dictatorship of the nothing' (*Diktatur des Nichts*), evidenced by the birth of nihilism, which, much like Christianity, was its own movement of faith, albeit in the opposite direction (Heidegger 2002, 163).[61] The nihilist, according to Nietzsche, is one who claims that the world as it is should not exist and the world that should be (the imagined 'true' world) does not exist (NF-1887,9[60]). One may thus regard the fifth epoch as being that of *nihilism*, which was, according to Nietzsche, to dominate for the next two hundred years (NF-1887,11[119]); it was thus a transitional historical movement. Nietzsche's thoughts on nihilism may appear to be contradictory – on the one hand, he pictures it as the source of the greatest crisis of the age (decadence) while it is also the only thing which can save us. Nihilism thus has two faces – the negative one, connected to the devaluation (Ger. *Abwertung*) of all values (values are deprived of their value), and the positive one, resulting in a revaluation (Ger. *Umwertung*) of all values (values are accorded new value). Thus, nihilism is a logical consequence of history; it has destructive power but at the same time it is a necessary condition of creative power. A catastrophe for Nietzsche would be a nihilism which became stuck in its negative aspect. What is necessary for the preparation

60 Ger. *Geist* means both spirit and mind.

61 And as the poet accurately points out, '[e]ven the most sublime nothingness gives birth to nothingness' (Hölderlin 1990, 67).

of a new spirit is complete nihilism, which 'must eliminate even the place of value itself, the supersensory as a realm; and it must accordingly alter and revalue values differently', as Heidegger put it (Heidegger 2002, 169). Nietzsche believes that when nihilism reaches its end, a strongly opposed, constructive force must arise – a creator of new values (GM-II-24). Nietzsche is thus not only a destroyer of values but rather a philosopher who notices and appreciates that human existence is a constant process of construction and destruction (GT-24), which one should accept joyfully and wholeheartedly participate in.

The sixth epoch which Nietzsche-Zarathustra foresees, and the one which we have not yet reached, is the epoch of the *Übermensch*. It will be a time when the division between the real and the apparent world is overthrown. The *error* which the fragment refers to is not the 'true world' but rather the division of the world into the true and the apparent. Nietzsche holds that this dualism was necessary for the internal growth of a person since it causes the tension necessary to make the soul fly (JGB-*Vorrede*). Christianity leads people to a maximum state of inner development (NF-1887,10[138]), creating a tension between the perfection of God and the sinfulness of a human being (NF-1880,6[357]), which was unknown in Ancient Greek culture.[62] That which was highest and most holy about a person was believed to be the working of the divine grace of the Lord (NF-1880,7[271]); God is also defined in opposition to a human being (Za-II-*Priester*; Za-II-*Tugendhafte*). Nietzsche admits in another place that in order to think about oneself, one must always formulate a counterpart, a rival (NF-1884,26[390]), and this is exactly the role which God may play in the development of a human being. The 'death of God' is necessary in order for the *Übermensch* to appear,[63] since this is when the tension between humanity and God becomes dangerous (JGB-262), when it begins to be seen as turning away from our human imperfections and towards a perfect God – it '*flows off* into a god' (FW-285) and impoverishes human beings at the expense of God (NF-1888,14[130]; NF-1885,34[204]; NF-1885,1[247]).[64] The lack of any tension is something even worse, however; the 'last men' described by Nietzsche are precisely those whose 'string of the bow will have forgotten how

62 In antiquity there was an opposition between the mortality of humans and the immortal gods (Snell 1953). Nevertheless, ancient religiosity stimulated the inner growth of spirit by mysteries in which one could experience the presence of the divine (Otto 1965).

63 Nietzsche compares losing faith in God to losing your milk teeth in order to grow permanent teeth later on (NF-1876,18[9]). See NF-1883,16[3]; Za-IV-*Mensch*-2.

64 Similar thoughts regarding the impoverishment of the world and man at the expense of the idea of God may be found in Feuerbach (see De Lubac 1998).

to whir!' (Za-*Vorrede*-5, Nietzsche 2006a, 9).[65] Nietzsche detects the weakening of the spirit in each successive doctrine imitating Christianity, from humanism, liberalism and Marxism to bourgeois morality, which he terms the 'euthanasia of Christianity' (M-92). A person should be as tense as a bow in order to be able to fire off new ideas.[66] He claims that the tension caused by Christianity should be replaced by the internal tension between the person who longed for oneself and the person that must be overcome to create something that is higher (NF-1882,1[86]; NF-1882,1[108]). Nietzsche, in summarising the most important period in the development of religion, writes that first mankind made sacrifices to their God; then they sacrificed for him their drives and instincts (by taking morality upon themselves); and finally, they sacrificed their own God and today we are the inheritors of that legacy and final sacrifice (JGB-55). Together with this final stage, humanity obtained an unprecedented ability to think in non-religious terms and the next stage should see an accompanying unimaginable leap in our abilities to think beyond morality (an immoral position), as posited by Nietzsche (NF-1880,3[70]).

It is no coincidence that the era of the *Übermensch* is described as the '*great noon*' (Za-I-*Tugend*; EH-GT-4).[67] Noon is the time when there is the greatest light (the sun is at its zenith and the shadows are shortest), the middle and, at the same time, the culmination of the day in terms of the movement of the sun. There are two crucial aspects to this metaphor, the first referring to human cognition and the second symbolizing spiritual development. The '*great noon*' is the crowning moment in human cognition and maturity (JGB-*Nachgesang*); it is the time of the greatest awakening of the mind of mankind (EH-M-2); a time of 'the consciousness that has become unconditionally and in every respect conscious of itself', as Heidegger notes (Heidegger 2002, 192). Hanna Buczyńska-Garewicz also calls attention to the mystical dimension of the '*great noon*' (Buczyńska-Garewicz 2013), which is a timeless moment full of the affirmation of being (NF-1881,11[196]; NF-1882,2[9]; NF-1883,18[48]).[68] The Platonic-Christian paradigm of top-down

---

65 The word 'bow' stems from the Greek *bios*, which also means life; cf. Heraclitus LXXVIII–LXXIX (Kahn 2001). See also Kerényi 1997; Jaeger 1948; Hadot 1999.

66 And when 'The bow is bent and drawn; make from the shaft', as King Lear says to Kent (Shakespeare 1965, 298).

67 Remarkably, Nietzsche wanted to entitle his life's work *The Great Noon*, a volume which he never wrote and of which all that remains is a plan in his notes (NF-1888,14[77]; NF-1888,18[17]).

68 An inspiration for Nietzsche in this regard may certainly have been Schopenhauer (cf. Schopenhauer 2010, § 54).

is replaced with that of a circle which restores unity to the process of becoming. Nietzsche calls himself a teacher of 'noon and eternity' (NF-1882,4[94]), while his Zarathustra not only speaks of the coming noon (Za-III-*Tugend*-3; Za-III-*Boese*-2), but also speaks to people from the noon itself (Za-*Vorrede*-10). The '*great noon*' is to be a landmark for humanity (NF-1883,21[3]), the source of a spiritual journey for humanity from the animal to the *Übermensch* (Za-*Tugend*-3; cf. Löwith 1969), a moment of change for mankind which would serve to aid them in new, great tasks (EH-GT-4).

A basic charge that one may levy against Nietzsche lies in the notion that events will become graspable and entirely understandable (see Jaspers 1961; Voegelin 1975). The conception described here encompasses a thought which Nietzsche negated in other philosophers, namely that human endeavours present stages in the development of the soul, that there is a deeper sense in them which may be revealed and that we may foresee further stages of development on the basis of previous ones and consciously shape them. All of these principles are not only far from obvious but they remain in large part contentious. Nietzsche in this regard is truly a man of his times. The division of human endeavours into stages in the development of the soul in which the interpretation of the world is changeable was itself a notion borrowed from the precursors of positivism, such as Turgot or Comte (Voegelin 1975). The latter identified three phases in the development of the mind: theological, metaphysical and positive ones, which lead to the rationalising processes of human thought. In Nietzsche, however, we have the development of the human spirit brought about by the manifestations of the will-to-power, where both the rationalisation and the idealisation of the human mind leads to the degeneration of the spirit, an aspect which I will return to in the next section.

3. The 'New Philosophy': beyond idealism and positivism

The philosophy of Nietzsche contains elements of both idealism and positivism, even though it was created by overcoming them. Nietzsche feels that both were responsible for the spiritual crisis in Europe at the time. The critique of idealism comes down to the critique of metaphysics, which attempted to capture reality in terms of timeless and universal ideas (Sedgwick 2013). The main charge laid against it is that in supporting the supersensuous world it opposed life, which was becoming. Positivism, which was focused on the empirical world, played an important role in awakening people from their metaphysical slumbers since faith in the 'true world' was beginning to fade. To stop at positivism is not enough, however, for in positivism it is not the spirit which binds people together but rather utility, which leads to 'the stifling of the spirit and to the atrophy of so many of our spiritual sources' as Charles Taylor put it (Taylor 2001, 107).[69] Nietzsche's method relies on using each of the approaches against one another in order to overcome both of them:

> From positivism and materialism, he took a weapon with which to fight idealism, and vice versa, as he wanted nothing more sincerely and profoundly than the destruction of all world views that had been devised by man (Shestov 1969, 281).

Paraphrasing Walter Benjamin, one may say that Nietzsche went into enemy territory in order to collect arguments (Taubes 1993). The fragments below show Nietzsche's feelings towards positivism and the oppositional method which he utilises:

> With stronger, livelier thinkers, however, thinkers who still have a thirst for life, things look different. By taking sides *against* appearance (…), [t]here is a *mistrust* of these modern ideas here, there is a disbelief in everything built yesterday and today; perhaps it is mixed with a bit of antipathy and contempt that can no longer stand the bric-a-brac of concepts from the most heterogeneous sources, which is how so-called positivism puts itself on the market these days, a disgust felt by the more discriminating taste at the fun-fair colors and flimsy scraps of all these reality-philosophasters who have nothing new and genuine about them except these colors. Here, I think, we should give these skeptical anti-realists and epistemo-microscopists their just due: the instinct that drives them away from *modern* reality is unassailable, – what do we care for their retrograde shortcut! The essential thing about them is not that they want to go 'back': but rather, that they want to get – *away*. A bit *more* strength, flight, courage, artistry: and they would want to get *up and out*, – and not go back! (JGB-10, Nietzsche 2002, 11–12).
> [P]hysics too is only an interpretation and arrangement of the world (…) and *not* an explanation of the world. But to the extent that physics rests on belief in the senses, it passes for more, and will continue to pass for more, namely for an explanation, for a long time to come. It has our eyes and our fingers as its allies, it has visual evidence and tangibility as its allies. This helped it to enchant, persuade, *convince* an age with a basically plebeian taste – indeed, it instinctively follows the canon of truth of the eternally popular sensualism. What is plain, what 'explains'? Only what can be seen and felt, – this is as far as any problem has to be pursued. Conversely: the strong attraction of the Platonic way of thinking consisted in its *opposition* to precisely this empiricism. It was a *noble* way of thinking, suitable perhaps for people who enjoyed even stronger and more discriminating senses than our contemporaries, but who knew how to find a higher triumph in staying master over these senses. (…) There was a type of *enjoyment* in overpowering and interpreting the world in the manner of Plato, different from the

69 The words of Hölderlin expressed a sentiment which Nietzsche certainly shared, '[y]ou have lost all faith in anything great; you are doomed, then, doomed to perish, unless that faith returns, like a comet from unknown skies' (Hölderlin 1990, 32).

> enjoyment offered by today's physicists, or by the Darwinians and antiteleologists who work in physiology, with their principle of the 'smallest possible force' and greatest possible stupidity. 'Where man has nothing more to see and grasp, he has nothing more to do' – this imperative is certainly different from the Platonic one, but for a sturdy, industrious race of machinists and bridge-builders of the future, people with *tough* work to do, it just might be the right imperative for the job (JGB-14, Nietzsche 2002, 15–16).
>
> Against the positivism which halts at phenomena – 'There are only facts' – I would say: no, facts are just what there aren't, there are only interpretations. We cannot determine any fact 'in itself': perhaps it's nonsensical to want to do such a thing (NF-1886,7[60], Nietzsche 2006b, 139).
>
> *Not* 'back to nature': for there has never been a natural mankind. The scholasticism of unnatural and *anti*-natural values is the rule, is the beginning; man arrives at nature after a long struggle – he never comes 'back'... Nature: i.e., daring to be immoral as nature is (NF-1887,10[53](182), Nietzsche 2006b, 185).

Positivism is also for Nietzsche the result of an old error stemming from dividing the world into the apparent and the true, with positivists siding with the world of the senses, regarding it as the only truth – the *real* world. Hence the use of the term 'philosophers of reality' in relation to the positivists, especially the French school (JGB-204). They opted for the sensuous world since the ideal world had not been attained – and thus their position was reactionary, one of resignation and pessimism; they were called the disenchanted romantics (NF-1885,2[131]). A powerful charge against positivism is that, as with idealism, they possessed a desire for certainty which leads to rational dogmatism, itself a symptom of the enduring presence of metaphysical superstitions such as the desire for truth (FW-344; FW-347). Positivist philosophy leads, as Comte noted, '"to regard all phenomena as subject to invariable natural *laws*." The discovery of these laws, their reduction to its smallest possible number is its sole aim' (Voegelin 1975, 164). Wittgenstein also recognised this, claiming:

> The whole modern conception of the world is founded on the illusion that the so-called laws of nature are the explanations of natural phenomena. Thus people today stop at the laws of nature, treating them as something inviolable, just as God and Fate were treated in past ages. (...) [T]he modern system tries to make it look as if *everything* were explained' (Wittgenstein 2002, 6.371–6.372, 85).

Positivism contributed to the fact that philosophy became subordinated to science. Thus, in the same way that philosophy was once in the service of theology, in positivism it became to be in service of science, something which Nietzsche regards as a 'plebeian instinct' which calls for a 'master' (JGB-204). He sees positivist philosophy as being dominated by biologists, doctors, psychologists and other specialists who were ignorant of philosophy and philosophers and whom they undervalued. This is a symptom of the crisis of philosophy for him, the price to be paid for the rejection of metaphysics. Positivists are for him not philosophers but rather critics who the philosophers of the future needed as tools to create their new philosophy (JGB-210), and they are intended to be used for quite primitive work, as we can see in the above fragment. The approach favoured by the positivists may seem naïve and incongruous, especially in comparison to the noble ways of reasoning presented by philosophers such as Plato. Nietzsche is not surprised therefore by contemporary idealists who oppose the pretence of the new reality; he praises their fastidious taste. He feels, however, that the philosophy of the future cannot return to the past, to outdated ideas, but should rather be able to go beyond them, taking pleasure from bringing new interpretations to the world as the great metaphysicians once did.

In the era of positivism, the spirit has been replaced with reason, something which the author of *Zarathustra* finds particularly painful. In both Nietzsche and Dostoyevsky one can find a critique of the kind of pure reason advocated by Kant, who gave us under the title *The Critique of Pure Reason* 'not a critique but an apology of pure reason', as Lev Shestov shrewdly observed (Shestov 1932, 396). Nietzsche thinks that this faith in the categories of reason, which gauged the values of the world but referred in fact to a world of fakes, is the main cause of the birth of nihilism (NF-1888,11[99]). The dogmatism of the rational interpretation of the world limited knowledge to that which was measurable and countable. As a result, contemporary philosophy reduced to a theory of knowledge, denies itself access to certain philosophical problems and only generates its own agony (JGB-204).[70] Positivism undervalues all problems that it is unable to solve and which do not fit with the scientific interpretation of the world:

> The strength of positivism lies in its ability to pass in silence over all problems regarded by it as fundamentally unsolvable, and to direct our attention only to those aspects of life in which there are no irreconcilable contradictions: after all, the limits of our knowledge end at precisely the point where irreconcilable contradictions begin. In this sense, Kantian idealism is, as we know, a most reliable ally of positivism (Shestov 1969, 274).

70 'A philosophy reduced to "epistemology," which is really no more than a timid epochism and doctrine of abstinence; a philosophy that does not even get over the threshold and scrupulously *denies* itself the right of entry – that is a philosophy in its last gasps, an end, an agony, something to be pitied. How could such a philosophy – *dominate*?' (Nietzsche 2002, 95). Hölderlin, whom Nietzsche had passionately read in his youth, had similar sentiments, '[m]ere intellect produces no philosophy, for philosophy is more than the limited perception of what is' (Hölderlin 1990, 68).

The similarity between positivism and idealism is that they both try to derive nature and morality from certain independent, a priori truths given to us and independent of human consciousness.[71]

Despite such a critical position towards positivist philosophy, the philosophy of Nietzsche is often interpreted as a form of naturalistic philosophy (see Leiter 2002; Clark 1990; Cox 1999; Schacht 1994; Janaway and Robertson 2012; Johnson 2010; Richardson 2004). Such interpretation puts emphasis on the positivist period of Nietzsche's philosophy and often neglects the other two. This stems from attempts to protect his philosophy from the postmodern interpretations which dominate French philosophy (see Derrida 1981; Foucault 1977; Deleuze 2002).[72] By *methodological naturalism* one may understand philosophical research which applies research methods based on those used in the empirical sciences (mainly the causal explanation of phenomena) and based on or supported by the best available scientific knowledge (Leiter 2002; Janaway 2006). Nietzsche frequently expresses his admiration for scientific research methods, leading many scholars to the conclusion that his methodology is strictly naturalistic. However, when Nietzsche writes that we should approach the study of our own life experience as a scientific experiment, or when he writes that physicists were the best scholars and should be imitated (FW-319; FW-335), he does not mean that scientific methods should be applied in philosophy. His analogy is intended to show the advantages of applying certain attributes to philosophical thinking, such as reliability, criticality, perseverance, a lack of presuppositions, openness, curiosity, patience, precision, etc. (Janaway 2006). The basic difference between Nietzschean and scientific research methods is his lack of neutrality, which he regards as a necessary condition of fruitful philosophising (FW-*Vorrede*-3; FW-345). Nietzsche believes that the limits to the scientific view of the world do not permit us to truly understand being (Jaspers 1979). Besides, he utilises many aphoristic arguments which are often expressed in a commanding tone, unsupported by any argumentation, let alone scientific research. These include some of his most important thoughts: the source of moral judgements lying in *ressentiment*; the concept of the will to power, the idea of the eternal recurrence, the *Übermensch*, etc. Nietzsche himself is also extremely sceptical of the idea of causality (FW-112; JGB-21, GD-*Irrthuemer*),

71 'In the beginning was the law', as Shestov ironically comments on Kant (Shestov 1932, 46).

72 The first chapter of Brian Leiter's book entitled *Nietzsche on Morality* poses the question in its title 'Naturalism or postmodernism?', with Leiter supporting the former (Leiter 2002, 1).

and thus feels some reluctance to engage with traditional epistemology and rejects the idea of objective truth (FW-345).

If by ontological naturalism we understand the position most frequently termed monism or ontological reductionism, which reduces all phenomena to natural facts, then ascribing it to Nietzsche is a serious error and may result in an oversimplification of his anti-metaphysical claims. Nietzsche rejects the existence of the supersensuous world (GD-*Fabel*), undermines notions such as 'free will' (JGB-19; JGB-21; GD-*Irrthuemer*-7; AC-14), and regards 'the self' as an illusion (FW-11; NF-1885–35[35]; NF-1885–40[16]; NF-1885–40[20], NF-1885–40[23]). At the same time, however, he sharply criticises social Darwinism and evolutionary psychology (GM-*Vorrede*-1–5; GM-I-1; GM-I-2; GM-II-13), which are the most radical forms of naturalism. He vigorously opposes materialism, physicalism and mechanism (FW-109; FW-373; GM-III-16; JGB-12; JGB-14), whose representatives are today considered to be the most representative groups of ontological naturalists. Nietzsche categorically rejects the possibility of ascribing psychological, aesthetic and ethical etc., phenomena to physical facts (Leiter 2002). He believes that there are no phenomena (facts) in themselves, as we can read in the first of the fragments quoted above, but only certain (moral, legal, physical or mathematical) *interpretations* of the phenomena (JGB-108). He feels, therefore, that one should not talk about 'the laws of physics' as if the world had been created together with a set of some laws, but rather only about necessities which appear in nature; the world is regarded by him as chaotic and not founded on laws; order is thus an exception rather than the rule in the world (FW-109).[73] The 'laws of nature' are only formulations which describe power relations (NF-1885,34[247]); they are not explanations of the world, only interpretations of it. Nietzsche holds

73 'The astral order in which we live is an exception; this order and the considerable duration that is conditioned by it have again made possible the exception of exceptions: the development of the organic. The total character of the world, by contrast, is for all eternity chaos, not in the sense of a lack of necessity but of a lack of order, organization, form, beauty, wisdom (…). [I]t is neither perfect, nor beautiful, nor noble, nor does it want to become any of these things; in no way does it strive to imitate man! In no way do our aesthetic and moral judgments apply to it! It also has no drive to self-preservation or any other drives; nor does it observe any laws. Let us beware of saying that there are laws in nature. There are only necessities: there is no one who commands, no one who obeys, no one who transgresses. (…) When will all these shadows of god no longer darken us? When will we have completely de-deified nature? When may we begin to *naturalize* humanity with a pure, newly discovered, newly redeemed nature?' (Nietzsche 2001, 109–110).

that our mental representations of the world refer not to the world itself but to other images of the world (Leiter 1994). Thus we may only talk about physical (JGB-14), mathematical (FW-246), and moral interpretations (JGB-108). They cannot be reduced to one unified and universal scientific interpretation as the advocates of ontological naturalism would like; none of them is, according to Nietzsche, epistemologically privileged.

There are, however, better and worse interpretations – the mechanistic view is an example of one which Nietzsche feels is too reductionist, too superficial and infertile, as we can read in the third fragment above; he terms it the 'philosophy of the façade' (NF-1885,34[247]; see NF-1885,35[15]). The limitations of this interpretation are illustrated by Nietzsche through the example of music (FW-373).[74] Music explained by reference to scientific explanation (the physics of sound) is senseless since it cannot provide us with understanding of what music *means* for us. This same analogy may be applied to other cultural products, including morality. In other words, the scientific interpretation of the world which is proposed by positivism is no 'crystal palace' within which humanity dwells but is rather more reminiscent of a hen house in which humanity can seek shelter from the rain. The metaphor is to be found in a writer dear to Nietzsche's heart, Dostoyevsky:

> You believe in a palace of crystal that can never be destroyed—a palace at which one will not be able to put out one's tongue or make a long nose on the sly. And perhaps that is just why I am afraid of this edifice, that it is of crystal and can never be destroyed and that one cannot put one's tongue out at it even on the sly. You see, if it were not a palace, but a hen-house, I might creep into it to avoid getting wet, and yet I would not call the hen-house a palace out of gratitude to it for keeping me dry. You laugh and say that in such circumstances a hen-house is as good as a mansion. Yes, I answer, if one had to live simply to keep out of the rain. But what is to be done if I have taken it into my head that is not the object in life, and that if one must live one had better live in a mansion? (Dostoyevsky 2006, 41).

---

74 'That the only rightful interpretation of the world should be one to which *you* have a right; one by which one can do research and go on scientifically in *your* sense of the term (you really mean *mechanistically*?) – one that permits counting, calculating, weighing, seeing, grasping, and nothing else – that is a crudity and naiveté, assuming it is not a mental illness, and idiocy. (…) Suppose one judged the *value* of a piece of music according to how much of it could be counted, calculated, and expressed in formulas – how absurd such a "scientific" evaluation of music would be! Nothing, really nothing of what is "music" in it!' (Nietzsche 2001, 238–239).

One may interpret the philosophy of Nietzsche as a form of naturalism but only broadly understood, encompassing the cultural-historical sphere of human life which cannot be reduced to the physical-biological sphere.[75] The philosopher himself sees it as a 'new philosophy' (MAI-*Vorrede*-I; JGB-42; JGB-43), a philosophy of 'free spirits' which is to replace and follow the era of nihilism. One might say that Nietzsche utilises naturalism to 'de-deify' nature, which does not mean reducing the world to natural phenomena but rather creating a new interpretation of humanity, moving beyond the dispute between naturalism and anti-naturalism. The naturalisation of humanity which manifested itself in numerous fields in the 19th century was not a return to nature from civilization, which Rousseau dreamed of, but rather the next stage of the development of that same civilization that the French philosopher rejected (NF-1887,10[53]). The newly liberated nature is one which has overcome all a priori assumptions and values – it is neither good nor bad, true nor false, ordered or chaotic – it just is, permanently becoming. By the 'naturalisation of man' or 'translating humanity back to nature' (JGB-230; cf. FW-109) Nietzsche understands interpreting humanity without referring to Platonic-Christian metaphysics. Naturalism is to serve to rid the human nature of guilt – in other words, it is the way to immoralism, as we can read in the last of the fragments above. I will develop this thought in subsequent chapters.

75 For the interpretation of Nietzsche's philosophy in terms of non-reductive naturalism see, for instance, Sedgwick 2013; Schacht 1983; cf. Acampora 2006; Cox 1999; Janaway 2006.

Chapter 2. 'The sponge to wipe away the horizon': the normative character of cognition

The lie made into the rule of the world.
Franz Kafka[76]

Dass jeder deutet sich die Welt in seinem Sinn,
Und jeder deutet recht; so viel ist Sinn darin.
Friedrich Rückert[77]

In the previous chapter the claim was made that, together with the loss of faith in God, the horizon would be wiped clear (FW-125). The metaphor of the horizon can be found in Plato (Plato 1998) and Kant (Kant 2000), and Nietzsche perhaps utilises it intentionally. The horizon here has many meanings, the first being the moral one – the horizon of good and evil. The second is the cognitive one – according to Nietzsche, in losing the metaphysical horizon we also lose the perspective necessary to interpret and order the world; the border between heaven and earth disappears so that we are left without points of reference, criteria and goals for our knowledge (NF-1881,14[25]). Both meanings are closely interrelated for Nietzsche as he regards evaluation as a means of interpreting the world and interpretation is a form of knowledge. As Gadamer writes:

> Since Nietzsche and Husserl, the word has been used in philosophy to characterize the way in which thought is tied to its finite determinacy, and the way one's range of vision is gradually expanded. A person who has no horizon does not see far enough and hence over-values what is nearest to him. On the other hand, 'to have a horizon' means not being limited to what is nearby but being able to see beyond it. A person who has an horizon knows the relative significance of everything within this horizon, whether it is near or far, great or small (Gadamer 2013, 313).

In his first works Nietzsche emphasises the importance of the horizon which gave unity to a culture. For him, this horizon was the myth of Dionysus and Apollo, providing the tension between the general and the individual. It was thwarted by Socrates whose philosophy gave rise to the birth of the 'abstract man' for whom culture has 'no secure and sacred place of origin' (GT-23, Nietzsche 2007b, 109). By culture Nietzsche mainly understands something more than the external decoration of life –

76 From *The Trial* by Franz Kafka (Kafka 2014, 415).
77 From *Die Weisheit des Brahmanen* by Friedrich Rückert (Rückert 2017, 12).

'culture as a unanimity of life, thought, appearance and will' (HL-10, Nietzsche 2007c, 123). That is the what and how a person lives, something which cannot be divided into the internal and the external. Culture as an expression of spiritual strength is the highest of values for Nietzsche (CV-CV3). Frederick Copleston thus aptly describes Nietzsche as a philosopher of culture, at the same time arguing that his war upon Christian values contributed to the degeneration of the very European culture that he so prized (Copleston 1975). The effect of this destruction are contemporary people in pursuit of their roots which they have deprived themselves of and are eternally unsatisfied as a result. Nietzsche comes to the conclusion that we must wholeheartedly and joyfully turn to face the open sea in order to create our own horizons, although he admits that this will be far from easy (FW-124).[78] Jose Ortega y Gasset was of a similar mind when he compared the 20th century to childhood:

> [I]s it not clear that the feelings of our time are more like the noisy joy of children let loose from school? Nowadays we no longer know what is going to happen tomorrow in our world, and this causes us a secret joy; because that very impossibility of foresight, that horizon ever open to all contingencies, constitute authentic life, the true fullness of our existence (Ortega y Gasset 1950, 24).

Ortega also saw danger lurking here, adding that the newly discovered world was terrifying since 'everything is possible, the best and the worst' (Ortega y Gasset 1950, 24).

A different meaning of horizon applies to the temporal nature of human existence. It features as a horizon in the work of Schopenhauer, who claims that a genius expands his horizons in art, going beyond his own experience, person and reality which he finds himself in – by breaking these boundaries, he creates a broader horizon pursuing it with a relentless desire and a dissatisfaction with the present (Schopenhauer 2010, §36). This aspect will be explored in the second part of the book.

I. A Critique of the will to truth

1. Knowledge as an adventure of the spirit

> In some remote corner of the universe, effused into innumerable solar-systems, there was once a star upon which clever animals invented cognition. It was the haughtiest, most mendacious moment in the history of this world (...). [F]ew things are more incomprehensible than the way in which an honest and pure impulse to truth could have arisen among men. They are deeply immersed in illusions and dream-fancies; their eyes

78 '*In the horizon of the infinite.* – We have forsaken the land and gone to sea! We have destroyed the bridge behind us – more so, we have demolished the land behind us!' (Nietzsche 2001, 119).

glance only over the surface of things and see 'forms'; their sensation nowhere leads to truth, but contents itself with receiving stimuli and, so to say, with playing hide-and-seek on the back of things (WL-1, Nietzsche 1911b, 173–175).

[W]hat do the people actually take knowledge to be? what do they want when they want 'knowledge'? Nothing more than this: something unfamiliar is to be traced back to something *familiar*. And we philosophers – have we really meant anything *more* by knowledge? The familiar means what we are used to, so that we no longer marvel at it (…). And isn't our need for knowledge precisely this need for the familiar, the will to uncover among everything strange, unusual, and doubtful something which no longer unsettles us? Is it not the *instinct of fear* that bids us to know? And isn't the rejoicing of the person who attains knowledge just rejoicing from a regained sense of security?… (…) For 'what is familiar is known': on this they agree. (…) Error of errors! The familiar is what we are used to, and what we are used to is the most difficult to 'know' – that is, to view as a problem, to see as strange, as distant, as 'outside us'… The great certainty of the natural sciences in comparison with psychology and the critique of the elements of consciousness – with the *unnatural* sciences (…) – rests precisely on the fact that they take the *strange* as their object, while it is nearly contradictory and absurd even to *want* to take the not-strange as one's object… (FW-355, Nietzsche 2001, 214–215).

In terms of knowledge, Nietzsche advances the idea that we do not have privileged access to the world. He emphasises the anthropomorphic nature of human cognition which reduced everything to a human perspective, unjustly positing that it is an objective and universal perspective. One cannot compare the manner in which a human being views the world with that of another being such as an animal since there are no objective criteria governing perception, as he goes on to say in the rest of the fragment cited above. This leads him to the conclusion that since the cognition of any being can be given priority and since there is no being that would guarantee correct knowledge, this means that we cannot talk about the existence of the world in itself but rather about different images of that world, none of which can have an exclusive claim to the truth (cf. FW-374). The assumption that the world by itself is apprehensible by humans may only be maintained when we accept that the world and humanity were *created* and that the world has a structure compatible with human perceptual capabilities. People were not, in the opinion of Nietzsche, equipped with any specific instruments for discerning the truth (FW-354).[79] He recognises that we are only skating over the surface, discovering thoughts created by us to interpret the reality around us which we have grown used to regarding as

79 'We simply have no organ for *knowing*, for "truth": we "know" (or believe or imagine) exactly as much as is *useful* to the human herd, to the species: and even what is here called "usefulness" is finally also just a belief, a fiction, and perhaps just that supremely fatal stupidity of which we someday will perish' (Nietzsche 2001, 214).

the truth. Images of the world which are created by the human mind and which are common to most people are regarded as necessary truths.

Still in Nietzsche's lifetime, *The Chautauquan* magazine posed the question of whether a tree falling on a desert island with no one there to hear it would make a sound.[80] The reply developed by another magazine, the *Scientific American*, was the following: no, since a sound is nothing more than a vibration of waves transmitted to our senses by our ears and only interpreted as a sound by our nervous system; thus even though the falling tree would bring about vibrations in the air, a suitable organ is required to interpret them as a sound. One may consider the question of the existence of colours in a similar manner. The human mind constantly generates detailed images of the surrounding reality which are, in a sense, delusions since they do not correspond to any objective external reality in itself, but are real representations in the same sense as human feelings of pain or joy. Nietzsche thus mocks the human drive for the truth, understood as access to the world in itself, recognising a human being as a creative animal – creating an image of the world in which it lives.[81]

The only privileged access that we have is to ourselves and thus the main goal of cognition is knowledge of oneself, constituting a source of experience for ourselves (MAI-292; FW-324).[82] Nietzsche identifies our knowledge of the world with the human nervous system (NF-1880,10[E95]). People do not uncover the world in itself but only their own conceptual apparatus (M-483), their own 'callipers' (NF-1880,10[D83]), and hence knowledge of self is the limit of knowledge of all other things (M-48). A similar thought is expressed by the Heisenberg paradox, in accordance with which 'man, whenever he tries to learn about things which neither are himself not owe their existence to him, will ultimately encounter nothing but himself, his own constructions, and the patterns of his actions' (Heisenberg in Arendt 1961, 86).[83] Knowing oneself, however, also entails two fundamental

---

80 The Chautauquan, June 1883, (3)9: 543; see Scientific American 1884, 218.

81 Nietzsche also focuses on the fact that since our organs create an image of the world which we regard as true, there would be no difference between a dream and reality, if only our dreams were repeated regularly (WL-1). And since life is only possible thanks to the creation of appearances, the world which we are interested in may just be a figment of our imagination.

82 'No, life has not disappointed me. Rather, I find it truer, more desirable and mysterious every year – ever since the day the great liberator overcame me: the thought that life could be an experiment for the knowledge-seeker – not a duty, not a disaster, not a deception! (...) "*Life as a means to knowledge*" – with this principle in one's heart one can not only live bravely but also *live gaily and laugh gaily*!' (Nietzsche 2001, 181).

83 Heisenberg formulates this thought in a different context among others in his book *Das Naturbild der heutigen Physik*, Hamburg 1956.

problems connected with the proximity to ourselves and, at the same time, the distance. It is hard to get to know ourselves as we are too close (FW-*Vorspiel*-25), and thus cannot see ourselves clearly. This is reflected in the metaphor of the eye, which sees everything beyond us but not ourselves (cf. Wittgenstein 2002, 5.633).[84] Another difficulty in knowing ourselves stems from the fact that we are locked in a delusive 'chamber of consciousness', that one has been separated from its own body by nature – from 'the convulsions of the intestines, the quick flow of the blood-currents' (WL-1, Nietzsche 1911b, 175–176).

In the second fragment cited above, Nietzsche warns that the common understanding of knowledge, which is not so different from the one adopted by most of the philosophers, leads to the *taming of the world* in which we live. That which we think we know is simply what we have become accustomed to. Nietzsche rejects knowledge as striving for certainty; for him, it is something which is the exact opposite – the constant questioning of all certainties, unmasking statements which stem from habit, it is an adventure, an expedition into the unknown, into danger, something which should make us shudder (FW-374; GD-*Deutsche*-7). Habits, much like dogmas, are harmful to thinking, which is rather an experiment and game (FW-51; Za-IV-*Wissenschaft*; EH-*Weise*-1).

2. The rejection of metaphysical truth: the will to appearance instead of the will to truth

> God is dead; but given the way people are, there may still for millennia be caves in which they show his shadow. – And we – we must still defeat his shadow as well! (FW-108, Nietzsche 2001, 109).
>
> [I]t is still a *metaphysical faith* upon which our faith in science rests – that even we knowers of today, we godless antimetaphysicians, still take *our* fire, too, from the flame lit by the thousand-year old faith, the Christian faith which was also Plato's faith, that God is truth; that truth is divine… But what if this were to become more and more difficult to believe, if nothing more were to turn out to be divine except error, blindness, the lie – if God himself were to turn out to be our longest lie? (FW-344, Nietzsche 2001, 201).
>
> '[N]othing is true, everything is permitted'… (…) Has a European or a Christian freethinker [*Freigeist*] ever strayed into this proposition and the labyrinth of its *consequences*? Does he know the Minotaur of this cave *from experience*?… (GM-III-24, Nietzsche 2007a, 111–112).

---

84 Wittgenstein in this context criticises the a priori nature of knowledge and the fictional metaphysical subject, claiming that the subject is not a part of the world but the limit of our experience of it.

The shadows may be identified with appearances and connected to the Platonic parable of the cave referred to in the first and last fragments. The cave described in *The Republic* is a symbol of the sensuous world and its inhabitants are prisoners of their own habits (Plato 2004). Their lives amount to looking at shadows on the wall of the cave which are the work of their deceivers (sophists), the reflections being caused by the manipulation of the artificial light of a fire (the Promethean gift of knowledge). The deceivers for Nietzsche may be the philistines he criticized in *Untimely Mediations*, accusing them of obscuring the difference between what was alive and what was dead, what was honest and dishonest, original and imitated, seeing the *living God* in totems and idols (DS-12). The Sage, however, is able to escape from the cave and to see the sun, the symbol of truth. Nietzsche's 'madman' is in many respects a counterpart to Plato's sage since he unmasks the deficiencies of the metaphysical notions utilized by philosophers. The difference between the cave of Plato and that of Nietzsche is in what this 'madman' discovers – that there is no independent source of light, no 'lining to the world'.[85] In other words, he also unmasks Plato as a great fraud of the type mentioned above.

Nietzsche recalls in his works that myths were, for the Ancient Greeks, the counterpart to the sun, which guarantees life, joy, beauty and truth, with the rest of life being darkness (MAI-261).[86] Ancient philosophers rejected myths, although they did not exactly want to live in darkness – on the contrary, they thought they would be better able to replace it with the light of *Logos*. Plato, the opponent of Homer, enriched the world with an unlimited number of copies, as Roberto Calasso notes, 'and illuminated those copies with the art of reason', obscuring the glamour of gods and goddesses (Calasso 1994, 290). In the opinion of Nietzsche, it had the opposite effect, with humans moving from the omnipresent light of sunbeams to the gloom illuminated solely by the flickering candle of reason. This reached its climax in the Enlightenment, which one may surmise from its very name, which was intended to bring the *illumination* of reason to philosophical problems and yet in fact brought a large degree of disenchantment.

In the Bible, which Nietzsche frequently referred to, God was the source of light, identified with the eternal, transcendental light which illuminated the faithful (Jn 1,5; Jn 8,12; Ps 4,7; Is 49,6, etc.). 'Light' is the symbol of religious truth and

---

85 I refer to Czesław Miłosz's poem entitled *Meaning*:

> And if there is no lining to the world? (...)
> And on this earth there is nothing except this earth? (Miłosz 1996, trans. Cz. Miłosz and R. Hass, 393).

86 In the mythical world, the sun that never set was associated with an omniscient God, the eye of Zeus (see Stolleis 2004).

moral good whilst 'darkness' represents delusion, error, and evil. Thus, announcing the 'death of God' in the fragment from *The Gay Science* analysed earlier, Nietzsche writes about the separation of the earth from the sun. What would the 'shadow of God' be if the existence of God was to be rejected? It would be a dead letter, an empty idea, a truth that would come to light in the rays of reason.

Nietzsche highlights the existence of a linguistic analogy between perceiving (*wahrnehmen*) and taking something as real (*Etwas-als-wahr-nehmen*) (NF-1885,34[132]). Perception is just one means of knowledge. As Arendt noted, thinking can be identified with the pursuit of meaning, and knowledge is focused on seeing truth or seeing something *in the light* of truth (Arendt 1981a). The connection of knowing truth with visual acuity can be found in the New Testament. In his famous hymn to love, St Paul writes: 'For now we see through a glass, darkly; but then face to face: now I know in part; but then shall I know even as also I am known' (1 Cor 13,12). The perfect knowledge which St Paul is referring to here is the knowledge of God since 'God, strictly speaking, does not know truth but *is* truth' (Kołakowski 2001, 84), truth made incarnate (Jn 14,6).

Furthermore, those who have been given the gift of faith and live in accordance with the will of God are also 'of the truth' (1 Jn 3,19). This knowledge is not derived from reason or the heart but acquired by our entire being. Thus, a desire for absolute truth is nothing other than a *desire for the Absolute*. Nietzsche poses the thesis that a desire to attain the truth does not indicate that there must be a satisfaction of this desire called the truth (MAI-131).[87] One should note here, however, that the opposite conclusion is also unfounded, as Leszek Kołakowski notes, i.e. a desire for something does not mean that what we long for is an illusion (Kołakowski 1988). Nietzsche believes that this great desire stems from a great lack of precisely that what is longed for, for example wanting strong faith is an expression of the fact that one does not have it (GD-*Streifzuege*-12). For him, human desire for absolute truth is an expression of the weakness of humanity, which is unable to bear the weight of its own contingency or rise to the challenge of rooting themselves. In rejecting God, one must be brave enough to reject all 'his shadows', including truth in itself, which may not be present in the world if there is nobody who could have hidden it in the world.

Nietzsche adopts the epistemological position of a sceptic, holding that since there are no epistemological Absolutes, then all attempts to establish universal

87 'Hunger does not prove that the food that would sate it *exists*, yet it wishes for this food. "Having a presentiment" does not mean knowing in any degree that something exists, but instead, taking its existence to be possible insofar as we wish for it or fear it' (Nietzsche 2000, 100).

criteria for binding knowledge about the world either lead to infinite regress or to a vicious circle and a paradox of self-reference (Kołakowski 1988). He claims that it is necessary to reject fragmentary truth, which becomes senseless without reference to all-encompassing truth; in other words, there is no 'ultimate certainty without God' (Kołakowski 2001, 81). Nietzsche's opposition to the concept of truth is thus a *metaphysical opposition*.[88] Nietzsche puts forward the notion that the development of modern science is fuelled by the Christian faith in a metaphysical absolute truth, from which knowledge constantly feels its impetus, even when this knowledge is anti-metaphysical and godless. He also claims that the final effect of this Christian 'discipline for truth' of the last two thousand years is radical atheism, since this pursuit of absolute truth has led to the creation of the 'scientific conscience' and intellectual honesty which have undermined Christian dogmas and revealed their weaknesses (FW-344; FW-357;[89] GM-III-24).

The last of the fragments to be considered refers to the resulting problem for morality in rejecting metaphysical truth. The above sentence, that since there is no truth then everything is permitted, is related to the famous line of Dostoyevsky's: 'If there is no God then everything is permitted'. Both are based on the assumption that it is unjustifiable to use the notion of 'truth' when one rejects the existence of an absolute mind (Kołakowski 2001). Nietzsche read Dostoevsky and deliberately changed the word 'God' into 'truth' in order to reveal the hidden dependency of truth (in a metaphysical sense) on God. The line is to be found in Nietzsche's works seven times and each time it is put in inverted commas, perhaps suggesting that it is meant to be read as a citation.[90] It suggests that Nietzsche distanced himself from the utterance, seeing it as an expression of nihilism and a natural consequence of the 'death of God'. He mocks the nihilist position by recounting the ancient paradox of the radical sceptic: if someone says that 'nothing is true, everything is permitted', then they must also accept that disagreeing with this

---

88 'Truth seldom dwells where people have built temples for it and have ordained priests.' A letter to Carl von Gersdorff of April 6, 1867 (Nietzsche 1996, 23).

89 'One can see *what* it was that actually triumphed over the Christian god: Christian morality itself, the concept of truthfulness that was taken ever more rigorously; the father confessor's refinement of the Christian conscience, translated and sublimated into a scientific conscience, into intellectual cleanliness at any price' (Nietzsche 2001, 219).

90 In *Thus Spoke Zarathustra* these words are spoken to Zarathustra by his shadow which has fallen upon him and from which he wants to escape (Za-IV-*Schatten*). He wrote in his notes that the quoted sentence is a sign of the utmost confusion (NF-1884,25[322]) and the most dangerous thinking (NF-1884,32[8]).

statement is also possible and realise that this means either that this sentence is not true or that it is – but in both cases there is a contradiction (NF-1884,31[51]).

People accepting and rejecting the existence of truth are like those who believe and who do not, they 'have no way of convincing each other, and their incapacity and doggedness reveal that their respective epistemological decisions are irreducibly different with no supreme judge in sight' (Kołakowski 2001, 76), as Kołakowski noted, adding further:

> [W]hen a sceptic says 'nothing is true' he means 'it is true that nothing is true'; thus his position is self-defeating as a result of an inescapable contradiction (…). This counter-argument is hardly convincing. A sceptic (…) may well be satisfied with contending that the predicate 'true' is needless and its use unjustifiable (Kołakowski 2001, 80).

Nietzsche moves in this direction, protecting his sceptical position by refusing the predicate 'true' in the field of knowledge, just as he refuses the predicate 'good' in the field of morality. The doubt which led Nietzsche to reject the properties of 'true', invalidated the same act of doubt which would be pointless without it.[91] Instead of freedom in the field of values, he adopts the freedom to create new values which are connected with greater responsibility. Both may only be undertaken by higher people who are in a position to endure nihilism to its bitter end and overcome it – the new philosophers, artists and lawgivers (NF-1885,34[201]), which I will later elaborate on.

An interesting connection between the parable of Plato's Cave and the mythological figure of the Minotaur surfaces in the last fragment – the monster locked in his labyrinth and feasting on young Athenians offered up to him in sacrifice until he was defeated by Theseus, who was able to escape thanks to Ariadne's thread. One should also note that Ariadne becomes betrothed to Dionysus, a fact which is of considerable significance to her role in Nietzsche's philosophy. The symbolic and intriguing figure of Ariadne is remarkably important in the later period of his philosophy (see Jaspers 1979; Kerényi 1971; Otto 1965). In this context, the analogy between the cave and the labyrinth indicates some kind of imprisonment. The connection of the two suggests that humanity is trapped in a world of illusions and that the way out is through knowledge, in both cases as a result of knowledge from the outside, from the 'true world'. As much as the sage of Plato manages to escape from the cave by himself thanks to the strength of his reason, the Greek hero needs the help of a woman. One may identify all those thoughts for which one sacrifices his

---

91 As Kołakowski writes, '[m]y act of doubting implies that I believe something to be true, but I am unable to decide what is. Once the quality "true" is abrogated, doubting is pointless' (Kołakowski 1988, 27).

or her instincts and which terrify humans with the Minotaur (cf. NF-1887,9[105]). Theseus is thus a philosopher who kills the monster and the thing that guides him through the labyrinth is the *will to truth* (Ariadne's thread). It transpires, however, that the person who was meant to save him – Ariadne – turns out to be his own personal labyrinth who leads him astray and leads him to face something much worse than a Minotaur; because of Ariadne mighty heroes perish (NF-1887,9[115]). In other words, if I decipher the symbolism correctly, the same will to truth which drives a philosopher beyond the world of the senses, leads to the falsification of the supersensuous and results in dooming a thinker to nihilism.

Assistance in this new labyrinth of delusion may be an entirely new philosophical position advocated by Nietzsche. This is that of the 'free spirits' (JGB-44) and the Hyperboreans who are 'full of malice', 'curious to a fault', 'researchers to the point of cruelty' (JGB-44, Nietzsche 2002, 41–42). They are interested in the labyrinth and, instead of killing the Minotaur, they want to get to know him (NF-1888,23[3]). They do not wish to escape from the labyrinth with the aid of a thread, which they see only as a rope which one can only hang oneself with. They discover that the apparent world is not the true world but rather the world 'adjusted' by us which we experience as real; beyond this world there is no other true world, but only a formless chaos which we are unable to know (NF-1887,9[105]). These new figures are known as 'the people of the labyrinth', who do not seek truth within it but rather *seek their Ariadne* (NF-1882,4[55]).[92] Ariadne is thus an eternal delusion and symbol of never-ending cognitive unease, a stimulation to create – it is reminiscent of the titular girl from the poem by Bolesław Leśmian, for whose voice twelve brothers devote their lives.[93] The symbol of the new philosophy is not Theseus, who has been a moralist destroyed by truth, but rather Dionysus – the experimenter and tempter,[94] who tests and allows himself to be tested, who seduces and lets himself be seduced

92 In Greek mythology, the labyrinth is not a circular route but rather a spiral, being like a *dance* (Kerényi 1997) which also matches Nietzsche's idea of comparing thinking to a *dance* – a certain art of movement, without a goal, an exit point (GD-*Deutsche*-7).

93 A poem by Bolesław Leśmian, entitled *A Girl*, [*Dziewczyna*], tells the story of twelve brothers who sacrificed their lives to rescue a girl whose voice they could hear from behind the wall; when finally the wall collapsed, beyond the wall there was not a thing:

> Nobody's eyes, nobody's lips! Mid flowers nobody's hidden fate!
> Because it was sound, only a sound, nothing else in any form of shape! (…)
> Then a horror of overwhelming silence on the earth and in the blue.
> Why do you so often sneer at that silence when it doesn't sneer at you? (Leśmian 2000, 124).

94 The German word *Versucher* captures both meanings in the same word.

(NF-1885,22[44]).[95] Dionysus is also a philosopher of becoming. When Dionysus replaces Theseus, the roles are reversed – he becomes a labyrinth for Ariadne, it is he who ensnares and torments, controlling her instead of letting her control him (NF-1887,9[115]; DD-*Ariadne*).

Stefan Zweig accurately captures the philosophical stance of Nietzsche, contrasting it with the method of Kant, who was driven by a desire for order and a desire to discipline the mind and whose 'relationship to truth was essentially monogamous', but his love of the truth lacked eroticism (Zweig 2012, 320). Contrary to Kant, Nietzsche applies one of the strongest spiritual passions towards the truth 'which arose from a totally different emotional world':

> For just as genuine seducers are forever seeking among womankind the one and only woman of their hearts, so did Nietzsche seek among all kinds of knowledge the unique knowledge of his choice, the knowledge doomed to everlasting unreality and eternally eluding his grasp. It was not desire for conquest and possession and sensual enjoyment which stirred him, thrilled him and reduced him almost to despair, but invariably questionings, doubts, the pursuit of knowledge. He loved insecurity not certainty (Zweig 2012, 321–322).

The philosopher in Nietzsche appears as a seducer (FW-99; NF-1885,40[50]),[96] the Don Juan of knowledge (M-327),[97] who does not desire truth in knowledge, often construed as feminine by Nietzsche (NW-*Epilog*-2; NF-1888–20[48]; JGB-*Vorrede*), but just the pure pleasure of knowledge.[98] The task of philosophy, as of

95 Nietzsche emphasizes that Dionysus is a philosopher (JGB-295; NF-1883,23[8]; NF-1883,23[13]; NF-1885,2[11]; NF-1885,35[47]) and considers himself a student of Dionysus (NF-1885,22[44]) to finally become Dionysus himself. It is worth mentioning that when he was on the edge of madness Nietzsche used to sign his last letters and cards written to friends, among others to Jacob Burckhardt and to Cosima Wagner, as Dionysus (e.g. BVN-1889,1250; BVN-1889,1249; BVN-1889,1246; BVN-1889,1245; BVN-1889,1242a).

96 Nietzsche identifies the following as great seducers: Plato (NF-1888,14[94]), Socrates (NF-1885,39[22]), Jesus (NF-1888,12[1]), Wagner (NF-1888,14[65]), and even Zarathustra (NF-1883,13[4], Za-IV-*Wissenschaft*, EH-*Vorrede*-4).

97 'The Don Juan of knowledge: no philosopher or poet has yet discovered him. He does not love the things he knows, but has spirit and appetite for and enjoyment of the chase and intrigues of knowledge – up to the highest and remotest stars of knowledge! – until at last there remains to him nothing of knowledge left to hunt down except the absolutely *detrimental*; he is like the drunkard who ends by drinking absinthe and *aqua fortis*. Thus in the end he lusts after Hell – it is the last knowledge that *seduces* him (…) – for the whole universe has not a single morsel left to give to this hungry man' (Nietzsche 2005a, 161).

98 As he scornfully writes, 'a beautiful woman has something in common with truth (…) they both make you happier in their pursuit than in their possession' (NF-1876,19[52], Nietzsche 1999 (trans. A. Shaw), vol. 8, 342).

art, is to *seduce us to live*, to create an illusion that the absurd and accidental nature of our lives is something bearable.[99]

The search for metaphysical truth may also be understood as pursuit of a unity of being which has plagued people since antiquity – the first source (*arche*) that we encounter for the first time in Parmenides. Nietzsche admits that he himself attempted to 'seek out the foundations' (FW-*Vorspiel*-61), the Archimedean point, which I will later elaborate on referring. Nonetheless, he rejected the philosophical obsession with monism,[100] opting for pluralism, and for *becoming* instead of being. The desire for truth stems from the human need for safety – seeking permanence in the world and a permanent point of reference that makes life possible. In this respect, 'logicising, rationalising, systematising', with the aid of which we constantly order the world and our experiences, are for Nietzsche 'life's resources', as we can read in his notes (NF-1887,9[91]). In the same place he adds that truth fulfils the role of reinforcing and 'reinterpreting into something that *is*' our experience. To make something real means to make it permanent and enduring. Truth, therefore, is not something to be discovered in the world but something that is created, which is a never-ending process and expression of our will to control the world. In the world nothing just is, because everything is constantly in the process of becoming and that which is coming into being cannot be fixed as a form of being (truth). Our belief in truth is thus only an anticipation of our power to create which depends on constantly 'inventing the world'. In contrast to the will to truth (the will to reality and permanence) is *the will to appearance* (the will to becoming and change), which Nietzsche ascribes an Apollonian-Dionysian character to and regards as being more metaphysical than the will to truth (NF-1888,14[18]). It is something which delights since it is the will to create and to shape, but also to demolish and destroy; the will to truth is only its consequence and it induces suffering, which if taken to the highest degree may itself become a delight. As a result, Nietzsche advises philosophers that instead of striving for 'truth at any price', which he himself treasured in his youth, they should fall in

---

99 In his earlier notes, Nietzsche wrote that 'the goal of beauty is to seduce one to life' (*Der Zweck des Schönen ist das zum Dasein Verführen*, NF-1870,7[27], Nietzsche 1999 (trans. A. Shaw), vol. 7, 144.). Religion is the opposite of art in this regard since it rejects everything that might be regarded as a temptation and holds that seduction undermines the value of life (HL-8).

100 As Kołakowski accurately points out, 'this obsession with monism, the stubborn passion to arrange the world in accordance with a single unifying principle, this search for a magic formula to make reality decipherable, proves to be more lasting' than anything else in our intellectual development (Kołakowski 1963, 316). Cf. Murdoch 1992.

love with the 'Olympus of appearances' and remain at a superficial level like the Greeks who had been 'superficial – *out of profundity*!' (FW-*Vorrede*-4, Nietzsche 2001, 8). The spirit, according to Nietzsche, is guided towards appearances and the surface level, and not to the depths, thus desiring life and joy rather than death and suffering (JGB-229).

2.1. Truth as a useful illusion

> *Origin of knowledge.* – Through immense periods of time, the intellect produced nothing but errors; some of them turned out to be useful and species-preserving; those who hit upon or inherited them fought their fight for themselves and their progeny with greater luck. Such erroneous articles of faith, which were passed on by inheritance further and further, and finally almost became part of the basic endowment of the species, are for example: that there are enduring things; that there are identical things; that there are things, kinds of material, bodies; that a thing is what it appears to be; that our will is free; that what is good for me is also good in and for itself. (…) Thus the *strength* of knowledge lies not in its degree of truth, but in its age, its embeddedness, its character as a condition of life. (…) [E]very kind of drive took part in the fight about the 'truths'; the intellectual fight became an occupation, attraction, profession, duty, dignity (…). Thus knowledge became a part of life and, as life, a continually growing power, until finally knowledge and the ancient basic errors struck against each other, both as life, both as power, both in the same person. The thinker – that is now the being in whom the drive to truth and those life -preserving errors are fighting their first battle, after the drive to truth has *proven* itself to be a life-preserving power, too. (…) To what extent can truth stand to be incorporated? – that is the question; that is the experiment (FW-110, Nietzsche 2001, 110–112).
>
> This unconditional will to truth – what is it? Is it the will not to let oneself be deceived? Is it the will *not to deceive*? For the will to truth could be interpreted in this second way, too – if 'I do not want to deceive *myself*' is included as a special case under the generalization 'I do not want to deceive.' But why not to deceive? But why not allow oneself to be deceived? Note that the reasons for the former lie in a completely different area from those for the latter: one does not want to let oneself be deceived because one assumes it is harmful, dangerous, disastrous to be deceived; in this sense science would be a long-range prudence, caution, utility, and to this one could justifiably object: How so? Is it really less harmful, dangerous, disastrous not to want to let oneself be deceived? What do you know in advance about the character of existence to be able to decide whether the greater advantage is on the side of the unconditionally distrustful or of the unconditionally trusting? But should both be necessary – a lot of trust *as well as* a lot of mistrust – then where might science get the unconditional belief or conviction on which it rests, that truth is more important than anything else, than every other conviction? (…) So, the faith in science, which after all undeniably exists, cannot owe its origin to such a calculus of utility; rather it must have originated *in spite of* the fact that the disutility and dangerousness of 'the will to truth' or 'truth at any price' is proved to it constantly.

> (…) No doubt, those, who are truthful in that audacious and ultimate sense which faith in science presupposes *thereby affirm another world* than that of life, nature, and history; and insofar as they affirm this 'other world', must they not by the same token deny its counterpart, this world, *our* world?… (FW-344, Nietzsche 2001, 200–201).
>
> It is no more than a moral prejudice that the truth is worth more than appearance; in fact it is the world's most poorly proven assumption. Let us admit this much: that life could not exist except on the basis of perspectival valuations and appearances (JGB-34, Nietzsche 2002, 35).

In the philosophy of Plato, knowledge is the striving for truth and the expression of this by means of rejecting the world of the senses and achieving the eternal world of ideas. This was the beginning of our philosophical tradition, yet 'nothing was left of this experience but the opposition of thinking and acting, which depriving thought of reality and action of sense, makes both meaningless', as Arendt claims (Arendt 1961, 25). Nietzsche wants to overcome this opposition, giving priority to life over thought (NF-1885,40[23]; 1885,40[24]). He inverted Descartes *cogito ergo sum* ('I think, therefore I am'), adopting instead: *vivo, ergo cogito* ('I live, therefore I think') (HL-10). One might say, in the words of a poet, that he wants the 'grey theory of the tree of knowledge' to return to its roots and become again 'the green-gold tree of life'.[101] This was to be achieved by recognising the entirety of our lives as experience, providing us with a source of knowledge (FW-324). Knowledge proposed by him has a broad significance and is not limited to the speculations of reason (cf. Dilthey 1996) but has a spiritual-physical character, meaning that people know and learn both when and how they experience – with their whole being (Za-I-*Veraechter*). Nietzsche adopts the Christian idea of the *truth incarnate* (incorporated) in life. However, he understands it in a completely different way, as miscellaneous old errors and habits which were rooted in humanity thanks to its experience and inheritance, as he notes in the section of *The Gay Science* quoted above. The power of knowledge is to be seen, therefore, to the extent that these truths are embedded in human beings, which depends on their enduring nature and the conditions of human life. All human drives play a role in their creation, not just the mind. Knowledge stemming from reason regarded as the absolute truth may in fact endanger one's life by revealing the appearance of old truths. In the opinion of Nietzsche, this is exactly the case with many thinkers and it leads to the collision of powerful drives – the drive for

---

101 I refer to Goethe's Faust, who says:

> Grau, teurer Freund, ist alle Theorie,
> Und grün des Lebens goldner Baum (Goethe 1972, 59).

truth and the drive for life. Both are expressions of the same – the will to power, which I will expand upon in subsequent parts of this book.

Truth in Greek (*aletheia*) means 'unconcealment' and 'revealing' (Heidegger 1991b; Heidegger 1977). Untruth may be associated with a shadow which, according to Nietzsche, hides those who fear the consequence of the truth (MAI-39). Shadows may symbolize appearances or illusions (Ger. *Schein*), which are something different from lies; they are a unique type of untruth which one often creates out of necessity. Nietzsche himself explains that by appearances one may understand reality and the only reality of things (NF-1885,40[53]). Shadows serve to make those things which occur more beautiful (MAI-151), allowing them to attain greater significance – disguising something automatically highlights something else, just like metaphor in language which I will turn to shortly. In our lives we need both trust as well as distrust – something which we can regard as certain as well as uncertain. Georg Simmel neatly encapsulates this by noting:

> We are simply so equipped that we not only (...) need a certain proportion of truth and error [*Schein*] (...) but also of clarity and ambiguity in the pattern of our life's elements. What we see clearly short of the latter foundation thus shows us just the limit of its attraction and prohibits the fantasy from weaving into it its possibilities, for the loss of which no reality can compensate us (Simmel 2009, 324).

In reference to the abovementioned opposition between knowledge and action, Nietzsche emphasizes that in order to act we need illusions and appearances (GT-7);[102] in striving for the uncompromising uncovering of everything, we succeed in paralysing action and this makes life impossible. The thought that knowledge of the truth is a panacea for a sickness (the suffering of humanity) which turns out to be more dangerous than the disease, was probably taken by Nietzsche from Leopardi.[103] He records in his notes that there is an amount of truth that the human soul is able to bear (NF-1888,16[32]), which we should understand as an ability to endure the 'unhidden' world, exposing the contingencies and transient (contingent) nature of human life. He presents the thesis that, deprived of illusions, the 'truth' of ourselves and our world is hard to bear since the 'truth is ugly' (the beginning of everything we praise are terrible). He categorically rejects the

---

102 'Knowledge kills action; action requires one to be shrouded in a veil of illusion' (Nietzsche 2007b, 40).

103 Leopardi frequently mentioned the necessity of lying and the usefulness of illusions, which are 'natural, inherent to the system of the world'; and the progress of reason which leads to extinction of illusions produces barbarism (Leopardi 2013, e.g. pp. 273, 298, 397).

Platonic trinity of the good, truth and beauty, regarding beauty, especially in art, as an illusion created so that we would be able to bear reality (NF-1888,16[40]; MAII,VM-174; FW-299).[104]

Thus, when Nietzsche criticises the desire for truth as an expression of bad taste, he has in mind the desire of 'truth at every price' which strives to remove all protective covers (FW-*Vorrede*-4). He compared truth to women, who should not *reveal* too much in order to retain their allure (NF-1882,3[1]). The truth is a notion which stems from its exact opposite – something hidden. It obtained its philosophical dimension in the work of Parmenides; in Homer it featured in an appeal to the muses who remembered everything that they saw since the Greek term *aletheia* also meant 'not forgetting' (Snell 1953). It also indicates that the truth, which had been a collective memory dependent upon human consciousness before it became in Parmenides and Plato an essence independent of consciousness. This certainly inspired Nietzsche, who wants to show the truth of being as an illusion which we have forgotten is an illusion. As Brzozowski comments, '[t]he truth is as real as far as we understand that it is a delusion' (Brzozowski 2012 (trans. A. Shaw), 50). Equally important, however, is the ability to verify this collective memory by researching the genealogy of human practices and notions together with the rejection of those which have become worthless under the changing conditions of human life. Nietzsche emphasises that we are never really concerned with the 'truth' in philosophy but always with something else, something which the 'truth' is only meant to serve: be it health, development, the growth of power, or life (FW-*Vorrede*-2). He claims that the majority of people desire not truth but rather the life-supporting consequences of 'truth'. Truth plays the role of a 'social contract' – it compels us to be adjusted, typical and predictable for others. The liar for Nietzsche is someone who overuses and abuses the conventions laid down by the community or who rejects them, thus endangering the existence of the group (WL-1). Thus, when we take as a criterion of knowledge the useful consequences of the 'truth', it may transpire in many cases that self-delusion is more useful than uncovering delusions.

One should not think, however, that Nietzsche embraces pragmatism, that our convictions are true if they serve our interests and wellbeing, since for him life itself is not an argument for truth (FW-121). He rather thinks there exist many different perspectives which are, to a greater or lesser extent, useful. The efficacy

---

104 'The ugly truth is: we have art so that we go not to the underlying truth' (Nietzsche 2012b, 173); 'Art should first and foremost *embellish* life, therefore make *us* ourselves tolerable' (Nietzsche 2013, 75). One may say that even if the universe were ugly, the theories describing it, both scientific and philosophical, might still be beautiful.

of biology requires the falsification of the world (adapting the world to meet useful ends) and in which the 'criteria of truth' also feature (NF-1888,14[153]). If truth is a kind of faith which conditions our lives then its criteria would depend on *the strength of that faith* and not on usefulness (NF-1885,40[15]).

Research on the issue of truth in Nietzsche sometimes focuses on the lines contained in the collection of his works falsified by his sister and entitled *The Will to Power*, in accordance with which a feeling of a growth in power is a criterion of truth.[105] This idea does not feature in the official collections of Nietzsche's works prepared by the author himself, even though the will to power is numbered as one of factors affecting the criteria of truth (NF-1888,16[86]). As Williams aptly noted, regarding the growth in the will to power as a criterion of truth is an error (Williams 2006). The growth in power may not be a criterion since one is not able to anticipate power in order to have the ability to foresee in which conditions it grows and which truth would best serve it. It would require the will to power to be considered as a perspective which is somehow external to existence whilst it is in fact an expression of existence.

2.2. Truth as a metaphor

> What therefore is truth? A mobile army of metaphors, metonymies, anthropomorphisms: in short a sum of human relations which became poetically and rhetorically intensified, metamorphosed, adorned, and after long usage seem to a nation fixed canonic and binding; truths are illusions of which one has forgotten that they *are* illusions; worn-out metaphors which have become powerless to affect the senses (WL-1, Nietzsche 1911b, 180).

As metaphor plays a remarkably important role in the philosophy of Nietzsche, it is worth considering it here in more depth. Metaphor relies on identifying in the same words something which is not the same, transferring meaning from one sphere to another (Schrift 1990). Nietzsche illustrates this in many places, showing the etymology of the words we use. One such example relates to the origins of the notion of being (*den Begriff des Seins*) (PHG[11], Nietzsche 1911a, 128). The word *esse* originally meant 'to breathe' (*athmen*), which was regarded as a sign of life. The term 'being' was understood to denote something living (breathing), and the notion was extended to all things, ascribing an anthropomorphic existence (*Dasein*) to them, as if everything breathed just like a human being. '*The essence of the metaphor is understanding and experiencing one kind of thing in terms of another*' (Lakoff, Johnson 2003, 6). It is

105 'Das Kriterium der Wahrheit liegt in der Steigerung des Machtgefühls [The criterion of truth lies in the increase of one's sense of power]' (in Williams 2006, 327–328).

useful when we do not experience something directly. Metaphors have a particular importance in relation to abstract notions and afford access to them. No metaphor can encapsulate the meaning of the problem but all pay attention to certain aspects which simultaneously reveal and obscure. By using metaphors we either refer to a similarity of the impression or to a similar function of the phenomena described by means of metaphors (Snell 1953). They serve to make the incomprehensible more understandable, as noted by Bruno Snell. They best explain by using an analogy to something which is closest to our experience, e.g. comparing something that occurs in the phenomenal world to a human creation, to something that can be opened up and explored, to something which is repeatable (e.g. the head as a container for thoughts, thought as an arrow etc.). These explanations reveal why Socrates explained what was good by referring to the *techne* of a craftsman or the biblical use of the trade metaphors to describe the notions of sin and redemption.

Nietzsche shows that metaphors are certain structures which are built not only into our language but also into our thoughts. In accordance with this, Iris Murdoch claimed:

> The development of consciousness in human beings is inseparably connected with the use of metaphor. Metaphors are not merely peripheral decorations or even useful models, they are fundamental forms of our awareness of our condition: metaphors of space, metaphors of movement, metaphors of vision (Murdoch 2014, 75).

Metaphors fulfil a similar role to myths:

> Metaphors can be a mode of understanding, and so of acting upon, our condition. Philosophers merely do explicitly and systematically and often with art what the ordinary person does by instinct. Plato, who understood this situation better than most of the metaphysical philosophers, referred to many of his theories as 'myths' (Murdoch 2014, 91).

As both myths and metaphors reveal the process of the development of the history of culture, researching their functions is not only a purely linguistic problem but a broad-ranging historical issue, as Snell points out (Snell 1953). In a similar manner to Nietzsche's approach to notions, Snell addresses metaphors, showing that one rarely creates new ones and relies instead on old ones which have changed their meaning (cf. GM-II-13; MAII,WS-33).

The philological precision of Nietzsche leads him to the conclusion that metaphors are the basic intellectual tool that allow us to domesticate the world; they are linguistic conventions which often serve us in unconscious ways. Defining the truth as 'a moving army of metaphors' means that the truth is to be identified with the most fundamental linguistic habits which allow us to function in the world. The term 'moving' illustrates the elasticity and changeable nature of the habits referred to as the 'truth'. Nietzsche focuses on the fact that people name the metaphors about which they have forgotten what they are: 'truths' (NF-1872,19[229]). 'Truth' is thus a widespread conventional identification of things – an effect of the law-giving (normative) nature of language (WL-1), which I will explore in the next section devoted to perspectivism.

II. Perspectivism

1. Language

Consciousness is really just a net connecting one person with another (...). [A]s the most endangered animal, he *needed* help and protection, he needed his equals; he had to express his neediness and be able to make himself understood – and to do so, he first needed 'consciousness', i.e. even to 'know' what distressed him, to 'know' how he felt, to 'know' what he thought. (...) [M]an, like every living creature, is constantly thinking but does not know it; the thinking which becomes *conscious* is only the smallest part of it, let's say the shallowest, worst part – for only that conscious thinking *takes place in words, that is, in communication symbols*; and this fact discloses the origin of consciousness. In short, the development of language and the development of consciousness (...) go hand in hand. One might add that not only language serves as a bridge between persons, but also look, touch, and gesture (...). [C]onsciousness actually belongs not to man's existence as an individual but rather to the community – and herd-aspects of his nature (...). At bottom, all our actions are incomparably and utterly personal, unique, and boundlessly individual, there is no doubt; but as soon as we translate them into consciousness, *they no longer seem to be*... That is what *I* consider to be true phenomenalism and perspectivism: that due to the nature of *animal consciousness*, the world of which we can become conscious is merely a surface- and sign-world, a world turned into generalities and thereby debased to its lowest common denominator (FW-354, Nietzsche 2001, 212–213).

'...How lovely it is that there are words and sounds; aren't words and sounds rainbows and illusory bridges between things eternally separated?
To each soul belongs another world; for each soul every other soul is a hinterworld.
Illusion tells its loveliest lies about the things that are most similar, because the tiniest gap is hardest to bridge.
For me – how would there be something outside me? There is no outside! But we forget this with all sounds; how lovely it is that we forget! (...)
It is a beautiful folly, speaking: with it humans dance over all things.
How lovely is all talking and all lying of sounds! With sounds our love dances on colorful rainbows'(Za-III-*Genesende*-2, Nietzsche 2006a, 175).

Words are acoustic signs for concepts; concepts, though, are more or less determinate pictorial signs for sensations that occur together and recur frequently, for groups of sensations. Using the same words is not enough to get people to understand each other: they have to use the same words for the same species of inner experiences too; ultimately, people have to have the same experience *base*. (...) (the history of language is the history of a process of abbreviation) (JGB-268, Nietzsche 2002, 163).

In the first fragment, Nietzsche highlights the close relation between the development of consciousness in humans and their linguistic abilities. Consciousness manifested itself relatively late in humans (FW-11). Nietzsche defines the history of human speech as the 'history of a process of abbreviation'. He understands by this the ability to mutually warn one another of dangers in the swiftest possible manner and whilst limiting potential misunderstandings to a minimum. This ability to understand one another happens the fastest when people live together and share experiences, where the meanings of words are shaped by common practice. In this manner we may be able to explain why people from the same family, social group or nation are better able to understand one another than those who do not share a common background. In this respect, since we do not share our experiences with animals, we are unable to understand other species, even if they developed the physical capabilities to produce language, as Wittgenstein points out in his famous phrase: 'If a lion could talk, we could not understand him' (Wittgenstein 1999, 223; cf. FW-374).

Conscious thought is the most superficial part of what we experience. What we are able to communicate to others is our 'average', what we all feel as a species. Our most valuable, most individual internal experiences can neither be transmitted nor expressed (GD-*Streifzuege*-26),[106] hence the difficulty in knowing and understanding ourselves and others. It is an unjustified conclusion to draw that those things which are inexpressible do not exist, that the limits of our language mark the limits of our existence (M-115). However, language certainly marks a boundary between our conscious knowledge and our world.[107] Speech as the ability to 'abbreviate' can be developed further with the aid of a metaphor. Notions are a result of the process of generalising our experiences; of ordering and mapping out reality; of passing over individual experience. The creation of ideas leads to their classification, hierarchisation and, at the same time, they are a means to exert control over the world and other people – and that is why truth is considered a form of power (JGB-211), which can rule, *nota bene*, by the army of metaphors.

Language creates the world in which we live, connected to perspectivism and phenomenalism in the Nietzschean understanding. It is not a defect of language that it is unable to furnish us with true knowledge of things, but the fault rather lies in thinking that thanks to language we will be able to acquire knowledge of

---

106 'Our true experiences are completely taciturn. They could not be communicated even if they wanted to be. This is because the right words for them do not exist' (Nietzsche 2005b, 205).

107 This recalls the famous formulation of Wittgenstein's: '*The limits of my language* mean the limits of my world' (Wittgenstein 2002, 5.6, 68).

the world in itself, as Nietzsche puts it in the words of Zarathustra above. Talking about faith in the existence of 'things in themselves' and language as a bridge between us and things is completely unjustified. Language is our product and cannot give us true information about anything which is beyond language (WL-1). Notions and metaphors refer to one another, remaining rooted in linguistic terms and not going beyond them.[108] With the aid of language we attempt to create a certain interpretation of the world which is in our consciousness – beyond it there is no 'true' world since such an appeal would require reference to the transcendence – to an external guarantor of the world in itself. The above expression of the will to power of giving meaning to the world is akin to the biblical example of Adam giving names to things, participating in the act of the creation of the world. This occurs via the creation of notions and interpretations.

2. Interpretation: lawfulness and justice

> How far the perspectival character of existence extends, or indeed whether it has any other character; whether an existence without interpretation, without 'sense', doesn't become 'nonsense'; whether, on the other hand, all existence isn't essentially an *interpreting* existence – that cannot, as would be fair, be decided even by the most industrious and extremely conscientious analysis and self-examination of the intellect; for in the course of this analysis, the human intellect cannot avoid seeing itself under its perspectival forms, and *solely* in these. We cannot look around our corner: it is a hopeless curiosity to want to know what other kinds of intellects and perspectives there *might* be; e.g. whether other beings might be able to experience time backwards, or alternately forwards and backwards (…). But I think that today we are at least far away from the ridiculous immodesty of decreeing from our angle that perspectives are *permitted* only from this angle. Rather, the world has once again become infinite to us: insofar as we cannot reject the possibility *that it includes infinite interpretations*. Once again the great shudder seizes us – but who again would want immediately to deify in the old manner *this* monster of an unknown world? And to worship from this time on the unknown (*das Unbekannte*) as 'the Unknown One' (*den Unbekannten*)? Alas, too many *ungodly* possibilities of interpretation are included in this unknown; too much devilry, stupidity, foolishness of interpretation – our own human, all too human one, even, which we know… (FW-374, Nietzsche 2001, 239–240).
>
> There are absolutely no moral phenomena, only a moral interpretation of the phenomena… (JGB-108, Nietzsche 2002, 64).

---

108 From this perspective, 'our culture is reminiscent of a large dictionary in which every word is explained with the aid of another word but yet we are lacking that first word', as Sławomir Mrożek humorously put it (Mrożek 1982 (trans. A. Shaw), 243).

As Hans-Georg Gadamer noted, the career of the word 'interpretation' began with Nietzsche and became a challenge for the whole of positivism (Gadamer 1983). Nietzsche utilises in his writings a number of different terms: *Interpretation, Auslegung* and *Ausdeutung*, which are often used interchangeably in everyday language. This last notion is the most rarely implemented by Nietzsche and in the narrowest sense: it may be understood as indicating a particular meaning (*Bedeutungen*) of what we are interpreting. The first, *Interpretation*, has the broadest scope of meaning. In the context of this notion, the widespread nature of interpretation emerges, together with interpretation games and 'justice of interpretation' (*Gerechtigkeit der Interpretation*). By interpretation Nietzsche understands the kind of valuations (*Wertschätzungen*) which every human constantly performs. The idea of *Auslegung* has a more technical nature and leads to the 'filling with sense' (*Sinneinlegung*) of what we are interpreting. As Nietzsche indicates, knowledge (*Erkentniss*) does not depend on explanation (*Erklärung*), but on interpretation that fills with (*Einlegung*) the sense of what it is we are 'knowing'. In other words, knowledge (*Erkenntnis*) is exegesis (*Auslegung*) (NF-1885,2[86]). In English language translations of Nietzsche and commentaries on his works, *Auslegung* is often translated as exegesis, which one may associate with dogmatic 'interpretation', limited by the authority of the text or some overriding or dominant actor, e.g. the author (Kaufmann 1975). Exegesis is primarily utilised in the context of biblical texts, which suggests that there exists one true meaning of a text and its *discovery* is the goal of exegesis. In Nietzsche, no interpretation may have a dogmatic character since there exists no 'correct' interpretation of a text (NF-1885,1[120]), and the sense of a text is not so much discovered as *created* along the way to interpretation. The interpreter-creator is not limited by any authority nor by any overriding goal of interpretation. In the case of teleological interpretation we would have to consider that we are looking in the text for something that we want to find in it.[109] Interpretation in Nietzsche has an antiformal and antidogmatic character reminiscent of the Heideggerarian 'woodland paths' (*Holzwege*), which do not lead anywhere except into the depths of the forest, to a place where lumberjacks work, constituting another beautiful metaphor for thought (Heidegger 2002).

The position within which the form of interpretation proposed by Nietzsche was developed has been termed *perspectivism.*[110] Perspectivism relies on the re-

109 As Nietzsche playfully puts it, '[i]f somebody hides a thing behind a bush, seeks it again and finds it in the selfsame place, then there is not much to boast of, respecting this seeking and finding' (WL-1, Nietzsche 1911b, 183).

110 Nietzschean perspectivism, including the theory of truth and knowledge, is one of the most frequently discussed themes in contemporary research into the philosophy of

jection of two presuppositions: the first is ontological (that there exist things-in-themselves) and the second is epistemological (that truth represents the goal and criteria of knowledge). It is intended to present an alternative to traditional epistemology and also to the unjustified absolutism of science, religion and philosophy. It is the rejection of a longing for the kind of unified world view that the Platonic-Christian approach affords.

Nietzsche rejects both striving to achieve objectivity and its counterpart strongly rooted in contemporary philosophy – that is, striving for impartial judgements. If we accept that what is epistemologically objective is that which is true or false independent of our personal attitude (e.g. a date of birth in contrast to an opinion on a picture) this contains the criterion of truth as the link between the world and a judgement. Nietzsche rejects this criterion. Thus, a date of birth is 'objective' for him only in the sense that it is a certain agreed interpretation of reality. No interpretation may be ontologically objective, however, since it is not independent of human experience (just like information or money). For Nietzsche, nothing is in this sense objective, because even mountains are only mountains thanks to our interpretation of certain experiences – if we have never experienced a mountain, it would be hard to say what and how they are things in themselves for other entities.

Impartiality, in turn, contains neutrality as a condition of the reliability of judgements. An impartial decision may be characterised as being generally and publicly defendable and which may not be rationally rejected by anyone.[111] In the opinion of John Rawls, impartial judgements may be attained without recourse to the notion of truth (Rawls 1993). What is of paramount importance, in his opinion, is only what conscious and rational agents may commonly agree on, permitting the development of the so-called reflective equilibrium (Rawls 1999).

Ridding ourselves of what is personal was characteristic not only of science but also of much of post-Enlightenment philosophy, something which is particularly visible in Kant and Hegel. In the opinion of the latter, the goal of philosophy is to overcome that which is individual in favour of abstract generalities, of being as such (Hegel 1991). On this assumption, the whole of modern liberal philosophy was founded, which was criticized so fiercely by Nietzsche, who opposes the impersonal approach to problems, especially the philosophical ones. In his opinion, great problems demand above all *love*, that is the most personal of approaches

---

Nietzsche. Among the broader literature on the subject one should mention: Danto 1965, Magnus 1978, Schrift 1990, Warnock 1978, Leiter 1994, Clark 1990.

111 Invoking Thomas Scanlon, one may say that impartiality is 'the idea of justifiability to others, on terms that no one similarly motivated could reasonably reject' (Scanlon 2000, 6–7).

(FW-345).[112] Even questions about truth ought to be the most personal (M-196). Nietzsche demands that thinkers engage in an issue, feel passionate about solving it and to approach it in a completely individual manner. He regards generalisation and abstraction in interpretation which is approved of by everybody as redundant since they are based on too many unjustified simplifications. The first of these is the simplification that individual entities may be reduced to some ideal types ('a human being in general') which are established on the basis of arbitrarily assumed criteria (e.g. rationality). Secondly, they maintain that we are able to take into account the perspective of everyone else. In the opinion of Nietzsche, looking from an angle other than our own is a hopeless case indeed. The perspectives of other intellects are not available to us and those which are similar to our own are only accessible in the aspects which we have in common. It would be ridiculous, according to Nietzsche, to maintain that there only exists our own, single perspective. There are an infinite number of perspectives and no means of synthesising them since that would mean accepting the existence of an Infinite Being, which Nietzsche explicitly rejects. The impossibility of epistemology that Nietzsche describes is connected with the problem of the elusiveness of the whole.

In the above fragment we can also see him refer to 'foolishness of interpretation' and this may be read in the spirit of Kołakowski's 'philosophy of the jester', who opposes the complete interpretation of the world and expresses a watchful negativity towards any kind of absolute, not with the assistance of any arguments but by adopting an extra-intellectual attitude (Kołakowski 1963). According to Nietzsche, the passion for knowledge requires the discovery of both the hero and the fool in ourselves (FW-107).

Nietzsche proposes a new form of interpretation – *a new interpretation of all events* (*neuen Auslegung allen Geschehens*) (NF-1885,39[1]), which is connected with the will to power described further on. As he mockingly describes it in the fragment above, being (*Dasein*) without interpretation is senseless (*ohne Sinn*), and thus nonsense (*Unsinn*). The world does not have value in itself but in its interpretations (NF-1885,2[108]), just like human lives, which we are supposed to *assign* sense to. We can also see in this fragment that there exist no moral phenomena but only moral interpretations of phenomena. Morality

112 '"Selflessness" has no value in heaven or on earth; all great problems demand *great love*, and only strong, round, secure minds who have a firm grip on themselves are capable of that. It makes the most telling difference whether a thinker has a personal relationship to his problems and finds in them his destiny, his distress, and his greatest happiness, or an "impersonal" one, meaning he is only able to touch and grasp them with the antennae of cold, curious thought' (Nietzsche 2001, 202).

(treating the world according to the values of good and evil) is thus just one of many interpretations which Nietzsche rejects in favour of immoral, all-too-human interpretation, which is the expression of the will to power (AC-2). According to Nietzsche, something which is harmful to life is a greater charge than 'false' judgements since that which is 'false' (the diverse illusions which were described) may support life and foster its growth, and may be ultimately essential for life (JGB-4). Thus interpretation, in the opinion of Nietzsche, instead of consisting of a pointless war of words should be focused upon deciding and testing whether one can live in accordance with such interpretations (SE-8), since philosophy, instead of being the 'art of searching for truth', should be the 'art of life' (NF-1887,9[57] (44)). One should remember that this task is an individual one, depending on a certain type of spirit.

Nietzsche believes in never-ending interpretation (FW-374) and that there is no such thing as a 'correct' one (NF-1885,1[120]), but this should not be mistaken for advocating that every interpretation is equally important and sensible. Interpretation depends on ordering (*Rangordnung*) a multitude of perspectives and evaluating them, which enables us to sort the superficial thinkers from the profound ones (M-446). A good interpreter must, in the opinion of Nietzsche, possess a difficult ability to command, to have power over internal contradictions and the ability to create an image of the world which depends on our honesty and justice (*Redlichkeit und Gerechtigkeit*) (FW-114). The first criterion refers to the linguistic aspects of the text which should not be obscured by the interpretation (AC-52). The second, and considerably more important, is connected with the fundamental role of philosophy which is that of a provider of norms and laws (NF-1885,34[201]; NF-1885,35[74]).

It is worth stressing that the term 'norm' (Ger. *Norm*) comes from the Latin term *norma*, used to describe a builder's square in antiquity (Railton 2003). The term 'rule' (Ger. *Regel*) comes from the Latin term *regulus*, which meant something akin to today's ruler (Ger. *Lineal*), used to make straight lines and measure objects. Thus, if the acquisition of knowledge leads to generalising, measuring, weighing and evaluating then it is, in other words, the *normativization of the world*. The philosopher driven by the will to appearances, as described earlier, effectively replaces the will to truth with the will to create, since knowledge is understood as the constant creation of interpretations of the world (JGB-211). Thus, knowledge has a normative character – it does not describe the world, but creates it, affecting its inhabitants. The concepts have normative character, as Christine Korsgaard notes, when 'they tell us what to think, what to like, what to say, what to do, and what to be' (Korsgaard 1992, 22). Concepts such as 'good' and 'evil', 'beautiful' or 'brave' may be considered as normative because they assume a certain measure of reality which is not derived from the empirical and is not reducible to a description of the world (cf. Audi 2013).[113] According to Nietzsche, their normative power stems from will to power – that is the power so strong that it is able to shape every being in its manner (Za-II-*Selbstueberwindung*).

The measure of normativity (defining values, confirming and assigning power) is justice, representing 'the highest representative of life itself' (NF-1884,25[484]) and 'a far-seeing function of the will to power' (NF-1884,26[149]). Indeed, the greatest injustice is, according to Nietzsche, an undeveloped life which persists at the expense of a more developed life (MAI-*Vorrede*-6),[114] then justice will be that which gives the greatest feeling of power and which aids the most developed life. He refers here to justice beyond good and evil which has a constructivist character and is at the same time selectively destructive, a form of governing and personifying the will to power which is the basis of Nietzsche's metaphysics (see Heidegger 1991a; Jaspers 1979). He defines justice as 'the rarest of all virtues' (HL-6), possessed by only the few 'higher people', who are able to judge (in order to judge, one must be higher than that which one pronounces judgement upon).[115] Such an expression of justice helps to foster the 'will to truth' which is no longer the will to discover (cold reasoning) but the will to *judge the world* – to order and

113 In this respect, the empirical description of the world does not contain ethical judgements in itself, as Wittgenstein puts it, '[i]f for instance in our world-book we read the description of a murder with all its details physical and physiological, the mere description of these facts will contain nothing which we could call an ethical proposition. The murder will be on exactly the same level as any other event, for instance the falling of a stone. Certainly the reading of description might cause us pain or rage or any other emotion, or we might read about the pain or rage, caused by this murder in other people when they have heard of it, but there will simply be facts, facts, and facts but no Ethics' (Wittgenstein 1965, 6).

114 'Above all, you must see with your own eyes where injustice is always the greatest: namely, where life has developed in the smallest, narrowest, neediest, most preliminary ways and yet still cannot avoid taking *itself* as the purpose and measure of things and, out of love for its own preservation, secretly and meanly and ceaselessly crumbling away and putting into question all that is higher, greater, richer' (Nietzsche 2000, 11).

115 'In truth, no one has a greater claim to our veneration than he who possesses the drive to and strength for justice. For the highest and rarest virtues are united and concealed in justice as in an unfathomable ocean that receives streams and rivers from all sides and takes them into itself. The hand of the just man who is empowered to judge no longer trembles when it holds the scales; he sets weight upon weight with inexorable disregard of himself, his eye is unclouded as it sees the scales rise and fall, and his voice is neither harsh nor tearful when he pronounces the verdict' (Nietzsche 2007c, 88).

punish, in other words to evaluate and create it. Nietzsche's justice requires forceful engagement with the problem, a loving immersion in it, the strongest flexing of the noblest internal values together with the artistic force of creation. Its task is to encompass all of the necessary processes at play in the process of becoming and to bring them to light. I will return to this issue in subsequent chapters.

Paul Ricœur describes Nietzsche's method of interpretation with the term 'reductive hermeneutics' and explains its character in the following manner:

> [It] is at the same time a kind of philology and a kind of genealogy. It is a philology, an exegesis, an interpretation insofar as the text of our consciousness can be compared to a palimpsest, under the surface of which another text has been written. The task of this special exegesis is to decipher this text. But this hermeneutics is at the same time a genealogy, since the distortion of the text emerges from a conflict of forces, of drives [*pulsions*] and counter drives, whose origin must be brought to light. It is evident that it is not a genealogy in the ordinary chronological sense of the word. For even when it refers to historical stages, this Genesis does not lead back to a temporal origin but rather to a possible source or, better, an empty place from which ethical and religious values emerge (Ricœur 1974, 442–443).

Ricœur uses the term 'reductive' in the context of the hermeneutics of Nietzsche and Freud because he feels their methods lead to uncovering the hidden role of instincts, fears, desires, drives and resentments in the lives and value systems of humans. He describes the hermeneutics of Marx in a similar manner, albeit for different reasons. He criticizes the 'hermeneutics of suspicion' opposing it with the 'hermeneutics of belief', which is not destructive, but rather aimed at restoring meaning (Ricœur 1974, xix). Nietzsche defends himself against the charge of naturalistic reductionism and his philosophy does contain some constructive elements (Nietzsche emphasises that the only ones who could destroy are those who can *build,* FW-58).[116] The most accurate description of his philosophical approach would therefore be the hermeneutics of the will to power, since to a large degree it is devoted to identifying the manifestations of the will to power and expressions of power in culture.

2.1. Linguistic interpretation

Linguistic interpretation requires of the interpreter not a correct but rather a *good* reading. The linguistic art of good reading depends on not falsifying the interpreted text. By falsification one may understand dishonesty as regards the text, an interpretation which does not match the text or reading the text without

116 'Only as creators can we destroy!' (Nietzsche 2001, 70).

the requisite sensitivity. As Nietzsche claims, one must read of one's own volition, patiently and with an open mind disposed to caution, precision and linguistic insights (J-*Vorrede*-5).[117] There are no a priori criteria as to what fits a text and what does not – they are verified by interpretation. The interpretation of a text must be *responsible*, as with every creation, and thus as Alan Schrift notes, the interpreter should have the 'textual ability to respond' (Schrift 1990, 193).

Nietzsche writes that the text is nothing other than interpretation, hence one may conclude that the text is not an independently existing object of interpretation as much as a collection of potential interpretations (NF-1885,2[108]). One may utilise the Nietzschean metaphor of the mirror here, which always reveals something that is not the mirror itself (MAII,WS-218). The text has an open character as it is not a collection of all of the interpretations which have been *conducted* but those which are *possible*. The text is something other than that which is defined by its interpretation but nothing other than a product of interpretation (Schrift 1990). In order to understand this better, one may utilise the metaphor of dance proposed by Schrift. It refers to the question posed by William Butler Yeats, '[h]ow can we know the dancer from the dance?'[118] According to Schrift, the same question can be asked of the text and its interpretation, which are also indivisible. Nietzsche also compares thinking to dancing (GD-*Deutsche*-7).[119] Dance symbolises lightness, joy, sensitivity to nuance and also the engagement of the whole person in the process of interpretation. Continuing this line of thought, one may add that it is impossible to divide the interpreter from the interpretation, the argument from the arguer.

Nietzsche uses the metaphor of 'great style' to define the highest lawfulness (*höhere Gesetzlichkeit*) (WA-Brief-8). The use of the term 'lawfulness' in terms of linguistic interpretation is in accordance with his assumption that interpretation is not only about inferring meanings but also *bestowing* them. The creative character

117 'Ordinary people don't know how much time and effort it takes to learn how to read. I've spent eighty years at it, and I still can't say that I've reached my goal' (Goethe in Hadot 1999, 109).

118 A poem entitled *Among School Children*, I quote after Schrift 1990, 196.

119 '[T]hinking wants to be learned like dancing, as a *type* of dancing (…). A *noble education* has to include *dancing* in every form, being able to dance with your feet, with concepts, with words; do I still have to say that you need to be able to do it with a pen too – that you need to learn to *write*?' (Nietzsche 2005b, 191); 'I wouldn't know what the spirit of a philosopher might more want to be than a good dancer. For the dance is his ideal, also his art, and finally also his only piety, his "service of God"' (FW-381, Nietzsche 2001, 246).

of interpretation imposes criteria other than truth, as Nietzsche illustrates with the example of a work of art which may be both alluring and shocking but not true or false in the classical sense.[120] The notion of style is not only an aesthetic category in Nietzsche. Great style is contrasted with decadent style, the former fostering development in life and the latter negating it. All kinds of dogmatism and absolutism in interpretation oppose life since they negate the fundamental condition of life, namely perspectivism. In this sense, the metaphysics to date is for Nietzsche a bad interpretation since it turns away from life and obscures perspective with the dogma of truth.

2.2. Genealogical interpretation

A model of active interpretation is for Nietzsche the genealogical one (GM-*Vorrede*-8), thanks to which we are able to synthesise our philosophical viewpoints (GM-*Vorrede*-4). This method relies on researching the origins of our notions, social practices and manners of evaluation in order to better understand them and verify their efficacy. Researching the history of ideas (*Entstehungs-Geschichte*) is for Nietzsche the basis for overcoming them (NF-1883,16[14]) in order to create new ones. It is not a straightforward historical analysis (locating the origin of ideas in a particular historical context), however, but a critical method, combining aspects of psychology, anthropology, sociology, philology, phenomenology and history (Williams 2006). The genealogical method for Nietzsche is far from a glorification of the past and the efforts of metaphysicians who are seeking the foundations on which the notions are based. The genealogy of Nietzsche does not rely on seeking out 'first causes' but rather on learning about the history of notions and etymology of words in order to understand our ways of thinking which have shaped these notions. He does not make references to any historical or anthropological research to support his thesis since history is used here as a means to achieve non-historical objectives – philosophical speculation regarding the manifestations of the will to power and the clash of drives in particular notions.

Alasdair MacIntyre contrasts the genealogical approach of Nietzsche with the encyclopaedic approach typical of the Enlightenment (MacIntyre 1994). The French encyclopaedia brought about a revolution in thought; it was the modern equivalent of the *Summa* of St Thomas, as Voegelin notes (Voegelin 1975). While the encyclopaedic approach stemmed from the belief in the unity of science, the

120 'Art is free, also in the domain of concepts. Who would refute a phrase by Beethoven, and who would find error in Raphael *Madonna*?' A letter to Carl von Gersdorff, of the end of August 1866 (Nietzsche 1996, 18).

genealogical one posited multiplicity and rejected a systematic and comprehensive approach to the problems posed; it was above all a critical approach and not a dogmatic one.

Nietzsche did not invent this method but rather adopted it from English empiricists whilst modifying it considerably. David Hume, in his research into human nature, as well as his speculations concerning the origins of religion, applied the genealogical method precisely (Hume 2002; Hume 1960). A direct inspiration for Nietzsche was the book of his friend Paul Rée *The Origin of the Moral Sensations* (*Der Ursprung der moralischen Empfindungen*), published in 1877. Despite finding it inspirational, Nietzsche criticized the book considerably, not agreeing with any of its findings (GM-*Vorrede*-4), something I will return to in the next chapter.

Chapter 3. The genealogical method and its philosophical applications

To the accumulated errors of their ancestors, they added [others] unknown to them,- Hesitation and Fear: therefore it came to pass that they vanished from the face of the earth, and a deep silence fell upon them.
Zygmunt Krasiński[121]

I. Psychological realism

> *Anti-Darwin.* – As far as the famous 'struggle for *existence*' is concerned, this seems to me to be more of an opinion than a proven fact at the moment. It takes place, but as an exception; the overall condition of life is *not* a state of need, a state of hunger, but rather abundance, opulence, even absurd squandering. Where there is a struggle, it is a struggle for *power*... (...) But assuming this struggle exists (and it does in fact happen), it is unfortunately the opposite of what Darwin's school would want, and perhaps what we might want too: namely to the disadvantage of the strong, the privileged, the fortunate exceptions. Species do *not* grow in perfection: the weak keep gaining dominance over the strong, – there are more of them, and besides, they are *cleverer*... Darwin forgot about spirit (– that is English!), *the weak have more spirit*... You have to need spirit in order to get it, – you lose it when you lose the need for it. Anyone with strength can do without spirit (...). You see that by spirit I mean caution, patience, cunning, disguise, great self-control, and everything involved in mimicry (which includes much of what is called virtue) (GD-*Streifzuege*-14, Nietzsche 2005b, 199).

According to some thinkers, the genealogical method adopted by Nietzsche is the most systematic attempt to naturalise morality (Leiter 2002). Nietzsche had a high regard for psychology, considering it the queen of the sciences (JGB-23), making him a precursor of the contemporary philosophy of mind in the eyes of many scholars (Acampora 2006). However, his view of psychology is somewhat unique: understanding it as a study of mutually compensating drives, he thus also sees the identification of moral content as being related to experience from other spheres of life. As a result of the last aspect, Bernard Williams holds that Nietzsche is concerned not with psychological naturalism but rather psychological realism (Williams 2006). He is concerned not only with a purely biological interpretation of humanity but also and foremost a cultural one, allowing his approach to be associated with broader naturalism of the type delineated by John McDowell

121 From the motto of *The Undivine Comedy* by Zygmunt Krasiński (Krasiński 1875, 173).

(McDowell 2002). Nietzsche criticizes reductionism, the naturalistic psychologists who, as materialists, seemed to turn people into 'thinking frogs', and lost in their analysis spirit and soul (FW-*Vorrede*-3; JGB-12). It is also worth recalling Nietzsche's critical attitude towards the evolutionary psychologists who he borrowed his methods from, albeit giving them his own personal twist.[122] The basic charge that Nietzsche makes against the scholars of genealogical research such as Paul Rée is that they are founded on certain a priori assumptions (described by Nietzsche as superstitions), which narrowed the scope of their research and warped its results. The main superstition they start with is an a priori assumption that altruism, mercy and an ego-less perspective have some value in themselves (GM-*Vorrede*-4–6). One may also direct similar criticism towards Schopenhauer's praise of mercy and the defeat of the ego (GM-*Vorrede*-5). These values are regarded as given although, in the opinion of Nietzsche, they are contagious superstitions which have developed alongside a particular kind of morality which he terms the slave one.

In contrast to philosophers such as Hume, Nietzsche sees the roots of moral judgements expressing altruism as being in *ressentiment* and not in feelings of sympathy or compassion (Hoy 1994). He rejects Hume's thesis concerning the existence of universal psychological (natural) and social (artificial) values. By recognising contemporary liberal morality as a universal value, the research of evolutionary psychologists leads to the pursuit of its confirmation in a pseudo-scientific manner. He believes that the researchers themselves are acting under the influence of Christian morality and that they think that they are analysing *morality itself* in their critical opinions towards Christian morality and its origins (FW-345). None of them has gone as far as Nietzsche, however, in presenting morality itself as a problem. They discuss mainly moral justifications or explanations but not morality itself. Morality may not be, after all, an abstract general problem but rather the most personal problem, need and torment. This is the approach favoured by Nietzsche, and one which I will present in the second part of the book.

Nietzsche mocks research which is based on the theory of natural selection and which leads from the 'Darwinian beast' to the contemporary 'moral weakling who "no longer bites"' (GM-*Vorrede*-7), but is full of care and empathy, denies the self and is keen to cooperate (cf. FW-345). The error committed by these scholars lies in the fact that they assume that what they want to prove – that there is a biological conditioning of non-egotistical moral feelings which are socially useful. This is

---

122 Nietzsche emphasised on many occasions that he had discovered 'his own country' of knowledge which was separated from the source of inspiration (GM-*Vorrede*-3).

the so-called moralistic fallacy, which means that something that is considered as moral is assumed to be natural (necessary). As we can see in the above fragment, Nietzsche approaches Darwinism critically, replacing the survival of the fittest with the will to power, which he terms his own interpretation of becoming (JGB-13). The argument, which often serves as the basis of naturalized morality, that the goal of morality is the development and self-preservation of humanity, is not as straightforward as it seems.[123] It is unclear *towards what* and *in what* humanity is supposed to grow, as Nietzsche notes (M-106). Some naturalists (such as Spencer) hold that it means the highest possible development of reason, that which separates the human species from all others. Such a line of argumentation, however, leads to a paradox, since the highest development of human reason may not be compatible with the survival of humankind since it may lead to our self-destruction. In nature we can observe development but natural development have no other objective than development itself. Furthermore, the process of development is accompanied by the processes of degeneration, disorganization, decay and entropy, and thus we cannot assume that the universe is going in any direction, let alone a 'good' one. He criticizes the thesis that the 'survival of the fittest' and natural selection could lead to the perfection of the species. In his opinion, Darwinism is better suited to explain the degeneration of a species, since the average, the largest number, always prevail and then eliminate the atypical examples (including the best as well as the worst ones) thanks to their numerical ascendency.

He also criticizes the naturalist approach advocated by Spencer or Rée, who sought a universal explanation for the remarkably complex matter of moral life (FW-373). In his opinion, interpreting responsibility, punishment, conscience and free will from the perspective of their utility to society rests on a superstition, a false simplification (see Copleston 1975; Hoy 1994). As Arendt notes, liberal utilitarianism, and neoclassical economics after it, accept as their basis the 'communistic fiction' of the compatibility of social interests as a whole, as a result of which the interests of its individuals are guided by an 'invisible hand', concerned with ensuring our prosperity and harmony (Arendt 1998; cf. Taylor 2001). For Nietzsche, there is no such thing as the 'greatest happiness' or the 'prosperity of all mankind' – they are purely fictitious notions created to attain a certain social, political or ideological goal. In the case of liberal-democratic societies, they were to be shaped by market forces and divided into employers and employees, their

123 The preservation of the species is not, on the grounds of this argument, an instinct but rather a duty and thus requires the existence of an ethical system. If instinct is to be a model, it cannot contain a hierarchy of instincts because it requires the adoption of the system (Lewis 2001).

lives organized around activity concerned with production, exchange and consumption.[124] Happiness understood as prosperity, pleasure, security and comfort is to be the discovery of the 'last men' (Za-*Vorrede*-6);[125] it is not a universal idea but a reflection of the bourgeois preferences of English merchants who tried to apply them to the whole of humanity (JGB-228; cf. M-230). For Nietzsche, it is the morality of the herd, of its average members, who found their strength in their number. He feels that the idea of a species-wide perspective on morality is wide of the mark since the essence of all evaluations is an individual perspective, particularly the perspective of the most remarkable individuals (NF-1886,7[9]). Happiness is something purely individual, it cannot be reduced to a common denominator, counted, gauged or even compared. He scoffs at the moralists who claimed to be able to show 'a way to happiness', which was a goal to be reached (M-108; NF-1888–23[3]). It is rather something internal, something which happens to us and not something which we strive for; there is no formula for happiness, on the contrary, any 'recipe for happiness' may only serve to be an obstacle to its attainment (JGB-198; AC-1).[126]

Nietzsche rejects the idea that every human being was consciously striving for happiness (JGB-I-13). If happiness were to be the goal of our activity, then unhappiness would have to be the cause of that activity (NF-1888,22[19]). At the same time, for Nietzsche, suffering or pleasure are not stimuli for activity, as the utilitarians would have them be, but rather their symptoms, their expressions (NF-1888,14[174]). Activity is not born from any need or goal of a human being but is rather its own type of necessity – a discharging of power which grows in a person and which may bring him or her pleasure (NF-1888,14[173]; NF-1888,22[17]). The desire for happiness, in turn, may not be seen or called a moral drive but rather a form of cowardice (M-343). Providing people with the greatest amount of pleasure and the least amount of suffering is an unattainable contradiction since

---

124 Arendt accurately diagnosed the utilitarian ideal of happiness as socio-economic conditioning, claiming that the ideal of utility permeates the society of craftsmen (this *homo faber* mentality means that everything is seen in terms of means and ends and subsequently causes the degradation of many goods through their instrumentalization), that the society of employees is dominated by the ideal of comfort and the market society is filled with the ideal of exchange (Arendt 1998).

125 Similar remarks were made by Hölderlin who wrote, 'it is very easy indeed to be happy and at peace, with a shallow heart and a narrow mind' (Hölderlin 1990, 30).

126 Nicolai Hartmann wrote in a similar vein, accepting that happiness or love were states which stemmed from our predispositions towards them and not by striving for them (Hartmann 2007a).

one conditions the other. Eliminating the ability to suffer also removes our capacity to enjoy the greatest joy (FW-12), it destroys life (see Lewis 2009). Every stage in human development has, for Nietzsche, its own state of happiness (M-108). There is no peak here, where happiness is to be found at its most sublime; there is also no way of comparing the happiness experienced at those different stages.

Nietzsche also focuses on the question of how we *understand* the world as posed by those concerned with researching nature, including Darwinists – a separate question from how we *organise* our lives; research on institutions (such as the state, punishment or marriage) becomes obscured when it is combined with Darwinism (DS-9). Furthermore, he holds that a person's personality type, their psychophysical makeup as well as the culture in which they were brought up condition their method of valuation and this in turn influences the way in which they view the world (cf. Leiter 2002; Janaway 2006). However, the values of both strong and exceptional people are very different from those who are weak or average. Thus, in this respect also, values are full of contradictory interpretations. In contrast to the evolutionary psychologists, Nietzsche does not seek to find any agreement between his own statements and study; instead, he focuses his philosophical efforts mainly on tracking the contradiction between thought and action. The genealogical method which he uses serves to help interpret the phenomenon. Nietzsche is aimed not at a research hypothesis about the origin of moral values but rather at an analysis of the value of a given morality. He is thus conscious of the dangers of the so-called genetic errors, which stem from drawing unwarranted conclusions about the value of a given phenomenon based on its origins, and, as a result, avoids them (Leiter 2002). When he claims that the source of all that is 'good' and beautiful is lots of blood and suffering (GM-II-3), he is not claiming that this origin discredits the present value of the practice or concepts. Digging up and exposing that which awakens disgust and horror in us plays the role of a stimulant for Nietzsche, designed to help us overcome our own prejudices (FW-347; NF-1886,7[7]). It is in this manner that we should understand Nietzsche's claim that a creation such as a tree depends on its seeds, not its fruits, which will only be consumed (MAII,WS-406). By fruit Nietzsche understands here the thoughts that grow in a thinker (GM-*Vorrede*-2).

Nietzsche proposes 'a realistic history of morality' (GM-*Vorrede*-7), which shows that there are better and worse genealogies and, therefore, criteria with which one may assess them (cf. Leiter 2002). A fundamental charge which may be brought against Nietzsche's interpretation is that it is not assumptions-free but that it rests upon hidden premises which may be regarded as prejudices too. The will to power, however, is not a dogma but rather a hypothesis for interpretation which Nietzsche regards as being helpful but which others may find to be harmful when they present other types of philosophical personality. Nietzsche also regards his moral interpretations as stemming from his own drive to individual life which resulted in the rejection of herd-morality based on universal obligations (NF-1888,6[123]). Those who do not have this drive, those who prefer the life of the herd, will not be able to regard this interpretation as being their own – and therefore binding. Nietzsche's interpretation is thus just one of many, it is certainly not an expression of a privileged epistemological interpretation, nor is it objective but it is rather an interpretation from a given perspective (the will to power) and serves a particular kind of person.

II. The origins of morality: *ressentiment*

Nietzsche explains the mechanism which leads to development of moral judgements with the aid of the notion of *ressentiment*. A notion stemming from a French term *ressentiment*, it refers to a deep feeling of insult, of resentment, and which is a reaction to disappointment, a sense of indignity or being offended by someone. Nietzsche used this notion for the first time in his notes in 1875 in the context of his considerations over the sense of law (NF-1875,9[1]). They were notes in the margin of a work by Eugen Dühring entitled *Der Werth des Lebens*, published in 1865. Amongst them was the observation that the sense of law (*Rechtsgefühl*) was based on *ressentiment* since the idea of justice also seems to incorporate and appeal to the sense of revenge. The notion surfaced in the notes of Nietzsche in 1887, and it is in *On the Genealogy of Morality* that he presents his ideas concerning the origins of moral judgements in the most complete form. He returns to this subject later, but in a somewhat piecemeal fashion, in *The Antichrist*, *Twilight of the Idols* and *Ecce Homo*. He thus made use of Dühring's idea but he applied it, somewhat interestingly, not in the field of law but rather that of morality. In his considerations of justice and the theory of punishment, he argues with Dühring, claiming that it is not law which is the product of *ressentiment* but rather morality. One may be tempted to venture the idea that Nietzsche's thesis was inspired by the works of Dostoyevsky, who he regarded as the only psychologist with anything to say and teach (BVN-1887,800; BVN-1888,1151).

Thanks to Dostoyevsky's *The House of the Dead*, Nietzsche came to learn of the Russian camps in which those who had been excluded from society showed themselves to be remarkably strong, as if they were 'cut from hardest wood' (GD-*Streifzuege*-45). In many of the Russian author's novels, especially in *Humiliated and Insulted*, amoral people, who are strong and devoid of any pangs of conscience, are contrasted with moral people who are weak and seek to bolster their moral position by means of blackmailing those who are stronger than they are. Dostoyevsky suggestively presents the psychological portraits of his characters, focusing mainly on the divide between the two types; whilst he is generally on the side of the good ones, he does not shy away from expressing his admiration of heroic villains either. Nietzsche may have used this psychological material as the foundation of his own theory of *ressentiment*. A precise self-analysis of the sick emotional state of the narrator of *Notes from Underground* could have served, in my opinion, as a direct influence on his considerations of *ressentiment*, as can be seen in this somewhat lengthy fragment:

> I sometimes have had moments when if I had happened to be slapped in the face I should, perhaps, have been positively glad of it. I say, in earnest, that I should probably have been able to discover even in that a peculiar sort of enjoyment – the enjoyment, of course, of despair; but in despair there are the most intense enjoyments, especially when one is very acutely conscious of the hopelessness of one's position. (…) The worst of it is, look at it which way one will, it still turns out that I was always the most to blame in everything. And what is most humiliating of all, to blame for no fault of my own but, so to say, through the laws of nature. In the first place, to blame because I am cleverer than any of the people surrounding me. (…) To blame, finally, because even if I had had magnanimity, (…) I should certainly have never been able to do anything (…) —neither to forgive, for my assailant would perhaps have slapped me from the laws of nature, and one cannot forgive the laws of nature; nor to forget, for even if it were owing to the laws of nature, it is insulting all the same. Finally, even if I had wanted to be anything but magnanimous, had desired on the contrary to revenge myself on my assailant, I could not have revenged myself on any one (…).
>
> With people who know how to revenge themselves and to stand up for themselves in general, how is it done? Why, when they are possessed, let us suppose, by the feeling of revenge, then for the time there is nothing else but that feeling left in their whole being. Such a gentleman simply dashes straight for his object like an infuriated bull with its horns down, and nothing but a wall will stop him. (…) For them a wall is not an evasion, as for us people who think and consequently do nothing (…).
>
> Well, such a direct person I regard as the real normal man, as his tender mother nature wished to see him (…). I envy such a man till I am green in the face. (…) [I]f you take, for instance, the antithesis of the normal man, that is, the man of acute consciousness, who has come, of course, not out of the lap of nature but out of a retort (…), this retort-made man is sometimes so nonplussed in the presence of his antithesis that with all his exaggerated consciousness he genuinely thinks of himself as a mouse and not a man. (…) Let us suppose, for instance, that it feels insulted, too (and it almost always does feel insulted), and wants to revenge itself, too. (…) Of course the only thing left for it is to dismiss all that with a wave of its paw, and, with a smile of assumed contempt in which it does not even itself believe, creep ignominiously into its mouse-hole. There in its nasty, stinking, underground home our insulted, crushed and ridiculed mouse promptly becomes absorbed in cold, malignant and, above all, everlasting spite. (…)

> Maybe it will begin to revenge itself, too, but, as it were, piecemeal, in trivial ways, from behind the stove, incognito, without believing either in its own right to vengeance, or in the success of its revenge, knowing that from all its efforts at revenge it will suffer a hundred times more than he on whom it revenges itself, while he, I daresay, will not even scratch himself. (...)
> [I]n that hell of unsatisfied desires turned inward, in that fever of oscillations, (...) — that the savour of that strange enjoyment (...) lies (Dostoyevsky 2006, 11–15).

In the fragment above, people of action are juxtaposed with those who think, who are endowed with excessive awareness that makes them unable to act and results in their contempt for one another. The first belong to the active group, they are natural creatures who are both healthy and strong; one may put the majority of the criminals that Dostoyevsky met in the camps in this category. Those in the second group, which includes the narrator, are passive figures who suffer as a consequence, secretly delighting in this suffering. Suffering for Dostoyevsky is the origin of consciousness and it is this consciousness which is human greatest unhappiness (Dostoyevsky 2006).

The similarities between the description of the internal struggles of the narrator of *Notes from Underground* and those of Nietzsche's ruminations on the genealogy of morality are too significant to be considered a mere coincidence. Dostoyevsky appeals to those who are stout of heart in his confession, just as Nietzsche addresses his to those who are strong enough to hear the sad truth. Both authors posit that moral conscience, which we typically regard as the peak of human properties, stems from very low feelings – from an insatiable lust for revenge, from humiliation and from an awareness of our own misery which shapes itself into a warped form of pleasure. In the parable of *On the Pitying*, which appears in the second part of *Thus Spoke Zarathustra*, Nietzsche writes that the guilty conscience of sinners are something harmful since 'bites of conscience teach people to bite' (Za-II-*Mitleidige*, Nietzsche 2006a, 68). A similar formulation can be found in Dostoyevsky's text, where the hero admits to pangs of conscience in the following manner:

> I was ashamed (...) and secretly, inwardly gnawing, gnawing at myself for it, tearing and consuming myself till at last the bitterness turned into a sort of shameful accursed sweetness, and at last – into positive real enjoyment! (Dostoyevsky 2006, 10).

Both authors focus on a fascinating psychological phenomenon related to the victims of violence who, unable to direct their anger at the perpetrator of the injustice, frequently turn it upon themselves, taking the blame for the injury they have suffered at another's hands. Primo Levi also noted this with startling clarity when he wrote:

[W]e have to recognize, sadly, that the offense is irreparable: it is protracted in time, and the Furies, in whom we are forced to believe, not only harass the tormentor (if they harass him, with or without the aid of human punishment) but also perpetuate his work by denying peace to the tormented (Levi 2015, 3475).

Nietzsche focuses, however, on another aspect of the role of conscience produced by *ressentiment* which also manifests itself in Dostoyevsky. It is supposed to make those who are weak and suffering feel happy since they have the moral high ground (it is described above as being *wiser*), in fact being unable to return the injustice. They thus use their weakness to forge a weapon to use against their stronger adversaries. Richard III has a similar thought in mind when he feels pangs of conscience bite before the decisive battle, '[c]onscience is but a word that cowards use, devised at first to keep the strong in awe. Our strong arms be our conscience, swords our law' (Shakespeare 2008, 186). In a similar manner Nietzsche sees the clash between the morality of the master, based on strength, and that of the slave, based on weakness and *ressentiment*, which I will examine in the subsequent sections.

1. The concept of *ressentiment*

Here are crucial fragments in which Nietzsche explains the notion of *ressentiment* and its role in the shaping of morality:

The beginning of the slaves' revolt in morality occurs when *ressentiment* itself turns creative and gives birth to values: the *ressentiment* of those beings who, denied the proper response of action, compensate for it only with imaginary revenge. Whereas all noble morality grows out of a triumphant saying 'yes' to itself, slave morality says 'no' on principle to everything that is 'outside', 'other', 'non-self': and *this* 'no' is its creative deed. This reversal of the evaluating glance – this *essential* orientation to the outside instead of back onto itself – is a feature of *ressentiment*: in order to come about, slave morality first has to have an opposing, external world, it needs, physiologically speaking, external stimuli in order to act at all, – its action is basically a reaction (GM-I-10, Nietzsche 2007a, 20).

– Would anyone like to have a little look down into the secret of how *ideals are fabricated* on this earth? Who has enough pluck?... (...) Lies are turning weakness into an *accomplishment* (...). '[I]mpotence which doesn't retaliate is being turned into "goodness"; timid baseness is being turned into "humility"; submission to people one hates is being turned into "obedience" (...). The inoffensiveness of the weakling, the very cowardice with which he is richly endowed, his standing-by-the-door, his inevitable position of having to wait, are all given good names such as "patience", also known as *the* virtue; not-being-able-to-take-revenge is called not-wanting-to-take-revenge, it might even be forgiveness (...). They are also talking about "loving your enemies" – and sweating while they do it.' (...)

'They are miserable, without a doubt, all these rumour-mongers and clandestine forgers, even if they do crouch close together for warmth (...).'
'They are now informing me that not only are they better than the powerful, the masters of the world whose spittle they have to lick (…) – not only are they better, but they have a "better time", or at least will have a better time one day. (…)'
You haven't said anything yet about the masterpieces of those black magicians who can turn anything black into whiteness (…). Would you suspect, if you just went by what they said, that the men around you were nothing but men of *ressentiment*?… (GM-I-14, Nietzsche 2007a, 27–28).

As we can see in the first fragment cited above, *ressentiment* has a negative character (it is an expression of enmity, frequently hidden), it is reactionary and defensive (but it is not a mere defensive reflex action, but rather a delayed reaction connected with a certain strategy) and it stems from weakness and powerlessness. *Ressentiment* is an attitude which encompasses such negative emotions as hatred, the need for revenge, envy and jealousy. Weakness is understood here as a dependence upon other, stronger people; strength is thus a reflection of freedom, mastery over oneself. Strength need not be regarded as a purely physical force, it is rather something internal, created by powerful acts which show the creativity and power of the spirit which Nietzsche terms the will to power. *Ressentiment* is thus a reaction stemming from physical-spiritual impotence, nourished on hatred and injury. It is born of an inability to act against a perceived wrong or the experience of frustrations, especially long term ones. When the opponent is too strong for us to repay the wrong visited upon us, we may only soothe our suffering with thoughts of imagined revenge.

Since the source of *ressentiment* is a feeling of powerlessness over an injury suffered, it is frequently connected with a feeling of inferiority for which one tries to compensate. *Ressentiment* poisons a person from the inside and is a strong, destructive force. It remains a contentious point if *ressentiment* expresses weakness or if it makes people weak (Solomon 2003); it seems that that both are true. *Ressentiment* may be experienced both by strong and weak individuals in an unpleasant situation which is beyond their control. In strong people, according to Nietzsche, *ressentiment* is overcome by action and does not result in the same kind of internal corruption and poisoning.

Ressentiment is a personal emotional attitude which may sometimes become a group experience shared by people who find themselves in a similar situation. *Ressentiment* may also surface even when there is no defined wrongdoer – instead, the person feels wronged by fate. This may in fact lead to the strongest type of *ressentiment* which Scheler called 'existential envy' (Scheler 1994, 35). It comes about when someone is so unhappy with their life that they feel that their fate compels them to seek vengeance and frequently manifests itself towards those who appear to have it better. A person suffering from this type of *ressentiment* cannot forgive others for their happiness – so unhappy are they that they want everyone else to be just as unhappy as they are.[127] The attitude that someone suffering from this has towards the person they are envious of is not simply that they are envious of what that person has, of something specific, but rather that they are not that person. Since they cannot be that person, they cannot forgive them for being who they are or, indeed, for their very existence.

In the above fragment one may identify three fundamental assumptions upon which Nietzsche builds his concept of *ressentiment*. These are: 1) the origins of *ressentiment*, 2) its characteristics and 3) its consequences.

The key to understanding what *ressentiment* stems from is the division of people into active and reactive, as Dostoyevsky writes. The former are men of action, in whom the creative emotion dominates. The latter are passive people, powerless to act and in whom are collected emotions which negate the importance of everything that is unattainable for them. The emotional state of the latter is a reaction against the image of the world which they find threatening and where the only salvation is the negation of everything that it represents. In other words, this reactive-negative state differs from the active state in that it is dependent upon it – it needs opposition, something to strain against. The active state is independent – it does not need anything external to rage against.

The origins of *ressentiment* highlight the characteristics of the emotional state that people filled with it find themselves in. Even when *ressentiment* serves to unleash a person's creative powers, the result will always be something inferior to that which it opposes because it has powerlessness as its source. It is crucial that *ressentiment*, which arises from an inability to affect the external world, forces this energy inside the person (leading to the suppression of emotions and internal turmoil). A person suffering from *ressentiment* is thus first of all separated from themselves and an effect is self-torment combined with a perverse form of delight in being the victim of this self-torture, as Dostoyevsky writes, and what Nietzsche understands as the spiritualization and deepening of cruelty which provided the foundations for almost everything we call 'higher culture' (JGB-229).

---

127 The problem is insightfully expressed in the dialogue written by Dostoyevsky, whereby Hippolite asks Prince Muishkin, 'how do you think I ought to die, now? I mean – the best, the most virtuous way? Tell me!?', and Prince Muishkin replies, '[y]ou should pass us by and forgive us our happiness' (Dostoyevsky 2011, 1062).

Ressentiment also has an impact on the way in which we value things, since this is supposed to work on the wrongdoer as well, serving to soothe the wronged. An important aspect of this long running process is that it leads to the development of a mental state which may determine the moral attitude of someone towards the world, not just particular behaviours or evaluations (Solomon 2003). The moral attitude is a judgmental reaction expressed in the categories of good and evil. It is at the same time a specific propositional attitude, that is a mental state (e.g. a conviction, a desire, an exception) which defines the relationship of the subject to the content of the judgement. When the moral attitude stems from *ressentiment*, this is a negative relation and one reliant upon an opposition to what is stronger or better than us. Internalizing our negative attitude towards the world occurs when our emotional states stem from failure and humiliation.

Ressentiment is thus not only an attribute of human nature, like the instinct for self-defence, but something much more – it is a *strategy* of the defeated intended to obtain or regain power (Solomon 2003). *Ressentiment* is initially directed towards those who have done us wrong, to those who have defeated us somehow. Its initial goal is thus purely negative – it means that the person who has injured us should also suffer. *Ressentiment* gives people pleasure in negating and defeating those who are above them. This is why it is so closely related to revenge or *Schadenfreude* (experiencing pleasure at others' misfortunes). This attitude is also connected with a constant comparison of oneself with others and when we do not measure up, we seek to level the playing field with the help of contempt and condemnation.

Nietzsche focuses in his reflections on the situation of a physically weaker person who has been wronged. Since he also takes into consideration, however, that the will to power manifests itself not only in the physically strong but above all in the spiritually robust, we may venture a more sophisticated psychological analysis of human attitudes. One of the most interesting situations is when the wrongdoer hates his victim for the harm that he has done and wants to take revenge on them for his own wickedness.[128] In this context, the vice (or bad deed) is an expression of weakness, as Nietzsche himself admits (Za-II-*Mitleidige*), and

128 This attitude was detected in Germans by the Israeli psychoanalyst Zvi Rex, who claimed 'Germans have never forgiven Jews for Auschwitz' (Uri Avnery, *Keine Sonderbehandlung*, Der Spiegel, 3.06.2002). We can also find an example of such an attitude in Dostoyevsky, 'he suddenly remembered being asked once before, at some point: "Why do you hate so-and-so so much?" And he had replied then, in a fit of buffoonish impudence: "I'll tell you why: he never did anything to me, it's true, but I once played a most shameless nasty trick on him, and the moment I did it, I immediately hated him for it."' (Dostoyevsky 1992, 72).

the innocent attitude is one of strength and victory, which may arouse *ressentiment* in the wrongdoer.

2. The reversal of values

In terms of the consequences of *ressentiment*, it can sometimes affect the *creative* process whose goal is the reversal of power between the weak and the strong. This utilises the mechanism of 'the reversal of values', the best example of which is the 'sour grapes syndrome' of Aesop (cf. MAII,WS-244; Scheler 1994). In the fable the fox cannot reach the grapes which it desires as they are too high on the tree. As a result, he decides that they must be sour and not worth the effort and that those who manage to get them are only worthy of derision.

The seizing of power by the weak is a result of them opposing strength and treating it as evil. As a result, Nietzsche describes those who create values based on *ressentiment* as 'counterfeiters' (NF-1880,4[249]) and fabricators of ideals who can make white black and vice versa. The figure of Lucifer in *Paradise Lost* by Milton exemplifies this – the fallen angel who had been the master of faking holiness; he was unable to find comfort in God because 'hatred, the mortal wound, had cut so deep' that instead of an unachievable good, he called for an even greater evil:

> So farewell hope, and with hope farewell fear,
> Farewell remorse: all good to me is lost;
> Evil be thou my good (Milton 2005, Book IV, verse 108–110, 108).

This kind of creation of values relies on the devaluation of higher values and replacing them with inferior – often contradictory – ones. This is exactly the case with the revolt of the slaves on moral grounds. In the value systems of masters and slaves, the terms 'bad' (used in master morality) and 'evil' (used in slave morality) mean precisely the opposite. One should stress here that the 'revaluation of all values' will be its own kind of value reversal by the people Nietzsche describes as higher (NF-1885,2[100]; NF-1886,7[45]), yet the values will not have their source in *ressentiment* as they come from their strength. The 'revaluation of all values' depends on experiencing and overcoming the values which we have obtained rather than rejecting unachievable values.

Value judgements stemming from *ressentiment* are characterised by the fact that they refer to choices made in the *comparative sphere*. The noble morality described by Nietzsche differs from the common one in that it is not formed by means of comparisons. In other words, a comparison with others is not a necessary condition of feeling one's own value in a 'noble person':

[a 'noble person'] has a completely naive and non-reflective awareness of his own value and of his fullness of being, an obscure conviction which enriches every conscious moment of his existence, as if he were autonomously rooted in the universe. On the other hand, the 'common' man (in the exact acceptation of the term) can only experience his value and that of another if he relates the two, and he clearly perceives only those qualities which constitute possible differences (Scheler 1994, 37).[129]

If we derive our self-esteem and worth from comparisons with others, we may display two different attitudes. The first manifests itself in the spirit of a ceaseless rivalry designed to prove the worth of our own values. The second consists of questioning the values that we are comparing but which remain unattainable. The latter is characteristic for *ressentiment* and it may be understood as a strategy utilised when we find ourselves in no position to demonstrate our power in competition with others.

3. *Ressentiment* and Christianity

Max Scheler conducted the most in-depth analysis of the phenomenological relation between *ressentiment* and the creation of moral judgements in his book *Ressentiment and Morality*. He expressed it in his praise of the remarkably detailed psychological awareness of Nietzsche which had contributed to our better understanding of the origins of moral judgements in people. At the same time, Scheler showed how Nietzsche interpreted Christian morality in a completely wrong way, especially in the fact that Nietzsche saw Christian love as the subtlest form of *ressentiment*:

[F]rom the trunk of the tree of revenge and hatred, Jewish hatred – the deepest and most sublime, indeed a hatred which created ideals and changed values, the like of which has never been seen on earth – there grew something just as incomparable, a *new love*, the deepest and most sublime kind of love (GM-I-8, Nietzsche 2007a, 18).

You crowd around your neighbor and you have pretty words for it. But I say to you: your love of the neighbor is your bad love of yourselves.

You flee to your neighbor to escape yourself and you want to make a virtue of it: but I see through your 'selflessness.' (…)

Do I recommend love of the neighbor to you? I prefer instead to recommend flight from the neighbor and love of the farthest! (…)

You invite a witness when you want someone to speak well of you; and when you have seduced him into thinking well of you, you then think well of yourselves. (…)

129 The author borrowed the term 'nobility' from Georg Simmel and both were influenced by Nietzsche in this matter.

> One person goes to his neighbor because he seeks himself, and the other because he would like to lose himself. Your bad love of yourselves makes your loneliness into a prison.
> Those farther away pay for your love of the neighbor; and even when you are together five at a time, always a sixth one must die (Za-I-*Naechstenliebe,* Nietzsche 2006a, 44–45).
> Human beings themselves, however, the seeker of knowledge calls: the animal that has red cheeks. (…)
> …Shame, shame, shame – that is the history of human beings!
> And that is why the noble person commands himself not to shame (…).
> Indeed, I do not like them, the merciful who are blissful in their pitying (…).
> And if a friend does evil to you, then say: 'I forgive you what you have done to me; but that you did it to *yourself* – how could I forgive that!'
> Thus speaks all great love; it overcomes even forgiveness and pitying. (…)
> …And what in the world causes more suffering than the folly of the pitying?
> Woe to all lovers who do not yet have an elevation that is above their pitying! (…)
> …[A]ll great love is above even all its pitying, for it still wants to create the beloved!
> 'I offer myself to my love, *and my neighbor as myself* – thus it is said of all creators (Za-II-*Mitleidige,* Nietzsche 2006a, 67–69).

In the first of the texts above Nietzsche highlights the paradox of the 'self-crucifixion of God for the *salvation of mankind*' as being 'the most dangerous bait' that he knew of and an expression of the most sublime vengefulness. Such an interpretation stems from the notion of love as self-sacrifice, which he sees as serving to shame enemies and become an instrument of revenge. He might have been inspired by the words of St Paul who calls for 'coals of fire on his [enemy's] head' (Ro 12,19–21).[130] The interpretation of the love of one's neighbour conducted by Nietzsche suggests that it is a passive (powerless) attitude in the face of violence (Lk 6,29).[131] The blessings mentioned in the *Sermon on the Mount* are in turn seen by Nietzsche as an example of God's kingdom as a simple reversal of the earthly world, constituting a form of compensation for those who possess the least in this life (Lk 6,20–25).[132]

---

130 'Dearly beloved, avenge not yourselves, but *rather* give place unto wrath: for it is written, Vengeance *is* mine; I will repay, saith the Lord. Therefore if thine enemy hunger, feed him; if he thirst, give him drink: for in so doing thou shalt heap coals of fire on his head. Be not overcome of evil, but overcome evil with good'.

131 'And unto him that smiteth thee on the *one* cheek offer also the other'.

132 'Blessed *be ye* poor: for yours is the kingdom of God. Blessed *are ye* that hunger now: for ye shall be filled. Blessed *are ye* that weep now: for ye shall laugh. Blessed are ye, when men shall hate you, and when they shall separate you *from their company*, and shall reproach *you* (…). Rejoice ye in that day, and leap for joy: for, behold, your reward *is* great in heaven (…). But woe unto you that are rich! for ye have received

However, as Scheler shrewdly observes, interpreting Christian love as a symptom of *ressentiment* is a result of a complete misunderstanding of Christianity and its system of values (Scheler 1994). Love in the Christian perspective certainly undergoes a considerable change but one cannot see it as being an expression of powerlessness – on the contrary, it is rather an expression of overcoming *ressentiment*. In antiquity, love was interpreted as spiritual strength directed from something below to something higher, of which the best example is the famous dialogue between Socrates and Diotima on the subject of *Eros* (Plato 1980). Christianity, on the other hand, goes in the opposite direction: that which is higher directs love towards that which is lower, elevating it with its love, the greatest source of which is God (1 Jn 4,16). When talking about charity, Christianity gives the example of the perfect love of God (Mt 5,43–48); it thus seems to have a noble character rather than a common one, generosity rather than envy. In the New Testament the term *agape* is used to denote love instead of the term *eros* (cf. Benedict XVI 2006). *Agape* is identified with spiritual love ('descending', oblative love), grounded in and shaped by faith, whilst *eros* is a sensual love ('ascending', possessing love) which imposes itself upon mankind. The one-way progress of man to the pinnacle of beauty and truth described in the *Symposium* of Plato is replaced by Jacob's Ladder, combining heaven and earth in a two-way relationship (see Rom 28,12; J 1,51).

The lesson from the Gospel about turning the other cheek does not mean adopting a passive attitude, as Nietzsche claims, but rather an active one which calls for more strength than the person striking the cheek. After all, we can read in the same section that we not only should not return the blow but we should go one step further and we should present the attacker with the other cheek to strike (Lk 6,29). It is similar to the idea of loving our enemies, which calls for more than just accepting the wrong done to us, 'and him that taketh away thy cloak forbid not to *take thy* coat also' (Lk 6,29). We can find a similar idea in Nietzsche, who admired those who were strong enough not to strike their attackers back as they are barely affected by them. He was unable, however, to recognise strength in the love of one's neighbour because he was influenced by the caricature of this idea that was at that time being produced in the form of humanitarianism and other socio-political doctrines. The same is true of the ascetic ideals which Nietzsche devoted so much attention to. The Christian idea of holiness contains an active attitude – the overcoming of the self, controlling our drives and a powerful love

your consolation. Woe unto you that are full! for ye shall hunger. Woe unto you that laugh now! for ye shall mourn and weep'.

which is not used to defeat an enemy but to elevate him to a position of love (the 'coals of fire' should symbolise the transformation and not the punishment). As Thomas Mann aptly put it, Nietzsche himself lived like a holy ascetic (Mann 1959), preaching through the mouth of Zarathustra the idea of overcoming and controlling both our senses and our virtues (Za-I-*Kind*).[133]

The second of the fragments above shows how Nietzsche understands love of one's neighbour. It is for him a form of escaping from ourselves to others, seeking to find confirmation of self-worth in them. It is an expression of need, of belonging to a group, of identifying with those who are close to us and from whom we seek acceptance. Nietzsche claims in the above fragment that those who cannot love themselves first love those who are close to them – we are concerned here only with a false love 'founded on *self-hatred* and *self-flight*' (Scheler 1994, 101). It should be emphasized here that the Christian commandment to love one another means precisely the opposite. Nietzsche seems to be describing something akin to altruism, which, whilst frequently appealed to in modern ethical theory, does not have much in common with Christian love since it springs from a different source – the humanitarianism of the Enlightenment which calls for an impersonal love of humanity. One may also add, after Dostoyevsky, that the more one loves humanity, the less one loves people.[134] The attitude of valuations is completely different here – in the case of altruism, it is about the happiness of the humankind whilst Christian love is about individual redemption. Furthermore, altruism (in contrast with love of one's neighbour) does not have a spiritual character and is not a form of love with transformative power. It is rather a 'hallucination of feeling' or 'it becomes an animal drive which continually grows in refinement and complexity through man's social evolution and intellectual development', spreading thanks to imitation (Scheler 1994, 94). Contemporary ethical theory often refers to the so-called kin altruism or reciprocal altruism in order to help explain altruistic behaviour with the assistance of evolutionary psychology wherein it becomes in reality a broad type of egoism in which we only care about others when it is in our common interest. The parable of *On Love of the Neighbour* seems to describe exactly this attitude.

In the third of the above fragments, Nietzsche uses Zarathustra to oppose *great love* to low and shameful love. He calls this humiliating form of love pity and

133 'Are you the victor, the self conqueror, the master of your senses, the ruler of your virtues? Thus I ask you' (Nietzsche 2006a, 51).

134 'I love mankind (…) but I am amazed at myself: the more I love mankind in general, the less I love people in particular, that is individually, as separate persons' (Dostoyevsky 1992, 46–47).

identifies it with the Christian love of one's neighbour, which is both a creator and source of *ressentiment* (GM-III-14).[135] There are a number of problems with this interpretation which are worth highlighting. The word *misericordia* is comprised of two words *miser* (unhappy) and *cordis* (heart), and thus *misericordia* literally means 'in our hearts we have merciful love because of the misfortune of another' as St Thomas wrote (Aquinas 1981, II–I, Question 30, 1754).[136] The love of one's neighbour (the Christian word *caritas* being the equivalent of the Greek *agape*) is thus the virtue superior to charity. Charity is just one of the external fruits of the virtue of love, as St Thomas also argued. As much as the love of thy neighbour is driven towards the general good of another, charity is powered by a desire to compensate for the lack of good (unhappiness) of the other person. It contains two key aspects: mercy and compassion. The former consists of the alleviation of sorrow, refraining from punishing or ascribing guilt, which does not stem from a desire to humiliate the other but only: a) from the generosity of the forgiver, who wants to remain true to oneself and one's own love (Hebr. *hesed*), or b) from compassion (Hebr. *rah mim*) (John Paul II 1980). The second aspect of charity, compassion, mainly manifests itself in Christian teachings.[137]

Aquinas distinguishes between charity which stems from sensual drives and is a feeling and charity which is a manifestation of will; it is the latter that he terms a virtue and that is a subject of commandments. The commandment in the New Tes-

135 In Nietzsche's opinion, only those who are higher can show pity to those who are lower. Pity contains a form of contempt which does not arouse gratitude but only *ressentiment*. The person who calls for pity (such as a beggar) is in danger of *ressentiment*, of wanting to bring you down to their level of unhappiness by making you feel ashamed of your own happiness (M-185; NF-1883,12[1]; Za-II-*Mitleidige*). It is a particularly accurate observation that pity based on contempt is mutually destructive. Pity (Ger. *Mitleid*) has a pejorative aspect which distinguishes it from compassion (Ger. *Mitgefühl*). *Mit-leiden* means to 'suffer from' or to 'suffer with' whilst *mit-fühlen* has a sense of 'co-feeling' which need not necessarily require suffering. The latter has neutral connotations in Nietzsche's work, it can be understood as 'empathy', although he also criticises it as weakening the spirit. Thus, instead of empathising with those who suffer, he proposes empathising with oneself (NF-1888,20[129]).

136 The term *misericordia* is very rich semantically and contains notions such as *clementia* (clemency) or *gratia* (grace) while also being connected with *humanitas* (philanthropy, charity) and *epieikeia* (cf. Aquinas 1981, II–I, Questions 120, 157).

137 The Gospel of Saint Luke is known as the 'Gospel of Mercy' since it contains the most parables and stories which show the compassionate face of mercy (especially those of the Good Samaritan in Lk 10,33; the prodigal son in Lk 15,20; and the widow of Nain in Lk 7,13).

tament that 'you shall love your neighbour as yourself' (Mt 22,39) and also in the Old Testament that 'you shall not take vengeance, nor bear any grudge against the children of your people, but you shall love your neighbour as yourself' (Lev 19,18) are a form of overcoming revenge and are reminiscent of the 'great love' that Zarathustra mentions in the citation above. There is one key difference, namely that Christian love is *rooted in God*. It is both given to and demanded of people.[138] It is the desire of God – one loves because of God. Nietzsche is amazed by this notion and rejects it claiming that it treats human love as something animal and requiring redemption (JGB-60).[139] Christian love, just as the 'great love' proclaimed by Zarathustra, is *affirming* and applies to human beings in their *entirety*. As Simone Weil writes, 'Among human beings, only the existence of those we love is fully recognized' (Weil 2002, 64). Love is precisely this deep conviction of both the existence of the other combined with the desire for its existence, for it to be. This is why the best definition of love is that furnished by the words ascribed to Saint Augustine: 'I love you – I want you to be' (Augustine in Heidegger 2004, 21).[140] The constructive and active character of love is also encapsulated by the words of St Augustine: 'There is no greater invitation to love than to precede [the other] with loving' (Augustine in Heidegger 2004, 74).[141]

The next argument against interpreting Christian love as an attitude of *ressentiment* is the fact that the Gospel teaches us not to focus on judging others but rather to focus on ourselves and our own improvement (e.g. Lk 6,41). This refers to the internal dimension of morality which is not based on comparisons (e.g. Mk 12,41–44). Nietzsche calls for exactly the same as Jesus does (JGB-19). The only difference is that while the Christian attitude stems from the supposition that we are all guilty (Jn 8,7), Nietzsche argues for the complete innocence of all, an aspect that I shall return to later. The revolutionary dimension of Christian thought is that it transformed the Old Testament doctrine of crime and punishment into one of mercy and redemption. The death of Jesus on the cross cannot be understood in terms of shameful pity, as Nietzsche would have it, but rather as an expression of the power of God's love and forgiveness (Mt 25,40).

---

138 'Since God has first loved us (cf. 1 Jn 4,10), love is now no longer a mere "command"; it is the response to the gift of love with which God draws near to us' (Benedict XVI 2006).

139 'To love humanity *for the sake of God* – that has been the noblest and most bizarre feeling people have attained so far (…) holy and admirable to us as the man who has flown the highest so far and has got the most beautifully lost!' (Nietzsche 2002, 54).

140 'Amo: volo ut sis' (Augustine in Arendt 1981b, 104).

141 'Nulla est enim maior ad amorem invitatio, quam praevenire amando' (Augustine, *De catechizandis rudibus*, lib. I, cap. IV, in *Patrologiae cursus completes. Seria latina (Migne)*, vol. XL, Sp. 314).

Forgiveness, whose transformational role in human relations was a major discovery of Christianity, is fundamentally something constructive, free from revenge, as Arendt remarks (Arendt 1998). Forgiveness does not preclude punishment but rather moves beyond it. The punishment for a particular crime is not enough to redress its consequences, but forgiveness does have a remarkable power to overcome evil. The forgiveness of sins has an ontological dimension equivalent to creation *ex nihilo*, as Kołakowski notes, since it annihilates the world as it was before forgiveness. Arendt claims that love is unworldly and thus unsuitable for establishing a legal-political system governing interpersonal relations. She proposes instead that in its place there should be the philosophical category of respect or recognition which served philosophers like Hegel or his followers, Charles Taylor and Axel Honneth. Nietzsche also values recognition (*Annerkenung*), which he juxtaposes with contempt (*Verachtung*), in his considerations of punishment and revenge (NF-1875,9[1]), and holds grace (*Gnade*) to be the highest form of justice, an aspect that I will turn to in a moment.

To sum up, the inaccurate interpretation of Christian love conducted by Nietzsche stems from two fundamental misconceptions as indicated by Scheler: 1) philosophical; and 2) historical-anthropological. Nietzsche claims that the metaphysical structure of the world and the morality based upon it was founded on *ressentiment* and fear. His philosophical error is, for Scheler, a result of an impossibility to evaluate the structure with the use of categories that lie beyond it without risking the charge of creating a competing image of the world which would be, from the perspective of the former, an expression of *ressentiment*. In other words, the error stems from evaluating Christian values with the external scheme of the will to power (vitality, growth) since they only had sense by reference to the idea of the kingdom of God in which they were rooted. According to Scheler:

> Nietzsche interprets Christianity from the outset as a mere 'morality' with a religious 'justification,' not primarily as a 'religion,' and he applies to Christian values a standard which they themselves refuse consciously: the standard of the maximum quantity of life (Scheler 1994, 84).

It seems that one may also interpret Nietzsche's philosophical error in a different manner. In my opinion, Nietzsche's basic and already emphasised error is to identify Christianity with a heretic idealism which was pagan in its roots and which posited a dualism of the sensuous world and the supersensuous world and which called for an escape from life into the afterlife. This type of spiritual Manichaeism which could be found in the superficially Christianized culture of the West generated tremendous tension which may be interpreted as a refined form of *ressentiment* towards Christianity itself.

The historical-anthropological error is founded on the fact that Nietzsche confuses Christian morality with bourgeois morality and modern ideas (humanitarianism, communism). Thus, the social notion of equality has nothing to do with equality before God, which does not call for any change in social relations or to the use of the same standard to refer to all; on the contrary, it calls for the separation of the kingdom of God from the earthly one and for the individual manner in which God learns what lies in the heart of every person (Scheler 1994). For Scheler, '*the core of Christian ethics has not grown on the soil of ressentiment*', but rather 'the *core of bourgeois morality*, which gradually replaced Christian morality ever since the 13th century and culminated in the French Revolution, *is rooted in ressentiment*' (Scheler 1994, 61).

4. *Ressentiment* as a source of contemporary spiritual crisis

> Ha! Up now, dignity!
> Blow, blow again,
> Bellows of virtue!
> Ha!
> Roar once more,
> Roar morally!
> As a moral lion
> Before daughters of the desert, roar!
> – For the howling of virtue, (...)
> Is more than all
> European fervor, European voraciousness!
> And here I stand already,
> As a European,
> I cannot do otherwise, God help me! (...)
> *The desert grows: woe to him who harbors deserts!* (Za-IV-*Toechter*, Nietzsche 2006a, 251–252).

Scheler analyses the conditions which foster the development of *ressentiment* and shows that many contemporary forms of evaluation are connected to a consciousness which has been at least partially shaped by *ressentiment*, including humanitarianism, communism, socialism, antisemitism, utilitarianism and ethical imperativism, all of which may be regarded as symptoms of spiritual degeneration. Many of them stem from *ressentiment towards the Judeo-Christian tradition.*[142]

142 The *ressentiment* of the common man 'wreaks vengeance on the *idea* whose test he cannot stand by pulling it down to the level of his factual condition' (Scheler 1994, 118). One may say that it resulted in the 'death of God' in contemporary hearts which are, furthermore, too weak to bear the weight of this death.

Their common trait is that they arose from their own moral impotency, transforming all previously hard-to-attain values into superfluous ones and thus making them widely available. A good example would be utilitarian ethics, on the basis of which we have seen an inversion of the relationship between values and desires. Instead of desiring something which is valuable (and thus something which is hard to attain) in the case of utilitarianism something becomes valuable when we desire it (cf. Mill 1871). This leads to a conclusion which is absurd from the ethical perspective, namely that the more people want something, the more it is worth.

A result of the 'revolt of slave values' is the triumph of the so-called 'last men' together with their cult of comfort, warmth, and pleasure (Za-*Vorrede*-5; cf. Heidegger 1968) – all those values which only serve to maintain and use up life and which were regarded in both ancient philosophy and Christian ethics as inferior. As Emil Cioran notes, contemporary civilized people resemble helots of antiquity, slaves to necessity and its creations, no longer masters of their own time.[143] This phenomenon diagnosed by Nietzsche has also been described by many other thinkers. Ortega y Gasset terms it the 'revolt of the masses' which relied on the dictatorship of the average:

> This is what (…) I laid down as the characteristic of our time; not that the vulgar believes itself super-excellent and not vulgar, but that the vulgar proclaims and imposes the rights of vulgarity, or vulgarity as a right (Ortega y Gasset 1950, 50).

This state is a result of the disappearance of the spirit in the masses, as Ortega claims:

> In the schools, which were such a source of pride to the last century, it has been impossible to do more than instruct the masses in the technique of modern life; it has been found impossible to educate them. They have been given tools for an intenser form of existence, but no feeling for their great historic duties; they have been hurriedly inocu-

143 Cioran claims that contemporary man lives under the delusion of his own freedom, but is in fact 'a convict on leave', a person being permanently 'at the mercy of the hours', eternally exhausted, busy and absent-minded (Cioran 1970, 68). They are just like those who, as Arendt writes, are stuck in a trap of their own needs and live a purely biological existence, that they are *animal laborans,* characteristic of contemporary consumer society and identical to a slave in antiquity since all their time outside of work is spent on the consumption of goods, which lasts for less time than it takes to make them and increases faster than the possibility to accumulate goods (Arendt 1998). As Nietzsche writes, '[f]undamentally, one now feels at the sight of work – one always means by work that hard industriousness from early till late – that such work is the best policeman, that it keeps everyone in bounds and can mightily hinder the development of reason, covetousness, desire for independence' (M-173, Nietzsche 2005a, 105).

lated with the pride and power of modern instruments, but not with their spirit. Hence they will have nothing to do with their spirit, and the new generations are getting ready to take over command of the world as if the world were a paradise without trace of former footsteps, without traditional and highly complex problems (Ortega y Gasset 1950, 36).

In contemporary society, the crisis of human spiritual identity which Nietzsche observed has strengthened – higher values have been replaced with a consumerist scale of values, in which the only 'responsibility' of a person is to maintain life and the maximisation of prosperity becomes the sole goal of all our efforts.[144]

In the fragment above Nietzsche writes with horror about the growth of the wasteland, which one can identify with the spiritual desolation of Europe whose apex is nihilism. For Heidegger, these words of Nietzsche are a cry for help:

> 'The wasteland grows.' It means, the devastation is growing wider. Devastation is more than destruction. Devastation is more unearthly than destruction. Destruction only sweeps aside all that has grown up or been built up so far; but devastation blocks all future growth and prevents all building (Heidegger 1968, 29).

What is interesting is that Nietzsche senses a paradox stemming from the 'death of God' which is to be found in the fact that one deprived of the ability to 'roar morally' is a burnt-out husk of a soul, as cold as stone and this is something no European fervour is in a position to change. This fragment refers to the three spiritual transformations and particularly to that of the lion who escapes into the desert which I will discuss in the fourth chapter. This fragment shows that Nietzsche-Zarathustra himself has doubts as to whether the spirit of contemporary people would be strong enough to overcome nihilism.

Ressentiment as a source of moral upheaval is best seen in all of the revolutions which have taken power away from the privileged ruling class, rejecting the values from which that class draws its power and authority and replacing them with their opposites. An example may be found in the Russian Revolution, where the values of the aristocratic class were replaced by those stemming from the worker-peasant class and thus the values relating to education or wealth were negated. Instead of 'do not steal', the popular slogan becomes 'you should not have assets', as Nietzsche writes (WC-II-285). In this manner people seek to level the playing field equalizing power of different groups in society through the negation of the source of the previous power. The most fertile ground for such an inversion of values

144 Vaclav Havel claims that the technocratic and consumer societies are post-totalitarian, just as all societies based on ideology (Havel 1985).

is a long-term sense of injury and hatred felt by the weaker (the disadvantaged) towards the stronger (the privileged).

Scheler puts forward the hypothesis that the wider the difference between the formal-legal status of groups in society and the actual balance of power (reflected in the access to goods), the stronger *ressentiment* becomes (Scheler 1994). Thus the most ripe for revolt are constitutional democracies if there is a substantial gap between the privileged and disadvantaged ones; more so than in a caste-based society, such as Hindus, or the feudal society of medieval Europe, where particular groups do not intermix, where there is little movement between them and everyone accepts their place in a hierarchically-ordered world as their destiny, which is reinforced by different customs, laws and beliefs. From the other perspective, the democratic political system may be seen as an invention which enables and facilitates the diffusion of *ressentiment* amongst less privileged social groups by involving them in shaping the community.

III. The origins of laws: degrees of power

Nietzsche refers directly to the philosophy of law only once:

> Yes, the philosophy of law! It is a discipline which, like every moral science, is not even in its infancy! Even the most free thinking lawyers, for example, do not appreciate the oldest meaning of punishment – they have no idea: and as long as legal science is not established on new foundations, namely those of history and the comparison of nations, it is doomed to fight out pointless battles on the field of false abstraction which the 'philosophy of law' presents us with today and which is completely detached from the people of today. Contemporary man is, however, in such a complicated muddle, in his legal values [*rechtlichen Werthschätzungen*] too, that it allows for various interpretations (NF-1883,8[13], Nietzsche 1999 (trans. A. Shaw), vol. 10, 334).

In the first few lines of one of the most important works in contemporary philosophy of law entitled *The Concept of Law* the author, Herbert L.A. Hart, claims that '[f]ew questions concerning human society have been asked with such persistence and answered by serious thinkers in so many diverse, strange, and even paradoxical ways as the question "What is law?"' (Hart 1994, 1). In the opinion of Hart, no other academic discipline so persistently poses itself the question of its essence and considers it to be the main subject of its reflections as does the theory of law. Questions of the type 'what is chemistry' do not occupy much of a place in the literature of the subject as they are answered by a simple definition. Law, on the other hand, is a different matter. The problem has nothing to do with the inability to use the term 'law'. An average person, regardless of their knowledge of law, is in a position to identify when law is applied and to provide examples of legal regulations. The difficulty of the question which Hart is concerned with and which has occupied the philosophy of law since antiquity rather lies in other areas. They may be summarized in a few points such as: the problem of distinguishing laws form other norms (e.g. moral) and customs; the problem of validity and justification of law; the problem of the ontological and epistemological status of legal norms; the problem of the aims and function of laws, etc. The representatives of different philosophical schools, from natural law through positivists, realists, hermeneutics and the contemporary variant of the critical school, have all tried to answer this question (cf. Stelmach, Brożek 2011). Some researchers have attempted to order the philosophy of Nietzsche according to one of these trends, e.g. legal hermeneutics, whilst others, in contrast, have seen him as a defender and precursor of positivism and still others wish to regard him as a representative of legal realism, the forebear of *critical legal studies*, or even as the voice of legal nihilism (see Mootz, Goodrich 2008; Goodrich, Valverde 2005). Nietzsche was not a representative of any of these doctrines and it is not the intention of this work to examine any of these trends.

Nietzsche regards the philosophy of law as being *one of the moral sciences* and recommends an approach to law which is the same as his approach to morality (NF-1883,8[13]), typical of the 19th-century scholars. Instead of concentrating on a critique of particular details of legal-philosophical theory, which would only be a criticism of the notions of law, Nietzsche is interested in presenting *law as a problem* (FW-345). The philosophy of Nietzsche encourages the posing of questions but they are not to be questions such as what law or how to justify law; they should rather be concerned with *why law* as well as *what is the value of law*. In these questions, legal-philosophical issues become intertwined with those of moral philosophy since the effect of asking these questions boils down to asking what the mechanism of norm-giving is and how it works, in what conditions and circumstances values arise, including legal values, what is the meaning of notions such as justice, obligation, responsibility, etc. Nietzsche, like Wittgenstein, is more interested in researching the foundations than building some towering creation.

What is characteristic of the genealogical method applied by Nietzsche is that he does not strive to find the only correct meaning of a notion or legal-social institution; quite the opposite, his task is to uncover the wealth of meanings of legal or moral notions. It is not possible to define anything that has its own history (GM-II-13), our task is rather to consider its creation in order to understand it. Nietzsche compares words to a pocket in which different and often simultaneously contradictory meanings and opinions may be found (MAII,WS-33). He emphasises that, just as words obtain new meanings, often new ideas and notions are to be found in old institutions which frequently play a role in conserving them (MAI-466),[145] something particularly visible in law (the best example would be the contemporary debate over the institution of marriage and its value).

Oliver Wendell Holmes, representative of American legal realism and Supreme Court Justice, proposes a similar approach to law (Holmes 2009). He claims that the social objectives of law are obscured by the gradual development of history. No legal scheme had been created in its entirety at once, legal norms having developed over the years and mainly on the basis of imitation and tradition. In order to understand them and interpret their power correctly, it is necessary to analyse their history. The main task of jurisprudence is researching legal norms and institutions by uncovering what led to their creation, how they came to be as they are, what goals they are meant to achieve, whether those goals are still desirable and what are the costs involved in their realisation (that is, what do we give up in return and are they worth the price?). Holmes argues that many legal rules exist as blind imitations of past laws while the goal which they had been formed to achieve no longer has significance for us. The genealogical examination of law should therefore be a part of legal study whose goals are the attainment of useful legal norms, as he illustrates with the metaphor of the dragon:

> [I]t is the first step toward an enlightened scepticism, that is, towards a deliberate reconsideration of the worth of those rules. When you get the dragon out of his cave on to the plain and in the daylight, you can count his teeth and claws, and see just what is his strength. But to get him out is only the first step. The next is either to kill him, or to tame him and make him a useful animal (Holmes 2009, 24).

Similarly to Nietzsche, Holmes ascribes great power to legal norms since they generate greater and more enduring forms of power than any other previous means of control:

> To an imagination of any scope the most far-reaching form of power is not money, it is the command of ideas (…). Read the works of the great German jurists, and see how much more the world is governed today by Kant than by Bonaparte (Holmes 2009, 40).

It thus seems that the relationship of Nietzsche to the law is closest to legal realism, both in its sociological and psychological variants, although with its own distinct features which I will try to outline below. The unique nature of Nietzsche's inter-

145 'The overthrow of institutions does not follow immediately upon the overthrow of opinions; instead, the new opinions live for a long time in the desolate and strangely unfamiliar house of their predecessors and even preserve it themselves, since they need some sort of shelter' (Nietzsche 2000, 249–250).

pretation provides legal interpretation from the perspective of *the will to power.* This is visible, for example, in the genealogical research of the notion of justice which Nietzsche regards as closest to active people and furthest from spiritual reactivity.

1. Law in the metaphysical sense: justice as pre-established order

In the oldest surviving philosophical texts in the Western cultural milieu, Anaximander uses the notion 'justice' (*diké*) in relation to the laws governing the cosmos. *Diké* is identified with the cosmic order:

> 'Whence things originated, thither, according to necessity, they must return and perish; for they must pay penalty and be judged for their injustices according to the order of time' (PHG-4, Anaximander in Nietzsche 1911a, 92).[146]

Justice (*diké*) manifests itself alongside its opposite, injustice (*adikia*), which it is intended to neutralise; they are connected by their characteristic mutual exchange. Justice is not understood as something in itself here, as an objective or an ideal, but rather a function of creating and restoring a balance which has been disturbed by injustice; injustice is thus prior to it, justice is a form of reaction. As a result, many philosophers feel that justice can be best understood by its opposite (cf. Heraclitus LXIX in Kahn 2001; Mill 1871; Shklar 1990). In Anaximander's text, justice does not have a retributive character but is rather a part of a certain process which constitutes order; it is a reaction but a *positive* and *creative* one – it is not repaying like with like (as is the case with *ius talionis*), but instead it provides a new element. The *status quo ante* cannot be restored, it can only be *reconstructed.* Justice is an effect of the struggles of a cosmic power, one side of which leads to chaos and the other to order. Order may not be something permanent or unchanging and thus justice frequently becomes a constant process of restoring order, just as the nature which surrounds us is engaged in a constant cycle of renewal. In Anaximander's thought, there is something more than a mere explanation of nature; as Werner Jaeger stresses, one may find here the first philosophical theodicy (Jaeger 1948).

---

146 After quoting this passage Nietzsche writes, '[e]nigmatical utterance of a true pessimist, oracular inscription on the boundary-stone of Greek philosophy, how shall we explain thee?' (Nietzsche 1911a, 92). Cf. Anaximander in Heidegger 2002, 242; and David Farrell Krell's translation based on Martin Heidegger's quotation, '[b]ut where things have their origin (*genesis*), there too their passing away (*phthora*) occurs according to necessity (*kata to chreon*); for they pay recompense (*tisis*) and penalty (*dike*) to one another for their recklessness (*adikia*), according to firmly established time', (Anaximander in Oppermann 2003, 45–46).

In this first idea, justice was introduced to restore harmony to the universe. However, for Anaximander the 'cosmic rhythm' is more than 'a law of nature' in our understanding; it has a character of inscrutable force. These forces govern the cosmos and humanity in an equally ruthless manner and are the subject of many of the tragedies and epics of antiquity. Just as night follows day, so punishment must be visited upon the patricidal Oedipus and Orestes cannot escape responsibility for the death of his mother, as Martha Nussbaum notes:

> After summer comes fall, after fall comes winter, after day comes the night, and the fact that Agamemnon was not the killer of Thyestes' children is as irrelevant to *diké* as the fact that the night did not deliberately aggress against the day (Nussbaum 1999, 159).

In reading the deliberations of Anaximander, one may wonder if the idea of justice came about as a result of observing nature and was the application of cosmic laws to the social reality or whether it was the opposite and that nature may be understood by means of interpersonal relations. Nietzsche favours the second path. As Heidegger emphasises, the Pre-Socratic *diké* did not have a moral dimension but rather, for Nietzsche, it had a metaphysical character which sometimes led to the birth of moral order (PHG-4).[147] Anaximander reveals the internal inconsistencies of our world which negate themselves. He was the first to pose the question of the sense and justification of all existence, regarding it as the sum of all the injustice (*Ungerechtigkeiten*), that we have to endure in life until death, until we pass on; he creates the idea of universal judgement and punishment for existence; existence is guilty, it requires justification (*Rechtfertigung*), which the Ancient Greeks sought in their gods (NF-1872,19[134]; NF-1872,19[239]; PHG-4; GM-II-23). Anaximander begins, in Nietzsche's opinion, to consider the deepest ethical problem there is – the right to exist (*ein Recht zu sein*) and the injustice (*Unrecht*) of death, from which the Greek philosopher escapes to his 'metaphysical castle'. Existence inextricably linked to death is regarded here as a curse. These considerations led subsequent philosophers towards a moral interpretation of existence – as guilt paid for through the punishment of passing. The pessimistic view of Anaximander brings to mind the words of Silenus, companion of Dionysus, quoted by Nietzsche:

> Wretched, ephemeral race, children of chance and tribulation, why do you force me to tell you the very thing which it would be most profitable for you not to hear? The very

147 Cf. Heidegger 2002, where the author conducts a precise examination of the cited words of Anaximander which he feels were superficially interpreted by the young Nietzsche.

best thing is utterly beyond your reach not to have been born, not to be, to be nothing. However, the second best thing for you is: to die soon (GT-3, Nietzsche 2007b, 23).[148]

According to Nietzsche, to overcome Silenus's curse the Greeks needed gods and the mystery of tragedy, which could bring them a metaphysical consolation.

The existence which Anaximander covered by a mystical darkness is illuminated momentarily by philosophy of Heraclitus who Nietzsche particularly appreciated:

> 'I contemplate the Becoming,' (…) 'and nobody has so attentively watched this eternal wave-surging and rhythm of things. And what do I behold? Lawfulness, infallible certainty, ever equal paths of Justice, condemning Erinyes behind all transgressions of the laws, the whole world the spectacle of a governing justice and of demonically omnipresent natural forces subject to justice's sway. I do not behold the punishment of that which has become, but the justification of Becoming. (…). Where injustice sways, there is caprice, disorder, irregularity, contradiction; where however Law and Zeus' daughter, Dike, rule alone, as in this world, how could the sphere of guilt, of expiation, of judgment, and as it were the place of execution of all condemned ones be there? (PHG-5, Heraclitus in Nietzsche 1911a, 97).

Heraclitus rejects the dualist picture of the world – the separation of the physical from the metaphysical, division into being and nothingness, into defined and undefined qualities, the opposition between multiplicity and unity. He sees only eternal and constant becoming due to the struggle of opposites, which Nietzsche in turn took as his interpretation of existence. Heraclitus' vision presents a cosmodicy, as Nietzsche notes, a justification of all becoming in the enduring reign of the eternal laws of justice (the wonderful regularity which he discovered in becoming). In this metaphysical vision, which Nietzsche admires, the world appears as 'the game of Zeus' – a world-creating power that is only really playing with itself (PHG-6). In contrast to the moral interpretation of existence, this vision assumes complete innocence of becoming and regards the existence of contradictions and suffering as a result of the fragmentary apprehension of the world by a human being. Death may be seen as a punishment, and destruction as the opposite of creation, only when they are taken out of context and treated separately (PHG-7). By approaching becoming in its entirety, existence is seen as a child's game[149] or an artistic-creative one, a completely innocent game in itself. This aspect, inspired

148 Cf. *Theognidea*, 425–428 by Theagenes of Megara, the subject of a paper by Nietzsche when he was a Professor of Ancient Philology.

149 Cf. Heraclitus XCIV, '[l]ifetime is a child at play, moving pieces in a game. Kingship belongs to the child' (Kahn 2001, 71).

by the philosophy of Heraclitus, was to inspire Nietzsche's later concept of the eternal recurrence, which I will return to in the final chapter.

The motifs of game and chance in the context of justice are also to be found in the *Iliad* of Homer, where Zeus makes a judgement concerning the outcome of the Trojan War and the fate of Achilles in his battle with Hector (Homer 2007, 79–85, 161 and 478–484, 267). In both instances he uses the scales onto which he casts the fates of both Greeks and Trojans and the two heroes. The attribute of the scales ascribed to the Greek deity of the law, *Themis*, or that of justice, *Dike*, is to symbolise balance and indicate a deliberated verdict, the maintaining of proportion and the employment of due measure in judgements. The same attribute was originally attributed to the deity that governed fortune and destiny, *Tyche* (Lat. *Fortuna*), symbolising the chance nature of the manner in which human fates are decided upon. The relation between law, chance and accidents is strongly rooted in our thinking concerning justice and is to be found in many of the original legal institutions (especially in customary law can one detect traces of fate, which has a role to play today in, for example, sporting rivalry when both sides achieve the same result) and in language (Huizinga 1980).[150] Many contemporary psychological experiments show that the unequal distribution of goods, including profits and losses, is not regarded as unjust if it is a matter of chance; the same unequal result would most often be regarded as unjust and rejected if it stemmed from a decision.[151]

By the same token, the blindfold over the eyes, a symbol of impartial and objective justice, originally symbolised blind luck. The symbol of a sword is also ascribed to *Themis*, representing the execution of law, but was borrowed also from another deity – this time that of revenge, *Nemesis*. The connection of all of these mythical images into one allegory of justice illustrates Nietzsche's approach par-

---

150 Both in Greek and Hebrew there is a connection between the words 'right' and 'casting' (*thorah* – meaning right, justice, law; but also casting lots, shooting); the element of chance is visible in Old German customs, where the boundaries between possessions were settled by throwing an axe, races, drawing lots, etc.; with time, luck became replaced by trials of strength such as duels (Huizinga 1980). A contemporary, rational, formalized legal process gradually replaced irrational arguments, trials of strength, magic and luck; on the magical, irrational sources of many aspects of the legal system see Weber 1978.

151 On the difficulty on drawing the boundary between bad luck and injustice see Shklar 1990. Contemporary philosophical liberals like John Rawls take into account the natural lottery of life, recognising that the division of goods by nature is neither just nor unjust – what may be unjust is that our institutions exploit these divisions and differences (Rawls 1999).

ticularly well as it shows how this notion is comprised of diverse and frequently opposing drives and intuitions.

Aristotle, like the Pre-Socratics, identified justice as a kind of *balance* between excess (committing of an injustice) and scarcity (suffering from an injustice) and with order (Aristotle 2000). However, in his work it attains an ethical-legal dimension; justice is equated with being a virtue. The virtue of realising justice in a broader sense was for Aristotle identified with ethical perfection, it is a virtue which may be understood as moderation and a determination to act in accordance with the other virtues – as a result, it is an attribute of all other attributes (a meta attribute). In a narrow sense, it is just one of the virtues connected with positions, safety and maintaining the balance between profit and loss. It is precisely the second meaning of justice which becomes the subject of Aristotle's analysis in Book V of the *Nicomachean Ethics*, which became one of the main inspirations for philosophers concerned with justice. Justice was presented there as order identified with the 'rule of law' which attains a moral dimension since the political order (the justice of the *polis*) is inextricably connected with ethics (internal justice).

The case is similar in Plato, where justice appears in two contexts – as political justice and justice relating to a human being (spiritual order). In antiquity, virtue was defined as excellence, prowess (Lat. *virtu*), which formed a whole related set of attributes (wealth, expertise) in a person (AC-2; cf. Huizinga 1980). In this sense, everything had its own external ideal – be it a horse, knife or eye. Strength and health become attributes of the body while prudence, temperance and fortitude – those of the soul; justice thus becomes the internal harmony of these. In Book IX of *Republic*, Plato divides the soul into three parts according to the desires which drive them; in the just soul[152] reason rules over other parts (spirit and appetite), constituting a kind of internal policy of a person; the just soul is one in which balance, geometric proportion and the unity of all its components rule (Plato 2004). Only the just can build a truly just *polis*, according to Plato. The just meant the same as adhering to the divine laws or living in full conformity with the will of God – such a meaning can be found in the *Antigone* of Sophocles as well as in the Old and New Testament and the works of St Augustine and St Thomas.

In contrast to the philosophers mentioned above, Nietzsche presents his own political realism in relation to justice, rejecting the supernatural origins of laws. Inspired by Greek metaphysical thought, he utilises a fundamental intuition that

152 The terms 'just' and 'just soul' are used here to denote a word in Greek, *dikaios* (Lat. *justus*), which does not have a good equivalent in most contemporary languages (cf. Mauthner 1923, entry 'Recht').

justice is its own kind of harmony and is an expression of normative control over the world. He understands justice as a form of expression of the will to power which can be seen in the laws adopted by a society and its individuals. Justice as a ceaseless renewal of order is thus the Apollonian objection to the Dionysian chaos (see Linarelli 2008; Sedgwick 2013). As an active expression of creative power, it is also the best way to overcome *ressentiment*.

2. Justice as mutual advantage

> Justice (fairness) has its origins among people of approximately *equal power*, as Thucydides correctly understood (in the terrible dialogues of the Athenian and Melian ambassadors); where there is no clearly discernible superiority and a struggle would lead to ineffectual damages on both sides, the thought arises of coming to an understanding and negotiating the claims of both sides: the character of *exchange* is the original character of justice. Each satisfies the other, in that each receives what he values more than the other. We give the other person what he wants, as henceforth belonging to him, and receive in return what we wanted. Justice is therefore requital and exchange under the assumption of an approximately equal position of power: thus, revenge originally belongs in the domain of justice; it is an exchange. Likewise gratitude. – Justice naturally goes back to the point of view of judicious self-preservation, hence to the egoism of this reflection: 'why should I uselessly harm myself and still perhaps not attain my goal?' – So much for the *origin* of justice (MAI-92, Nietzsche 2000, 70).
>
> Our duties — are the rights of others over us. How have they acquired such rights? By taking us to be capable of contracting and of requiting, by positing us as similar and equal to them, and as a consequence entrusting us with something, educating, reproving, supporting us. We fulfil our duty – that is to say: we justify the idea of our power on the basis of which all these things were bestowed upon us (…). The rights of the others can relate only to that which lies within our power (…). Expressed more precisely: only to that which they believe lies within our power. The same error could easily be made on either side: the feeling of duty depends upon our having the same *belief* in regard to the extent of our power as others have (…). My rights – are that part of my power which others have not merely conceded me, but which they wish me to preserve. How do these others arrive at that? First: through their prudence and fear and caution: whether in that they expect something similar from us in return (protection of their own rights); or in that they consider that a struggle with us would be perilous or to no purpose; or in that they see in any diminution of our force a disadvantage to themselves, since we would then be unsuited to forming an alliance with them in opposition to a hostile third power. *Then*: by donation and cession. In this case, others have enough and more than enough power to be able to dispose of some of it and to guarantee to him they have given it to the portion of it they have given: in doing so they presuppose a feeble sense of power in him who lets himself be thus donated to. That is how rights originate: recognised and guaranteed degrees of power. If power-relationships undergo any material alteration, rights disappear and new ones are created – as is demonstrated in the continual disap-

pearance and reformation of rights between nations. (…) Where rights *prevail*, a certain condition and degree of power is being maintained, a diminution and increment warded off. The rights of others constitute a concession on the part of our sense of power to the sense of power of those others. If our power appears to be deeply shaken and broken, our rights cease to exist (M-112, Nietzsche 2005a, 66–67).

In the first of the fragments above, Nietzsche emphasises that justice is possible only when the relations between the two sides are of *equal power* (M-112), something that finds agreement in the works of other philosophers concerned with justice, such as Aristotle, for whom the master-slave relationship *ex definitione* ruled out justice because of the dependency of one upon the other (Aristotle 2000). Following this lead, contemporary theorists hold that one of the necessary conditions of justice is equality between the sides which it applies to (cf. Hume 2010; Hart 1994), hence the problem of justice between states. Nietzsche, however, takes this line of argumentation one step further and interprets justice through the prism of power and motivation based on one's own benefits, as illustrated by the famous dialogue between the Athenians and the inhabitants of Melos described by Thucydides.[153] This type of position was ascribed during antiquity to the Sophists whom Aristotle and Plato had long argued with.[154] For most contemporary philosophers, the behaviour of the Athenians is an expression of the highest injustice. The thought of Nietzsche does not lead to the justification of the behaviour of the Athenians. Instead, the thesis which he poses is the following: justice is an expression of power and thus may manifest itself between equal partners but also between a stronger and a weaker party where the former bestow power on the latter. The second case requires such disproportionate strength that the weaker party is no threat to the stronger, and the stronger party is so strong that it may afford sharing power with the weaker, as we shall see in further considerations.

Pascal writes in a similar spirit of legal-political realism:

Justice without strength is powerless. Strength without justice is tyrannical. (…) So justice and strength must be joined (…). So, having been unable to strengthen justice, we have justified strength (Pascal 1999, 135, 34).

---

153 The small island of Melos wanted to remain neutral during the Peloponnesian War and utilised the idea of justice in its defence. For the stronger Athenians, this argument was insufficient and they demanded the participation of Melos on their side or else they would exterminate the population of the island – with the inhabitants choosing the latter in order to preserve their honour (see Thucydides 2009, V, 84–116, 301–307). The role of Thucydides in revealing the mechanism of foreign policy is often compared to that played by Machiavelli in revealing the mechanisms of internal running of a state.

154 We can find this kind of Sophist argumentation in Thrasymachus (Plato 2004).

These words may be interpreted as a bitter assertion that what we call justice is only a disguised expression of force as true justice is impossible on Earth. Nietzsche rejects the idea of heavenly justice but at the same time regards it as perfectly natural that legal-political justice is an expression of power. As a result, justice either demonstrates a balance of power (fulfilling functions of conservation and exchange) or it bestows power (playing a creative and lawgiving function).

Nietzsche accepts that justice stems from a *contract* and is based on the *mutual benefit* of both parties. Nietzsche's idea of justice matches the naturalistic theory of *justice as mutual advantage* which, in contrast to the anti-naturalistic theory of *justice as impartiality*, does not require moral arguments for its justification (see Barry 1989). The idea of justice, according to Nietzsche, came about as a result of the need and care to avoid wasting effort on needless arguments when we do not have sufficient power over the other party to guarantee our success. In order to obtain what we want and without injuring ourselves in the process, we enter into an exchange and create legal norms to that end. Justice is thus a certain refined form of self-preservation, a drive with its roots in an animal instinct (M-26), which holds people back from conflict when it is clear that neither side will profit from it. Norms and legal relations are thus temporary measures and not ends in themselves, they serve to lay down the borders of the dispute and guarantee the *modus vivendi.*[155] In a situation where the balance of power shifts to unduly favour one of the parties, the stronger has to take care to maintain the legal relations with the weaker, giving them the same rights in order to achieve the same effect –the least amount of effort wasted (MAII,WS-26). In his opinion, the position of being inferior is often better than being equal.

This interpretation returns and is developed in the second of the fragments above and which Nietzsche entitled *On the natural history of rights and duties.* In Nietzsche's interpretation, rights are a manifestation of power – both of those who create them and those who are covered by them. If every right is correlated with a duty, then our duties are a reflection of the rights of others towards us and our rights are reflected by the duties of others towards us. In both cases, rights

155 The idea of international justice based on the balance of power was criticized by Kant who claimed that 'balance of power is a pure illusion, like Swift's story of the house which the builder had constructed in such perfect harmony with all the laws of equilibrium that it collapsed as soon as a sparrow alighted on it' (Kant 1999, 92). In his opinion, a stable notion of justice should be built on the basis of principles leading to the balance of power rather than on the basis of the balance of power making out of it a principle, which would be akin to the building of the house starting from the roof in Gulliver's *Travels* .

and duties define the *scope of the power* of those that they apply to in their mutual relations. The subject bestowing a right is always stronger than the one to whom it applies. At the same time, rights only refer to what is in our power (which gives us the Roman aphorism *Impossibillium nulla obligatio est*), and thus the issuing of rights may be equated with the confirmation or giving power to the one to whom they apply. The source of rights is thus a form of agreement (MAI-446) which fosters *exchange*. When we fulfil certain obligations, we are confirming that we have the power to reciprocate what we have committed to and we regain our sense of power. Furthermore, laws only attain normative force when those covered by them agree to respect and comply with them, which in turn forms the basis of the contractual nature of law which Nietzsche refers to in the third fragment. Blind obedience to the law is insufficient for the law to function without excessive repression, which is costly and does not guarantee stability. It is necessary to make those covered by the laws *legal subjects* (MAII,WS-303), which is connected with giving people the power to make promises and be responsible for themselves and the obligations they undertake. Then laws cease to be the orders of a sovereign power and become self-refraining measure.

For example, in Roman law a particular legal status (*persona*) was ascribed to all Roman citizens, which meant they were accorded certain legal rights connected with the role they played in the society; it guaranteed that their voices would be heard in court where one would appear not as a person in the natural sense but in the legal one – as 'a right-and-duty-bearing-person' (Arendt 1990, 107). The equality before the law ascribed to all free men in Athens or in the Roman Empire was not a natural equality but a legal-political one. The conferring of rights, as Joel Feinberg emphasises, has a great significance for the status of those entitled to use them since the law is different from requests or begging for something: it means that someone is *entitled to* something and that it should be executed without any feelings of shame or embarrassment (Feinberg 1966). Rights in this sense are *an assurance of a recognised degree of power.*

Rights conserve power relations and prevent reductions in power as well as increases. This is why all radical shifts in power relations most often come about because of revolution or war in which laws are either suspended or lifted. Another route is the increase in power which may stem from the threat of an external power or a transformation in living conditions which necessitates a change in the internal power structure. The introduction of rights may stem from an excess of power held by the lawgivers, who surrender part of this power to those who are the subjects of the law. The giving of power to those who are weaker by those who are stronger is also in the interests of the latter since they want the former to retain some useful amount of power. They must be strong enough to be allies of the ruling classes in their conflict with a stronger third party.

A good illustration of this would be the history of Polish feudal law, where the sovereign first guaranteed a broad range of rights and privileges to one social group – the nobility. The legal status obtained by landowners, largely between the 14th and 16th centuries, was known as the Golden Liberty and gradually led to the reversal of the role and power relations between the king and this particularly influential social group. These rights were also a means whereby lesser nobles were protected from being dominated by the aristocracy and this ensured the dignity of this class and the equality of its members.[156] With time, this privileged social group began to extend basic legal protection to other social groups, including the bourgeoisie and the peasantry. This transpired because the nobility felt sufficiently powerful to share their power with other classes who no longer posed a threat to them. Another cause of this 'guarantee of power' for the lower classes was the need to turn them into a stronger ally necessary to help regain independence of the Republic of Poland, a state of affairs that had meant the ruling class had actually lost a degree of their power and their influential position.

In writing about the natural roots of law, Nietzsche understands the concept in a manner different from some representatives of legal realism. One of the main figures in this movement, Alf Ross, compares the normativity of law to that of the idea of taboo which operated on an island in the South Pacific. What they called *tû-tû* was a secret power which made people 'impure' and required their ritual purification (Ross 1957). Normative notions like obligation, responsibility, guilt or possession are for Ross similar magical notions with a metaphysical source. They do not refer to anything which was physically present in the world (they do not describe anything) but are rather meaningless linguistic crutches which may be disposed of.

Nietzsche's position is different since rights and responsibilities for him not only confirm but also *establish and shape* power in society. The key to understanding this notion, as with legal obligations, is to recognise a defined practice as being required by those using the law (cf. Hart 1984). If we assign rights to someone, then, according to this interpretation, we are giving them the power to do something – in other words, rights not only reflect the current state of affairs but rather give the rights holders reasons for acting so that they can broaden the

---

156 In accordance with Nietzsche's interpretation, this aspect of equality may be regarded as a result of the *ressentiment* of the lesser nobility, or the power of the aristocracy who did not feel threatened by the petty nobility and needed their help in obtaining their independence from royal authority.

scope of their power. One may say that the fundamental function of law is to give a certain *status* (a meaning, function) to things, people and their practices and also entities (including legal persons). Legal persons, such as a university, cannot be reduced to a sum of its people and buildings which make it up but are rather only metaphorically described by using an analogy to a physical person (using terms like 'has headquarters in', 'accepts responsibility', 'intends to', etc.). They are not empirical facts or metaphysical entities but their own type of legal entity which is often not purely fictional since it has realistic effects in our world.

In order to explain this idea of status further, I would like to use the example of the boundary wall which comes from John Searle and which is an excellent metaphor for the creation of legal institutions (Searle 2010).[157] Searle describes a tribe that built a high stone wall around their settlement in order to protect themselves by physically limiting access to their settlement. In time, the wall decays and eventually only traces remain. Let us say that both the inhabitants of the village and their guests accept that one cannot cross the line without permission, even though there is no physical impediment to them doing so. In this manner, something is constructed in social practice which people ascribe normative force to – *a border*. A certain physical structure evolves in time into a mental limitation which only functions in the minds of people – the line has the status of a border which may not be crossed just because there is a collective recognition of the border. Legal institutions, just like many other social constructs (such as money) exist and have effects simply because *people act as if they physically existed*. As Searle succinctly puts it, ascribing the function of status to certain things, people or entities is different from the mere disposition which may be seen in animals (Searle 2010). If a dog is taught, by using punishments and rewards, not to cross a certain line, then the situation is different from the example described above in which people recognise the existence of the border and which is connected to the defined prohibition. The same is true when we award someone the status of a leader. A wolf pack led by an alpha male is different from a society with a leader in that the wolf relies on direct control over others, building both fear and respect. The authority of leaders, however, is built on their subjects' recognition of a status which entails certain prerogatives and which is based on legal norms, do not so much reflecting the reality of power but rather *creating*.

157 The metaphor is particularly accurate since the Greek word *nomos* (law) comes from *nemein* (distribute), as Arendt elucidates, and thus the connections between law and property and fencing are tight, 'the word *polis* was originally connoted with something like a "ring-wall" surrounding a city' (Arendt 1998, 63–64).

An interesting example of according of all humans with legal status is the conception of human dignity (see Soniewicka 2017). According to the dictionary, one may understand 'dignity' as:

1. 'The quality of being worthy of honour or respect;
2. a way of appearing or behaving that suggests formal reserve or seriousness of manner, or language and self-control;
3. high rank, office, or position;
4. a legal title of nobility or honour' (Merriam-Webster 2016, entry 'dignity').

Both the term 'dignitary' and 'dignity' come from the Latin *dignitas* which 'in Roman usage (…) embodied the idea of the honor, the privileges and the deference due to rank or office' (Waldron 2009, 225). The physical manifestation of this dignity was walking with up straight. In other words, dignity was understood as a particular status of a given person who belonged to a privileged class or who performed an important public function which required them to be treated with respect. To this day, the notion of dignity is used in the same sense when we talk about the dignity of the position of the President or of a judge, which enjoys legal protection. The idea of the inherent and inalienable human dignity, however, has another meaning and its source lies in antiquity. The Judaeo-Christian tradition re-evaluated the Roman conception of legal-political dignity and transformed it into the *internal dignity* as the essence of humanity, independent of one's external social status. Everyone had been created in the image of God which granted them *a particular moral status* amongst other beings, an inherent dignity in the eyes of God (Mt 10, 28; Mt 23,27–28). With reference to this, Kant ascribes dignity to every rational being able to order their will in accordance with universal moral law; he defines dignity as an absolute internal value which may not be ordered, measured or compared as we do with everything else that has its price (Kant 2002b). The contemporary notion of human dignity, applied to law, draws upon all of these traditions at once, retaining aspects of the Roman, Judaeo-Christian and Kantian conceptions. In this manner, the historical conception of dignity in an egalitarian frame became 'nobility for the common man', as Jeremy Waldron puts it since it gave a special status to every human being, guaranteeing a minimum of legal protection (Waldron 2009, 210). At the same time, there is a legal distinction between innate dignity, accorded to all on the basis of their humanity, and personal dignity, which depends on our own merits.

Nietzsche approaches the metaphysical aspects of law critically, calling notions such as 'human dignity' and 'human rights' phantoms, hallucinations (NF-1871,10[1]) and 'fine words of seduction and pacification' (GT-18), which have no ground. He regards natural law as a superstition (MAII,WS-9) and, like Hobbes, holds that 'there exist neither natural rights, nor natural wrongs' (MAII,WS-31). If we apply his model of interpretation, the legal recognition of the dignity of all would have the source of *ressentiment* in the weak.[158] Human dignity obtained legal status after World War II as a response to genocide and a legal safeguard against any repetition of such atrocities. From the Nietzschean perspective this may be interpreted as a necessity arising from accepting the normative equality of people in order to permit a minimum level of justice not only within countries (where equality before law has been guaranteed previously by other legal norms) but on a global scale.

2.1. Rectificatory justice

> Neither punishment nor reward is something that comes to anyone as *his due*; they are given to him for reasons of utility, without him being able to lay claim to them in justice (MAI-105, Nietzsche 2000, 81).
>
> The community is in the beginning the organization established by the weak for *balance* against threatening powers. (...) *Balance* is therefore a very important concept for the oldest theories of law and morality; balance is the basis for justice. If in more barbarous ages justice says, 'an eye for an eye, a tooth for a tooth,' it presupposes the attained balance and wants to *maintain* it by means of this recompense: so that if someone transgresses against another, the other person no longer takes revenge in a blindly embittered way. Instead, by virtue of the *jus talionis* the balance in power relations that has been disturbed *is reestablished*: for having one eye or one arm *more* than another is in such primitive conditions like having a bit more power, a heavier weight than him (MAII,WS-22, Nietzsche 2013, 164–165).
>
> Throughout most of human history, punishment has *not* been meted out *because* the miscreant was held responsible for his act, therefore it was *not* assumed that the guilty party alone should be punished: – but rather, as parents still punish their children, it was out of anger over some wrong that had been suffered, directed at the perpetrator, – but this anger was held in check and modified by the idea that every injury has its *equivalent* which can be paid in compensation, if only through the *pain* of the person who injures (GM-II-4, Nietzsche 2007a, 40).
>
> [T]he community has the same basic relationship to its members as the creditor to the debtor. You live in a community, you enjoy the benefits of a community (...), you live a sheltered, protected life in peace and trust, without any worry of suffering certain kinds of harm and hostility to which the man *outside*, the 'man without peace', is exposed (...). The lawbreaker is a debtor who not only fails to repay the benefits and advances granted to him, but also actually assaults the creditor: so, from now on, as is fair, he is not only deprived of all these valued benefits, – he is now also reminded *how important these benefits are* (GM-II-9, Nietzsche 2007a, 46–47).

---

158 From the Christian perspective, according moral dignity to all mankind does not stem from *ressentiment* but from the elevation of humanity by God; it is God who shares his power with a human being and not the other way round.

Nietzsche treats contractual relations – trade, exchange – as the original social relations and the source of law and morality; this also explains the etymology of many words used in the legal and moral language such as guilt, duties and obligations as being connected with trade (GM-II-6), an aspect I will return to in the second part of the book. Measuring and comparing is a source of valuation and norm-giving and thus of morality and law (GM-II-8). Law and morality became influenced by an idea typical of trade relations, namely that everything has its price and everything may be paid for, both right and wrong actions. In this manner, justice in rectification arose, the justice of punishment and rewards (cf. Aristotle 2000).[159] Exchange exists in every society; in practice problems arise when there is a question concerning whether the exchanged goods have the same value and how to gauge this correctly. For example, 'an eye for an eye, a tooth for a tooth' does not claim that every eye or tooth is equal but only the eyes and teeth of *the same class of people*. What was established as having 'equal value' became a rule, and when the mechanism of obeying the rules became based on this equality what today we call justice came into being, as Bergson elucidates in his thoughts on the mercantile origins of justice (Bergson 1963).

The oldest and most naïve canon of justice as retribution mentioned by Nietzsche is *ius talionis*, which stemmed from a strongly rooted idea that one can repay like with like (evil for evil, good for good). This is founded on an illusion since the suffering endured by the villain does not remove nor relieve the suffering of the victim (the idea of compensating for suffering is made on the false assumptions concerning the interchangeability of suffering and its conversion) – nor does it bring back what was lost. In his opinion, the original cause of punishment was anger: the punishment for an injury with anger was similar to how parents punish children; to justify this punishment one developed an idea of responsibility and free will. Upon these a theory was constructed whereby someone who breaks a societal norm becomes in some way indebted towards the society (they are guilty and should be punished) and this debt may be repaid through their suffering or other valuable goods, as we can read in *On the Genealogy of Morality*.

If we adopt the classical notion of justice which was formulated by the Roman jurist Ulpian: *suum cuique* – to each his own due (cf. Acquinas 1981, II–II, Question 58), the retributive theory of punishment holds that punishment as the deliberate infliction of pain upon the villain is justified as evil *deserves* to be

159 On criminal justice by Nietzsche see Balke 2005; Valverde 2005; Petersen 2008.

punished.[160] When we say that a villain deserves to be punished and the victor deserves the prize, we utilise a notion with a moral dimension – it is a certain category by which we conduct valuations (Feinberg 1970). We use the notion of *desert* in relation to acts depending on our will, as distinct from the notion of *merits* which are ascribed to people and which are independent of their will. The evolution of the legal system depended to a large extent on the fact that it came to be seen as rewarding and punishing people not because of who they were but because of *their actions*. The fundamental problem of grounding justice on moral desert is that it is particularly difficult to separate what we owe to our own effort from what we owe to our innate abilities or other arbitrary factors whose influence was tried to be limited. On the other hand, it contradicts our intuitions that the greater reward goes to a less talented person who has achieved the same result but with the expenditure of much more effort than someone who has great talent and need not work as hard.

This lack of consistency was noted by Nietzsche, who says that we should punish someone who has committed a solitary crime more severely than a recidivist since the latter has a much stronger likelihood of committing a crime than the former, and thus the recidivist must expend more effort to prevent himself from any wrongdoing. Taking into account that what we do stems from who we are and that every act has its own history in other acts, Nietzsche questions in the above fragment the assumption that we may act otherwise, proclaiming that no one deserves anything in the moral sense. In other words, no one is entitled to anything *as theirs* but just in terms of something else, for instance the benefit to the community. The theory of justified punishment and rewards based on moral desert is a fiction which overshadows the utilitarian function of reward and punishment. They are not aimed at those who are punished and rewarded but at others to act as either a deterrent or an incentive.[161]

---

160 Kant was a radical advocate of retributive justice, regarding the obligation to punish to be justified independently of whether or not there was a society, in contrast to the utilitarian justification of punishment, '[e]ven if a Civil Society resolved to dissolve itself with the consent of all its members (…) the last Murderer lying in the prison ought to be executed before the resolution was carried out. This ought to be done in order that every one may realize the desert of his deeds, and that bloodguiltiness may not remain upon the people; for otherwise they might all be regarded as participators in the murder as a public violation of Justice' (Kant 1887, 198).

161 Nietzsche also emphasises that punishment does not serve to arouse feelings of guilt but rather the opposite – it inhibits them (GM-II-14).

The utilitarian function of punishment is not its sole one; Nietzsche devotes considerable space to different interpretations of punishment understood as disposal, retribution, isolation, deterrence, elimination, education, compromise, and celebration (sacrifice), etc. (GM-II-13). The beginnings of our legal system and states, as with the beginning of everything, are soaked in blood and connected with great suffering (GM-II-3; GM-II-6). In Michel Foucault we can find a precise description of the evolution of the Western penal system, which until recently (to the French Revolution and in many respects until the 20th century) focused on public punishment (Foucault 1991). The creation of tortures such as breaking on the wheel, impalement on a spike or burning at the stake did not only lead to the infliction of pain but also, and above all, had a ceremonial character intending to shame the perpetrator and to cleanse the society of the wrong that had been done and that had affected the whole community (Foucault 1991). They were more reminiscent of a religious ritual sacrifice, as Nietzsche writes, than of a rational system of justice (GM-II-13; cf. M-9). The suffering, the ostentatious and furious dimension of the punishment had a political character – it was about confirming and renewing power; the response of the rulers to the violence of the guilty party was even greater violence and had the goal of a show of strength (in the execution of a punishment, the roles are reversed and it is the perpetrator that suffers evil).

The power to punish is nothing more than the power to control disobedience. The stronger the power becomes, the less ostentatious its displays of power become; with time, punishment as a spectacle disappears and repression becomes hidden within the shadow of justice, obscured by abstract and impersonal administrative procedures. The use of violence began to be seen as inappropriate, as we have already seen in the shame of the position of the executioner. Together with the growth in the strength of society, justice began to serve to protect the criminal from those he had harmed and their revenge. It is not only the limiting of physical punishment which shows the strength of a modern state but it is also reflected in a shift in attitude towards criminals, who begin to be seen as sick, degenerate, in need of both treatment and help rather than punishment (M-202). The gradual weakening of the system of punishment is often termed the 'civilizing of society' or humanitarianism. Nietzsche explains this in two ways. The first is that it may be a sign of the strength of a community that no longer feels threatened by the actions of individuals and thus may show them mercy (GM-II-10). It may also be a sign of the weakness of a society, where customs have begun to lapse and they no longer have the strength to discipline its members. Most frequently, however, violence on the part of the state is a sign of its weakness since rule by fear stems most often from hatred and a sense of threat, as Nietzsche writes expressing his opposition to militarism (MAII,WS-284).

The general social function of the execution of justice is the application of punishment in order to maintain order in the community. Punishments are thus not meted out because of individuals or even because of specific actions but rather for the sake of the society and for the sake of restoring the balance which has been disturbed. Nietzsche's precise observations show the universal and abstract dimension of justice, which, in contrast to revenge, focuses on the community as a whole rather than on particular interests or harm of individuals. Revenge was originally an obligation of the harmed and their family, allowing them to let off steam and gain some measure of satisfaction in the suffering of the other. In time, an endless cycle of violence, destructive for the society, is thus replaced with the idea of redress determined by the community; its goal is to end the argument and restore order. A confirmation of this can be found in Max Weber, who shows that the trial is the oldest form of legal action, based on a contract – an agreement to redress (Weber 1978). Trial proceedings usually took place in public (they were social gatherings), with the judgement given in public but the execution of the law in private; this is also where the idea of the 'pledge' comes from – someone who has been sentenced in public was detained (taken as a pledge) until what is required by the verdict was fulfilled, giving rise to the form of punishment we know today as prison (Weber 1978; Huizinga 1980; Foucault 1991). In Old German law, described by Weber, inter-familial conflict had been resolved by elders and punishment was shaped within the home (Weber 1978). Initially there was no distinction between civil and criminal proceedings; a judgement was only executed by a community when the actions had threatened the whole community, a consequence of which is the public prosecution office of today.

The actions of individuals against the norms of a community disturb its balance and are thus regarded as a threat to all (M-9).[162] The punishment of a criminal by a society is thus connected with the neutralization of an indirect harm inflicted upon the community rather than a direct harm visited upon a particular indi-

162 'The community can compel the individual to compensate another individual or the community for the immediate injury his action has brought in its train; it can also take a kind of revenge on the individual for having, as a supposed after-effect of his action, caused the clouds and storms of divine anger to have gathered over the community – but it feels the individual's guilt above all as *its own* guilt and bears the punishment as *its own* punishment – : "customs have grown lax", each wails in his soul, "if such actions as this are possible". Every individual action, every individual mode of thought arouses dread' (Nietzsche 2005a, 12).

vidual. Balance, in the context of justice, should not be confused with full equality, which Nietzsche rather equates with the end of justice; all of law and justice demands the existence of a *certain degree* of inequality, which permits development; equality would mean stagnation (GD-*Streifzuege*-48; AC-57; cf. Clark 1999).[163] A community is founded on general norms applied to the majority to guarantee their safety from the threat posed by stronger individuals – the excess power of the stronger individuals is tamed by punishment. Interpreted in the spirit of trade, a community brings all of its members benefits, stemming from cooperation and a guarantee of security – and is based on obliging its members to respect norms in order to enjoy the benefits of its existence (GM-II-3). In this respect, members of a community are its debtors and society is their creditor. An individual must thus work off his or her debt towards society and since it is a debt which cannot be paid (it accumulates over the generations) an individual is a slave to society. In this understanding, a criminal is understood as one who breaks the covenant and draws an undue advantage (he or she takes more than is promised in the contract). The task of justice is thus to take back these ill-gotten gains. It originally did this by the most radical means to exclude the villain from society (exile and shame), as the subsequent fragments describe.[164] The more contemporary approach of equalising mainly leads to depriving the person who breaks the contract of goods held valuable by the society, the most highly prized of them being freedom. As a result, the idea of imprisonment became widespread in Western societies from the end of the 18th century, despite the economic and resocialisation inefficiencies associated with this form of punishment (Foucault 1991).[165]

Nietzsche's argument of justice as the balance of entitlements and requirements may be seen to anticipate the position adopted in contemporary philosophy of law and political philosophy which rejects the notion of moral desert understood

---

163 Maudemarie Clark does not interpret Nietzsche as an opponent of democracy or political equality but rather a preacher of spiritual and personal inequality destroyed by the revolt of the people and the herd against those who are in a higher position.

164 Exile was connected with being taken beyond the protection of the law and with stigmatization, which allowed anyone to kill such a person. The reversal of this situation can be found in the story of Cain, who God punished for the killing of Abel by banishing him and marking him with a sign which forbade others to kill him (Gen 4,10–14); here it was about an internal punishment – a moral-spiritual one (guilt), and not an external-physical one (killing).

165 An additional consequence of the contemporary system of punishment is the changing social status of the punished person, who after a legally binding verdict at trial becomes a person with a criminal record, which may affect their societal relations (applying for work, performing public functions, etc.)

as a pre-institutional, independent criterion of justice prior to practice and rules (Scheffler 2008). For example, Hart bases the justification of punishment on the principle of reciprocity (Hart 2008) found in Rawls's idea of a society as a 'cooperative venture for mutual advantage' (Rawls 1999, 4). He adopts the argument, similar to Nietzsche's, that all members of a community enjoy the same benefits from the existing legal order and bear the same burdens connected with obeying those laws; breaking the rules of the 'game' means they enjoy excessive benefits which, according to the principle of *fair play*, must be taken from them. The difference between Nietzsche's position and the philosophers mentioned stems from the origins of their legal communities. For Nietzsche, this is not a result of a contract made on normative arguments but rather it stems from violence and years of different power arrangements which in time have led to a balance of power, making the contract and subsequently the laws connected to it possible. It is a temporary and changeable phenomenon and not an enduring order resting on universal justifications.

2.2. Customary law and statutory law: the role of custom and coercion

> Jurists disagree as to whether the legal code that has been most completely thought through or the legal code that is easiest to understand prevails. The first sort, whose highest model is the Roman law, appears to the lay person as incomprehensible and therefore not as an expression of his sense of justice. Popular codes of law, such as the Germanic, were crude, superstitious, illogical, in part foolish, but they did correspond to quite specific, inherited, indigenous customs and feelings. – But wherever the law is no longer a tradition, as it no longer is for us, it can function only by *command* or compulsion; none of us has a traditional feeling for the law any more, so we must therefore be content with *arbitrary laws* that are the expression of the necessity that there *must be* some law. In this case, then, whatever is the most logical is the most acceptable because it is the *most impartial*: even conceding that in every case the smallest unit of measure in the relationship between transgression and punishment is arbitrarily established (MAI-459, Nietzsche 2000, 247).

> Laws go back in the first instance to *custom*, custom to a onetime *agreement*. At some point in time, people were mutually satisfied with the effects of the agreement they had made and yet too lazy to renew it formally; so they lived on as if it were always being renewed and gradually, as forgetfulness spread its fog over the origin, they believed they had a holy, unalterable condition upon which every generation *had* to build further. Custom was now *compulsion*, even if it no longer produced the advantages for the sake of which they had originally made the agreement. – The *weak* have at all times found their firm refuge here: they tend to *eternalize* the onetime agreement, the granting of a favor (MAII,WS-39, Nietzsche 2013, 177).

Since it is crucial for the individuals of a community to obey its norms regardless of their own interests (and, indeed, often against their own interests), a community creates people who are strongly connected to its traditions and customs, which in turn become gradually replaced by an obedience to increasingly abstract laws. Nietzsche writes about the ties we have to tradition, something which he refers to as a combination of a moral sense (*Gefühl der Sittlichkeit*), and the power of custom. Obedience in terms of tradition relies on respecting customs regardless of their benefits but rather because they are required – they call for the repression of individuality (M-9). Fear of and obedience towards customs, and subsequently the law, is the fear of something higher than the individual, something greater than the personal. One may find a similar thought in Pascal when he writes that '[c]ustom is the whole of equity for the sole reason that it is accepted. That is the mystical basis of its authority', and concludes, '[i]t would therefore be a good thing if the laws and customs were obeyed because they were laws (…), we should follow only those already accepted' (Pascal 1999, 94, 24; 454, 110).

Writing about the roots of law, Nietzsche shows in the second fragment that the maintenance of traditions conserves the community and favours the weak, who thanks to custom are able to turn temporarily bestowed power into stronger laws which cement their position. It is the weakest whom Nietzsche calls 'the model of injustice', scrupulously hanging on to regulations and wanting them to be eternalised out of fear of loosing their position; they are also willing to abandon their own freedoms in favour of a strong leader in order to resolve the problem (NF-1884,31[61]). In this manner they commit themselves to abiding by laws or customs which no longer bring the benefits which they were established for (MAI-96, MAI-459, J-9).

In the first fragment, Nietzsche considers the difference between customary law, based on the strength of tradition and custom, and Roman law, which will be taken as an example of modern statutory law. He focuses on the irrational nature of customary law, using the example of Germanic law, and holds that when the strength of tradition upholding it ceases to function, it must be replaced by more rational, cold, logical, impartial and arbitrary statutory laws, the obeying of which does not require emotional involvement.[166] The power of its compulsion rests on the very fact of its establishment and the conviction of the necessity of law in

166 The distinction between rational and irrational law can be found in Max Weber: irrational law is based on emotions and habits; rational law is abstract law based on reason, logic and form (Weber 1978).

general, as we can read in the above fragment. Pascal wrote in a similar vein on the arbitrary nature of law:

> [W]e see nothing, just or unjust, which does not change in quality with a change in climate. Three degrees of latitude overthrow jurisprudence. A meridian determines the truth. (...) It is an odd kind of justice to have a river for its boundary. Truth lies on this side of the Pyrenees, terror on the other (Pascal 1999, 94, 23).

Nietzsche shows two key factors in shaping obedience to the law (including moral laws): coercion and custom. Both permit the socialisation of individuals, turning them into 'collective individuals' (MAI-99). In the eyes of Nietzsche external coercion precedes morality – first, a certain behaviour is induced in us (acting according to norms in order to avoid suffering), subsequently they become voluntary acts (customs or obligations) and, finally, when they are our habits and bring us pleasure, we begin to see them as virtues (MAI-99). Hence the conclusion that the tables of human laws are tables of their customary habits (Za-I-*Ziel*). He also claims that the original cruelty of punishment mentioned above lit the flame of human cooperative behaviour (GM-II-3).[167] The effect of discipline by cruelty is the 'embodiment' of a custom, accompanied by the development of emotions in individuals in accordance with the enduring habit (cf. Petrażycki 2002; see Sedgwick 2013). Embodied knowledge, even if it is full of errors and mistakes, represents an important stage in the human development, it is our 'second nature' (HL-3),[168] which is comprised of the drives termed good and evil (M-38). Second nature in the conception of Nietzsche is not the rational nature as proposed by McDowell in his idea of expanded naturalism (McDowell 2002). For Nietzsche, second nature is an effect of the battle between our drives and social pressure.

---

167 '"A thing must be burnt in so that it stays in the memory: only something that continues *to hurt* stays in the memory" (...). [H]ow much blood and horror lies at the basis of all "good things"!...' (Nietzsche 2007a, 38–39).

168 'For since we are the outcome of earlier generations, we are also the outcome of their aberrations, passions and errors, and indeed of their crimes; it is not possible wholly to free oneself from this chain. If we condemn these aberrations and regard ourselves as free of them, this does not alter the fact that we originate in them. The best we can do is to confront our inherited and hereditary nature with our knowledge, and through a new, stern discipline combat our inborn heritage and implant in ourselves a new habit, a new instinct, a second nature, so that our first nature withers away. It is an attempt to give oneself, as it were *a posteriori*, a past in which one would like to originate in opposition to that in which one did originate (...). [T]his first nature was once a second nature and that every victorious second nature will become a first' (Nietzsche 2007c, 76–77).

Customs which come from outside seem to be the opposite of our inner moral norms. However, the self-regulation of the autonomy of individuals – calculating, able to promise, free to command and be judge and jury over themselves – is a product of a custom which has made and formed people through the generations to make just such an individual possible. A self-governing individual is possible thanks to centuries of the shaping of individuals by customs and, at the same time, the overcoming of a 'person of custom'. The development of individuality and individual responsibility which accompanies it (FW-117) is not a source of law but the result of a great and deep transformation in the human freedom (GM-II-1), since the privilege of responsibility depends on the power to control oneself and is called conscience (GM-II-2) or the soul (GM-II-16). It is a process of 'human internalization', which means that instincts are subject to sublimation, one often directs them inwards into oneself (GM-II-16–17). *Ressentiment* is at work here, as I have discussed previously. A 'bad conscience' destroys a person and poisons our inner self; however, since the conscience is a necessary part in the shaping of an individual, with the power to control oneself (GM-II-4; GM-II-16), this in turn makes it possible to overcome the self-imposed, shameful customs which are no longer necessary for such a noble individual (cf. M-207). Nietzsche compares 'bad conscience' to a physical condition akin to pregnancy – thanks to it, people are able to give birth to themselves – which shapes their internal life (GM-II-19). The point is that at the very moment of becoming a mature, moral person, one should be able to overcome one's own conscience in order to become the true master of oneself and not become one's own victim. Even when one is unable to strip off the 'shirt of obligations' which clings to one's body, Nietzsche wants us to learn to freely 'dance in [our] chains' (JGB-226).

This process of the human internalization which Nietzsche writes about was termed by Norbert Elias the 'civilizing process' (Elias 2013), by which he understood the complete change dependent on the evolution of the behaviour and feelings of people and connected with changes of forms of human co-existence (social structures). Together with the growth of society there was an increase in and a greater diversity of human functions, as well as more interaction between them and thus a greater degree of interdependence. This led to the gradual creation and increasingly complex interweaving of human activities which in turn required greater and increasingly precise harmonization, a result of which was the transformation of the human psyche whereby thanks to external coercion a greater degree of internal coercion arose and replaced it. Individuals who became adjusted to the new societal structures by habit and behaviour most often do not sense the legal-social violence that they were subjected to and that stemmed from the existence of the law and state. The monopoly of the state on violence did not lead to the elimination of violence in the public sphere as such but rather to the creation of a newer, more subtle variant of violence hidden behind the scenes of public life (e.g. economic and verbal violence, discrimination, lack of recognition, etc.). Physical abuse of power in a well-functioning state is only potential and foreseeable (it takes place when we break the rules) and the threat of punishment is not exactly a direct motive for us not to break norms. Those who refrain from committing crimes are generally motivated by their own mental pressure or the pressure of their immediate surroundings; they are often incapable of committing crimes (especially those most serious of crimes, such as murder). The external apparatus of control corresponds to the internal apparatus of self-control and habit and also the production of fears stemming from the reconstitution of human psyche. It is all about control, calculability and predictability, thanks to which humans are not a game of fate or a game of their passions, thanks to which they and their surroundings become safer. In contrast to antiquity, which was a civilization of spectacle (GM-II-7), modernity is a civilization of surveillance, whose culmination is totalitarianism (Foucault 1991). When the all-seeing eye[169] becomes an internal one, surveillance takes on its worst form since one becomes a prisoner of one's own psyche. No one expressed this better than Franz Kafka in the form of his protagonist, Josef K., who presents himself for judgement and decides on his own punishment.[170]

Only an individual who is noble and strong enough may overcome both custom and morality which make up the 'herd instinct within the individual' (FW-116) and which utilise the 'impersonal eye' (GM-II-11). From the perspective of society, such an individual will be a criminal but not a degenerate murderer (an animal, driven by their atavistic behaviour) nor 'the pale criminal' who has sinned

169 The 'judging eye' has an interesting history as a metaphor with its source in the religion and metaphysics, which is presented by Michael Stolleis in his book *Das Auge der Gerechtigkeit;* it is described as a symbol of God, truth, omnipresence, objectivity, control, repression, protection, omniscience, and intelligence; in modern societies, the law (*Gesetz*) and state replace God in the omniscient role of the witness to actions (Stolleis 2004).

170 '"The court doesn't want anything from you. It accepts you when you come and it lets you go when you leave"' (Kafka 2014, 417). There is a similar situation in another tale of Kafka's, where the sight of the gallows in the courtyard of the prison is such a terrifying spectacle that the main character becomes convinced that it is for him and thus one night hangs himself on it (this story features in the third book of notes edited and published after the death of Kafka by Max Brod entitled *Die Acht Oktavhefte*, on the 25th of January1918).

blindly and is ashamed of one's actions but rather a *heroic type* who forges one's own fate, exerting influence on others and their era.[171] This is the person that begins where the state ends (Za-I-*Goetzen*).

3. 'The genius of justice': the self-sublimation of justice in love

> There is also, to be sure, a quite different species of genius, that of justice; (…) it wants to give everything its due, whether it be something living or dead, real or imagined – and for that purpose it must perceive things clearly; hence, it places everything in the best light and goes over it with a careful eye (MAI-636, Nietzsche 2000, 301).
> '…A wrong shared is half a right. (…)
> It is more noble to pronounce oneself wrong than to remain right, especially if one is right. Only one has to be rich enough for that.
> I do not like your cold justice; and from the eyes of your judges gazes always the executioner and his cold steel.
> Tell me, where is the justice found that is love with seeing eyes?
> Then invent me the kind of love that not only bears all punishment but also all guilt!
> Then invent me the kind of justice that pardons everyone, except the one who judges! (…)
> But how could I want to be thoroughly just! How can I give to each his own! Let this be enough for me: I give to each *my* own (Za-I-*Natter*, Nietzsche 2006a, 50–51).

As mentioned above, Nietzsche considered whether the law stems from *ressentiment* but came to the conclusion that it usually comes from a force giving or abdicating power; it is also a means to overcome and soothe the *ressentiment* of the victims (GM-II-11). Justice may, however, become exhausted when a reactive spirit (the spirit of revenge) comes to dominate the active spirit. Through the mouth of Zarathustra, Nietzsche calls this 'cold justice', stemming from *ressentiment*, in which judges are like executioners – harmful to those who are stronger than themselves yet their own iniquities are more grievous and they are often unable to commit the crimes they wished to commit, therefore they judge those who are able to do so (Za-II-*Tugendhafte*, M-412).[172] This is a phenomenon more frequently encountered on moral grounds rather than on legal, as Nietzsche often mentions, writing in *Thus Spoke Zarathustra* with irony about the 'good and the just' for whom justice is expressed in conquering and shaming others under the guise of compelling them to become more virtuous. In justice in legal terms, the

171 For Nietzsche, an example of the heroic type was Napoleon. The three types of criminals in the work of Nietzsche are distinguished by Lukas Gschwend (Gschwend 1999).
172 'And when they say: "I am just [*gerecht*]," then it sounds always like: "I am just avenged [*gerächt*]!"' (Nietzsche 2006a, 73).

active power triumphs only when it stems from force and not from a desire to compensate for weakness and when it focuses neither on the wronged nor on the wrong-doer but rather on the society and its order. Law reaches its peak when it overcomes the reactive spirit since it then enables the treatment of acts of criminal wilfulness as acts against the law and power of the community and not as personal injury of the victim (GM-II-11).

The term 'the genius of justice' used by Nietzsche in the above fragment does not relate to legal relations and it would be a grievous error to draw legal-political conclusions from it. With the help of the analogy of laws based on justice, Nietzsche expresses an *existential postulate* concerning the relation of a person to his or her being in the world, something which will be the subject of my considerations in the next part of the book. In this sense, the notion of justice appears in the context of knowledge, as I wrote in the previous chapter. Nietzsche was from a young age concerned with the possibility of justice, as we can learn from his notebooks (NF-1885,40[65]). Here he writes about giving to everything that exists its due – justice thus understood is impossible since it would require us to consider it from the perspective of infinity – and one always looks at things from one's own perspective ('from his or her own angle').

In elucidate this point, I would like to appeal to the three levels of power which Nietzsche mentions in his notebooks (NF-1887,9[145]). The first degree is 'free will', an attitude which features in the aspirations of all slaves and to which I will return. Freedom is desired when one does not have it and thus where there is no freedom, there can be no power either. The second degree present in the strongest people is the 'will to justice'; already enjoying power (*Macht*), they want even more (*Übermacht*), and, when this proves unattainable, they settle for justice as the 'balance of power' (NF-1887,10[82]). In time, justice may evolve into *fairness* whereby it becomes the maintenance of balance in relations between people which are not regulated legally (MAII,WS-32). The highest degree of the will to power is *love*, a symptom of the greatest possible power and the desire to share it with others. A discussion of what this love entails exactly will be offered in the second part of the book.

The greatest cause of disharmony in existence stemming from our own injustice is that we are entities which evaluate; perfect justice would require the overcoming of the 'judging eye' for the sake of an approach which affirms all kinds of existence (MAI-32) and which is only possible thanks to love. At this level, justice overcomes itself, becoming mercy, which is 'being beyond law' (GM-II-10) and this is the basis for the 'genius of justice'. The 'judging eye' is gradually replaced by the 'impersonal eye', which finally becomes the 'loving eye'.[173] Love becomes a gift which moves beyond justice since we give people more than is their due; love is not giving everyone what is theirs but what is our own. Hölderlin encapsulates this idea perfectly in the words: 'he whom you encounter with your love and wisdom – let him either run away or become like you! Meanness and weakness cannot survive beside you' (Hölderlin 1990, 7).

173 This idea is reminiscent of the Christian doctrine of love so criticised by Nietzsche. The dichotomy between the law (letter) and faith (spirit, love) expresses the idea of overcoming the ethics of moral commands and prohibitions (Ro 2,29; Ro 3,21; Ro 3,28–31; Ro 6,14; Ro 10,4; Col 2, 17); it is also illustrated by the Christian transformation of Judaism which does not destroy the law but rather changes it from within (Bergson 1963); in this respect, Alain Badiou contends that St Paul was more of a rival to Nietzsche than an enemy (Badiou 2003).

Part II. Nietzschean Anthropodicy

Chapter 4. Metamorphoses of the spirit: the normative character of the will to power

Ought! Do you think that anything is strong enough
to impose oughts on a passion except a stronger passion still?
George Bernard Shaw[174]

If one wishes to obtain a clearer picture of the depiction of man in the philosophy of Nietzsche, it is worth focusing on the three metamorphoses of the spirit that are to be found in *Thus Spoke Zarathustra*:

> Three metamorphoses of the spirit I name for you: how the spirit becomes a camel, and the camel a lion, and finally the lion a child. (…)
> All of these heaviest things the carrying spirit takes upon itself, like a loaded camel that hurries into the desert, thus it hurries into its desert.
> But in the loneliest desert the second metamorphosis occurs. Here the spirit becomes lion, it wants to hunt down its freedom and be master in its own desert.
> Here it seeks its last master, and wants to fight him and its last god. For victory it wants to battle the great dragon.
> Who is the great dragon whom the spirit no longer wants to call master and god? 'Thou shalt' is the name of the great dragon. But the spirit of the lion says 'I will.'
> 'Thou shalt' stands in its way, gleaming golden, a scaly animal, and upon every scale 'thou shalt!' gleams like gold.
> 'The values of millennia gleam on these scales (…).
> … 'Indeed, there shall be no more "I will!"' Thus speaks the dragon. (…)
> To create new values – not even the lion is capable of that: but to create freedom for itself for new creation – that is within the power of the lion.
> To create freedom for oneself and also a sacred No to duty: for that, my brothers, the lion is required.
> To take the right to new values – that is the most terrible taking for a carrying and reverent spirit. Indeed, it is preying, and the work of a predatory animal.
> Once it loved 'thou shalt' as its most sacred, now it must find delusion and despotism even in what is most sacred to it, in order to wrest freedom from its love by preying. The lion is required for this preying.
> But tell me, my brothers, of what is the child capable that even the lion is not? Why must the preying lion still become a child?
> The child is innocence and forgetting, a new beginning, a game, a wheel rolling out of itself, a first movement, a sacred yes-saying.

174 From *Man and Superman* by George Bernard Shaw (Shaw 2003, 59).

> Yes, for the game of creation my brothers a sacred yes-saying is required. The spirit wants *its* will, the one lost to the world now wins *its own* world (Za-I-*Verwandlungen*, Nietzsche 2006a, 16–17).

The first metamorphosis of the spirit for Nietzsche is represented by the camel, symbolising the morality of the herd which says that 'thou shalt' do something. The spirit gradually sinks under the weight of the external moral commandments placed upon it (the grammatical form of 'thou shalt' contains a reference to another's will). It is a beast of burden, unable to give thanks for what it has, unable to increase its assets but only able to waste them (SE-2). Such a spirit is characterised by obedience, helplessness and infertility. Since camel is a slave, its spirit wants to obtain freedom. The spirit thus escapes into the desert, which for Nietzsche represents the sterilization of the soul whilst at the same time heralding a metamorphosis which is clearly linked to the *Bible*.[175]

The second stage of the development of the spirit is that of a lion, symbolizing pride – but also in Nietzsche the free spirit ('God's murderer') – who says 'I will'. This stage may be identified with the liberation from the idea of God, which is an act of will rather than the intellect, as noted by de Lubac (De Lubac 1998). At this stage 'ought' is replaced by 'will', which means that one begins to decide what they will order themselves. This breaking of chains is only for 'noble' spirits and for all those who seek to break the chains and for those who are not noble this may prove both dangerous and destructive (MAII,WS-350). The metaphor of the dragon which fights the lion is one which is reminiscent of the biblical Leviathan – the sea monster which comes from Phoenician mythology and represents the power immersed in the original chaos. The greatest threat posed to the free spirit is to be found here, namely nihilism. The lion is a predator (a 'wild beast'), one who becomes a victim of its own freedom – the spirit is able to secure its freedom from the herd mentality but is unable to make its own values. As a result, the lion's fate is lawlessness and madness.

In order to avoid this fate, it is necessary to move to the third stage, in which there appears the figure of the child who says 'I am'. Despite being free of 'ought',

---

175 In the Bible, the desert was a place of metamorphosis and challenges, as symbolized by the wanderings of the Chosen People following their flight from Egyptian slavery. It also served as the place where Jesus prepared himself for the next stage of his journey; the desert fathers are the Christian monks who, from the earliest days of Christianity, looked for God through contemplation in the desert. At the same time, the desert is a place of the greatest trials and temptations which become a necessary condition of improving oneself and becoming one with God (in mysticism, the equivalent of the desert is the 'dark night' of the soul).

the lion is unable to create since its essence is negation; it must become a child, symbolizing complete innocence and affirmation, in order to be *free to create*.[176] This final stage sees the birth of a new person (the *Übermensch*) that says 'yes' to being and to eternal recurrence, putting humanity onto another track entirely.

I. The ethics of duty: 'Thou Shalt'

Let us begin with the analysis of a few citations which show the general view of Nietzsche towards moral ought:

> For there is no longer a Thou Shalt; morality, insofar as it was a Thou Shalt, has been as thoroughly destroyed by our way of viewing things as religion (MAI-34, Nietzsche 2000, 41).
> But there is no doubt that a 'thou shalt' still speaks to us too, that we too still obey a stern law set over us – and this is the last moral law which can make itself audible even to us, which even we know how to *live*, in this if in anything we too are still *men of conscience*: namely, in that we do not want to return to that which we consider outlived and decayed, to anything 'unworthy of belief', be it called God, virtue, truth, justice, charity; that we do not permit ourselves any bridges-of-lies to ancient ideals (M-*Vorrede*-4, Nietzsche 2005a, 4).
> '*Morality for morality's sake*' – an important stage in its denaturalisation: it appears as the ultimate value itself NF-1887,10[194](288), Nietzsche 2006b, 206).
> A law was therefore legally, that those to whom it was to give an undertaking to keep it. 'Contract' for the law. Initially, the various representatives of the people committed themselves introduced to the attitude of the 'Law' (NF-1887–11[377], Nietzsche 2012a, 113–114).[177]

In the fragment above from *Human, All Too Human*, Nietzsche sees ought as having been defeated; in 1884 he noted that the *moral 'ought'* is only an expression

176 As Hölderlin puts it:

> ...But our concepts are only of what has degenerated and been repaired; of childhood, of innocence we have no concept.
> When I was still a child and at peace, knowing nothing at all that is about us, was I not then more than now? (...)
> Yes, divine is the being of the child, so long as it was not dipped in the chameleon colors of men.
> The child is wholly what it is, and that is why it is so beautiful.
> The pressure of Law and Fate touches it not; only in the child is freedom (Hölderlin 1990, 4–5).

177 Reference here is made to the covenant between Yahweh and the Chosen People which made both sides contracting parties, providing Israel with its laws. These remarks were made by Nietzsche after reading the book of Julius Wellhausen on the history of Israel of 1883 (first published in 1878 as *Geschichte Israels*), (Wellhausen 2001).

of human will – something that we sought to overcome with the construction of God or conscience (NF-1884–26[347]). He believes that ascribing the creation of moral commandments to God rather than humans robbed the latter of their own creativity and was an expression of spiritual laziness which obstructed further development. Nietzsche appeals to moral voluntarism, proponents of which had been philosophers such as Thomas Hobbes or Samuel Pufendorf. Such philosophers, adopting the modern scientific outlook emphasised by Korsgaard, recognised that moral values do not exist in the world but are rather given to it; moral obligations have their source in the authority that guides them (Korsgaard 1992).[178] In contrast to the authors mentioned, stemming from his adoption of the idea that 'God is dead' in the people's hearts, Nietzsche rejects the idea of God as a moral authority. In resigning from the 'Commander' (the 'Supreme Authority') one must have the courage to free oneself from his orders (cf. Gauthier 1963), since nothing is more despotic than a dead law (M-14).

In his notes from 1887 Nietzsche points out the origins of moral law in the Old Testament tradition of the contract between God and his Chosen People (in the New Testament this contract is replaced by the love-relationship).[179] Laws were not imposed on people but people *committed themselves* to obey them and in return obtained the promise of salvation. In the context of the 'death of God', the agreement ceases to be binding since there is no authority to guarantee it. Obligations in spite of his death are a kind of paradox which is reminiscent of the tale of Kafka about the herald carrying a message from the dying emperor.[180] The herald of God, separated from God, becomes a herald of nothingness.[181]

---

178 Nietzsche also rejected the assumptions of moral realism, as discussed previously (JGB-108).

179 One may find a similar comment in Arendt, showing the strong presence of authority of obligation in both Roman law and Judaism which is founded on an alliance between man and God, where Abraham of Ur becomes the prime example of fulfilling promises (Arendt 1998). In Christianity, as Scheler writes, '[t]he old covenant between God and man, which is the root of all "legality," is replaced by the love between God and his children' (Scheler 1994, 72).

180 'The Emperor—so they say—has sent a message, directly from his death bed, to you alone, his pathetic subject, a tiny shadow which has taken refuge at the furthest distance from the imperial sun. He ordered the herald to kneel down beside his bed and whispered the message in his ear. (…) And in front of the entire crowd of those witnessing his death (…) he dispatched his herald. The messenger started off at once, a powerful, tireless man' (Kafka 2017).

181 Lucifer was just such a herald, as noted by de Rougemont (De Rougemont 1992).

Modern moral philosophy tried to overcome this paradox by appealing to the notion of morality in itself whose source is the autonomous will of the moral agent, as proposed by Kant. Nietzsche claims that the subordination of people to the ought in itself (the last moral law) is a lie since the authority of God is replaced by a weaker version – the authority of universal practical reason. Nietzsche does not ask how to justify the moral norms that remain after the old metaphysical order but rather poses the question of the *value of this morality* (JGB-186).[182] In other words, he questions the a priori notion of moral obligation, thus the Kantian question of '[w]hat ought I to do?' (Kant 2000, A 805-B833, 676) is replaced with the question, 'why ought Ought exist?'.

In his opinion, people created moral norms in order to serve them as a *bridge to ideals* (M-*Vorrede*-4). This is well illustrated by the classical scheme for moral reasoning, which is comprised of three elements, as highlighted by MacIntyre:

a) Empirical assumptions concerning the nature of man ('man-as-he-happens-to-be');
b) Normative assumptions concerning the nature of man ('man-as-he-could-be-if-he-realized-his-essential-nature');
c) Moral norms (representing the best way of moving from point a to point b; in other words, the best way to achieve certain ideals) (MacIntyre 2007, 52–53).

Modernity saw the rejection of the metaphysical ideal in which the norms were rooted whilst the norms themselves were retained (MacIntyre 2007). In MacIntyre's opinion, this was the source of the failure of the Enlightenment project since it had created an *incomplete* moral theory – it focused on what principles one should respect but was unable to justify them. In other words, the norms were bridges to nowhere.

In his notes from 1885 Nietzsche claims that the whole of German philosophy, from Leibniz through Kant, Hegel and Schopenhauer, was an expression of nostalgia for a lost world in which one might feel at home (NF-1885,41[4]). This

182 'Philosophers have all demanded (with ridiculously stubborn seriousness) something much more exalted, ambitious, and solemn as soon as they took up morality as a science: they wanted morality to be *grounded*,– and every philosopher so far has thought that he has provided a ground for morality. Morality itself, however, was thought to be "given." (…) As strange as it may sound, the problem of morality itself has been *missing* from every "science of morals" so far: there was no suspicion that anything was really a problem. Viewed properly, the "grounding of morals" (as philosophers called it, as they demanded it of themselves) was only an erudite form of good *faith* in the dominant morality, a new way of *expressing* it; as such, it was itself already situated within the terms of a certain morality. In the last analysis, it even constitutes a type of denial that these morals *can* be regarded as a problem' (Nietzsche 2002, 75–76).

nostalgia for a lost paradise is for him a manifestation of our spirituality and all of its symptoms, from antiquity and Christianity, are regarded as subtle and refined, in sharp contrast to the plebeian reality, stripped of its spirit (practical and mundane) that had overcome Northern Europe and found its father figure in Luther. This is also why he identifies German philosophy (and especially German idealism) as being a kind of counter-Reformation. The bridge to where one felt at home had been burnt (FW-124; NF-1880,8[97]; FW-137), and all that remained is a 'rainbow-bridge of concepts' (NF-1885,41[4]).[183] The rainbow is a deceptive illusion (NF-1885,40[20]).[184] Thus the 'rainbow-bridge of concepts' is for him a 'rainbow of lies' (NF-1885,40[59]), 'a bridge of words' begun between a false earth and a false heaven (Za-IV-*Schwermuth*-3).[185] For Nietzsche it is necessary to reject the outdated 'bridges of ideas' just as we reject the ladder up which we climb (SE-1), or the scaffolding that we remove once the building is finished (MAII,WS-335). In place of the 'rainbow-bridge of concepts', one is to become one's own bridge, one's own entrance and exit (SE-1; Za-I-*Vorrede*-4; GM-II-16), and it is the next step to becoming the *Übermensch* (NF-1883,10[21]; Za-I-*Vorrede*-9). One is to find the ladder of one's own knowledge and development, to use one's own expertise and experience to find one's own obligations, to look deep inside oneself to 'the dark well of [his or her] being' (MAI-292, Nietzsche 2000, 195).

1. Ought, obligation, duty

When trying to understand a certain problem we often encounter words and terms around it which contribute nothing to the meaning, and our linguistic habits are so strong that it would be easier to break a leg than to abandon the associations 'long decided' that accompany the word (M-47). Jaspers writes in a similar vein, noting that in the 'disenchanted' world:

---

183 'Man ist nirgends mehr heimisch, man verlangt zuletzt nach dem zurück, wo man irgendwie heimisch sein kann, weil man dort allein heimisch sein möchte: und das ist die griechische Welt! Aber gerade dorthin sind alle Brücken abgebrochen, — ausgenommen die *Regenbogen* der Begriffe!' (Nietzsche 1999, vol. 11, 678).

184 In the *Bible* the rainbow symbolises the covenant made by God with people (Gen 9,13).

185 As we can read in Nietzsche the following:

> Auf bunten Regenbogen,
> Zwischen falschen Himmeln
> Und falschen Erden,
> Herumschweifend, herumschwebend, –
> Nur Narr! Nur Dichter! (Nietzsche 1999, vol. 4, 372).

> Work with the old words can appear as a mere veil which hid the preparing powers of chaos from our anxious eyes. This work seemed to have no other power than that of a long continued deception (Jaspers 1955, 23).[186]

For Nietzsche, moral ought is something of an outdated term, a notion which is inextricably linked with the biblical Commandments (Mauthner 1923, entry 'Sollen'). In the original version of the Old Testament, as well as in the *Vulgate*, the German modal *du sollst* or the English *you ought to* are nowhere to be found, with the commandments expressed with different grammatical forms such as imperatives (orders), optatives (wishes) or future forms. It is only in later translations of the Bible that the notion of ought surfaces and becomes the source of the phenomenon in ethics (*Urphänomen*), a worthy counterpart to the *cogito* for post-Cartesian epistemology. Kant is to be thanked for the philosophical significance of the Ought since he put this term at the heart of his moral theory and wrote about *das Sollen* in, as Maria Ossowska notes, a remarkably pompous tone (Ossowska 2004).

Ossowska holds that obligation expressed with the aid of orders (such as 'do not kill') is different from that expressed by a norm (such as 'one ought not to kill') and not merely in the expressive sense. In her opinion, an order expresses a kind of will (it has its own defined sender and target) whilst a norm need not express a will, it is 'nobody's order' since it has ceased to be an order (Ossowska 2004). For Nietzsche, it becomes purely a kind of grammatical distinction, applied in an attempt to obscure the lack of authority behind the moral norm expressed.

It is worth adding here that whilst the Decalogue has the form of imperatives (orders and prohibitions), in Christian terms they are not just the expression of the will of God since God is equated with moral laws.[187] It is worth emphasizing that '[t]he language of the Sacred is not normative in a semantic sense, as though it was "ultimately" reducible to moral commandments with nothing more left. Nor is it normative in a psychological sense', as Kołakowski argues (Kołakowski 2001, 164). Prescriptive, factual and evaluative content, despite being discernible analytically, is regarded as a unified whole on the grounds of religion and may only be fully understood in terms of faith since '"faith" is not an act of intellectual

---

186 For Jaspers, the philosophers who rose to the challenge of modernity in the most authentic manner were Nietzsche and Kierkegaard. Cf. MacIntyre's notion of the fragmentation of contemporary moral language which he describes by means of the metaphor of the world after a catastrophe (MacIntyre 2007).

187 Thus, questions such as whether God must obey the laws which he created or whether God commands something because he is good or something is good because God commands it are meaningless (Kołakowski 2001).

assent to certain statements, but a moral commitment involving in one indivisible whole both intellectual assent and an infinite trust, immune to falsification by facts' (Kołakowski 2001, 51).[188]

Obligation is the state of being obliged to do something (Ger. *verpflichtet sein*), which contains within it a certain limit on behaviour (compulsion – a negative element) as well as a certain relation (creation – a positive element). Obligation creates a mental relation between people which imitates ties of a physical nature (cf. Brandt 1964).[189] The binding metaphor in the context of promises is related to the interests of the community. This is to be clearly seen in the etymology of the English word *obligation*, derived from the Latin verb *ligo, ligare*, meaning to tie, to join together.

In German *Verpflichtung* (commitment) and *Pflicht* (obligation) are derived from the verb *pflegen* (to care for, to look after), which is also the origin of *Rechtspflege* (understood as the administration of justice or law enforcement). The German *Pflicht* has equivalents in the English words *plight* (in the sense of being in danger but also promising and swearing to do something – 'I plight my troth', for example) and *pledge* (Huizinga 1980). The most important common element of these terms is their relational character. The relations which are created between subjects are defined in legal terms as a relationship of obligation – in Ger. *Schuldverhältnis,* and bear certain legal consequences such as claim-rights or duties. Obligations may differ depending on their source – they may be moral, legal, social or customary obligations.

Some philosophers distinguish between *obligation* and the notion of *duty*, showing how obligation stems from the relations tying the sides together which were freely made and may be rejected, e.g. dissolving a contract (Hart 1955; Brandt 1964). A duty, however, may be the expression of the will of another imposed on us or may stem from certain relationships which are ascribed to us independently of our will (such as social role or status). However, duty and obligation are far from irresistible, in contrast to the laws of nature, and rather require the cooperation of our will in *acting in accordance with them* (Railton 2003). It is often shown that to the same extent that necessity belongs to the language of logic, the language of morality depends on ought. *You ought to* is a weaker form of *you must*, even though it also contains a certain degree of predictability. The uncertainty of the future is connected to the use of the notion of 'ought'. To the same degree that

188 Cf. Heb 8,10: 'I will put my laws into their mind, and write them in their hearts'.

189 The metaphor of 'blood ties' is similar since it explains heredity in terms of physical connections.

logic is dependent upon the opposition of true and false, morality founded on ought is linked, in the opinion of Fritz Mauthner, with the juxtaposition of freedom and necessity, the field within which one struggles with norms (Mauthner 1923, entry 'Sollen'). In this respect, submitting to a moral law is different from giving in to violence or having an inclination for something (Kant 2002b). As Kant stressed, fulfilling an obligation is neither an act of necessity nor weakness but an *act of free will.*

In Kantian philosophy, '[d]uty is an authority from within', says Scheler, 'a command that comes from us and resounds in us' (Scheler 1985, 193). Yet saying 'you ought to do so-and-so' is based on a relation, it requires the one who commands and the one who follows the commands, it creates a sort of obligation. 'Every idea of duty is based on the obligation of an order', Scheler writes, 'It makes no sense to speak, as Kant does, of a duty that is floating in the air, as it were, a duty vis-à-vis no one, and which is not imposed by the order of an authority' (Scheler 1985, 211). In this understanding, the Kantian obligation floating above us may seem as absurd as Lewis Carroll's idea of the grin of a cat without a cat in *Alice in Wonderland.* Kant regards this internal duty as the price of dualism – distinguishing between the empirical and the transcendental 'I'.

2. Guilt, responsibility

The notion of obligation is connected with that of guilt and both, as Nietzsche writes, have their source in contract law and trade, as many other moral notions, which was the subject of the previous chapter (GM-II-6). In German, the words *Sollen* and *Schuld* come from the same root of 'skul' and were developed together. The words for 'excuse' and the expression of an apology in German (*Ent-schuldigung*) are derived from the term 'guilt'. In German, the word *Schuld* (*Verschuldung*) means both guilt and debt. These connections between the language of trade and morality are clearly discernible in the Bible: where redemption from slavery becomes a metaphor for salvation (the redemption of sin).[190]

Responsibility, just like obligation, is one of the sources of morality and the law, without which it would be hard to characterise one as a moral agent. The etymology of the word *responsibility* suggests that it is to be understood as the *ability to respond.* The history of the term is connected with the law and, as stressed by many scholars, it lies in the Latin word *responsium*, which was connected with

190 '[T]he very key term of Christianity – redemption – originally had a purely economic meaning – to redeem, to purchase a slave, and to set him or her free' (Sedlacek 2011, 167).

justifying one's action in court (Picht 2004; Schwartländer 2004). In Roman law, the verb *respondēre* (respond) was used by legal scholars during the Roman Republic to describe the practice of responding to legal questions (*responsa*). The Latin *respondēre* contains the verb *spondēre* or *spondee*, meaning to promise, to commit to, to make a vow. This is why the notion of responsibility may be understood on the one hand as the ability to reply to a legal question (including the ability to respond to charges in a court of law) but also as the ability to commit to something, being a subject who is able to independently shape his or her own rules and obligations (which was replaced by the concept of the legal capacity for legal action). As Friedrich von Hayek puts it:

> The assigning of responsibility is based (…) on what we believe will be the probable effects of encouraging people to behave rationally and considerately. It is a device that society has developed to cope with our inability to look into other people's minds and, without restoring to coercion, to introduce order into or lives (Von Hayek 1978, 77).

Responsibility thus comprises both a positive element connected with directing actions and guaranteeing their outcomes and a negative element of bearing the consequences of our own actions. One may say that responsibility connects the future with the past.

As Harry G. Frankfurt claims, the person 'will not be morally responsible for what he has done if he did it only because he could not have done otherwise' (Frankfurt 1969, 839). This reveals the close connection between the notion of freedom and responsibility, which Hayek regards as complementary and indivisible notions:

> Liberty not only means that the individual has both the opportunity and the burden of choice; it also means that he must bear the consequences of his action and will receive praise or blame for them (Von Hayek 1978, 71).

The freedom mentioned in this context is neither internal freedom, which Hayek terms metaphysical, nor 'the physical ability to do what I want', but rather freedom from being compelled to do something by other parties, that is the 'independence [from] the arbitrary will of another' (Von Hayek 1978, 12–16). Hayek shows that in the legal context '[o]riginally liberty signified the quality or status of the free man' (Von Hayek 1978, 428), that is someone who enjoyed the status of a member of a legal community and the legal protections that it entailed. The confirmation of this intuition may also be found in etymology since the German word *frei* (free) originally meant someone who was not defenceless or deprived of their rights; the Latin *liber* and Greek *eleutheros* 'seem to derive from words denoting membership in the tribe' (Von Hayek 1978, 428). Freedom from compulsion is understood as the ability to control our own behaviour; one may distinguish between internal and external compulsion. External compulsion may either be physical (*vis absoluta*) or moral (*vis compulsiva*). An example of the first one would be a situation when someone forces us to pull the trigger on a gun we are holding in our hands, resulting in the death of another. An example of the second may be threats (such as threatening to kill us) that are so serious that we perform the will of another. Internal compulsion depends on the lack of awareness, of consciousness. In such situations, compulsion removes any liability.

The notion of responsibility is not equated with that of guilt (Feinberg 1968). First of all, law envisages situations where the ascription of responsibility does not depend on guilt (for example, in civil law, there is the idea of strict liability which makes a person responsible for damage regardless of culpability). When a weapon kept at home goes off and kills someone, no one is guilty but the owner of the gun will be held liable for the accident on the basis of it being his property. This kind of responsibility is connected with the idea that if something goes awry and damages are incurred, a liable subject must be found in order to make redress. Other examples of responsibility separated from guilt are those of collective responsibility (a whole group being held responsible for the actions of one or more members of the group);[191] the responsibility of collective agents; and also delegated responsibility (where superiors are held responsible for the actions of their employees). The opposite may also be true, when someone is guilty of an action but due to mitigating circumstances he or she is not held responsible for the action. Moral guilt, with one exception stemming from Christian theology, is strictly individual and cannot be passed on.

'Because the law requires clear tests to decide when a person's action create an obligation or make him liable to punishment' (Von Hayek 1978, 75–76), institutions were created which ascribed responsibility, in accordance with 'Subject X takes responsibility for action y', if 1) X performed (or failed to perform) action y; 2) action y is not permitted (in cases of failure: is prescribed); 3) X acted in a free manner (cf. Hart 2008). In other words, legal responsibility is connected with the manifestation of a certain unwanted state of affairs violating legal norms as a result of the performance or non-performance of an action. A necessary conditions of legal responsibility are: the existence of a causal link between the action or omission and the undesired state of affairs; as well as the agent's freedom from compulsion.

---

191 Co-responsibility (or shared responsibility) is another matter, where two or more agents are ascribed responsibility for a given action (e.g. a crowd may be held responsible for the death of a person who was trampled upon by them and thus all are found to be co-responsible for his death).

Moral responsibility is more complicated and is based on metaphysical premises such as free will, understood as something more than just independence *from* the arbitrary will of others – it is an ability *to* direct our own fate and it constitutes agency. This is exactly the idea of responsibility which Nietzsche criticises, undermining its assumptions. Before I turn to the problem of free will, I will explain what led Nietzsche to reject also the ethics of duty, of which Kant was the most influential representative.

3. A critique of the ethics of duty

> The older morality, notably Kant's, demands from the individual those actions that one desires from all people: that was a beautiful, naive thing; as if everyone would immediately know which modes of action would benefit the whole of humanity, hence which actions would generally be desirable; it is a theory, like free trade, presupposing that a general harmony *must* result of itself according to innate laws of improvement. Perhaps a future survey of the needs of humanity will make it appear not at all desirable for all people to behave in the same way (MAI-25, Nietzsche 2000, 34–35).
>
> One more word against Kant as a *moralist*. A virtue needs to be our *own* invention, our *own* most personal need and self-defence: in any other sense, a virtue is just dangerous. Whatever is not a condition for life *harms* it: a virtue that comes exclusively from a feeling of respect for the concept of 'virtue', as Kant would have it, is harmful. (…) The most basic laws of preservation and growth require the opposite: that everyone should invent his *own* virtues, his *own* categorical imperatives. (…) Nothing ruins us more profoundly or inwardly than 'impersonal' duty, or any sacrifice in front of the Moloch of abstraction. – To think that people did not sense the *mortal danger* posed by Kant's categorical imperative!… (AC-11, Nietzsche 2005b, 9–10).

Nietzsche's opposition to the ethics of duty may be summarised under the following charges: a) the universal and abstract nature of duty; b) the formalism of duty; c) the mechanistic character of the ethics of duty; d) the negative nature of duty.

The indifference of general rules to individuals stems from the fact that Kant based his ideas on the natural and legal sciences (Simmel 2010). The whole of rationalist ethics, from Socrates to Kant, attempts to subordinate life in all of its particular, individual manifestations to general notions – norms. As Fichte noted, having in mind the general, universally binding ideal of morality, '[i]f all people could become perfect, (…) then they would all be fully the same as each other' (Fichte in Simmel 2010, 114). Nietzsche opposes this, claiming that you cannot demand the same from all people since every person, and every action, is different, finding themselves in different circumstances and situations and thus may not be subjected to the same measure and standards. What is right for one person may not be right for another for Nietzsche, and demanding a common measure for all is damaging for the most remarkable, the higher people – it thus becomes a fruit of *ressentiment* amongst average people, an issue I have already discussed (JGB-228). Even people holding the same principles are guided by them in different ways (JGB-77). Attempts to justify the existence of universal moral laws have a hidden, circular nature: we accept that the norm obliges one to do something, since it applies to all and it obliges all since it applies to one (Simmel 2010). Moral law is not then proven but rather assumed, as Nietzsche mockingly puts it (WL-I). For Nietzsche that which requires justification is of little value. Instead of justifying obligation, which is a sign of its weakness, one should begin to command oneself again since being one's own commander is the mastery of one's drives and thus a sign of strength (GD-*Sokrates*).

The ethical formalism of Kant, in which the categorical imperative is deprived of content, is a consequence of striving to implement a universal and abstract obligation. One of the fundamental charges laid against formal ethical obligation is that it does not take into account the whole life of a person, only focusing on 'what ought I to do', underestimating the much more fundamental questions of 'who am I?' and 'who must I become?'. Here arises a problem which becomes more discernible when we separate the two questions. For an obligation to become universal and general, it must transcend individuals and thus have a transcendental source, beyond individuals and things. To this end, Kant reduces the moral subject to an abstract, impersonal, rational self which directs its own will, disregarding the fact that a person is an integrated whole. As Brzozowski rightly notes, Nietzsche, in opposition to Kant, tries to formulate the content of categorical imperatives, which I will consider in the next two chapters, whose foundation is entirely personal and applies to the person as a whole (Brzozowski 2012). This is because what is personal is able to move a person deeply and to have a lasting effect upon them. In this manner he completes the ultimate internalisation of ought, which Kant began. Bergson's formulation is particularly useful in this context, namely that obligation is not only a tie to someone but above all what ties us to the world.[192] Simmel adopts a similar line, showing that obligation is 'a categorical *Ur-phenomenon*', concerned with an individual life and penetrating it completely (Simmel 2010, 102).

For Nietzsche, applying the categorical imperative of Kant to particular human actions is based on a false and harmful simplification. This is the charge of the mechanistic or atomistic attitude to morality, a consequence also of Kant's interest in the sciences. The desire to separate individual actions from the context of

192 Bergson derives the idea of obligation from human need of 'taking up its position in the part of us which is socialized' (Bergson 1963, 14).

a whole life in order to assess them independently falls into a paradox similar to that of Zeno's arrow – it results in obstructing becoming, just as the arrow paradox prevents movement. Spiritual life is a certain process, something indivisible and irreducible to particular actions or choices, it is something 'that goes on continually' (Murdoch 2014, 36).

Duty, as Scheler notes, has a negative character since if there is something that we ought to do, it means that there is something which is not as it should be; when the duty is fulfilled, it disappears (Scheler 1985). Nietzsche mockingly writes that for Kant, who was 'a fanatic of the notion of "ought"' (NF-1887,10[11]), the greatest source of pride was the replacement of happiness with the absolute obedience to duty, making an ideal out of placing the most value in that which brought the least pleasure (NF-1883,7[36]).[193] Nietzsche sees the origins of this line of thinking in communal customs, where a person who is an individualist disrespectful of tradition is regarded by the community as the least decent whilst the person who devotes the most attention to customs is regarded by the community as the most decent (J-9).

Besides, Kant's reasoning is counterintuitive because as a rule we have greater admiration for the person for whom doing good is rather effortless. Nietzsche regards effort as a charge against morality here; for him, truly good actions (in the non-moral sense) are instinctive, light, necessary and joyful (GD- *Irrthuemer*-2). Transgressions are thus not for him a cause of degeneration and decline of our instincts but rather their symptom. Nietzsche compares an evil deed to an ulcer which grows within us and is a sign of illness (Za-II-*Mitleidige*). Where life is the lowest, one will find the most laws (NF-1888–20[128]).[194] Only moral impotence and *ressentiment*, as Scheler argues, may bring about the devaluing of good inclinations in favour of sacrifice and inner struggle to conform to a moral duty (Scheler 1985). It is a mistake reducing obligation to these unusual situations in which we are reminded of abiding by an obligation despite its being painful to ourselves; it is as if the pain and effort connected with the healing of a broken leg were to be identified with the pain of walking, as Bergson notes (Bergson 1963). The drive behind obligation is thus for him power, 'the quintessence of innumerable specific habits of obedience to the countless particular requirements of social life' (Bergson 1963, 23). It also raises an important question of whether reason is

193 Kant identifies virtue with conforming to a moral duty by sacrificing one's own inclinations, 'virtue is here worth so much only because it costs so much' (Kant 2002a, 195).

194 'Where life frozen, towered to the law' (Nietzsche 2012b, 221).

indeed strong enough to persuade people, with all their conflicting impulses, to moral action. As Bergson points out:

> Our admiration for the speculative function of the mind may be great; but when philosophers maintain that it should be sufficient to silence selfishness and passion, they prove to us – and this is a matter for congratulation – that they have never heard the voice of the one or the other very loud within themselves (Bergson 1963, 87).

II. The Will: 'I will'

The notion of free will may be understood in different ways, for example as an ability to make a choice or something more – such as the ability to initiate things and events, as noticed by St Augustine and developed by Kant. In this second sense, free will becomes the power to initiate and plan the future, which Nietzsche regards as a theological invention to assign guilt to a human being – and as one of the greatest errors of humanity (GD-*Irrthuemer*-7).[195] Here I will provide a brief overview and discussion of the notion of free will so that the critique of Nietzsche is rendered more understandable.

1. Free Will

As Arendt notes, people in Ancient Greece, including philosophers, were thinking in Homeric terms, and Homer's 'circling years' provided the background against which life had appeared and stories were being told (Arendt 1981b, 17). The cyclical nature of time and life together with the Aristotelian conception of potentiality and actuality meant that the Greeks did not need the notion of free will and did not even have a word which might have expressed something which we would equate with the state of mind before an action.[196] The future was regarded as the

---

195 'People have lost sympathy for the concept of "free will": we know all too well what it is – the shadiest trick theologians have up their sleeves for making humanity "responsible" in their sense of the term, which is to say *dependent on them*... (...) Whenever a particular state of affairs is traced back to a will, an intention, or a responsible action, becoming is stripped of its innocence. The notion of will was essentially designed with punishment in mind, which is to say the desire to *assign guilt*. (...) People were considered "free" so that they could be judged and punished – so that they could be *guilty*: consequently, every act *had* to be thought of as willed, every act *had* to be seen as coming from consciousness' (Nietzsche 2005b, 181).

196 Arendt identifies a few words which are closest to our expression of free will and mainly rooted in actions: *thelein* – to be ready, to be prepared for something; *boulesthai* – regarding something as being desired; *pro-airesis* – the choice between two options or preferences dictating our choice (Arendt 1981b, 15).

logical consequence of the past since the potential transforms into the actual. It was only with the adoption of a linear conception of time under Christianity that a human being and the world obtained its beginning and its end,[197] meaning that will as an individual, autonomous mental state became a necessary attribute of a person connected with the ordering of the future.

In pre-Christian philosophy we can only find the notion of freedom which means free action, 'freedom was localized in the I-can; freedom was an objective state of the body, not a datum of consciousness or of the mind' (Arendt 1981b, 19). Christianity shifted the criterion of freedom from I-can (act) to I-will (will). Christian ethics moves beyond the Hebrew commandments by paying attention not only to actions but first and foremost to the volitional element of a person. It is not enough to do good, one must also *want* to do so as well since then people will be judged not only for their actions but also for their thoughts that accompany their actions. This focus on the internal motivations for actions (the Latin *motus* meant movement or motion) lead to the discovery and identification of the forces determining human actions. The Greeks recognised the existence of consciousness and the thought process but as the harmony of thought and action. Yet the will identified by St Paul and treated autonomously manifests the conflict in people between the forces of desire and of expressing their free will or, as the Apostle aptly put it: 'For that which I do I allow not: for what I would, that do I not; but what I hate, that do I' (Rom 7,15).[198] This conflict was regarded by St Paul as the battle of good and evil within a person and the only way in which it could be resolved – and the salvation of a human being secured – was in the grace of God (Rom 9,15). Will is free in its very nature, it has the power to dictate our behaviour, allowing us to be free from compulsion and necessity in either respecting or breaking the Law. There is a certain paradox here, however, seen in its dualistic nature, a division into will and anti-will, which represents the conflict between 'I-will' and 'I-will-not', paralysing it. Resolving this conflict, as St Paul does in the grace of God, eradicates the anti-will and prompts one towards good – which seems even more paradoxical than the conflict itself since it reveals a potential contradiction between human free will and the will of an Almighty God. St Paul was painfully aware of this problem.

---

197 All of the works of God are to be found in time, as St Augustine writes, '[t]hey have a beginning and an end in time, a rise and fall, a start and finish, beauty and the loss of it. They have in succession a morning and an evening' (Augustine 1998, 745).

198 We can find a similar inner conflict but differently understood in Ovid's *Metamorphoses*, when Madea says, 'I am dragged along by a strange force. Desire and reason are pulling in different directions. I see the right way and approve it, but follow the wrong' (Ovid 2004, 249).

St Augustine, whom Arendt calls 'the first philosopher of the will', took up the subject of human freedom opened by St Paul and tried to find a philosophical solution to it.[199] By the notion of free will he understood solely the faculty of reason, that which was responsible for willing and which in the ontological sense is an integral element of the rational nature of a human being. The internal conflict of the will in a person described by St Paul is not a conflict of two laws for St Augustine, not of the body and the soul, but rather a 'sickness of the soul' which stems from the force of habits and sin (Augustine 1998).

The conception of free will was formulated by St Augustine partially in his polemic against the Stoics and Manicheans and also in his arguments with the Pelagians. The Stoic philosopher Epictetus in his pantheistic vision of the world explained the weakness of will as determinism, the only solution which should temper the strength of the will being the acceptance of fate (*apatheia* – apathy, inaction). Thus, the main goal of the will is not the desire to obtain that which it cannot nor to oppose that which it cannot avoid. In other words, the Stoic imperative says: 'in order "to live well" it is not enough to "ask *not* that events should happen as you will"; you must "let your will be that events should happen as they do"' (Epictetus in Arendt 1981b, 123).[200]

The Manichean perspective, regarded by the Catholic Church as heresy, talks about two opposing human natures – the good and the evil, which have their roots in the dualistic vision of the world, arising from the struggle between absolute good and pure evil. One does not bear responsibility for his or her actions since a truly free will does not participate in choosing evil. St Augustine appeals to the Gospels in order to show that free will is an ontological trait of a human being which allows people to direct themselves and frees them from the determinism of the laws of nature. In his search for evil, St Augustine finds its psychological source in the human free will (Augustine 2010).

The Pelagians in turn went in a completely different direction, regarding the human free will as their sole and overriding controller, responsible for all human activity. This led to the conclusion that salvation lies solely in the hands of people, something that met with considerable opposition from the Catholic Church, which regarded the Pelagian doctrine as heresy. St Augustine distinguished between freedom as the power to act – possessed by every person – and freedom of action, which a person owed to God. Sin warped and coerced a person, meaning

199 He also devoted another text solely to this purpose, *De libero arbitrio voluntatis,* but many of the subjects may be found explained more simply in his other works such as: *On the Trinity*, *The City of God*, *Confessions.*

200 Epictetus, *Encheiridion*, 8, 459.

that even though one had the power of free will, one did not in fact have any true freedom in one's actions. Free will is not enough to secure the highest good by its efforts alone (Augustine 2010), it needs God's grace. This grace does not deprive people of their free will since God does not force us to do good. It is rather a movement towards God, a disposition to *love* which permits us to abide by 'the [true and unchangeable] rules and beacons of the virtues' (Augustine 2010, 53). It creates in us an authentic freedom, it awakens a desire for the good for which reason everyone was created; it does not destroy free will since it is only with its help that it can achieve its goal in the hearts of people.[201]

Referring to Aristotle, St Augustine regarded a human being as the highest form of being since it not only exists (a stone can exist, for example) and lives (like an animal does) but it is also conscious of this thanks to reason. A human being was made in the image and the likeness of God but, unlike God, it is an entity rooted in time, going from birth to death and, after death, to eternal life. The temporal nature of a human being means that one must be equipped with the ability to-will and not-to-will, to be directed towards the future. St Augustine distinguished three parts of the soul in his *Confessions*: memory, sight and expectation (Augustine 1998). Memory is the property of the soul which is meant to commune with the past, sight (recognising, knowing) deals with the present whilst expectation (waiting, willing, wanting) is concerned with the future. These three spheres work together and form a cohesive whole. A key role is played in this triad by the will, since it is the only active one of the three which unites them all, producing thought (*cogitatio*) (Augustine 2003). St Augustine further distinguished between different types of action, namely those which are natural (purely mechanical and ordered by the laws of nature, such as falling from some height, for which we bear no responsibility) and free (conscious actions which are characteristic of rational, sentient beings who direct their own actions). Thus, the antithesis of freedom is compulsion, whilst necessity, which is connected to the laws of nature, does not eliminate human freedom as it does not deprive one of the ability to choose. The human freedom is limited by sin and is not to be equated with autonomy since a human being is a relative being (in terms of time) and derivative one (created in the image and likeness of God).

201 In his later works, St Augustine's views on the subject of grace became more radical, with him claiming that it was arbitrarily bestowed by God, regardless of our actions and will, which became one of the causes of the debate between the Jansenists with the Jesuits regarding the question of predestination during the Reformation (see Kołakowski 1995).

St Augustine distinguished between the ontological and the ethical sense of freedom, leading to a distinction between free will, the power of humans to make choices and determine their actions, and good will, which is 'a will by which we seek to live rightly and honorably, and to attain the highest wisdom' (Augustine 2010, 21). The will is independent, it alone decides and chooses a happy life (which is directed by moral virtues and wisdom) or a shameful one (where reason is governed by our lusts and desires). Will cannot be explained in terms of causality and the question of what causes the will to want something inevitably leads to regress. Free will is good even when it leads to sin:

> [F]or just as even a wandering horse is better than a stone that does not wander off because it has no perception or movement of its own, so too a creature that sins through free will is more excellent than one that does not sin because it does not have free will (Augustine 2010, 84).

It is not absolute good in itself but rather a means to secure that good.

Kant adopted the doctrine of free will as a causative factor of action and made the concept of autonomy central to his moral philosophy. In his understanding, this notion becomes the rational ability to direct our will according to universal moral law (Kant 2002b). As mentioned above, '[a]utonomy is thus the ground of the dignity of the human and of every rational nature' (Kant 2002b, 4:436, 54).

2. Weak and strong wills

> Philosophers tend to talk about the will as if it were the most familiar thing in the world. (…) Willing strikes me as, above all, something *complicated*, something unified only in a word – and this single word contains the popular prejudice that has overruled whatever minimal precautions philosophers might take. (…) [I]n every act of willing there is, to begin with, a plurality of feelings, namely: the feeling of the state *away from which*, the feeling of the state *towards which*, and the feeling of this 'away from' and 'towards' themselves. But this is accompanied by a feeling of the muscles that comes into play through a sort of habit as soon as we 'will,' even without our putting 'arms and legs' into motion. Just as feeling – and indeed many feelings – must be recognized as ingredients of the will, thought must be as well. In every act of will there is a commandeering thought, – and we really should not believe this thought can be divorced from the 'willing,' as if some will would then be left over! Third, the will is not just a complex of feeling and thinking; rather, it is fundamentally an *affect*: and specifically the affect of the command. (…) A person who *wills* –, commands something inside himself that obeys, or that he believes to obey. (…) [T]he one who wills believes, in good faith, that willing *suffices* for action. (…) 'Freedom of the will' – that is the word for the multi-faceted state of pleasure of one who commands and, at the same time, identifies himself with the accomplished act of willing (JGB-19, Nietzsche 2002, 18–19).

> The *causa sui* is the best self-contradiction that has ever been conceived (…). The longing for 'freedom of the will' in the superlative metaphysical sense (which, unfortunately, still rules in the heads of the half-educated), the longing to bear the entire and ultimate responsibility for your actions yourself and to relieve God, world, ancestors, chance, and society of the burden – all this means nothing less than being that very *causa sui* and, (…) pulling yourself by the hair from the swamp of nothingness up into existence. Suppose someone sees through the boorish naiveté of this famous concept of 'free will' and manages to get it out of his mind; I would then ask him to carry his 'enlightenment' a step further and to rid his mind of the reversal of this misconceived concept of 'free will': I mean the 'un-free will,' which is basically an abuse of cause and effect. We should not erroneously *objectify* 'cause' and 'effect' like the natural scientists do (and whoever else thinks naturalistically these days –) in accordance with the dominant mechanistic stupidity (…). *We* are the ones who invented causation, succession, for-each-other, relativity, compulsion, numbers, law, freedom, grounds, purpose; and if we project and inscribe this symbol world onto things as an 'in-itself,' then this is the way we have always done things, namely *mythologically*. The 'un-free will' is mythology; in real life it is only a matter of *strong* and *weak* wills. (…) '[U]n-freedom of the will' is regarded as a problem by two completely opposed parties, but always in a profoundly *personal* manner. The one party would never dream of relinquishing their 'responsibility,' a belief in *themselves*, a personal right to *their own* merit (…). Those in the other party, on the contrary, do not want to be responsible for anything or to be guilty of anything; (…). When they write books these days, this latter group tends to side with the criminal; a type of socialist pity is their most attractive disguise (JGB-21, Nietzsche 2002, 21–22).

Nietzsche is opposed to the notion of free will understood as an independent power of the intellect which permits action. If we accept that neither the world nor a human being was created by anyone, we must also reject the assumption that a human being is a sovereign being possessing the metaphysical properties necessary to allow it to direct its own destiny. The assumption that a person is the author of his or her own actions is, for Nietzsche, an illusion, which he describes as acting. The feeling of power, the idea that we ourselves have caused something, leads people to the false conclusion that it was this that they wanted. For Nietzsche, one does the most wonderful things unconsciously, in an unwanted way and from the depths of one's soul (NF-1888,14[127]).[202] It is this conscious state of being the cause of evil or good that leads us to feel guilty or worthy and brings about the idea of moral responsibility for one's own actions (cf. Wojtyła

202 '[Perfect acting is] unconscious and no longer wanted, that consciousness expresses an imperfect and often pathological human condition. The personal perfection as conditioned by the will, as consciousness, reason with dialectic is a caricature, a sort of self-contradiction… The level of consciousness makes it impossible' (NF-1888,14[128], Nietzsche 2012b, 67).

2000), which Nietzsche categorically rejects, together with the whole Christian conception of free will (MAI-99). For him, the notion has so deeply penetrated the consciousness of people that it has become a permanent illusion accompanying our actions, produced by our minds and especially in situations where we feel a tension between the will to act (wanting) and reality (action). The feeling of will as the power over oneself and one's future requires something that can be overcome – it requires resistance to be detected, just as pleasure is better experienced when we know the meaning of sorrow (cf. Arendt 1981b).

The notion of the will itself is, however, remarkably important for Nietzsche, which may be discerned in the citations above. The will (wanting) is identified with the effect which is manifested in the form of *commanding* oneself and being *obedient* to those commands (NF-1884,27[19]; NF-1884,25[389]; JGB-230). The will is thus understood by Nietzsche as a kind of instinct of the mind (cf. Buczyńska-Garewicz 2010), it unifies what commands us with that which is obedient to our interests whilst giving us at the same time the illusion that we are on the side of the commander. Nietzsche believes that this illusion is wrongly associated with free will or the spirit (self, soul). He rejects the existence of free will as power, as the human command centre; it is for him only a linguistic expression of a metaphysical belief (GD-*Vernunft*-3). This is why he suggests in the above citation that the notion of free will should be replaced with the more adequate notions of *the weak and strong will*. The continual struggle between our drives and impulses becomes a dialectic of the will – between obeying and controlling, whose arena is both the human body and the universe upon which Nietzsche projects what he sees in the human form. The unique aspect of the will for Nietzsche and something of central importance for his whole philosophy is that it is strictly individual. Arendt focuses on this, claiming that 'while reason reveals what is common to all men, and desire what is common to all living organisms, only the will is entirely my own' (Arendt 2003, 114).

3. The will to power

It is no accident that the main work of Nietzsche's, intended to be the crowning achievement of his philosophy and described in his notebooks but never written, was to be entitled *The Will to Power.*[203] It is, after all, one of the key elements of his

203 In his notes and letters, Nietzsche frequently referred to this unwritten work which was to be so controversial that he feared its copies would be confiscated in Germany, as Nietzsche jokes in one of his letters (BVN-1888,1049). Nietzsche never went beyond preparing the table of contents of his planned work. A book bearing the title of *The*

philosophy;[204] it is to be found in many citations, of which two are particularly helpful to understand it:

> The river is not your danger and the end of your good and evil, you wisest ones; but this will itself, the will to power – the unexhausted begetting will of life. (...)
> How does this happen? I asked myself. What persuades the living to obey and command, and to still practice obedience while commanding? (...)
> Wherever I found the living, there I found the will to power; and even in the will of the serving I found the will to be master.
> The weaker is persuaded by its own will to serve the stronger, because it wants to be master over what is still weaker: this is the only pleasure it is incapable of renouncing. (...)
> And this secret life itself spoke to me: 'Behold,' it said, 'I am that *which must always overcome itself*' (Za-II-*Ueberwindung*, Nietzsche 2006a, 88–89).
> Will to Power psychologically (...). We are used to keep the design of an immense variety of forms compatible with an origin from the unit. That the will to power is the primitive form of affect that all other emotions are but his designs: Is that there is a significant education, instead of the individual 'happiness' each striving for the survivors to put power: 'it strives for power, for more in power' – lust is only a symptom of the feeling of power reached a differential awareness (...) desire accompanied not feel like moving... That all the driving force is the will to power, there is no physical, mental or dynamic force also... (...) [T]he change does not stop (...). The proposition (Satz) of Spinoza by the self-preservation would actually put a stop to the change: but the proposition (Satz) is false, the opposite is true. Just to all living things most clearly show that it does everything so as not to receive such, but more to be... (NF-1888,14[121], Nietzsche 2012b, 61–62).

The will to power (*Wille zur Macht)* is the will to *seek* power; when it disappears, life perishes with it. Will thus understood is not the faculty of mind but rather an ontological category which does not belong to a human being alone but rather to the whole process of the becoming of the universe. The word power (*Macht*) should not be identified with that of rule (*Herrschaft*) or violence (*Gewalt*). In opposition to them, power is a type of strength which is neither intentional nor targeted (Heidegger 1991b). The German word *Macht* comes from *mögen* (to be able), *möglich* (possible), which indicates its potential character (the Latin equivalent is *potentia*) – power means that one may do something (Arendt

---

Will to Power appeared in 1901, a year after his death, but it was a compilation of his thoughts made by his sister, Elisabeth Förster-Nietzsche and was full of distortions. It was this title that gave Nietzsche the dubious fame of being regarded as the source of many Nazi ideas, precisely as his sister, a supporter of National-Socialist ideals, wanted him to become.

204 An extensive interpretation of the will to power was conducted by Heidegger (Heidegger 1991a; Heidegger 1991b).

1998); all-mightiness means that one can do everything. Power manifests itself, for Nietzsche, throughout the universe and may be found in both the organic and inorganic world, in short, everywhere where there is life and becoming, it is becoming itself (NF-1888,16[51]). Everything strives to extend its force – which is the manifestation of the will to power (NF-1888,14[186]).

The will to power is the will to create, to transform and tame oneself (NF-1885,35[60]); it is the desire to be something more (NF-1888,14[121]), which is also associated with taking full responsibility for creating oneself.[205] The will to power has a normative character but not in the sense of the normativity of will itself but rather the normativity of power. It is to be seen in everything, even in the spiritual manifestations which the will to power rejects, such as religion, society, art, or morality (NF-1888,14[72]). When Nietzsche writes about the will to power in 'nature' or in 'the laws of nature' he usually employs quotation marks since the power which he refers to is a spiritual power rather than a physical one; it is a notion which is used to interpret the world and not to describe it. Nietzsche frequently emphasises that the will to power is his interpretation of the world (NF-1885,2[73]), an interpretation of the world of events (NF-1885,40[50]), an interpretation of all becoming (NF-1885,1[35], NF-1885,1[35]). It is meant to be a new interpretation that will help to form the foundation of a new philosophy (NF-1885,40[50]). One may say that the will to power is its own kind of way of combating the entropy of the universe (where each decay conditions the growth of the will to power) – it is not a 'law' but rather a perspective which Nietzsche regards as particularly fruitful. In his opinion, '[t]he world seen from inside (…) would be just this "will to power" and nothing else' (JGB-36, Nietzsche 2005a, 44).

The will to power is not, however, to be identified with the desire to preserve life, as has already been discussed, nor the striving for pleasure. Pleasure is neither the goal nor the driving force behind an action, it is only a symptom which accompanies commanding. Bliss is the sense of excess, a feeling of growing (NF-1886,5[63]). The will to power cannot stem from a lack of power – it is not the 'inability to power' (AC-16).[206] On the contrary, it stems from the exertion of strength, the feeling of power which desires itself and wants to increase. Its op-

205 According to Jacek Filek, 'der Wille zur Macht' should be understood as 'der Wille zur Selbstverantwortlichkeit' (Nietzsche 1999, vol. 6, 139; vol. 14, 431), Filek 2003.

206 'Ohnmacht zur Macht' (AC-16, Nietzsche 1999, vol. 6, 183). A lack of power was a source of *ressentiment* for Nietzsche (ZGM-I-7) and a symptom of Christianity (NF-1888,22[4]) and decadence (NF-1888,17[6]; NF-1888,17[1]). The will to power, as Jonathan Yovel noted, should not be regarded '*as will that wants power, but power that desires*' more power (Yovel 2005, 29).

posite is the disappearance of strength and vitality which Nietzsche describes with the term decadence (NF-1888,17[4]; NF-1888,14[72]. As Shestov shrewdly observes, the thought of Nietzsche is a traditional one, one frequently held until the advent of Christianity, which was the first in our culture to claim the opposite, 'blessed *are* the poor in spirit: for theirs is the kingdom of heaven' (Mt 5,3) and '[f]or when I am weak, then am I strong' (2 Cor 12,9) (Shestov 1969; Taubes 1993). In this respect Nietzsche regards Christianity as a plot stemming from the *ressentiment* of the weak majority against the stronger minority. He accuses it of being on the side of weakness, of opposing the timeless dialectic of power and shaping people in ways which were harmful for them. The problematic nature of these charges was discussed in the previous chapter.

Life should instead be an expression of the will to power, that is it should be strong, healthy and robust. Nietzsche understands by this life in a biological-spiritual manner and not in a purely biological or spiritual sense. Permanently afflicted by illnesses, he was fully aware of his own physical weakness which did not allow him the spiritual extravagance he desired. He was remarkably hard on himself and, despite his physical suffering, continued to constantly create, which he felt was an expression of the victory of his will to power over his powerlessness (BVN-1881,142). The will to power as a spiritual instinct need not have a manifestation in physical health but rather help to shape the whole life of a person, both in terms of combating illness and overcoming physical limitations.

4. The conception of agency and agent

In order to understand the importance of the will to power in the life of an individual, it is important to consider how Nietzsche understands the relation between willing something and acting, as well as his idea of the subject.

4.1. Will (willing) and acts of will (acting)

> Our habitual, imprecise observation takes a group of phenomena as one and calls them a fact: as it thinks, it adds an empty space in between it and another fact, it *isolates* every fact. In truth, however, all of our acting and knowing is not a consequence of facts and empty spaces in between, but rather a continual flow. Now the belief in freedom of the will is incompatible with the representation of a continuous, homogeneous, undivided, indivisible flowing: it presupposes that *every individual action is isolated and indivisible*: it is an *atomistics* in the realm of willing and knowing (MAII,WS-11, Nietzsche, 2013, 156–157).
>
> *What is willing!* – We laugh at him who steps out of his room at the moment when the sun steps out of its room, and then says: '*I will* that the sun shall rise'; and at him who cannot stop a wheel, and says: '*I will* that it shall roll'; and at him who is thrown down in

wrestling, and says: 'here I lie, but *I will* lie here!' (...) [A]re we ourselves ever acting any differently whenever we employ the expression: '*I will*'? (M-124, Nietzsche 2005a, 77).

I learned to distinguish the cause of acting from the cause of acting in a certain way, in a certain direction, with a certain goal. The first kind of cause is a quantum of dammed-up energy waiting to be used somehow, for something; the second kind, by contrast, is something quite insignificant, mostly a small accident in accordance with which this quantum 'dischargers' itself in one particular way: the match versus the powder keg. (...) The usual view is different: one is used to seeing the *driving* force precisely in the goals (purposes, professions, etc.), in keeping with a very ancient error; but it is only the *directing* force – one has mistaken the helmsman for the stream. And not even always the helmsman, the driving force... Is the 'goal', the 'purpose', not often enough a beautifying pretext, a self-deception of vanity after the fact that does not want to acknowledge that the ship is *following* the current into which it has entered accidentally? That it 'wills' to go that way *because it – must*? That it certainly has a direction but – no helmsman whatsoever? (FW-360, Nietzsche 2001, 225).

In his notes from 1887, Nietzsche writes simply that there is no such thing as free will, merely acts of will (NF-1887,11[73]). On the one hand, he distinguishes between *willing* as a mental operation in opposition to 'thou shalt' and in anticipation of 'I can' (in which 'will' is not limited by 'can', one may want a limitless amount or even have infinite desires, which means it is possible for a people to continually go beyond themselves). On the other hand, he also distinguishes *acting*, so acts of will accompanied by feelings of power (the victory of what orders us over what is subordinate in us), and which is often confused with the causative power (NF-1888,14[81]). This distinction is, however, purely theoretical since in reality, according to Nietzsche, it is impossible to separate acting from willing for they regard the same subject which is involved them. Nietzsche *equates acting with willing*, just as Wittgenstein was later to do when he said that '[t]he will is an attitude of the subject to the world. (...) The act of will is not the cause of the action but is the action itself (Wittgenstein 1998, 87). It could even be argued that for Nietzsche in the beginning there was not the word but rather the will together with action, which is primary to thinking (cf. Jn 1,1).[207]

Nietzsche undermines the traditional (mechanistic) understanding of the concept of causality in a manner akin to Hume, alleging that it is only a delusion resulting from the generalization of observation. In seeking an explanation of a particular phenomenon, one chooses a factor in an arbitrary manner, com-

207 Goethe wrote that in the beginning was the Act ('Im Anfang war die Tat', Goethe 1972, 38). Yet, Zarathustra, the teacher of the will, proclaims: '"Go ahead and do whatever you will – but first be the kind of people who *can will*!"' (Za-III-*Tugend*-3, Nietzsche 2006a, 137).

pletely out of context, and ascribes causality to it in the manner mentioned in the first citation. It is not only arbitrary and oversimplified but also nothing like an explanation, it only gives an illusion of one. For Nietzsche, this mechanistic understanding of causality is a worthless fiction since the world of entities is something apparent; what is not apparent is the process of becoming which is a sort of continuum and not a group of related facts (FW-112), as has already been discussed. Nietzsche applies the notion of will to refer both to affect and the state resulting from the battle of affects (AC-14)[208] while understanding human affective life in terms of the will to power (JGB-36). At the same time, Nietzsche rejects classical determinism, regarding the notion of the un-free will as being as senseless as that of free will if we reject the assumption that one is the causative origin of actions (JGB-21). Nietzsche compares the human will to the waves which form with every movement of the sea (FW-310; NF-1882,21[12]). The metaphor of the sea may help understand the process of becoming which encompasses the whole universe and whose swells are our desires (FW-302; NF-1880,1[70]).

Just as Nietzsche questions the notion of causality, he also undermines the idea of goal-oriented actions, as described in the above fragment. The ideas of a purpose (*Zweck*) and purposefulness (*Zweckmäsigkeit*) are only interpretations rooted in metaphysics, they beautify appearances required to understand the world and give it meaning (NF-1885,2[147]). They have a regulatory character and are purely fictional (NF-1885,35[35]); they are metaphors (MAI-38). They do not represent the driving force of our actions but are rather an addition to them. The notion of purposefulness is closely related to reasonableness (*Vernünftigkeit*), just as 'purpose' is to sense (*Sinn*), as Nietzsche highlights (NF-1873,29[31]). They serve to show that one is able to make predictions. In this respect, the purposeful actions become one of the conditions of rational behaviour which society demands of its members. If we are unable to answer the questions 'for what purpose are you doing this?' or 'why did you do that?' then we can regard our actions as irrational or caused by hidden (unconscious) reasons. Asking about the purpose of actions is as pointless as asking us why something tastes – it simply does (NF-1880,7[218]), and the pleasure which accompanies eating something does not serve any particular goal or purpose but is manifested in the course of a certain

---

208 'People were once endowed with "free will" as their dowry from a higher order of things: today we have taken even their will away, in the sense that we do not see it as a faculty any more. The old word "will" only serves to describe a result, a type of individual reaction that necessarily follows from a quantity of partly contradictory, partly harmonious stimuli: – the will does not "affect" anything, does not "move" anything anymore…' (Nietzsche 2005b, 12).

action. Talking about purposes in the case of our drives is a great fraud. Purposefulness or usefulness are only something extra (accessories) to an action and not their causes or motives (NF-1884,27[34]). A frequent error in considerations of the purposefulness of human actions is the identification of the purpose of the action with the purpose of the agent (NF-1880,10[D69]).

In the whole of human history there has never been anything like a purpose, only accidents (NF-1880,1[63]). Nietzsche calls this an error of inference since the ability to live infers purposefulness and purposefulness infers legitimacy of life (*Rechtmässigkeit*); he also claims that an assumption that what is useful is good (justified) is also false (MAI-30) – there is no logical inference here but only certain assumptions. Purposefulness and usefulness in actions are a philosophical invention thanks to which the reasons for acting began to be sought in the mind whereas their true source lies in our instincts (JGB-191). The purpose of an action is often conflated with its result, its final outcome being subsequently regarded as its original aim (NF-1880–6[254]; NF-1883,7[239]). Establishing the purpose or the meaning of an action is a simplification, we simply choose certain affections which suit our interpretation and regard them as our motives or objectives, even though this choice is arbitrary (NF-1884,25[374]). Since we are unable to understand purposeless actions, we accept that all actions in the world must also have some kind of purpose and that the universe must also be explainable in similar terms, as Nietzsche claims (NF-1880,6[250]; NF-1885,36[15]), and as I wrote in the first chapter.

Nietzsche regards the philosophical conception of acting as a consequence of will as being caused by a grammatical error, the inability to distinguish between the active and the passive (M-120).[209] As we can read in the second fragment, the expression 'I will' may only be said as a confirmation of an existing state of affairs and not prior to one which we wish to transpire as a result of our willing it to be. Nietzsche mockingly says that our willing something to occur is a superstition, not the driving force behind our actions (NF-1880,5[43]), and is no different from wanting, at sunrise, for the sun to rise. Nietzsche does not negate action but, as Williams aptly puts it, he undermines the *moral interpretation of acting* initiated by a will which might make one responsible and subject to guilt, something which I will examine in the next section (Williams 2006).

209 '"I have no idea how I am *acting*! I have no idea how I *ought to act*!" – you are right, but be sure of this: *you will be acted upon*! at every moment! Mankind has in all ages confused the active and the passive: it is their everlasting grammatical blunder' (Nietzsche 2005a, 76–77).

Since will is the internal struggle of certain aspirations in humans, the correct act is one in which the strongest instance of our will triumphs; the act which is most our own. A sea without waves is an image of victory but also of the death of the will. It is perhaps worth considering whether the strongest will could not lead to its opposition – the disappearance of will. Following this line of thought, Arendt sees in the Nietzschean conception of will a developed version of that of Epictetus, in which we should want that which happens (Arendt 1981b).

The Christian paradox of freedom described above is expressed by the formula, 'I want Your will, my Lord, to be done, not mine'. This formula shows that we may want something (such as immediate pleasure) and at the same time sincerely hope that what we want does not transpire in order to realise the will of God, who knows better than us what is good for us. It is not that we do not want to desire at all (as it is in Epictetus) but we want to not desire something which is not in accordance with the will of God. In other words, we want to do what God wants us to do. Perfect faith depends on completely entrusting ourselves to God's will, suspending our own, the best example being the figure of Abraham, who was willing to sacrifice his own son to the will of God (Gen 22,1–19).[210]

Nietzsche, in rejecting God, also rejects the idea of any kind of adjusting ourselves to any other will – he directs his thought towards powerful individuals who are their own masters. The attitude of a strong individual against the universe proclaimed by him does not entail so much the renunciation of will, but rather the affirmation of everything that fosters growth – the whole process of becoming. By saying 'be the will to power' we are saying 'let things grow' – after all, it will happen anyway. The affirmation is to show that our will is not in opposition to growth but rather fosters it, uniting the individual human will with the will to power of the universe, of which a human being is both a part and the arena. In the place of Christianity, which calls for the submission of the self to God, Nietzsche proclaims the submission to the self (the individual will to power which permeates us). What distinguishes the Nietzschean conception from the Stoic one is the assumption that the will to power is an internal desire-bliss and it has the same power for transforming a human being as metaphysical desire, elevating a human being, with the reservation that its movement is circular rather than linear (will

210 'There was one who was great by virtue of his power, and one who was great by virtue of his wisdom, and one who was great by virtue of his hope, and one who was great by virtue of his love, but Abraham was the greatest of all, great by that power whose strength is powerlessness' (Kierkegaard 1983, 16); 'If it had been otherwise with Abraham, he perhaps would have loved God but would not have had faith, for he who loves God in faith reflects upon God' (Kierkegaard 1983, 37).

increases and disappears). It is the desire to command themselves and the joy of carrying out these orders, the delight in giving into the internal struggle of drives and affections. A human being is thus in this conception, or at least may be, as much a slave to oneself as a master. Desiring oneself, one desires both one's own growth and demise.

The conception of the will to power is closely related to the conception of time as adopted by Nietzsche. In the linear, Christian conception of time, a person cannot wish to return but only to move forward – one may be the cause of things in the future and, as such, be responsible for the past. Nietzsche returns to the idea of time as a circle, widespread in antiquity and in many other cultures. He adopts a modified version of the idea, claiming that in an endless cycle of death and rebirth, the *same things* occur endlessly and thus the will to power must become an affirmation of the whole process of becoming, a point I will turn to in the final chapter.

4.2. The construction of the subject

Nietzsche's conception of willing identified with acting is connected to the conception of the subject, which I will now present.

> What separates me most deeply from the metaphysicians is: I don't concede that the 'I' is what thinks. Instead, I take the *I itself to be a construction of thinking* (…), a *regulative fiction* with the help of which a kind of constancy and thus 'knowability' is inserted into, *invented into*, a world of becoming. Up to now belief in grammar, in the linguistic subject, object, in verbs has subjugated the metaphysicians: I teach the renunciation of this belief. It is only thinking that posits the I: but up to now philosophers have believed (…) that in '*I* think' there lay something or other of unmediated certainty and that this 'I' was the given cause of thinking, in analogy with which we 'understood' all other causal relations (NF-1885,35[35], Nietzsche 2006b, 20–21).
>
> Consciousness (*Bewußtheit*) is the latest development of the organic, and hence also its most unfinished and unrobust feature. Consciousness gives rise to countless mistakes that lead an animal or human being to perish sooner than necessary (…). One thinks it constitutes the *kernel* of man, what is abiding, eternal, ultimate, most original in him! One takes consciousness to be a given determinate magnitude! (…) Sees it as 'the unity of the organism'! (…) The *task* of *assimilating knowledge* [*das Wissen sich einzuverleiben*] and making it instinctive is still quite new (FW-11, Nietzsche 2001, 37).
>
> 'Body am I and soul' – so speaks a child. And why should one not speak like children? But the awakened, the knowing one says: body am I through and through, and nothing besides; and soul is just a word for something on the body.
>
> The body is a great reason, a multiplicity with one sense, a war and a peace, one herd and one shepherd.

> Your small reason, what you call ‘spirit’ is also a tool of your body, my brother, a small work- and plaything of your great reason.
> ‘I’ you say and are proud of this word. But what is greater is that in which you do not want to believe – your body and its great reason. It does not say I, but *does* I (Za-I-*Veraechter*, Nietzsche 2006a, 22–23).
> And just as the common people separates lightning from its flash and takes the latter to be a *deed*, something performed by a subject, which is called lightning, popular morality separates strength from the manifestations of strength, as though there were an indifferent substratum behind the strong person which had the *freedom* to manifest strength or not. But there is no such substratum; there is no ‘being’ behind the deed, its effect and what becomes of it; ‘the doer’ is invented as an afterthought, – the doing is everything (GM-I-13, Nietzsche 2007a, 26).

Let me begin from the last of the cited fragments since it serves as a bridge between action and understanding the subject. The distinction between the ‘I’ who is acting and the action is for Nietzsche a superstition which has led to the myth of causality (NF-1885,1[35]). He compares it to the common understanding of thunder as somehow separated from lightning and causally prior it. As Williams accurately notes, Nietzsche identifies the fallacy of ‘counting double’, whereby the doer is separated from the act; conscious action (first-person consciousness) is something other than the consciousness that a certain state of affairs is the result of our actions (third-person consciousness) (Williams 2006). In Nietzsche’s opinion, the agent is not the cause of the action but is rather identified with the action. In the fragment above, he claims that this ‘doubled action’ – with the desire being both the cause and effect of actions – was formed to meet the needs of Christian morality, which recognised the existence of subject endowed with free will and thus could make the subject responsible and guilty for its actions. From Nietzsche’s perspective, this is a certain fiction which stems from *ressentiment*, whereby the victim cannot avenge oneself on their stronger adversary so tries to find them morally guilty of committing an evil (to be condemned) and in this sense compensate for own lack of strength and, furthermore, deprive the enemy of strength *ex post*. In other words, the abovementioned conception of responsibility is deemed by him to be exactly the opposite of what it appears to be, and is instead a construction resulting from impotence and intended to secure compensation.

It is worth mentioning here that Nietzsche, in his understanding of will and the subject, shatters the distinction between the active and passive sides of human nature, which is the crux of different philosophical traditions: the rationalistic and the naturalistic (Korsgaard 1989). Humans as rational beings can, in Kant’s view, perceive themselves from two different perspectives:

a) As objects of theoretical study (wholly determined by natural forces, the mere undergoers of their experiences);
b) As agents (free and responsible, the authors of their actions) (Korsgaard 1989, 120).

The first of these perspectives is the domain of empirical research which regards a person as a passive subject of experience whose behaviour may be studied in order to explain their motives and predict their future behaviour. This is the perspective adopted by the naturalistic approach. The second perspective, the practical one which is the traditional domain of morality, places emphasis on the active side of human nature, understanding a person as an agent – the author of his or her thoughts, the helmsman of his or her life. In this domain, the understanding of the reasons directing the actions of the agent is crucial. Both perspectives understand actions differently and the choice of one of the perspectives leads to fundamental differences in understanding morality. From the rationalist perspective, what is crucial in morality above all is what we do and why we do it; the naturalistic focuses on what happens to us (moral behaviour is a kind of experience). Nietzsche abolishes the distinction between the willing subject (expressed by 'I will') and the subject of willing (signalled by saying 'I feel like'), crucial to Christian philosophy, as well as the distinction between the agent and the subject of experience happened to a person (cf. Wojtyła 2000). By invalidating this distinction, Nietzsche subscribes neither to the active nor the passive conception but to their unification.

As the above citations show, Nietzsche rejects the conception of the metaphysical subject which he regards as the foundation of Christianity (NF-1885–40[16]). He harshly criticises Cartesian dualism, in accordance with which the existence of 'I' is the condition of thought, regarding it as a naïve faith in grammar (NF-1885–40[16]; NF-1885–40[20]; NF-1885–40[23]);claiming that the philosopher should move beyond a mere faith in grammar (JGB-34). In his opinion, it is precisely the opposite – thinking is the condition of the 'I', which is a purely mental construction. As I mentioned before, he changes the Cartesian formula of 'I think, therefore I am' (*cogito ergo sum*) into 'I live, therefore I think' (HL-10). Nietzsche finds the Cartesian line of argumentation to be a vicious circle since what begins in the *sum* (self), is initially rooted by him in the *cogito.* 'I' does not provide a beginning for things and actions nor is it a 'synthesis initiating thought' (NF-1885–40[16]); in Nietzsche's conception there is no permanent 'I' (FW-11), it is only a fiction which arose with philosophers connected to Christian morality.

As Buczyńska-Garewicz notes, rejecting the significance of the concept of essential identity, the Cartesian *ego* or the transcendental self, is not the same as a refutation of the individual identity of a person nor of a depersonalised and fragmentary 'I' (Buczyńska-Garewicz 2010). On the contrary, it is the basis for a deeper analysis and attempt to understand individuality and uniformity in human lives, in which there is no essence which may be extracted and generalised. The illusion of the 'I' may be useful from the perspective of Nietzsche when it enables an individual to focus sufficiently large amounts of the will to power to transform oneself, providing us at the same time with joy in this transformation (NF-1885,35[68]; FW-11). The factor limiting the perspective of the will to power and concentrating it in an individual is egoism (selfishness), which is for him a condition of the temporary existence of everything individual at every level of development. The highest will to power is demonstrated when one uses its will to mark its individual being in the process of becoming (NF-1887,7[54]).[211] It is the desire to feel being someone who is separate and unique, like a drop of water aware of itself and mentally discernible in an ocean.

Nietzsche emphasises the fact that the subject cannot prove itself since a certain external point of reference is required, which is absent if one is as 'fleeting and apparent as a rainbow' (NF-1885–40[20]). The 'self-reflecting soul' may only lead to false self-interpretation, which may, at the same time, be useful for us (NF-1885–40[21]). It is worth considering in this context the distinction stemming from St Augustine concerning the difference between the questions of 'Who am I?' and 'What am I?' (Augustine 1998, 411). The first question, which concerns the identity of a person, is answered by everyone based on their own lives, something that I will turn to in the following chapter. The answer to the second question, however, requires an external perspective on the person and is in St Augustine a question which is posed to God-the Creator: 'What is my nature?' (and the immediately following question of, '[w]hat then ought I to do?', Augustine 1998, 500–501). It is a teleological question, as Arendt aptly notes, a question about the purpose and the ideal of humanity – a question by which one poses an unsolvable problem for onself (Arendt 1998).[212] Together with the rejection of Christian metaphysics and the accompanying transcendental perspective afforded by God, the problem of human nature remains and reaches its apogee in modernity, as emphasised by Scheler (Scheler 1991).

The third of the above fragments shows that Nietzsche calls for attention to be directed towards the subject understood psychologically (physiologically) instead of the metaphysical subject which philosophers had concerned themselves with until this point. Inverting the tradition, Nietzsche proposes something which he

---

211 'Dem Werden den Charakter des Seins aufzuprägen — das ist der höchste Wille zur Macht' (Nietzsche 1999, vol. 12, 312).

212 '"[H]eal me" (...). In your eyes I have become a problem to myself, and that is my sickness (Augustine 1998, 532).

calls 'inverted Platonism' (NF-1870,7[156]; cf. Arendt 1961). An interesting observation of Nietzsche's is that the rejection of the Cartesian dualism of mind and body leads to the adoption of 'embodied reason' which is not to be confused with consciousness. Since consciousness is the most recent aspect of the organic world and the least developed one, the unity of the subject should not be sought in the subject's consciousness but in their body and physiology (NF-1885–40[20]), of which consciousness is but a small part. The body is a field of battle for all of our affections and the closest, and hardest, subject of our knowledge. The embodiment (*einverleiben*) of knowledge is its best use (*verleben*) and the deepest proof of our own experience (*erleben*) of knowledge, as we have seen in the previous chapters. It means making knowledge instinctive in order to remove it from the field of consciousness. The best example of this for Nietzsche is morality which he describes as 'the sickness of the chains' (MAII,WS-350). Its goal is to distinguish human beings from animals, the effect of forcing the embodiment of morality was the subsequent ennobling (spiritualization) of humanity. However, for Nietzsche this is only halfway from the animal world to human, the next step will be the noble human casting off the chains that bind them and regaining their spiritual freedom. Morality is tyranny and rape but, at the same time, it is necessary for the ennobling of the spirit, thanks to which the refined European soul would arise (JGB-188).

Animal nature is completely determined by natural factors, thanks to which we can define what a certain animal is based on their biological traits and on this basis answer the question of what that animal requires in order to have a good life of the type it leads. With people, however, it is somewhat different since, as Arendt points out, the natural conditions of our existence 'can never "explain" what we are or answer the question of who we are for the simple reason that they never condition us absolutely' (Arendt 1998, 11). What is characteristic of a human being is that one is able to distance oneself from one's own nature and thus become that which can be overcome. Every 'second nature', which was discussed in the previous chapter, was always some kind of first nature – human beings have no permanent first or second nature but are rather an arena for these changes (HL-3).

III. The total innocence of becoming: 'I am'

Liberation from imposed duties which are symbolized by the lion is not enough to restore creative power to a human being. For this, a total innocence of becoming must be restored and it is symbolised by the child. The notion of Original Sin adopted in the Judaeo-Christian worldview means that people are sinful by nature and that no one is without sin or guilt (Ps 51,7; Jn 8,7; Mk 10,18). It is an expression of human weakness, of the contingency and finite nature of life, whereby Christianity may be considered as an expression of that in human misery which it is impossible to remove by human effort alone.[213] The doctrine of Original Sin thus only has meaning in the context of salvation, which brings to a human being once again innocence lost together with paradise (Mt 18,1–5; Mk 10, 13–16; Lk 18,16–17).

The motif of guilt and indebtedness also appears in cultural contexts other than the Judaeo-Christian one. It is most frequently expressed in terms of a debt towards the world, a people, a tribe, a society which the individual must pay for with his or her life. The debt grows with subsequent generations and becomes one which is not to be repaid; a debt to our origins becomes a debt towards God (GM-II-19). The Christian solution to this problem is somewhat astonishing: the Creditor sacrifices himself for his debtors (GM-II-21).

Nietzsche rejects the ethics of guilt and redemption (NF-1883,7[7]), announcing the *innocence* of humankind and the innocence of becoming (MAI-39; MAI-107; FW-68; NF-1881,11[83], GM-II-20), a 'second innocence', the innocence of the child and the rebirth which the Gospels heralded (M-321) but which was later distorted by Christianity in his opinion. For him, the teachings of Christ should be read as *lifting the burden of guilt* (AC-33) as well as the *annihilation of law* (M-69).

The Nietzschean critique of the notion of Original Sin is rooted in the modern worldview and may be divided into three distinct arguments: the secular, the naturalistic and the individualistic one. The first maintains that since God is dead, then it is necessary to remove metaphysical guilt.[214] Following the loss of God, there is no longer any objective measure, any external perspective on our lives which may gauge the value of actions – they may not be evaluated by their consequences either, which remain to a large extent unknown since we do not know

213 This aspect was regarded by Nietzsche as particularly treacherous and thus he regarded Christianity as 'a rebellion of the withered branch against the resilient tree' (Kołakowski 2001, 188). However, awareness of the corruption of human nature has a transformative sense in Christianity – it allows for a change of heart and it is why humility is such a great Christian virtue and pride such a great sin (cf. Arendt 1998). This doctrine is a particular challenge in today's day and age, where modern humanism put human beings in the centre of everything and psychoanalysis has identified guilt and shame as a form of cultural oppression leading to an illness which should be treated (Kołakowski 2001).

214 One may not, in the opinion of Nietzsche, judge a person, neither his or her conscience nor reason may judge him or her since if they were judged by them, then the problem would arise as to who would be their judge (Shestov 1969).

them in their entirety. The value of actions may not be evaluated by the feelings which accompany them either since they are subjective (NF-1888,14[185]). As much as 'Kant had the courage to acquit man of the consequences of his deed, insisting solely on his motives' (Arendt 1998, 235), Nietzsche went even further and found people out of guilt, emphasising the complete innocence of becoming, from which all of these acts emerge. The second argument is a consequence of accepting the first: since humanity is a part of nature and nature is neither good nor evil, then human beings also may not be and thus are innocent.[215] The third argument maintains that since every human being is separate and completely unique, one may not share in the guilt of others; also, one may not inherit guilt since one is only responsible for oneself and its whole life.

It is unjustified to judge one morally not because of our limited cognitive abilities, as Simmel notes, but rather because of the structure of the subject, which does not allow particular aspects of its existence to be distinguished since '[i]t is every "part" of an individual pervaded by the life of the whole' (Simmel 2010, 128). The idea of a life described by Nietzsche is best illustrated by the Heraclitan metaphor of the flowing stream (MAII,WS-223; cf. Heraclitus L–LI in Kahn 2001). The flow of life proceeds in one direction, with every moment constantly leading to another. One is present in its entirety in all of its actions and every act is a creation of its whole life (Simmel 2010). It is thus meaningless to talk about certain behaviours as being exceptional in the life of a person – it is more important that one was able to do this than the fact that one did it, that the acts were rooted in one's life and became a manifestation of it. Ascribing to someone *the permanent ability to act* which ceases to be regarded as a point in someone's life but is rather extended throughout one's entire existence becomes a heavy load to bear. Christianity takes into account the enduring ability of a person to commit sins by adopting the doctrine of Original Sin. Nietzsche, on the other hand, based on similar assumptions, comes to opposite conclusion and opts for the complete innocence of becoming.

No one is responsible for who they are (in the sense of being guilty) and thus they are not responsible for what they do (MAI-39). He thus proposes that instead of limiting our drives, we should learn to use them to develop the human life and power (NF-1882,4[94]; Za-I-*Veraechter*). The complete innocence of humanity is a state in which one becomes the master of one's virtues and sins, when one is

215 As we can read in Schiller the following:

> Das Leben ist der Güter höchstes nicht,
> der Übel größtes aber ist die Schuld (Schiller 1879, V,9, Chor).

completely responsible for one's life and oneself (NF-1884,26[179]). Responsibility takes for Nietzsche a new meaning. Here we are faced with the 'great responsibility' for our lives which accompanies our complete innocence (NF-1884,26[47]) and which has, for Jacek Filek, an ontological-existential character (Filek 2003). It should not be regarded in terms of judgement and punishment but rather in terms of will to power.

The fundamental relation of a person to the world for Nietzsche is one of *valuation* (creation, norm-giving) and not obligation (being guilty, indebted, obedient). Valuing is a way of perceiving the world, becoming a perspective from which one can see the world. It is a natural trait of a person, almost identical with thinking, which permits us to function in the world – to order the world. Nietzsche defines a human being as a measuring being (GM-II-8), as one who weighs and measures, as one who values (MAII,WS-21). Norm-giving is thus the most important example of human valuing. In this the measure of reality – the norm – does not exist in reality (either empirically or ideally) but in a human mind (MAI-111).[216] By rejecting the division of the world into the real and the apparent ones, norm-giving ceases to be a process of re-creating (discovery) and becomes instead a creative one which is responsible for creating values (FW-335; GD-*Sokrates*). Nietzsche understands norms primarily as an expression of the will to command; if God can no longer command, then this tremendous responsibility to command falls on the shoulders of human beings themselves, one should not escape into the obedience of the herd or into the abstractions of duty in itself (JGB-199). At the same time, obligation is understood as a thought appearing where initially there are only drives and where a certain drive compels another to become a norm (NF-1880,6[123]; NF-1886,7[60]).

Nietzsche opposes rationalist moralizers in the Kantian mould, which may be detected in the words of Goethe that he borrows, "'[i]n any case, I hate everything that merely instructs me without augmenting or directly invigorating my activity'" (HL-*Vorrede,* Nietzsche 2007c, 59).[217] One must then ask the question of where in us lies the strength to revive us and overcome these contradictory impulses, to incline us to action. It seems that Nietzsche, similarly to Scheler or Bergson, shows here a certain kind of *desire*, which is for him the highest expression of the will to power: a desire of creating, giving and loving. Telling us to do something that love propels us to do is pointless and offensive to our love. Commanding our

216 'Humanity is the rule, nature *the absence of rules*' (Nietzsche 2000, 90).

217 A letter of Goethe to Schiller of December 19, 1798. 'Übrigens ist mir Alles verhasst, was mich bloss belehrt, ohne meine Thätigkeit zu vermehren, oder unmittelbar zu beleben' (Goethe in Dollinger 1948, 238).

passion or love to do something, if they are strong enough, also seems absurd from the Nietzschean perspective since passions can only be commanded by stronger passions. In the degrees of the will to power mentioned above the pinnacle is to be found in the love which enables the richest loving spirits impose power upon themselves and others (NF-1887,9[145]). Love, as he writes, gives a person the highest sense of power and shows that humans are in position to do much more than they would in the service of a duty; love has greater transformational power than any obligation (NF-1888,14[130]).

Obligation transformed into love is the most personal, it finds itself at the centre of our lives and becomes an integral part, engaging us in our entirety and not just our reason – it is only love which is able to command our drives. This is best illustrated by the example of an affirmation of life claimed by Nietzsche. When we consider why we are alive, there are a number of immediate answers. The first and the most obvious one is that something keeps us going which is akin to instinct and which we may call the most primary duty that does not require reason and is strongly rooted in our instincts (cf. Bergson 1969). The second answer that we may offer is that life is our choice – we carry on living because of the will to exist or the will to live. The position adopted by Nietzsche is different. Life is not an obligation for Nietzsche but an experience which does not require justification. He thinks that there is no such thing as a 'will to exist' (*Wille zum Dasein*), as the will manifests itself together with existence and cannot be separated from it – if we do not exist, we cannot will, and if we exist, we should not need to want to exist (Za-II-*Ueberwindung*). At the same time he questions the idea of the 'will to live' (*Wille zum Leben*), since a living person values many things more than his or her life and the will to maintain life is one of the lowest manifestations of the will to power. The affirmation of life in Nietzsche is not just the desire to live or to survive but rather a *love for the necessity of our own life*. If we love life, it is not because we have grown used to it but rather that we have grown used to loving (Za-I-*Lesen*). This specific necessity of life which I have already discussed and will continue to do so in the following chapters is close to the thought of Meister Eckhart:

> If a man asked life for a thousand years, 'Why do you live?' if it could answer it would only say, 'I live because I live.' That is because life lives from its own ground, and gushes forth from its own. Therefore it lives without Why, because it lives for itself. And so, if you were to ask a genuine man who acted from his own ground, 'Why do you act?' if he were to answer properly he would simply say, 'I act because I act.' (Eckhart 2009, Sermon 13b, 110).

Chapter 5. The creative will as an expression of the self overcoming life

We 'want to be' like this, rather than that, too much,
and the result is that we 'are' too little.
Witold Gombrowicz[218]

My soul seethes over itself and will no longer
be confined to the old circle.
Friedrich Hölderlin[219]

I. The necessity of becoming oneself

1. Willing a self

> 'You should become who you are.' (FW-270, Nietzsche 2001, 152).
> Whatever you are, serve as your own source of experience! (...) [P]ardon yourself for your own self (...). You have it in your own hands to succeed in dissolving everything you live through – the experiments, wrong turns, errors, delusions, passions, your love and your hope – into your goal without any remainder. This goal is that you yourself become a necessary chain of the rings of culture and from this necessity draw conclusions about the necessity in the course of culture in general (MAI-292, Nietzsche 2000, 194–195).
> [*W*]*ill* a self, and you *become* a self (MAII,VM-366, Nietzsche 2013, 136).
> And assuming your imperative (...) basically amounts to 'living according to life' – well how could you *not*? Why make a principle out of what you yourselves are and must be? (JGB-9, Nietzsche 2002, 10).

Rejecting idealistic and spiritualistic metaphysics, Nietzsche proposes instead a naturalistic and vitalistic one. The common-abstract obligation becomes in these terms a personal-vital obligation which leads to the becoming of self (FW-335; MAI-263; EH-*Klug*-9).[220] When we decide that we are going to live in accordance

218 From *Diary* by Witold Gombrowicz (Gombrowicz 2012, 331).
219 From *Hyperion* by Friedrich Hölderlin (Hölderlin 1990, 116).
220 The formulation of becoming of self is to be found, among others, in the subtitle of *Ecce Homo*, which reads: *How to Become What you Are.* This was inspired by the famous passage (Line 73) from the Second Pythian Victory-Ode (BVN-1882,239). Nietzsche formulated a similar recommendation not only in his works but also in letters to his friends, an indication of how important it was to him (see letters to Lou Salomé of the end of August 1882, and of November 24, 1882). Similar idea was expressed by

with our lives and become who we are, the question arises as to the purpose of this directive since we are always going to be who we are, after all. This questions only surfaces when we accept the assumption that ought implies freedom and resides in a world that is devoid of necessity. However, as I have already written, obligation for Nietzsche is not regarded as an external order but rather the result of our experience and the internal struggle between our passions; thus, it is not an opposition to necessity but rather an expression of it. The adoption of such a sense of obligation, which cannot be separated from a life, may be understood as an affirmation of life and of the will to power, that is intensifying our own spiritual vitality.

Basing on the fragments above, one may come to the conclusion that in order to accomplish the task of becoming oneself one must: 1) want to become oneself and not someone else; 2) not sense or presume who one is. The first condition assumes the complete innocence of the process of becoming with the accompanying passions, drives, illusions and errors this entails. The idealistic approach, which assumes that one constantly strives towards an unattainable ideal that will order one's life, was for Nietzsche rather a *negation of life*. Adopting a common model of life is for him an expression of the greatest injustice since it ignores the unique individual nature of human life – adjusting to an ideal resembles placing life on the bed of Procrustes, and depriving life of all that is the most valuable, all that is above average. Assuming that there exists an individual model, however, requires the adoption of an external, metaphysical instance which shapes our souls and thanks to which we can derive the necessary power to satisfy the requirements of our life. In the Judaeo-Christian tradition, it is only God, who created us, that can know us in our entirety and in this respect only he can show us the way to lead our lives and tell whether we got lost (Ps 139).[221]

Hölderlin, '[e]veryone follows his own trade (…). He must follow it with his whole soul, must not stifle every power in him (…), let him be what he is, earnestly, lovingly, then a spirit lives in all that he does' (Hölderlin 1990, 128).

221 As we read in Psalm:

> O Lord, thou hast searched me, and known me.
> Thou knowest my downsitting and mine uprising, thou understandest my thought afar off.
> Thou compassest my path and my lying down, and art acquainted *with* all my ways. (…)
> Thou hast beset me behind and before, and laid thine hand upon me. (…)
> For thou hast possessed my reins: thou hast covered me in my mother's womb. (…)
> My substance was not hid from thee, when I was made in secret, *and* curiously wrought in the lowest parts of the earth. (…)

The Christian striving for holiness does not include condemning our own nature but rather directs it towards that which is good for us. St Augustine defined the virtue making us live well as the order of love (*ordo amoris*), which became the spiritual core of a person, strictly personal and dynamic axiological structure (Augustine 2000, XV, 22; cf. Pascal 1999; Scheler 1998). It is not to be identified with the biological structure of a human being since it is rather an effect of distancing ourselves from it and consciously shaping it, the means of which is to be, above all, love. 'The heart has its reasons of which reason knows nothing', as Pascal said, and thus this love depends on stirring the soul and not teaching (Pascal 1999, 680, 158; Pascal 1999, 329, 85).[222] The axiological structure of a person may be described as our individual ethos, the values which determine our worldview and our manner of participating within it; it is 'a property which he carries with him everywhere' and a window through which he sees the world (Scheler 1998 (trans. A. Shaw), 124–125).[223] An ethos is not something which is given to us but rather *demanded*, something closely related to the idea of the self-realisation of a person, and the authenticity of being oneself. As Władysław Stróżewski notes, '[m]an-the creator is above all a creator of his own self', and his axiological structure is something which is realised throughout his whole life (Stróżewski 2013, 266).

If we accept the 'death of God' then, according to Nietzsche, we should reject the individual ethos ascribed to us together with the dualism of the 'I' which is and the 'I' which should be. Since one cannot hope for the grace of God which would allow humans to overcome the weakness of their nature, it means that this unattainable ideal becomes an indictment of human nature. Nietzsche proposes therefore that we forgive our own 'I' as it is only then that we can love ourselves. This forgiveness is connected with innocence, the recognition that all of our internal contradictions are necessary for our existence (MAI-*Vorrede*-6); this is

---

Search me, O God, and know my heart: try me, and know my thoughts:
And see if *there be any* wicked way in me, and lead me in the way everlasting.

222 In this sense one should also understand the words of Jesus who said he came to Earth to bring fire (Lk 12,49); equally important are his words to his disciples: 'Did not our heart burn within us, while he talked with us by the way, and while he opened to us the scriptures?' (Lk 24,32).

223 Cf. Simmel who writes, '[o]nce a firmly individualized life exists as an objective fact in the full sense, then its ideal Ought is there also as an objectively valid thing, in such a fashion that true and false notions about it can be formed, both by its subject and by other subjects' (Simmel 2010, 142).

to lead us to merge our highest peaks and deepest abysses (Za-III-*Wanderer*).[224] In as much as morality and customs tell people to control themselves, they are something that the suitably formed and spiritualised person will not need to heed since such a person will already know what they have the right to do – what is in their power (MAI-*Vorrede*-6).[225]

Becoming oneself requires *the will to become yourself*. Just as it is not enough to do good in order to be good because one must also will good, for Nietzsche it is not enough to live to be yourself because we must also *will* to live our life. Nietzsche proposes that we do not put up any resistance against this but rather embrace our becoming with joy and lightness since it is in this way that we are able to obtain innocence in our becoming.

The already mentioned problem of the resistance of the will, that is the lack of internal integrity in a person, may be better understood by adopting the analytical distinction between the two levels of desires, as made by Harry Frankfurt, using the example of someone who is addicted to something.[226] For Frankfurt, one is not completely autonomous when one is alienated from its desires. Autonomy depends on being able to be free to have the will one wants (Frankfurt 1971).[227]

For Nietzsche, the separation of different volitional levels is purely theoretical; one is a battlefield between different drives and one's freedom is to be expressed in the ability to affirm the strongest drives in one's soul. By freedom he understands being honest (*wahrhaftig*) to oneself and others (HL-5). Addiction is a sign of the weakness of the soul, the triumph over dependencies is a sign of strength (the will to power operating within us) – in each of these cases we should know and accept our own 'fatum'. The fundamental difference of the Christian approach is that it relies 'on saying yes to that which is valuable in us', as Stróżewski notes (Stróżewski 2013, 265), which Nietzsche replaces with saying *yes* to that which is

224 '"Only now do you go your way of greatness! Peak and abyss – they are now merged as one! (…)" From the deepest the highest must come into its height' (Nietzsche 2006a, 121–122).

225 '"You must become master of yourself and master of your own virtues as well. (…) Above all, you must see with your own eyes (…). You must" – enough, the free spirit *knows* by now which "you must" he has obeyed and also what he now *can* do, what he now for the first time – is *permitted* to do…' (Nietzsche 2000, 11–12).

226 Frankfurt uses the example of a drug addict who wants to end his addiction but cannot do it since his desire to give up drugs (a second order desire) comes into conflict with the all too strong physiological conditioning which his addiction has caused (a first order desire) (Frankfurt 1971).

227 In Christian terms, autonomy depends on the freedom to desire what God wants for us, which has already been discussed.

most ours. The inability to order our drives according to an objective scale leads to the replacement of the order of love (*ordo amoris*), with the love of fate (*amor fati*).

Nietzsche frequently mentions our 'spiritual *fatum*' – something which is inside us and which cannot be changed (JGB-231). What he has in mind here are our individual conditioning and drives which are given to us together with our existence and which form our personality and decide on our fate.[228] The only way, for Nietzsche, to regain control over our own lives depends on the complete affirmation of one's necessity. No one is the maker of their own fate but rather fate reveals who they are (cf. Arendt 1998). Here we can see the Nietzschean fascination with the heroes of Greek tragedy. As Calasso writes, a hero does not choose his actions but rather the actions precede him and 'come to meet him, like a towering wave' (Calasso 1994, 709). We cannot choose our fates but we can *will* them. Only with the full acceptance of the self can a person will to be oneself and not anyone else. Nietzsche recommends that we treat ourselves as *fatum* and not will ourselves as somebody else (EH-*Klug*-6). The paradox of wanting to be someone else was noted by Leibniz, who warned that if someone wanted to be the Emperor of China, he actually really wanted to cease to exist since the Emperor of China would exist in their stead (Williams 1973). Nietzsche teaches us therefore to love ourselves and become someone who would desire to be oneself for all eternity, which will be discussed in the next chapter.

The second condition of becoming oneself may seem surprising, as it seems impossible to become someone without knowing who we are to become. Yet 'feeling ourselves' may be limiting since it is connected with a top down assumption of what we are and what we are to become. Nietzsche neither wants us to adopt an

---

228 A beautiful and moving insight about this deep abyss in a person can be found in the *Third Elegy* by Rainer Maria Rilke:

> It was not you, alas, not his mother
> that bent the arc of his brow into such expectation.
> Not for you, girl, feeling his presence, not for you,
> did his lips curve into a more fruitful expression.
> Do you truly think that your light entrance
> rocked him so, you who wander like winds at dawn?
> You terrified his heart, that's so: but more ancient terrors
> plunged into him with the impetus of touching.
> Call him…you can't quite call him away from that dark companion.
> Of course he wants to, and does, escape: relieved, winning
> his way into your secret heart, and takes on, and begins himself.
> Did he ever begin himself, though?
> (Rilke 2017).

ideal version of ourselves nor to have a static conception of 'I' but rather to regard the self as changeable (M-326). If a person is not a finished product at any moment in their life, then that feeling which is based on the knowledge of ourselves being a closed whole, those 'present truths' (FW-307), may limit us since they refer to a fossilized form of our existence.[229]

Nietzsche understands life in a dynamic way and this is why he talks about 'becoming' and not 'being'. The essence of life escapes us when we try to capture it, when we try to make it tangible; we experience a paradox in which 'it is as if the "I" were always chasing itself, without ever being able to overtake itself' (Simmel 2010, 10). The maxim 'know thyself', carved on the Temple of Apollo in Delphi, expressed a difficult task (Plato 2002, 343b, 36). Nietzsche finds this maxim as maliciousness of gods (FW-335; cf. Heraclitus XXVIII–XXIX in Kahn 2001), since it meant that human beings ceased to be concerned with themselves because that which became explained ceased to concern us (JGB-80). For him it is more important to experience ourselves (a similar idea can be found in the works of St Paul).[230] In the same manner that studying the self in Christianity is to lead to discovering one's call, analysing the self in Nietzsche is intended to lead to the will to power. Knowledge thus has a normative and assumptionless character – its goal is thus to create the self and to achieve this objective it is necessary to eliminate all of the usual habits about thinking of the self. The overcoming of prejudices concerning ourselves is presented in *Ecce Homo* in the form of a genealogical analysis of Nietzsche's own personality and things which had shaped it (emphasising the role of diet, surroundings, climate, reading).

2. Creating the self and our laws

> 'Be your self! All you are now doing, thinking, desiring, is not you yourself.' (…) [T]he fact of our existing at all in this here-and-now must be the strongest incentive to us to live according to our own laws and standards (…). [W]e possess only a shortlived today in which to demonstrate why and to what end we came into existence now and at no other time. We are responsible to ourselves for our own existence (…). No one can construct for you the bridge upon which precisely you must cross the stream of life, no one but you yourself alone. There are, to be sure, countless paths and bridges and demi-gods

229 A similar thought was accurately expressed by Gombrowicz in his *Diary*: 'I am. I am too much. And even though I could still do something unpredictable for myself, I no longer want to. I can't want because I am too much. Amid this in delineation, changeability, fluidity, under the ungraspable sky I am made, finished, delineated… I am and I am so much that this casts me beyond the limits of nature' (Gombrowicz 2012, 211).

230 'Examine yourselves (…); prove your own selves' (2 Cor 13,5).

> which would bear you through this stream; but only at the cost of yourself (…). There exists in the world a single path along which no one can go except you: whither does it lead? Do not ask, go along it. (…) But how can we find ourselves again? How can man know himself? (…) Let the youthful soul look back on life with the question: what have you truly loved up to now, what has drawn your soul aloft, what has mastered it and at the same time blessed it? Set up these revered objects before you and perhaps their nature and their sequence will give you a law, the fundamental law of your own true self. Compare these objects one with another, see how (…) they constitute a stepladder upon which you have clambered up to yourself as you are now; for your true nature lies, not concealed deep within you, but immeasurably high above you, or at least above that which you usually take yourself to be (SE-1, Nietzsche 2007c, 127–129).
>
> …Do you want to seek the way to yourself? (…)
>
> …Then show me your right and your strength to it!
>
> Are you a new strength and a new right? A first movement? A wheel rolling out of itself? Can you compel even the stars to revolve around you? (…)
>
> You call yourself free? Your dominating thought [*herrschenden Gedanken*] I want to hear, and not that you escaped from a yoke.
>
> Are you the kind of person who had the *right* to escape from a yoke? There are some who threw away their last value when they threw away their servitude.
>
> Free from what [*Frei wovon*]? What does Zarathustra care! But brightly your eyes should signal to me: free *for what [frei wozu]*?
>
> Can you give yourself your own evil and good and hang your will above yourself like a law? Can you be your own judge and the avenger of your law? (…)
>
> But the worst enemy whom you can encounter will always be yourself; you ambush yourself in caves and woods. (…)
>
> You must want to burn yourself up in your own flame: how could you become new if you did not first become ashes!
>
> Lonely one, you go the way of the creator [*Weg den Schaffenden*]: you will create yourself a god out of your seven devils!
>
> Lonely one, you go the way of the lover [*Liebenden*]: you love yourself and that is why you despise yourself as only lovers despise.
>
> The lover wants to create because he despises! What does he know of love who did not have to despise precisely what he loved! (…)
>
> …I love him who wants to create over and beyond himself and thus perishes. – (Za-I-*Schaffender,* Nietzsche 2006a, 46–48).

Since antiquity, the way has symbolised spiritual activity, on the one hand, in the moral sphere and, on the other, in terms of the knowledge of truth, with both spheres closely related to each other. The metaphor also plays a key role in the Gospel where Jesus says 'I am the way, the truth and the life' – the only way to salvation (Jn 14,6). Nietzsche mentions in his works *the way of the creator*. The creator is also described with the term 'the higher man' (Za-IV-*Menschen*). 'Higher men' are heralds for the *Übermensch*; a synthesis of the creative material with the creator, the non-human with the *Übermensch* (GM-I-16; NF-1887,9[154]; NF-1883,10[25]). They are great in both what is beautiful and what is terrifying, they grow upwards as well as inwards (Za-III-*Wanderer*; Za-III-*Boese*-2; Za-I-*Baum*[231]).

Nietzsche developed his mystical notions of the will to power and *Übermensch*, as Voegelin notes, as a counterweight to the bereft soul of the post-Enlightenment bourgeois culture which he despised (Voegelin 1975). The opposition to the 'higher men' are the 'last men', for whom culture is but a decoration obscuring a hollow shell which shatters at the slightest contact. The 'last men' only pursue happiness and pleasure, they use desensitizing means (which include consumption, entertainment as well as social institutions), thanks to which they can experience life as painless but which in turn makes them incapable of experiencing anything great (neither positive nor negative). They regard this state as their highest achievement arguing that they have invented happiness which, as already mentioned, they identify with their own indolence and comfort. Their spiritual strengths are so insignificant that they no longer even know what is love, creativity and yearning (three key notions for the idea of overcoming the human).[232]

The creator's way is one towards oneself and beyond oneself, on this way one cannot follow in anybody's steps – in scaling our heights we must use our own legs and to reach our own heavens we must use our own wings, as Nietzsche repeats (Za-IV-*Menschen*-10; Za-III-*Siegel*-7; Za-II-*Stunde*; Za-III-*Wanderer*). One must cast away the ladder which rungs we have used and lose our teachers and masters in order to have the power to continue independently down our way (Za-I-*Tugend*-3).[233] To paraphrase the famous aphorism attributed to Kafka, the paths of our life are made by walking (*Wege entstehen dadruch, dass man sie geht*).

---

231 '...But it is with human beings as it is with this tree.
The more they aspire to the heights and the light, the more strongly their roots strive earthward, downward, into darkness, depths – into evil!' (Nietzsche 2006a, 29).

232 They confuse love with desire or need which comes from the lack of something. 'You call hunger love' as Hölderlin writes (Hölderlin1990, 36).

233 'You had not yet sought yourselves, then you found me. All believers do this; that's why all faith amounts to so little.
Now I bid you lose me and find yourselves; and only when you have all denied me will I return to you' (Nietzsche 2006a, 59). It is another evident attack on the Gospel, echoing and distorting the teaching of Jesus concerning the fact that one can only find oneself through God (Mt 10,39; Lk 9,59; Mk 10,52; Jn 10, 1–18; Jn 14,1–14;Jn 21,19).

Nietzsche compares the human life to a work of art (cf. Buczyńska-Garewicz 2010; Buczyńska-Garewicz 2003).[234] The highest power manifests itself through giving form to human life – this was the role of myths and religions. In his first works, Nietzsche wrote about the Dionysian mysteries in which one sees oneself as a work of art created by 'artistic forces of nature' (GT-1; DW-2). Experiencing the creative forces of nature and the joy of existence which allowed us to unite with the entire creation (the experience of fusion with the species world – *zoé*) brought about the madness. For Nietzsche, 'taking possession of himself' is only possible for man when he reminds himself of his self, when he allows his apparent needs to vanquish and when he is honest with himself (HL-10).

It is here that we can see the most important concept in the way of the creator – it may be a way *to freedom*. In Ancient Greece, people who were completely independent of life's necessities and were free to involve themselves in things which were neither necessary nor useful (such as philosophising or contemplating beauty) were considered to be free (Arendt 1998). Freedom meant the ability to detach oneself from the purely biological existence in which the entire energy is usually spent to maintain the life of an individual (through working, the effects of which we strive to consume as fast as we create them) and the species (through procreation) (NF-1870,7[16]).[235] Christianity, with its introduction of the distinction between the *sacrum* and *profanum*, brings freedom to the human heart, freeing people from the circumstances of the external world which is temporal and transient, as I have already discussed. Nietzsche rejects the Christian approach, regarding it as an escape to an imaginary, transcendental world. At the same time, he decides to heroically challenge the necessity of passing, approaching the problem of freedom differently from Ancient Greeks. Instead of starting

234 The idea had been present since antiquity and acquired a particularly strong character during the Romantic period. The prime example is Goethe who expressed this thought in his famous autobiography entitled *Aus meinem Leben. Dichtung und Wahrheit* (*From my Life: Poetry and Truth*).

235 Contemporary enthusiasm towards sexual freedom in antiquity lies in a complete misunderstanding of the Ancient consciousness, as Kyle Harper emphasises. The sexuality of the period needs to be understood in a certain cultural context, which first and foremost had a close relationship with slavery (slaves were the main source of physical pleasures whilst the family served for procreation) and, secondly, in its own understanding and rooting of a human being in nature. Ancient sexuality was not, therefore, an area of freedom. Christianity did not bring sexual slavery or repression, as it is frequently assumed, but rather *liberation* – it made one free and responsible, separate from nature and the master of themselves and their bodies which can never be treated as mere objects (Harper 2013).

from *freedom from necessity* as the condition of freedom, Nietzsche sees *freedom to create* that which is not necessary as the condition of overcoming necessity. Just like the Greeks, he recognises that the majority of things that people pursue and which surround them in their lives (procreation, work, life goals) have nothing in common with freedom, freedom is to be found in creation (NF-1883,12[19]).

Nietzsche distinguishes between negative freedom (to be free *from* something) and positive freedom (to be free *to/for* something).[236] The first is a poor substitute of freedom. It is not enough to cast off one's chains to be free but one must have the power to enjoy that freedom, which is something that only the strong enjoy. True freedom is individual, creative, it is the freedom to order oneself and may be the pre-condition of liberation (Za-II-*Inseln*), and not the opposite. Nietzsche compares it to health (NF-1876,16[43]). Ordering oneself is seen as a sign of affirmation; who someone is and who they will become may be seen by the laws they enforce upon themselves (see Buczyńska-Garewicz 2010). As it was discussed, law for Nietzsche is a sign of power – only one who has the power to create one's own laws and be responsible for it is truly free.

It may seem that we can find here a similarity to the idea of autonomy mentioned in the previous chapter and which in the Middle Ages, long before Kant, was expressed by the maxim *persona est sui iuris* ('a person is something in his own right' – i.e. is a being which is able to ascribe laws to itself, it has the ability of self-possession and self-control and the creativity of a person is identified with his agency, Wojtyła 2000 (trans. A. Shaw), 152).[237] The fundamental difference

236 The distinction between negative and positive freedom was diffused in modern philosophy with the help of Isaiah Berlin (it had also been present in Protestant theology and in *The Fear of Freedom* of Erich Fromm). Berlin writes that positive freedom means 'being one's own master' – that our decisions and our lives depend entirely upon ourselves (Berlin 1969, 131). In turn Fromm believes that positive freedom is best explained in relation to the doctrine of Original Sin and the myth of heaven, which serves to alienate one from nature and to lose their animal innocence in the process. Opposing God's commandments is the first step to freedom which will bring humanity to the highest level of existence, '[h]e is alone and free, yet powerless and afraid. The newly won freedom appears as a curse; he is free from the sweet bondage of paradise, but he is not free to govern himself, to realize his individuality' (Fromm 2001, 28). The interpretation of Original Sin as a human 'awakening to freedom' and an escape from nature comes from Jean Jacques Rousseau and is not in accordance with the teachings of the Church.

237 As Wojtyła writes, 'human ability is an expression of creativity. It is that creativity whose first creation is man himself. Man, through his actions, primarily shapes himself' (Wojtyła 2000 (trans. A. Shaw), 120).

between Christian thought and that of Nietzsche is that in the first case one has the task of finding one's own obligations, of striving to live up to one's own axiological structure which has been given by God. Our actions only flow from our hearts when they are strongly rooted in it, when we are able to remain ourselves, as Roman Ingarden notes:

> There are my free and responsible deeds which I perform in life's difficult moments – sometimes in the face of death – and which spring forth from the deepest interior of the ego, as it has become in the past and sustains itself to this day, to the moment of the deed. These deeds can be accomplished only insofar as I, who have previously become as I am, remain such to this day. From this strength engendered in the past, and accumulated from the beliefs which I fostered, from the attachments with which I lived and from the desires which I tried to realize, is born the power which must be *alive* in me if I am to succeed in accomplishing the deed. In my innermost essence, which at any rate is not ordinarily manifest to me and which finds its outlet in this deed, I must *remain* such as I have become in the past (Ingarden 1983, 48).

In the case of Nietzsche, living 'according to our own laws and standards' depends on living in accordance with our immoral axiological framework – with our valuations which result from our lives, experiences and habits, and have a vital character (spiritual-physical). It is an individual structure of the will to power. One should measure the world according to their own perceptual abilities and their own power to act (HL-9). 'The right to its proper identity' may be discovered by gazing into 'the dark well of your being' (MAI-292), looking into our highest and strongest desires in life, their essence and hierarchy which is an expression of our law, as can be seen in the above fragment. The meaning of life (the law hanging over our life) is the interpretation which strong people give to their own internal power structure and meet its terms. In this manner, Nietzsche proposes a radical shift from the common-rational morality to vital-individual obligation. Everyone must become oneself and their individual obligation is not a signpost given in life but *is their life*.[238]

---

238 Nietzche's thought is aptly illustrated in Kafka's parable of a man standing before the gate of the law (Kafka 2014, 402–414). Even though the gate is open, the guard refuses to let him in and he does not enter. When after years of waiting in front of the gate the man is about to die the guard reveals that he could have entered if he really wanted; no one else but the man could enter through this gate, because it was meant only *for him*. Interpreting this parable in the spirit of Nietzsche's philosophy, we can say that the basic problem of man in relation to the law is that the man forgets that he is the lawmaker, making himself subject to law and treating law as something desired, unattainable, and, ultimately, unattained.

The freedom to create our own laws should be distinguished from the permissive freedom which is characteristic of the 'last men' and nihilists, and which is passive, typified by its accidental and necessary nature. Freedom in the Nietzschean sense is expressed by its active nature, it is something which one always seeks to attain (ZB-*Streifzuege*-38), expressing it with love. We cannot choose ourselves or to cease to be who we are but we have the potential for the affirmation and negation of the self in which precisely manifests our freedom.[239] It is done through a constant analysis of our inclinations and conditions as well as a consideration of our actions which do not have a fixed measure (FW-355). Individual obligation brings 'no easing of the moral claim, but on the contrary tends to narrow the domain of "mitigating circumstances"', since even that which we regard as remarkable about our behaviour is a confirmation of who we are and who we are becoming (Simmel 2010, 151). As Simmel writes, 'a whole life answers to a single action and a single action for a whole life' and thus prior to every tiny action one should ask themselves the question, '[c]an you desire that this action of yours should define your entire life?' (Simmel 2010, 151). Here we can clearly see the 'great responsibility' which is connected with adopting our own laws (ZB-*Streifzuege*-38) and means that:

> [W]e are now not only responsible for the question of whether we obey an existing law or not, but also even for the question of whether this law is valid for us; for it is valid for us only because we are these specific people whose being is somehow modified by every completed deed, and therewith the Ought-ideal steadily flowing from it is modified in the same instant (Simmel 2010, 200).

Only creators have the right to destroy values and laws (FW-58), since only they are able to create law and bear the burden of being the 'avenger of their own law' (Za-II-*Ueberwindung*) – the burden of responsibility for their own existence before themselves alone.

To be the way to oneself has two main meanings. Firstly, it is that one is 'a wheel rolling out of itself', that is that we find the source which gives us life and compels us to act within us. Secondly, it means that by going down our own way, we are losing ourself and perishing, we are 'a *crossing over* and a *going under*' (Za-*Vorrede*-4). As Hartmann notes, '[t]he highest value of life is inevitably a spending

239 As accurately Cioran puts it, '[o]nly the mirage of freedom is real – without it, life would scarcely be practicable, or even conceivable. What incites us to believe we are free is our consciousness of necessity in general and of our shackles in particular; consciousness implies distance, and all distance provokes in us a feeling of autonomy and superiority, which, it goes without saying, has only a subjective value' (Cioran 1970, 179–180).

of life' (Hartmann 2007b, 337); Janion understood this in a similar vein, writing that 'in living, we die' (Janion 2001 (trans. A. Shaw), 10–11). However, in creation the creator loses oneself but immediately creates a new self anew. Thus, the way of the creator does not lead to nowhere but rather to fading and growing and from growing to fading.[240] Hence, there are the comparisons of creation to self-immolation as well as Zarathustra to fire – one is to burn oneself and arise from the ashes of its former self like the phoenix.[241] Creating something from ashes symbolises crating something *ex nihilo* which is characteristic of God-Creator (cf. Kołakowski 1988).

Nietzsche uses the term *unerschöpft* (unextinguished) in relation to a human being (Za-I-*Tugend*-2). Here also *Schöpfer* means creator (a term which for a long time was only used in relation to God) and *Schöpfung* means creation or a created work. By claiming that a human being is *un-er-schöpft*, Nietzsche is saying that it is a non-created being but rather a self-created one and thus incomplete, unfinished. A human being is also the creator of everything radically new in the world and not derived from any other notion – if gods existed, this kind of creativity would be impossible (Za-II-*Inseln*; see De Lubac 1998; Brzozowski 2012). Nietzsche appeals to the mythological figures of Proteus and Dionysus here as symbols of constant change and rebirth (NF-1885,35[68]; NF-1888,14[89]).[242]

Nietzsche calls the creator 'the one who loves' (*der Liebende*) since the most creative force which engages humans in their entirety is the desire called love. 'In our personal lives there is nothing more creative than love' as Ortega y Gasset remarks (Ortega y Gasset 1989 (trans. A. Shaw), 6). Nietzsche expresses this in the words of Hölderlin, 'for in loving the mortal gives of his best' (MAI-259, Nietzsche 2000, 175).[243] This passion in which one creates is beautifully described by Stróżewski who writes, '[t]he essential thing is not only to be oneself, but to be oneself completely' (Stróżewski 2013, 259). Creation shows the individual nature of a person in its best possible way. The creator is 'pregnant with oneself' which

240 Cf. Heraclitus CIII, '[t]he way up and down is one and the same' (Kahn 2001, 75).

241 Fire was also a symbol of change in Heraclitus (Kahn 2011), as well as 'Dionysus' weapon' (Kerényi 1997). In the Bible, it is the symbol of God (Ex 13,21; Ex 24,17), and has the power to cleanse one of sins and bring about spiritual change (Ps 65,10; Ps 16,3); it both creates and destroys since he who would be reborn in faith must first die (Jn 3,3), it illuminates as well as burns; in the New Testament, the metaphor of fire and the burning heart refers, above all, to love (Lk 12,49; Lk 24,32).

242 Dionysus also symbolises madness, excess, joy, intoxication, fertility, the pleasure of being alive etc. For more on the subject of Dionysus, see Kerényi 1997.

243 The passage comes from Hölderlin's poem entitled *The Death of Empedocles*.

means that through creating one gives oneself to the world (Za-IV-*Menschen*-11), creating both its whole self and, simultaneously, everything beyond it.[244] Creation comes from the deepest passions which do not serve anything other than the pleasure of creating, it is a luxury and draws on the surplus generated by the spirit; it is not needed to maintain life or to reproduce it.[245] To create, just like to love, is not a matter of wanting it but a *capability*, a power to not want at all, to create completely innocently (MAIIVM-336).[246] Hence, Nietzsche frequently says that those who love are the great *despisers* – it means that in order to love one must despise all objects of love (Za-II-*Mitleidige*), rejecting all kinds of 'for', 'in order to' and 'since' (Za-IV-*Menschen*-11), for only love for the sake of love is something creative.

3. The desire to give the self: the bestowing virtue

> Uncommon is the highest virtue and useless, it is gleaming and mild in its luster: a bestowing virtue [*schenkende Tugend*] is the highest virtue. (…)
> This is your thirst: to become sacrifices and gifts yourselves, and therefore you thirst to amass all riches in your soul.
> Insatiably your soul strives for treasures and gems, because your virtue is insatiable in wanting to bestow.
> You compel all things to and into yourselves, so that they may gush back from your well as the gifts of your love.
> Indeed, such a bestowing love must become a robber of all values, but hale and holy I call this selfishness [*Selbstsucht*].
> There is another selfishness, one all too poor, a hungering one that always wants to steal; that selfishness of the sick, the sick selfishness.

244 A similar thought was expressed by many artists, including Gombrowicz, who writes, '[a] writer does not write with any mysterious "talent" but with "himself." That means, he writes with his sensitivity and intelligence, heart and mind, with his entire spiritual development and that intensity, that steady excitement of the spirit, which Cicero says is the essence of all rhetoric' (Gombrowicz 2012, 126).

245 'Art is a luxury, freedom, play, dream, and power. Art arises not from poverty, but from riches. (…) Hegel does not have much in common with us because we are dance', writes in a similar spirit Gombrowicz (Gombrowicz 2012, 292).

246 'It does not suffice to do what is *good*, we must have wanted to do it and, as the poet said, admit divinity into our *will*. But we should not want what is *beautiful*, we must *be capable* of it, in innocence and blindness, without any curiosity of the soul' (Nietzsche 2013, 130). For Scheler it is the opposite – he claims that one may not want and pursue good since it would be a kind of hypocrisy but instead one should desire beauty and do good as a result (Wojtyła 2006).

With the eye of the thief it looks at all that gleams; with the greed of hunger it eyes those with ample food; and always it creeps around the table of the bestowers.
Sickness speaks out of such craving and invisible degeneration; the thieving greed of this selfishness speaks of a diseased body.
Tell me, my brothers: what do we regard as bad and worst? Is it not *degeneration*? – And we always diagnose degeneration where the bestowing soul is absent.
Upward goes our way, over from genus to super-genus. But a horror to us is the degenerating sense which speaks: 'Everything for me.' (…)
When your heart flows broad and full like a river, a blessing and a danger to adjacent dwellers: there is the origin of your virtue.
When you are sublimely above praise and blame, and your will wants to command all things, as the will of a lover: there is the origin of your virtue. (…)
It is power, this new virtue; it is a ruling thought and around it a wise soul (…).
Remain faithful to the earth, my brothers, with the power of your virtue! Let your bestowing love and your knowledge serve the meaning of the earth! (…)
Do not let it fly away from earthly things and beat against eternal walls with its wings! Oh, there has always been so much virtue that flew away!
Like me, guide the virtue that has flown away back to the earth – yes, back to the body and life: so that it may give the earth its meaning [*ihren Sinn*], a human meaning! [*Menschen-Sinn*] (…)
Still we struggle step by step with the giant called accident, and over all humanity thus far nonsense has ruled, the sense-less.
Let your spirit and your virtue serve the meaning of the earth, my brothers: and the value of all things will be posited newly by you! Therefore you shall be fighters! Therefore you shall be creators! (…)
…[A]ll instincts become sacred in the seeker of knowledge; the soul of the elevated one becomes gay. (…)
There are a thousand paths that have never yet been walked; a thousand healths and hidden islands of life (Za-I-*Tugend*-1,2, Nietzsche 2006a, 56–58).

The idea of creation is closely tied to the bestowing virtue. It is the sole virtue because it concerns human beings in their entirety and not their attributes or drives. A similar claim that there is only one virtue can be found in Plato (Plato 2002) who assumed the idea of the unity of all virtues and subordinating it to the ordering virtue – *dikaiosynē* or justice. In Christian ethics, the role of the meta-virtue is played by love which stems from our internal structure, as discussed above. Nietzsche calls the virtue unifying a person with his or her all passions and drives *the bestowing virtue* – it is also a form of love, yet different from the way in which it is understood in Christianity. The bestowing virtue is the most personal virtue – the 'own true self' of a person (Za-II-*Tugendchafte*; Za-I-*Leidenschaften*; Za-I-*Schaffender*).

According to Nietzsche, the common moral virtues developed not from life but rather from the rejection of life – they are identified with everything that one was not. In this way, they took on the form of apparent virtues, in reality representing our inhibitions, habits, vindictiveness, conformity, servitude, desire to control others, our pettiness, as well as our cowardice (Za-II-*Tugendchafte*; Za-III-*Tugend*; Za-I-*Naechstenliebe*).[247] He emphasises that virtue is not a means to obtain happiness, as many often think, but rather a result of happiness (spiritual strength), whilst vices and debauchery (the pursuit of ever stronger stimulation) stem from unhappiness (spiritual degeneration) (GD-*Irrthuemer*-2).[248]

The bestowing virtue is *a desire to give,* independent of any moral values or intellectual predispositions on the part of the giver (Hartmann 2007b). Giving regards here spiritual goods and flows from the 'full heart' (Za-*Vorrede*-1) and not from a need. The giver is thus a person who has something to give; the giver belongs to the few who are like 'a cup runneth over', they have souls which are 'deep and cavernous'. Spiritual goods offer themselves, they only require our will's acceptance.[249]

In order to have the power to give, one must first desire onself and be able to love onself (Za-II-*Mitleidige*).[250] Nietzsche defines the bestowing virtue as *Sehnsucht* (longing) and *Selbstsucht* (selflove) (Za-III-*Boese*). The German word *Sucht* means 'yearning' and *suchen* means 'to search for' and thus the word *Selbst-sucht* may be translated as a longing for oneself as well as the search for the self. This is confirmed by the parable in which Zarathustra talks to his soul (Za-III-*Sehnsucht*), and such conversations of the soul, according to Heidegger, have been called thinking since the days of Plato (Heidegger 1967). 'Longing is the agony of the nearness of the distant', as Heidegger goes on to write (Heidegger 1967, 417). Longing is fed by distance and thus the further away from onself that one is, the more one longs for oneself.

---

247 Hölderlin writes in a similar manner about the virtues of the Germans (Hölderlin 1990).

248 In a similar way Scheler, argues that 'happiness is the root and source of virtue', not the goal of a virtuous person; thus 'only a happy person acts in a morally good way', and not a person who seeks happiness and satisfaction in his or her acts (Scheler 1985, 359).

249 This is reminiscent of the idea claimed by Thomas Aquinas – *bonum diffusivum sui* – that the goodness tends to spread and to expand itself (St. Thomas Aquinas, *De Virtutibus* 2.2c). Cf. 2 Cor 7,9; Mt 5,13–16.

250 '"I offer myself to my love, *and my neighbour as myself*" – thus it is said of all creators' (Nietzsche 2006a, 69). It is thus a reference to the Gospels (Mt 19,19; Mt 22,39; Mk 12,31; Lk 10,27). In his notes Nietzsche also remarks that the sight of man in love with himself must arouse a certain malicious pleasure in God (NF-1885,43[1]).

In loving oneself, one must at the same time spurn the self (Za-IV-*Mensch*), which should be interpreted as the loving person not only thinking of themselves alone or preserving themselves but desiring that desire itself in which one loses the self.

There is a distinction to be made here between 'sanctified' selfishness ('a robust, healthy selfishness which flows from the powerful soul', Za-III-*Boese*) and degenerate selfishness ('which is poor, hungry and always ready to steal', Za-I-*Tugend*-1). The former is a sign of spiritual richness and requires the self to be squandered in order for it to grow. The latter is a type of unhealthy greed, where the desire to obtain goods stems from their lack; wanting everything only for oneself, wanting to keep our existing self and everything that it has. Nietzsche rejects any kind of poverty of the soul, as well as the 'poverty of the soul by two' which he calls marriage (Za-I-*Kind*), and discards the souls' avarice in everything, including sinning (Za-*Vorrede*-3).

The bestowing virtue is a certain type of love which is not directed to the needy ones (such as love of one's neighbour) or to any concrete people which we may feel some affection for (such as the love of one's spouse); it is directed to everyone and no one – to those who are able to take it (Za-*Vorrede*-9; see Hartmann 2007b).[251] It is a love beyond good and evil (JGB-153), similar to the sun in that it shines on everyone – the just and the unjust alike.[252] The giver longs for the one who accepts his or her gifts, as it was for Zarathustra with those who gravitated towards his wisdom (Za-*Vorrede*-1). There is no greater loneliness than that of the giver who has no one to give to – such a giver is like the sun without anyone to shine upon (Za-II-*Nachtlied*).[253] Accepting spiritual gifts is accorded the same value as bestowing them, it is an expression of love towards the giver which frees them of a great weight (Za-III-*Sehnsucht*).[254] The giver does not impoverish oneself through giving; on the contrary, giving enriches the giver. There is no mutual relationship

251 Zarathustra paraphrases the Holy Gospel, 'who still has ears for the unheard of, I shall make his heart heavy with my happiness' (Nietzsche 2006a, 15). Cf. Mk 4,9; Mk 4,23; Mk 7,16; Lk 8,8; Lk 14,35.

252 Cf. Mt 5,45. Hölderlin writes, 'man is a sun, all-seeing and all-illuminating, when he loves' (Hölderlin 1990, 61).

253 '…Alas, there is thirst in me that yearns for your thirst!
It is night: alas that I must be light! And thirst for the nocturnal! And loneliness!' (Nietzsche 2006a, 83).

254 '"Who of us is supposed to be thankful?
– does the giver not have to give thanks that the receiver received? Is bestowing not a bare necessity? Is receiving not – mercy?"
Oh my soul, I understand the smiling of your melancholy: your super-richness itself reaches out with longing hands!' (Nietzsche 2006a, 180). Cf. Kierkegaard, who wrote

here, giving and taking are separated by a broad chasm, although neither of them is possible without the other.

The bestowing love, as Nietzsche terms this virtue, is an internal desire which fights 'the giant called accident', meaning that it is a force that can rescue us from the realm of necessity, leading us from the level of the species and the impersonal to that of the individual and the personal. Love, like hatred, is not a passive emotional state which happens to us but rather has a volitional and active character, it is directed *beyond* the self. In as much as hatred has a destructive character for both the hater and the hated, love also builds up and perfects the subjects who are engaged in it, it has the power to create. Love is engaged in going beyond what is common in us all to gain the self (that which is individual, unrepeatable) and something more than the self (something completely new – the fruits of our love).

This prompts the association with the Platonic *Eros*, and the Christian love called *agape*, the affirmation and transformation of being. The Platonic *Eros*, the son of Resource and Poverty, inherited a natural affinity to the beautiful and the good from his father and an eternal restlessness from his mother, as Plato writes (Plato 1980). It is thus an eternally unsatisfied desire that drives us onwards without ever letting us reach the summit. Nietzsche argues that Christianity poisoned Eros (JGB-168), including love in the moral order of things and placing human sexuality in the realm of guilt, which in turn led to the creation of asceticism which is a negation of life – the extinguishing of the instincts and a spiritual sickness. However, Christianity does not reject sensual love but rather tries to integrate it with spiritual love (incarnation rather than negation). Paradoxically, it is the pagan cult of Eros and its glorification of instincts which leads to idealization and sublimation of love in the supersensuous world (De Rougemont 1968). As I have written earlier, Christian love is not a passive acceptance of what there is but an active pursuit of what we love: 'love is the eternal sustaining, creating and protecting of that which we love' according to the Augustinian doctrine of love interpreted by Ortega y Gasset (Ortega y Gasset 1989).[255] Love is different to other feelings such as kindness in that it does not seek its affirmation in the maintenance of existence but rather in its perfection and, as a result, is dynamic.

---

about 'the little mystery that it is better to give than to receive (…), it is far more difficult to receive than to give' (Kierkegaard 1983, 104).

255 Hölderlin expressed Nietzsche's thought that only creators are allowed to destroy (FW-58) invoking love which has the power to bring life in the form of an accusation, 'you can kill, but you cannot bring life, unless it is done by love, which proceeds not from you, which you did not invent' (Hölderlin 1990, 129).

The fundamental difference between love in the Nietzschean and the Christian sense lies in the fact that the bestowing virtue is not rooted in a transcendent entity. Love separated from the Absolute may not be at ease and thus endless restlessness becomes its goal.[256] This causes tremendous tension between a person and his or her creative sustenance since pleasure is interwoven with pain. By placing the weight of human desire within us, Nietzsche also separates love from its objects, which are not important in themselves but rather serve as a pretext to generate love. Love is not understood as a desire for the good of what we love but rather a desire for the sake of desire itself which belongs beyond good and evil,– it is love not to anyone or anything but love to loving itself (crave for its intensity and power). The bestowing virtue is its own axiological peak, as Hartmann notes, and finds its ultimate confirmation within itself; it does not serve anyone beyond itself and contains its goal within itself (Hartmann 2007b). It desires itself and thus goes beyond the giver, providing one with a feeling of participating in eternity, and intensifies the desire for it (Za-IV-*Nachtwandler*-11).[257] In this manner, one finds in the bestowing virtue its own *anthropodicy,* as remarked by Hartmann (Hartmann 2007b).[258] Anthropodicy, which is intended to replace theodicy, is an attempt to find the sense of human existence in their spiritual creative strength and passionate love, a subject to which I will return later.

One may discern in the project of Nietzsche an attempt to return to the cult of Eros only in the sense that it overcomes a division between the sensuous and supersensuous worlds (he rejects the lie of idealism as well as its counterpart, pure animal instinct); it is a spiritual passion which serves 'earthly things', the highest degree of the will to power. Nietzsche regards the passionate as undoubtedly the noblest and rarest of souls, which allows the creative will to arise. Through its intensity and strength to go beyond humanity, it gives the illusion of completeness and freedom; it is the highest phase of our aesthetic lives, which Kierkegaard contrasted with the ethical-religious. Nietzsche wanted to give it an existential-ethical character, which will be discussed in the next chapter.

---

256 The Christian account of metaphysical desire is wonderfully presented by the Gospel scene by the well where Jesus talks to the Samaritan (Jn 4,13–14).

257 '[A]ll joy wants itself (…). Joy wants the eternity of *all* things, *wants deep, wants deep eternity*!' (Nietzsche 2006a, 263).

258 It is a term consisting of two Greek words: *anthropos* – which means human beings, and *diké* – which means justice. It was coined with reference to the notion of 'theodicy' (*théos* – God) introduced by Leibniz and used in considerations of how evil is possible in a world created by a perfect God.

II. Overcoming the human

1. Transcending without transcendence

> …Human being is something that must be overcome [*überwunden*]. What have you done to overcome him?
> All creatures so far created something beyond themselves; and you want to be the ebb of this great flood and would even rather go back to animals than overcome humans? (Za-*Vorrede*-3, Nietzsche 2006a, 5).
> And this secret life itself spoke to me: 'Behold,' it said, 'I am that *which must always overcome itself*' (Za-II-*Ueberwindung*, Nietzsche 2006a, 89).

The above citation from the Prologue to *Thus spoke Zarathustra* often appears in many parts of the book and tends to be regarded as its main message. The maxim that 'human being is something that must be overcome' (*Der Mensch ist eine Sache, die überwunden werden soll*) frequently appears in Nietzsche's notes (e.g. NF-1882,4[165]; NF-1883,11[8]; NF-1884,25[454]). The notion of overcoming (*Überwinden*) the human being is close to the idea of transcendence understood as going beyond (*Übersteigen*) human condition.[259] The prefix 'trans' may be translated in German as *über*, the very prefix that Nietzsche used in his crucial notions of the *Übermensch* and *Überwinden.*

The idea of the human transcendence was one which was familiar to people in ancient times and which took on a new dimension under Christianity in terms of its relationship to God. Pico della Mirandola, in his *Oration on the Dignity of Man* emphasised the human ability to go beyond its nature as proof of the miracle that is a human being:

> We have set you at the centre of the world so that from there you may easily gaze upon whatever it contains. We have made you neither of heaven nor of earth, neither mortal nor immortal, so that you may, as the free and extraordinary shaper of yourself, fashion yourself in whatever form you prefer. It will be in your power to degenerate into the lower forms of life, which are brutish. Alternatively, you shall have the power, in accordance with the judgment of your soul, to be reborn into the higher orders, those that are divine (Pico della Mirandola 2012, 117).

---

259 The notions of immanence and transcendence were incorporated into the philosophical discourse from the Scholastics and were revived by Spinoza before Kant gave them a new significance; by transcendental he meant 'to go beyond human notions', 'knowledge of that which we know nothing' (Mauthner 1923, entry 'transcendental' (trans. A. Shaw), 294–316).

One may see a connection between the words of Pico della Mirandola and Zarathustra in relation to the unique status of humankind as 'trans' or 'between'[260] (animal and non-animal world), which can be also found in the notes of Nietzsche where he claims that a human being is something between a plant and a phantom (NF-1882,4[116]). Zarathustra compares a human being to an animal, indicating the evolutionary fact that human beings descended from lower species. When he calls for the human to be overcome, however, he does not have in mind the purely biological development. Instead, he thinks, in a manner similar to Pico, of a spiritual development which will distinguish the human being from every other species. Pico della Mirandola, as Nietzsche, compared a human being to Proteus in his ability to transform, believing that the human 'fluid nature' was our greatest attribute as it allowed us to create ourselves anew (Pico della Mirandola 2012). However, it should be stressed that the manifesto of the Renaissance was firmly rooted in the Platonic-Christian tradition which Nietzsche so firmly rejected.[261]

Blaise Pascal also wrote on the unique duality of the human condition, expressed by the overcoming the human being by reference to God, '[i]s it not as clear as day that man's condition is twofold?' (Pascal 1999, 164, 42). According to Pascal, our infinite capability for growth is a particular property of the duality of human nature. For Pascal, as for St Augustine, it is only the external perspective given to people by faith that allows them to understand human nature and go beyond it.[262]

One may say that Nietzsche accepted the Christian notion of human existence as an existence which seeks to *overcome itself*, yet depriving the process of a reference to a Transcendent Being. This is transcending without transcendence (Jaspers 1979),[263] the interpretation of which can be found in Heidegger:

260 In Platonism, the term *metaksy* was used in reference to a human being situated between this which is mortal and this which is immortal, in order to describe the eternally unfulfilled desire (*Eros*) as a means of communicating with the absolute (Plato 1980). Simone Weil illustrated it with the metaphor of a wall which divides two prisoners and at the same time, since they can knock on it, is their only means of communicating with one another (Weil 2002).

261 Pico believed that man was a being created by God, that his main goal was to be elevated alongside God and that 'he must reject earthly things in order to gain his heavenly kingdom' (Pico della Mirandola 2012, 47).

262 For a wide-ranging and precise account of the Christian (personalistic) idea of the transcendence of a person in agency whose basis is, as in Nietzsche, the will, see Wojtyła 2000.

263 As Jaspers writes, after removing the idea of supernatural world, there remains 'pre-immanence as becoming' (Jaspers 1979, 253), the will to power as 'transcending without transcendence' (Jaspers 1979, 335–341).

Transcendence means surpassing [*Überstieg*]. That which accomplishes such surpassing and dwells in this surpassing is transcendent (transcending). As an occurrence, this surpassing pertains to something that is. Formally speaking, surpassing may be grasped as a 'relation' that passes 'from' something 'to' something. To surpassing there thus belongs that *toward which* such surpassing occurs, that which is usually, though inaccurately, called the 'transcendent.' (…) Transcendence, however, is that surpassing that makes possible such a thing as existence in general, thereby also making it possible to move 'oneself' in space (Heidegger 1998, 107–108).

The vitality of the human soul is manifested in transcending in every sphere of life; it is founded on a certain internal antimony of human life which is a 'boundless continuity and, at the same time, a boundary-determined ego' (Simmel 2010, 9). It is worth stressing here that Nietzsche understands overcoming the human being as a certain type of spiritual development and thus something more than just individuals surpassing their own weaknesses and conditionings. Nietzsche attributes to this phenomenon the ability to surpass everything living in the universe; in Zarathustra's conversation with life we learn that life is something that must constantly overcome itself, it is a constant striving for growth and contraction and thus a manifestation of the aforementioned will to power. This process has no goal, no ends beyond itself; by taking part in it, the human being must remain 'faithful to the earth' (Za-*Vorrede*-3; Za-I-*Tugend*-2). Nietzsche emphasises that the overcome human was the father of the *Übermensch*, which means that the overcoming of the human has been happening for a long time and has allowed humans to reach beyond themselves in the spiritual sense to a higher level (NF-1883,18[56]).

2. *Übermensch*

'Mankind is a rope fastened between animal and overman – a rope over an abyss [*Abgrunde*]. (…)

What is great about human beings is that they are a bridge and not a purpose: what is lovable about human beings is that they are a *crossing over* and a *going under*.

I love those who do not know how to live unless by going under, for they are the ones who cross over.

I love the great despisers, because they are the great venerators and arrows of longing for the other shore.

I love those who do not first seek behind the stars for a reason to go under and be a sacrifice, who instead sacrifice themselves for the earth, so that the earth may one day become the overman's.

I love the one who lives in order to know, and who wants to know so that one day the overman may live. And so he wants his going under [*Untergang*]. (…)

I love all those who are like heavy drops falling individually from the dark cloud that hangs over humanity: they herald the coming of the lightning, and as heralds they perish.

Behold, I am a herald of the lightning and a heavy drop from the cloud: but this lightning is called overman. –' (Za-*Vorrede*-4, Nietzsche 2006a, 7–9).

The Superman (Der Übermensch, <overman>)

:it's not my question, what separates the men: but what kind of person elected as higher values (höherwerthige), wanted to be bred...

Humanity is not a development for the better; represent or higher; or stronger in the sense in which it is believed today: the Europeans of the 19th century, is in their value (Werthe <worth>), far below the European of the Renaissance; development is absolutely no necessity of any increase, increase, gain...

in a different sense, it gives out a continuing success of individual cases in various locations around the world and from diverse cultures, which in fact represents a higher type: something that is in proportion to the overall-humanity a sort of 'superman'. Such good fortune of great success have always been possible and perhaps always be possible. And even whole tribes, sexes, nations may under certain circumstances such a hit... (NF-1887,11[413], Nietzsche 2012a, 126–127).

Together with the 'death of God', the *Übermensch* is the notion most frequently associated with Nietzsche but also one which has garnered many misunderstandings, even during his lifetime.[264] As he emphasises, the most frequent error lies in thinking of the *Übermensch* in idealistic or Darwinist terms (EH-*Buecher*-1; BVN-1888,1135). In his notes he expresses the idea that it is a metaphor used to define a specific expression of the surplus of will which is manifested in the most complete, ambitious and creative individuals (NF-1887,10[17]). It is a Dionysian vision of the abundance of life (*Überfülle des Lebens*, NF-1882,4[75]).[265] All societies are characterised by the averaging out of their members, aligning their forces, e.g. by means of universal and general moral norms, customs and laws. This leads to the stagnation and weakening of individuals, but also allows forces to be gathered together in society, which erupt in the form of individuals who go beyond the limits of the given society and its conditions, sometimes pulling the society along with them towards new horizons and values (NF-1882,4[94]; Za-I-*Tugend*-

---

264 Amongst his published works, the term most frequently occurs in *Thus spoke Zarathustra*, which is, in accordance with what is said in its Prologue, a lecture on the subject of the *Übermensch*. An interesting interpretation of the *Übermensch* is proposed by Heidegger (Heidegger 1968).

265 Ger. *Überfülle* means magnitude but the verb *überfüllen* means to fill, to load up; thus, the magnitude stems from being filled up.

2).[266] The *Übermensch* is described in terms of a thunderbolt hidden in a human being (NF-1882,4[116]; Za-*Vorrede*-7), meaning that one is the culmination and release of power in which one oneself disappears.[267]

The metaphor of the *Übermensch* is used to describe 'the *highest type of everything that exists*', but in the spiritual rather than the biological sense (EH-ZA-6). As Nietzsche himself frequently stresses, his notion does not refer to any Darwinist principles such as the survival of the species.[268] Darwinist principles were fostered by the attitude of *mimicry*, adapting and economising own energy (obtaining the maximum effect for the minimum effort). The idea of the *Übermensch* shows something completely different – breaking free from our surroundings, the tremendous waste in nature, extravagance, disdain for life. That which counts is not life but power, growth, the feeling of strength. It is not about preserving human beings but surpassing them (Za-IV-*Menschen*-3) and that which is worthy of admiration and love in human beings is their ability to make this kind of crossing (*Übergang*) while 'going under' (*Untergang*), to which this crossing inevitably leads (Za-IV-*Menschen*-3). In this respect another term is used in relation to the *Übermensch* – madness. Nietzsche plays a subtle game of words, since in one respect the *Übermensch* is to be the sense of the earth (*Sinn der Erde*), whilst on the other hand the teachings on the *Übermensch* give the sense to the human existence (*Sinn ihres Seins*), and in yet another way, the *Übermensch* is the imaginary sense – *madness* (*Wahnsinn*) – in which one wishes to squander oneself (Za-I-*Vorrede*-3–7).

The aforementioned madness (*Wahnsinn*), is almost certainly intended to recall the frenzy and ecstasy which overtook the participants in the ancient Dionysian rites and which Nietzsche longed for. This frenzy was 'the highest state of the expression of the vital power of man, where both the conscious and the unconscious come together in some kind of tremendous wave' (Kerényi 1997 (trans.

---

266 In a similar context Bergson used the example of the founders of religions and mystics as an 'army of conquerors' who 'have broken down natural resistance and raised humanity to a new destiny' (Bergson 1963, 42).

267 Cf. Heraclitus LXXVI, '[a]ll beasts are driver by blows' (in Kahn 2001, 65); the thunderbolt was a weapon of Zeus, the symbol of his ruling and power.

268 The goal is the *Übermensch* and not humanity, as Nietzsche writes (NF-1884,26[232]). The associations with Darwinism may stem from the unfortunate expression 'human herd' which Nietzsche uses in this context. As Buczyńska-Garewicz notes, however, for Nietzsche the term herd was connected with treating oneself as a fruit of nature and one's own work, trusting one's instincts and affirming one's internal necessities; the term was also meant to refer to individuals and not the population at large (Buczyńska-Garewicz 2010).

A. Shaw), 119; cf. Otto 1965). Plato, through Socrates, praised madness as a state of intoxication stemming from gods, a passion which moved sensitive souls and allowed them to experience a passion similar to that of *Eros*. As Schelling writes:

> Since Aristotle it is even customary to say of people that nothing great can be accomplished without a touch of madness. In place of this, we would like to say: nothing great can be accomplished without a constant solicitation of madness (Schelling 2000, 104).

In contrast to those who are gripped by 'divine madness' are those intellectuals who are 'sober spirits', denied of the gift of creating since they lack the madness which feeds the intellect (Schelling 2000). Nietzsche ascribes considerable importance to this understanding of madness, maintaining that it leads to new ways of thinking and gives us the power to overcome our embedded habits. In his opinion madness 'awoke in the bearer of a new idea himself reverence for and dread of himself and no longer pangs of conscience and drove him to become the prophet and martyr' (M-14, Nietzsche 2005a, 14). He believs that innovators in every field need madness in order to authenticate themselves and their thoughts and if they are not truly insane then they must adopt the appearance of being so; this is why the most productive people of all time have always asked the gods for madness (M-14).[269] Reading these poignant words, one may agree with Shestov, that the prayer of Nietzsche was heard and the gods drove him insane (Shestov 1969). Nietzsche might have said, in the words of the poem of Tadeusz Miciński, '[i]n choosing my fate, I *chose* madness' (Miciński 2000 (trans. A. Shaw), 58).[270]

Together with the 'death of God', human life became deprived of its higher sense and thus returned to the grip of necessity, degrading itself in the process, ceasing to grow spiritually. Setting themselves mundane goals, people are in a position to forget the absurdity of their life. However, by setting their goals higher than life itself, human beings can break free from the embrace of accident and necessity, to regain control, albeit illusory, over their lives, to emerge into the endless flow of life in the twinkling of an eye and showing their individuality within it. Existence itself does not require justification (no 'why' or 'what for'), whilst existence which is to surpass itself obtains a new 'raison d'etre' (the interpretation of being, NF-1885,35[73]), which Zarathustra expressed using the metaphor of the *Übermensch* (NF-1887,10[17]). The *Übermensch* is the new hope and harbinger of

269 '"Ah, give me madness, you heavenly powers! Madness, that I may at last believe myself! Give deliriums and convulsions, sudden lights and darkness, terrify me with frost and fire such as no mortal has ever felt, (...) make me howl and whine and crawl like a beast: so that I may only come to believe in myself!"' (Nietzsche 2005a, 15).

270 Poem entitled *Suicide* [*Samobójstwo*]), emphasis M.S.

happiness, a new spiritual peak (Za-I-*Tugend*; Za-II-*Inseln*; Za-IV-*Menschen*-2), an anthropodicy.[271]

As Cioran accurately notices, for the man 'to believe it is his responsibility to transcend his condition and tend toward of the *Übermensch* is to forget that he has trouble enough sustaining himself *as man*' (Cioran 1970, 183). The spiritual attitude to be found beyond good and evil and proposed by Nietzsche is its own mixture of aesthetic attitudes with vitality, which Novalis described as the most dangerous creation of our times since its worst adherents are to be found amongst the weakest spirits which it was intended to protect against:

> The ideal of morality has no more dangerous rival than the ideal of supreme strength, of a life of maximum vigor, which has also been called (…) the ideal of aesthetic greatness. That life is in truth the ultimate attainment of the barbarian, and unfortunately in these days of civilization's withering it has won a great many adherents. In pursuance of this ideal man becomes a hybrid thing, a brute-spirit, whose cruel mentality exerts a horrible spell upon weaklings (Novalis in Mann 1959, 168).

It is worth noting that the origin of the *Übermensch* reaches back to the ethics of Kant, even though it developed in opposition to it. The moral subject of Kant is the product of the age of science – it is independent, alone, strong, brave, it believes in rationality but is also conscious of its limits and its own alienation, as Iris Murdoch claimed. Post-Kantian ethics were sown in the same ground as the *Übermensch* since, as the author maintains, at its heart:

> [I]s the notion of the will as the creator of value. Values which were previously in some sense inscribed in the heavens and guaranteed by God collapse into the human will. There is no reality. (…) The sovereign moral concept is freedom, or possibly courage in a sense which identifies it with freedom, will, power. (…) Act, choice, decision, responsibility, independence are emphasized in this philosophy of puritanical origin and apparent austerity (Murdoch 2014, 78–79).

According to Murdoch, 'the Kantian man appeared already in his most impressive incarnation almost one hundred years before in the work of Milton: his real name

---

271 In his first creative period Nietzsche wrote that the only justification for the absurdity of existence may be found in art. In *The Birth of Tragedy* he wrote that 'only as an aesthetic phenomenon is existence and the world eternally justified' (GT-5, Nietzsche 2007b, 33); this same thought was repeated (GT-24); and at the end Nietzsche added that Dionysian art and tragedy 'justify (…) the existence of even the "worst of all worlds"' (GT-25, Nietzsche 2007b, 115). The thought of Nietzsche evolved and he rejected the need for any kind of metaphysical justification of existence. He remained faithful, however, to the idea that creation gave such pleasure as to allow one to love life with the eternal recurrence of pain, as I will discuss in the next chapter.

was Lucifer' (Murdoch 2014, 102). Lucifer in *Paradise Lost* is understood in the Anglo-Saxon world as the personification of the *will of man* in opposition to the will of God,[272] who proudly exclaims:

> ...Farewell, happy fields
> Where joy forever dwells: hail horrors, hail
> Infernal world, and thou profoundest hell
> Receive thy new possessor: one who brings
> A mind not to be changed by place or time.
> The mind is its own place, and in itself
> Can make a heaven of hell, a hell of heaven.
> What matter where, if I be still the same, (...)
> ...Here at least
> We shall be free; (...)
> ...and in my choice
> To reign is worth ambition though in hell:
> Better to reign in hell, than serve in heaven (Milton 2005, I, 249–263, 24–25).

The new incarnation of Lucifer manifests itself in the 'masochistic heroism of revolt' against Kantian ethics of duty (De Rougemont 1992 (trans. A. Shaw), 42). The *Übermensch* is a child of existential philosophy, the epoch of decadence and doubt, it no longer believes in reason but places unlimited faith in the will which is to be a mighty weapon in the battle with the absurdity of existence. The *Übermensch* was about to be a human peak, but it seems to be more of a dead end than a new beginning since, as Cioran observed, 'the will (...) turns against those who abuse it', and once one accedes to the rank of *Übermensch* 'he will doubtless explode and fall back upon himself' (Cioran 1970, 183).

272 Cioran shows that the fall of man was foreshadowed by the fall of an angel (Lucifer); there is a similarity between them as they both sought to separate themselves from God and questioned his order after they emerged from their original unconsciousness (Cioran 1970), the cause in both cases being pride (*hubris*).

Chapter 6. The will to return – *amor fati*

Let's plunge into time's torrent,
Into the whirlpools of event!
Then let joy, and distress,
Frustration, and success,
Follow each other, as well they can:
Restless activity proves the man! (…)
My soul will grasp the high and low,
My heart accumulate its bliss and woe,
So this self will embrace all theirs,
That, in the end, their fate it shares.
Johann Wolfgang von Goethe[273]

If we agree with Schopenhauer that a philosopher should be the philosopher of a single thought to which all other thoughts are only a commentary or a prelude (Schopenhauer 2010), in the eyes of Heidegger, Nietzsche was the philosopher of the thought of *the eternal recurrence of the same*, without which his philosophy would be like a tree without roots (Heidegger 1991a). I will attempt to explain why the idea of the eternal recurrence is the crowning achievement of Nietzsche's philosophy and the key to understanding his metaphysics.

Some intuitions concerning the eternal recurrence of the same (*ewige Wiederkunft des Gleichen*) or the eternal return of all things (*ewige Wiederkehr aller Dingen*)[274] may be found in Nietzsche's earliest works where they resemble the beliefs of the Pythagoreans (HL-2). However, this idea as his own and new concept appeared only in 1881 in the form of a sudden revelation which I will discuss in the final section of this chapter. It was then developed further in his publications – in *The Gay Science* it appears as a prelude whilst in *Thus Spoke Zarathustra* it becomes the main motif of the book (EH-ZA-1), the hero

273 From Part I of *Faust* by Johann Wolfgang Goethe (Goethe 2003, 1754–1776, 70).

274 Some Nietzsche scholars focus on the difference between the much less frequently used notion of *Wiederkehr* (the eternal return as a scientific hypothesis connected to the idea of time as a closed circle) and the more popular *Wiederkunft* (eternal recurrence as a philosophical proposition which is accompanied by certain existential-metaphysical conclusions). From the perspective of the research conducted here, the distinction does not have much significance. It is worth to highlight the similarity between words like *Wiederkunft* (return) and *Zukunft* (future), which indicates Nietzsche's view that the future is not something which follows on from something but rather something which returns, which comes back.

of which – Zarathustra – is referred to as the teacher of eternal recurrence (Za-III-*Genesende*-2).

A rich literature has developed from the idea of the eternal recurrence (see Heidegger 1991a; Heidegger 1991b; Löwith 1997; Kaufmann 1968; Buczyńska-Garewicz 2013), but it has not ceased to be a riddle. In my analysis I will focus on the following four overlapping interpretations which I find to be the most significant: I) cosmological; II) ethical-existential; III) metaphysical; IV) mystical.

I. The cosmological interpretation of the idea of eternal return

The cosmological speculations concerning the idea of the eternal return are hinted at in some of Nietzsche's notes where he presents his idea of the universe:

> And do you know what 'the world' is to me? Shall I show you it in my mirror? This world: a monster of force, without beginning, without end, a fixed, iron quantity of force which grows neither larger nor smaller, which doesn't exhaust but only transforms itself, as a whole unchanging in size, an economy without expenditure and losses, but equally without increase, without income, enclosed by 'nothingness' as by a boundary, not something blurred, squandered, not something infinitely extended; instead, as a determinate force set into a determinate space, and not into a space that is anywhere 'empty' but as force everywhere, as a play of forces and force-waves simultaneously one and 'many', accumulating here while diminishing there, an ocean of forces storming and flooding within themselves, eternally changing, eternally rushing back, with tremendous years of recurrence [*Wiederkehr*], with an ebb and flood of its forms, shooting out from the simplest into the most multifarious, from the stillest, coldest, most rigid into the most fiery, wild, self-contradictory, and then coming home from abundance to simplicity, from the play of contradiction back to the pleasure of harmony, affirming itself even in this sameness of its courses and years, blessing itself as what must eternally return, as a becoming that knows no satiety, no surfeit, no fatigue – this, my *Dionysian* world of eternal self-creating, of eternal self-destroying, this mystery world of dual delights, this my beyond good and evil, without goal, unless there is a goal in the happiness of the circle, without will, unless a ring feels good will towards itself – do you want a *name* for this world? A *solution* to all its riddles? A *light* for you too, for you, the most secret, strongest, most intrepid, most midnightly? – *This world is the will to power – and nothing besides!* And you yourselves too are this will to power – and nothing besides! (NF-1885,38[12], Nietzsche 2006b, 38–39).

These notes (also NF-1886,5[71](6)) may lead to the conclusion that the idea of the eternal return is considered by Nietzsche as a scientific hypothesis describing the universe (cf. Stöltzner 2012; Vaas 2012). The cosmological hypothesis of the eternal return is based on the assumption that the universe comprises a fixed amount of energy (NF-1886,5[54]), which undergoes constant change and is without a final purpose – and if this purpose were to be achieved, it would have been achieved a long time ago (NF-1888,14[188]). By adopting the infinite nature of time, every possible combination could become realised an infinite number of times in the same sequence – it is a vision of 'the world as a circle' (NF-1888,14[188]).[275]

Nietzsche frequently emphasised, as I have already discussed, that all normative categories (including the scientific ones) are only interpretations, thus he could not have adopted the cosmological hypothesis as an objective truth the existence of which he has denied. In fact, in the aforementioned fragments he used conditional forms and used the term 'hypothesis'. One may therefore assume that Nietzsche considered this interpretation as something supplementary, something that would make the 'Dionysian vision of the world' more convincing. Regardless of the scientific verifiability of this hypothesis, Nietzsche was concerned with the question of the influence it would have upon human existence and a vision of a human being.

II. The ethical-existential interpretation of the idea of the eternal recurrence

The considerations of the eternal recurrence first appeared in *The Gay Science* in the section entitled *The heaviest weight* [*Schwergewicht*]:

> What if some day or night a demon were to steal into your loneliest loneliness and say to you: 'This life as you now live it and have live it you will have to live once again and innumerable times again; and there will be nothing new in it, but every pain and every joy and every thought and sigh and everything unspeakably small or great in your life must return to you, all in the same succession and sequence (…). The eternal hourglass of existence is turned over again and again, and you with it, speck of dust!' Would you not throw yourself down and gnash your teeth and curse the demon who spoke thus? (…) If this thought gained power over you, as you are it would transform and possibly crush you; the question in each and every thing, 'Do you want this again and innumer-

275 'In infinite time, every possible combination would be reached eventually, even more, it would be infinite number of times achieved. And since between every 'combination' and their next 'return' all at all possible combinations would have expired and each of these combinations, the entire sequence of combinations in the same row conditional, a circular movement of absolutely identical series was proved that the world as a cycle has already repeated itself infinitely often and plays its game in infinitum. This conception is not simply a mechanistic: as it were, it would not condition an infinite recurrence [*Wiederkehr*] of identical cases, but a final state. Because the world has not reached it (ihn), the mechanism must apply to us as imperfect and merely provisional hypothesis' (Nietzsche 2012b, 103).

able times again?' would lie on your actions as the heaviest weight! Or how well disposed would you have to become to yourself and to life to *long for nothing more fervently* than for this ultimate eternal confirmation and seal? (FW-341, Nietzsche 2001, 194–195).

On the basis of the above fragment, it may be assumed that the idea of the eternal recurrence is a radical thought experiment conducted on an individual (NF-1881,11[141]). What proves that is the use of the conditional ('what if…'). The experiment concerns the temporal human nature, one of the basic attributes of our existence and a fundamental one for all of our ethical considerations. Morality regards thus our adjustment to time: to the past and the future. The human ability to manage *the future* is shown in our ability to place obligations upon ourselves by swearing oaths, creating contracts and making promises. In this way one learns to be predictable for onself and others, as I have already discussed. Keeping a promise is, on the one hand, an attempt to deal with an unpredictable future (with the freedom of another); on the other, it is an attempt to manage our own lack of knowledge of self (our own freedom). By undergoing constant changes and not knowing who we will be tomorrow, we try to control ourselves by making promises and plans – we thus strive for a relative permanence and tangibility of ourselves in time. As Nietzsche writes, one may only promise what one will do but not what one will feel. Thus when someone promises love to another, they make a promise that they think lies in their power – to express love in their actions, regardless of feelings which are changeable (MAI-58). As Arendt aptly notes, the ability to make and keep promises, creates 'islands of predictability and signposts to reliability' (Arendt 1998, 244).[276]

Human ability to deal with *the past*, is expressed by the notion of responsibility as the ability to take the consequences of our actions, which is closely connected with the notions of guilt and punishment. Christianity introduces here a revolutionary change in the moral context, replacing the categories of guilt and punishment with those of love and forgiveness, as we have already seen. The assumption of the 'death of God' forced Nietzsche to reject Christian mercy and the idea of salvation which, once separated from God, become for him an expression of *ressentiment*. The idea of the innocence of the state of becoming proposed by

276 Arendt describes this aspect of the human condition in the following words, '[m]an's inability to rely upon himself or to have complete faith in himself (which is the same thing) is the price human beings pay for freedom; and the impossibility of remaining unique masters of what they do, of knowing its consequences and relying upon the future, is the price they pay for plurality and reality, for the joy of inhabiting together with others a world whose reality is guaranteed for each by the presence of all' (Arendt 1998, 244).

the philosopher does not free a human being from the weight of the past (it is no accident that the fragment discussed was entitled *The heaviest weight*), nor does it invite them to live in the moment, regardless of what was and what will be. Doing so would be synonymous with adopting the very nihilism which Nietzsche strove to overcome. It is not about lifting the weight of time from our shoulders but rather teaching us how to regard it as light (NF-1876,16[7]).[277] The innocence which he proposes, therefore, depends on accepting every moment of our lives as a necessary element of who we are. Every moment hinges all other moments; humans are suspended in time not only bearing their past but also their future. In the idea of eternal recurrence, Nietzsche magnifies infinitely the weight of time, making every human life on earth their eternal life (NF-1881,11[183]).

Just as Christian forgiveness which annuls the past requires love stemming from God, the idea of the eternal recurrence of the same requires love rooted in the will to power (NF-1884,25[493]), a complete affirmation of our fate (*amor fati*). A test of our self-love and our ability to affirm our existnece is precisely the thought experiment from which the Nietzschean categorical imperative may be derrived: *act as if your had to live the same life an infinite number of times and that your every action were to repeat in perpetuity* (NF-1881,11[163]). This imperative is connected with the creation of our own values and ourselves (FW-335), as I have discussed, that is self-determination and self-responsibility. Following Simmel's interpretation, the categorical imperative stemming from an individual life may be framed by the following three questions:

a) 'Can you desire that you exist at all?';
b) 'Can you desire that a world, in which you exist, exist at all?';
c) 'Can you desire that a world in which you exist should exist infinitely often?' (Simmel 2010, 129).[278]

Adopting the idea that the Nietzschean imperative presented above is an ethical one often arouses objections. One of them is the concern regarding the possibility of adopting individual ethics, since ethics is a field of action which has meaning in relation to other people. Ethics concerns our relations with other people although this does not exclude the idea that the criteria for our actions are dependent on

277 This is confirmed by the Nietzschean motto, '[d]o not make life light but take it lightly' (Nietzsche 1999 (trans. A. Shaw), vol. 8, 288). Elsewhere we can read '[i]f one takes the hump from the hunchback, then one takes his spirit too' (Za-II-*Erloesung*, Nietzsche 2006a, 109).

278 *Amor fati* is expressed in the idea that one should be the person that one wants to be for all eternity (Buczyńska-Garewicz 2013).

the internal relations of a person with oneself, as Arendt claims (Arendt 2003). Morality is not just concerned about care for others but, above all, care for oneself. Both the Christian message of love and the imperative of Kant 'all take as their standard the Self and hence the intercourse of man with himself', as Arendt argues. 'In our context it does not matter whether the standard is self-love as in the Hebrew Christian precepts or the fear of self-contempt as in Kant' (Arendt 2003, 76). One may interpret the thought of Nietzsche in a similar manner yet I should emphasise that in both the thought experiment and the imperative of the eternal recurrence, Nietzsche is concerned with the *immoral* sense of life. As a result, I think it is more appropriate to refer to this interpretation as the existential or the ethical-existential.[279] The affirmative relation postulated here depends on the will to power and love which are categories beyond good and evil (JGB-153).[280]

Mauthner writes about the practically valueless nature of the eternal recurrence, accusing Nietzsche of contradicting himself when he tried to replace the Kantian imperative with that of his own, since the idea of eternal recurrence and its influence on human behaviour cancel each other out (Mauthner 1923, entry 'apokatastasis').[281] In order to accept the idea that eternal recurrence may influence our behaviour, we must assume that our behaviour can change and therefore that things can happen in a different manner, thus rejecting in the process the very idea of the eternal recurrence. However, by adopting the idea of the eternal recurrence we assume that everything that we do and will be doing has already happened an infinite number of times and will continue to recur, and reject the possibility that this idea may influence our actions which are subject to repetition. The typical response to this argument is that the notion of the eternal recurrence is only a hypothesis but one which is so shocking that it has the force to change the internal makeup of a person to the same extent that salvation and redemption have had for thousands of years (NF-1881,11[203]), despite the seeming impasse in consolidating the notions of free will and grace.

---

279 Here I am concerned with ethics broadly understood, as concerned with the idea of a flourishing life and not only an ethics concerned with moral judgements and their justification.

280 'Whatever is done out of love takes place beyond good and evil' (Nietzsche 2002, 70).

281 A similar argument can be found in Löwith's work, who argued that 'wherever he tries to develop his doctrine rationally, it breaks asunder in two irreconcilable pieces: in a presentation of eternal recurrence as an objective fact, to be demonstrated by physics and mathematics, and in a quite different presentation of it as a subjective hypothesis, to be demonstrated by its ethical consequences' (Löwith 1957, 222).

It is worth stressing here that Nietzsche regards the teaching of the eternal recurrence as the emphasis of life (NF-1881,11[141]), translated above as weight or burden (Ger. *Schwergewicht*). It has, however, a more subtle meaning – it is a point of reference to our way of living and thinking, which gives them weight and, at the same time, maintains them in balance. As Heidegger argues:

> A burden hinders vacillation, renders calm and steadfast, draws all forces to itself; gathers them and gives them definition. A burden also exerts a downward pull, compelling us constantly to hold ourselves erect; but it also embodies the danger that we will fall down, and stay down. In this way the burden is an obstacle that demands constant 'hurdling,' constant surmounting. However, a burden creates no new forces, while it does alter the direction of their motion, thus creating for whatever force is available new laws of motion. (Heidegger 1991a, vol. 2, 21–22).

For Nietzsche, Christianity placed the emphasis of life beyond existence – in the resurrection of Jesus (A-43; A-42). For St Augustine, the weight, described as a force of gravity, was love rooted in God and directing towards life, giving it sense – gravitating towards that which attracts us, that which we love.[282] Nietzsche finds the world beyond life as a Platon's lie and the resurrection of Jesus as a fabrication made by St Paul's, concluding from it that since the weight was placed in nothingness, life was robbed of its weight. An effect of this is the current state of weightlessness that we find ourselves after we killed our instincts and denied of ourselves (adopting an impersonal morality), we are in void and no longer gravitating towards anything (EH-M-2; EH-*Schicksal*-7). Nietzsche attempts to move the weight back to life itself. 'The thought of eternal return is to be a burden – that is, is to be determinative – for our envelopment within beings as a whole', as Heidegger comments (Heidegger 1991a, vol. 2, 21–22). One should recall here that an inappropriate burden may be dangerous and drag us down – it ma y become a weight which is too great to bear, a 'spirit of gravity' (Za-III-*Gesicht*-2). In the above cited fragment, the thought of the eternal recurrence is deliberately described as coming from a demon reminiscent of Silenus, the companion of Dionysus who was mentioned in the third chapter.

Thought about the eternal recurrence, which is elusive, has to have the power (and Nietzsche compares it sometimes to *violence*) to transform people. Nietzsche

282 After St Paul, St Augustine regarded love as the force of gravity which leads to God, as he writes in the Platonic spirit, '[a] body by its weight tends to move towards its proper place. (…) My weight is my love. Wherever I am carried my love is carrying me. By your gift we are set on fire and carried upwards: we grow red hot and ascend. We climb "the ascents in our heart" (…) and sing "the song of the steps"' (Augustine 1998, 694). Cf. Weil 2002.

neither means purely mental speculations nor a theoretical argument but rather a thought which is an expression of the deepest feelings and is strong enough to take control. This type of powerful thought (*mächitger Gedanke*), this thought above thoughts, was for him the one which concerned God (NF-1881,11[199]; MAII,WS-80), although at the same time he believed that the idea of God was harmful as it was opposed to what was human (NF-1888,16[26]; Za-II-*Inseln*). God had become the weight for the world, everything around God became the world (JGB-150) – meaning that God is the idea which orders the world, which gives it sense, direction and a structure of values. It is no accident that the idea of eternal recurrence appeared for the first time in *The Gay Science* alongside the announcement of the teachings of Zarathustra in paragraphs §341, §342, which directly follow paragraph §343 concerning the 'death of God' (Löwith 1987). The idea of the eternal recurrence is Nietzsche's answer to the 'death of God'. 'Nietzsche did not hesitate to say what great Christian teachers had always argued: the universe deserted by God is an absurd universe', although, as Kołakowski accurately notes, Nietzsche claimed that it was something that had to be borne with dignity (Kołakowski 2001, 200).

Nietzsche sees the world as chaos, and this thought is not supposed to supply order to this chaos but rather to raise it to even greater heights in its power. It is a thought which is both *heroic and tragic* since everything around heroes becomes a tragedy, as Nietzsche writes (JGB-150), greeting the coming of Zarathustra in *The Gay Science* with the words *incipit tragoedia* (FW-342 – this comes straight after the presentation of the notion of the eternal recurrence). The paradox of finding the weight for life is that it turns back against the one who finds it. The words of Kafka provide an excellent match for the figure of Zarathustra:

> He found the Archimedean point, but then used it against himself; it seems that he was permitted to find it only under this condition (Kafka in Arendt 1998, 248).

III. The metaphysical interpretation of the idea of the eternal recurrence

While the notion of the eternal recurrence appears in *The Gay Science* as a thought experiment utilised to form an imperative, in *Thus Spoke Zarathustra* it becomes a metaphysical 'truth' – an interpretation of the world intended to serve life (Löwith 1987; Löwith 1957). In the words of Zarathustra, Nietzsche presents the idea of the eternal recurrence, saying in his prophetic language that he had uncovered the deepest secret of existence. It is worth exploring this secret further by outlining the broader context of the considerations of the philosopher.

1. Unhistorical, historical and suprahistorical consciousness

Thinking about the eternal recurrence is for Mauthner an old wives' tale which, thanks to Nietzsche, found its way into the philosophical lexicon where it does not belong (Mauthner 1923, entry 'apokatastasis'). Nietzsche, a classical philologist and Hellenist, knew the myth of the eternal recurrence and knew what philosophers had written about it, from Heraclitus (the idea of the cyclical conflagration of the world and its renewal, Heraclitus B 30–31), Empedocles (the eternal cycle of the creation and destruction of the cosmos), Anaximander (the birth and return of all great things to *apeiron*), Plato (the spiral movement of The Same, Plato 2008, V, 37d-39d), the Stoics, the Pythagoreans (the repetition of existence by all of its entities), or the Neo-Pythagoreans.[283] Nietzsche, fully aware of his antecedents, emphasises that his idea is *completely new*, and clearly rejects all other ideas of the eternal recurrence as doomed to serve theological and spiritualistic thinking which he wanted to free himself from (NF-1888,14[188]). In order to better understand the innovative nature of the thought of Nietzsche, let us first confront it with the apparently similar ontological conceptions which arose in answer to the problem of time and its passing.

As Buczyńska-Garewicz accurately notes, Nietzsche belongs among the great philosophers of time (Buczyńska-Garewicz 2013),[284] and the problem of the relation of a human being to its own historicity became one of his prime considerations. In a publication entitled *On the Uses and Disadvantages of History for Life*, Nietzsche presents his distinction between three types of consciousness: 1) unhistorical; 2) historical; 3) suprahistorical (Nietzsche 2007c, 60–67), which may be helpful in elucidating his idea of eternal recurrence.

The *unhistorical sense* (timeless) of living concerns animals which thanks to the ability to forget can 'dissolve in the present', and be 'happy' in contrast to human beings, who carry with them the burden of the past and continually think of the future, haunted by longing and uncertainty (HL-1).[285] The Biblical Fall

283 On the subject of the diverse accounts of the eternal recurrence in philosophy see: Eliade 1959; Mauthner 1923, entry 'apokatastasis'; Löwith 1987; Borges 1964. In modern philosophy, the following wrote about the eternal recurrence: D. Hume, J.S. Mill, B. Russel, J.G. Fichte, and most seriously F.W.J. Schelling.

284 Nietzsche was certainly a great inspiration in this regard to philosophers such as Heidegger, Dilthey, Bergson and many others, placing the problem of the temporal human nature at the heart of their thought.

285 'Consider the cattle, grazing as they pass you by: they do not know what is meant by yesterday or today, (...) fettered to the moment and its pleasure or displeasure, and thus neither melancholy nor bored. This is a hard sight for man to see; for, though he

symbolises, in the opinion of many philosophers including Cioran, the fall of man into time (Cioran 1970). In result of the fall, human beings irretrievably lost their innocence, as Hegel notes, which left them only with 'a nostalgia for the lost paradise of animality' (Hegel in Eliade 1959, 91). Perhaps it was precisely this longing which lay at the heart of the archaic vision of the world, whose collective memory was based on myths which were able to *negate* time. In accordance with the definition proposed by the German historian Barthold Georg Niebuhr, whom Nietzsche cites (HL-1), by myth one should understand 'a symbolical representation of non-historical truth' (Niebuhr in Lewis 2009, 71; cf. Snell 1953). In this respect, Miracea Eliade terms the traditional societies as *ahistorical.* He holds:

> [A]rchaic man (…) tends to set himself in opposition, by every means in his power, to history, regarded as a succession of events that are irreversible, unforeseeable, possessed of autonomous value (Eliade 1959, 95).

This brings to light one of the oldest cosmogonies of premodern societies, namely the idea of the renewal of time in the sequential cycles of nature which are characterised by the cosmic rhythm of growth and decay. This was characteristic of farming societies, hence the frequent references to the phases of the moon. It was believed that together with the cycles of nature, time itself was also renewed, freeing human beings from their past, creating a 'new era' in which everything had a completely new beginning and the universe was returned to the harmony it enjoyed before creation.[286] 'The renewal of time' was accompanied by diverse fertility rites, rituals and sacrifices (see Kerényi 1997). Myths concerning the cyclical destruction of humanity often featured a flood (also present in the Old Testament) or conflagration (in Heraclitus, for instance) and presented a vision wherein humankind was constantly beset by cataclysms. They are variations of the

---

thinks himself better than the animals because he is human, he cannot help envying them their happiness – what they have, a life neither bored nor painful, is precisely what he wants, yet he cannot have it because he refuses to be like an animal. (…) But he also wonders at himself, that he cannot learn to forget but clings relentlessly to the past: however far and fast he may run, this chain runs with him. And it is a matter for wonder: a moment, now here and then gone, nothing before it came, again nothing after it has gone, nonetheless returns as a ghost and disturbs the peace of a later moment. (…) [A]nd envies the animal, who at once forgets and for whom every moment really dies, sinks back into night and fog and is extinguished for ever. (…) Man, on the other hand, braces himself against the great and ever greater pressure of what is past: (…) it encumbers his steps as a dark, invisible burden' (Nietzsche 2007c, 60–61).

286 'Life cannot be restored but only re-created through repetition of the cosmogony' (Eliade 1959, 81).

myth of eternal recurrence which guarantees the ontological unity and stability of the world – the eternally recurring world turns out to be stuck in eternity instead of moving.[287] This myth is closely related to the non-linear conception of time in which its cyclical nature annuls irreversibility.

Another archaic ontology contained the idea of annulling secular time with mythical time, which references archetypes, ideals and paradigms existing beyond the scope of secular time. By imitating heavenly archetypes, one was able to repeat the divine act of creation and the 'transformation of chaos into cosmos', participating in the *sacrum* (Eliade 1959, 10). Everything which was under necessity of becoming and transformation existed in secular time and was regarded as insignificant. The acts of repetition were accompanied by rituals, often expressed through dancing, and heroic actions. Through the repetition of gestures symbolising the wrong done, repentance was duly expressed.[288]

Nietzsche longed for the ability to 'sink down on the threshold of the moment' (HL-2), to have the power to be in the present, to experience a pure joy of the moment which is best exemplified by children lost in play (cf. Safranski 2007).[289] Nietzsche's thought, however, is not based on any of these archaic ontological conceptions. He not only rejects the non-historical position based on archetypes (idealism) but also the archaic idea of the cyclical renewal of the world. The Nietzschean thought on the eternal recurrence is *affirmative* with regards to time, it does not seek to negate it; furthermore it is a radically individual thought – it implies the eternal recurrence of the same being, together with the exact repetition of the exact same life of an individual, not the cyclical renewal of an impersonal life. In other words, it stems from historical consciousness.

Historical consciousness is connected with the attainment of the complete consciousness which distinguishes a human being from the rest of the natural world. In the natural world there is no such thing as birth and death as we understand it, as Arendt claims, the natural world is repeatable and in this sense immortal (Arendt 1998). The birth and death of human beings are not ordinary natural processes for us since they concern unique and unrepeatable individual

287 The idea of the eternal recurrence of the world, which constantly shots from chaos to order, was also originally considered by David Hume. In his analysis of various systems of cosmogony, he invokes a revised by himself Epicurean hypothesis which drives him to the conclusion, that '[t]his is commonly, and I believe justly, esteemed the most absurd system that has yet been proposed' (Hume 2002, 113).

288 It was thought that guilt was not annulled by punishment but only by a repetition which gave a consciousness of guilt (Calasso 1994).

289 Rüdiger Safranski claims that play was the foundation of being for Nietzsche.

lives. People not only have a biological life (*zoé*), but also a life understood in the socio-historical sense (*bios*), thanks to which it can be claimed that they have their own biography (Arendt 1998; Arendt 1961). In this manner, from the repeating process of birth and death in nature emerges something radically singular, fragile, something with its own beginning and end – human life, placed in an endless, soulless, passing universe. As Arendt notes, '[i]n the beginning of Western history the distinction between the mortality of men and the immortality of nature (…) was the tacit assumption of historiography' (Arendt 1961, 43).

Historical consciousness, characteristic of modern times, reached its maturity in the Judaeo-Christian tradition which rejected the heaven of archetypes and overcame myths. The idea of cyclicality of nature was replaced with the opposite idea of the eternal existence in relation to God-the Creator, which has been described in Ecclesiastes.[290] The conception of cyclical time was replaced with that of linear time – going in one direction only, having its beginning and end in God and stretched between the timeless abyss of nothingness and eternity. In this tradition, history underwent a re-evaluation both in general terms and in individual ones through eschatology – God manifested himself in history and religious experience gained a new dimension. The term 'apocatastasis' (from the Greek term *apokatastasis* and Latin *restitutio*) signifying a complete renewal, and used also in the aforementioned archaic idea of the recurrence of the same, obtains a new meaning in the framework of the New Testament in terms of the Resurrection.[291] Through teachings on salvation, a human being and an individual human life obtained a unique value and time obtained its own unique sense (Ro 6,9; 1Pe 3,18). The revolutionary nature of the Christian approach lays in that immortality

290 As we can read in the Bible the following:

> *One* generation passeth away, and *another* generation cometh: but the earth abideth for ever.
> The sun also ariseth, and the sun goeth down, and hasteth to his place where he arose. The wind goeth toward the south, and turneth about unto the north; it whirleth about continually, and the wind returneth again according to his circuits. (…)
> The thing that hath been, it *is that* which shall be; and that which is done *is* that which shall be done: and *there is* no new *thing* under the sun. (…)
> *That which is* crooked cannot be made straight: and that which is wanting cannot be numbered. (…) [W]hatsoever God doeth, it shall be for ever: nothing can be put to it, nor any thing taken from it (…).
> That which hath been is now; and that which is to be hath already been; and God requireth that which is past (Ecc 1,4–15; Ecc 3,14–15).

291 The idea of apocatastasis (the time of renewal of all things) appears in the Acts of the Apostles (Ac 3,21), and was developed further by such Christian thinkers as Origen.

no longer refers to human species or the cycle of life but to the human soul (see Arendt 1961).[292]

St Augustine devoted considerable space and attention to refuting the idea of eternal recurrence in Book XII of his *opus magnum*, *The City of God*, which may bear witness to the strength of this particular myth and its influence over antiquity (Augustine 2000, XII, Ch.11–20). He focuses on two variants of the myth of time as a circle – the first held that twilight was returning and time would be reborn with the same things appearing as if new (thus repetitions only seem to be the same), whilst the second concerned the repetition of everything in exactly the same way (in a similar vein to Nietzsche). St Augustine regards such thoughts as the work of 'deceiving and deceived sages' and adds, 'far be it, I say, from us to believe it' (Augustine 2000, XII, Ch.13, 1219–1220). He appeals in his argumentation to the idea of the existence of the eternal being – God, who has no beginning, no end and who gave a beginning and end to humanity which was created in time.[293] St Augustine writes:

> Even though reason could not refute, faith would smile at these argumentations, with which the godless endeavour to turn our simple piety from the right way, that we may walk with them 'in a circle' (Augustine 2000, XII, Ch.17, 1235).

He also appeals to the idea of salvation, arguing that the awareness of future happiness in heaven is enough to help bear the pain and suffering of this world, whilst a soul which had known the highest pleasure would not be able bear the thought that it would return to the old misery.[294] The idea of the eternal recurrence assumes the existence of eternal unhappiness and suffering, cyclically interspersed with phases of false since only temporary happiness. In turn, the idea of salvation

---

292 This was beautifully put by Rainer Maria Rilke in his poem entitled *Die Zeit vertreiben* (available online), in particular in the last strophes:

> Berge ruhn, von Sternen überprächtigt; –
> aber auch in ihnen flimmert Zeit.
> Ach, in meinem wilden Herzen nächtigt
> obdachlos die Unvergänglichkeit.

293 In St Augustine's opinion, God preceded time in the ontological sense, not the temporal (Augustine 1998).

294 'Who, I say, can listen to such things? Who can accept or suffer them to be spoken? Were they true, it were not only more prudent to keep silence regarding them, but even (…) it were the part of wisdom not to know them. For if in the future world we shall not remember these things, and by this oblivion be blessed, why should we now increase our misery, already burdensome enough, by the knowledge of them?' (Augustine 2000, XII, Ch.20, 1245).

assumes the freedom of the human soul which is able to free itself from its despair, and in which, because of this, something radically new and unique occurs.

The notion of breaking free from the repetitive nature of time by an act of human will can also be found in the religions of the East, such as Buddhism (the negation of will) and Hinduism (the rejection of karma). Both of these cases are not as much concerned with history as the glorification of God's plan, but rather with an escape from history into a position which Nietzsche defines as *suprahistorical*. Suprahistorical consciousness requires finding happiness and eternity in a single moment which contains the entire human experience and in which the world appears in every particular moment as something which is complete and ready.

We can also find the suprahistorical position in Marcus Aurelius, who repeats the Stoic idea of the cyclical nature of time and the everlasting recurrence, maintaining that one may overcome the sense of the absurd of the cyclical existence by realising that we only live in this particular moment and it is only the present which we may lose; we may not lose what is to come or what has been and thus the everlasting recurrence cannot take anything from us or bring anything back (Aurelius 2006).

The idea of the cyclical nature of time and its overcoming through the suprahistorical position can also be found in Schopenhauer (Schopenhauer 2010). Nietzsche was undoubtedly in his debt but he eventually managed to overcome the spiritual master of his youth.[295] Schopenhauer was heavily influenced by the religions of the East from which he adopted many ideas to Western modern philosophy. We can read in his work the following:

> We can compare time to an endlessly spinning circle: the half that is always sinking would be the past, the half that is always rising would be the future; but on top, the indivisible point that touches the tangent would be the extensionless present: as the tangent does not roll with the circle (…). Or: time is like an unstoppable stream, and the present is like the rock that it breaks on but does not carry away (Schopenhauer 2010, §54, 306).

For Schopenhauer, the present is the only form of reality. Hence, he also accepts the idea that the essence of the world as a whole may be philosophically

295 As Shestov accurately describes, the greatest intellectual enemies of Nietzsche were the masters of his youth, including Schopenhauer; the idea of independent thought which consumed Nietzsche, required a radical separation from his former inspirations (Shestov 1969). A similar approach was expressed by Gombrowicz who says, '[d]on't I have to distinguish myself from current European thought? Aren't my enemies the currents and doctrines to which I am similar? I have to attack them in order to force myself into contradistinction and I have to force you to confirm it' (Gombrowicz 2012, 43).

experienced in the present moment, which exists eternally and invariably.[296] He holds that even though expressions of will are temporal and changing, the will is something in itself and is thus timeless. At the same time, he finds consolation to the transience of human life in the eternal 'procession of Nature' – which implies the transience of individuals but the permanence of the species.

In the abovementioned treatise, Nietzsche also poses the thesis that one needs history to live and that *history should serve life*; history is compared to a horizon in which a human beings lives (HL-1). The suprahistorical position is rejected since it threatens humanity with complete stagnation and a deprivation of the drive to live and create (HL-1).[297] It does not mean, however, that the historical position serves life in itself. Nietzsche regards Hegelian historicism as a particularly harmful form of historical consciousness. He regards the definition of history as 'God's sojourn on earth' as a joke since it is History that creates God in this philosophy, and not the opposite (HL-8). He sees in the philosophical belief in history the reason for the delay in overcoming Christian consciousness and remaining in God's shadow. Post-Enlightenment historicism is after all a secular form of historical consciousness which was built on the foundations of the Judaeo-Christian tradition. It borrowed from the latter the linear notion of time, the ideas of progress, the end and the sense of history.[298] The fundamental difference is that the bearer of sense

---

296 'Whereas history teaches us that at each time something different has been, philosophy endeavours to assist us to the insight that at all times exactly the same was, is, and will be. In truth, the essence of human life, as of nature everywhere, exists complete in every present time, and therefore requires only depth of comprehension in order to be exhaustively known. (…) History shows on every side only the same thing under different forms; but he who does not recognize such a thing in one or a few forms, will hardly attain to a knowledge of it by running through all the forms. The chapters of the history of nations are at bottom different only through the names and dates; the really essential content is everywhere the same. (…) [I]n spite of all these endless changes and their chaos and confusion, we yet always have before us only the same, identical, unchangeable essence, acting in the same way today as it did yesterday and always (…). The true philosophy of history (…) should see everywhere the same humanity, in spite of all difference in the special circumstances, in costume and customs' (Schopenhauer 1958, XXXVIII, 441–444).

297 According to Cioran, the suprahistorical approach means 'falling out of time' (Cioran 1970, 181). As Nietzsche adds, 'we will gladly acknowledge that the suprahistorical outlook possesses more wisdom than we do, provided we can only be sure that we possess more life' (Nietzsche 2007c, 66).

298 Belief in limitless progress was announced by Leibniz, but became dominant during the Enlightenment and popularised in the 19th century (Eliade 1959). See also: Voegelin 1975; Löwith 1957; Cioran 1970. Nietzsche criticised the European myth of progress

becomes humanity and not the individual person. In as much as Christianity assumed the existence of the sense and spiritual destiny of every human, secular history can only really have sense for humanity as a whole and not individuals. Besides, sense concerns the entire history which is never available to individuals. The Hegelian variant returns the transcendental aspect to history, assuming that the Universal Spirit is at work within it; human beings are only extras in the progress of history and the world is their stage. In Marx's conception, history is once again stripped of its transcendental sense and becomes the stage for class struggle which creates history; the role of the individual does not change, however, remaining the material in this conception (a human beings instead of being the 'salt of the earth' becomes its fertilizer, Löwith1957).

As Eliade aptly warns, historicism leads to the 'terror of history',[299] and this is why such philosophical conceptions could only arise in countries which had never truly experienced terror and certainly not in Eastern Europe with its 'fatality of history'.[300] History, which Schopenhauer defined as 'the long, heavy, and confused dream of mankind' (Schopenhauer 1958, XXXVIII, 443) might pose a greater threat to humanity than the controllable nature. Thus, the opposition to

(AC-4), especially the idea that the measures of progress were things like democracy or liberal values (NF-1887,11[413]). He also criticised moral progress (GD-*Streifzuege*-37). The world is not goal oriented and thus one cannot talk of any kind of progress in the world; it would only have sense when we agree that there is an objective by which we can gauge its progress (FW-360). The idea of 'the end of history', identified with the triumph of liberal democracy in the world, was revived and popularised by the contemporary political philosopher Francis Fukuyama (Fukuyama 1989). As Ortega y Gasset insightfully writes, this idea is based on an assumption that the world is finally as it should be, that it has attained a full, definite height, 'it is thought that the end of a journey has been reached, a long-felt desire obtained, a hope completely fulfilled. This is "the plenitude of the time," the full ripening of historic life. (…) But we are now beginning to realise that these centuries, so self-satisfied, so perfectly rounded-off, are dead within. (…) When a period has satisfied its desires, its ideal, this means that it desires nothing more; that the wells of desire have been dried up. That is to say, our famous plenitude is in reality a coming to an end' (Ortega y Gasset 1950, 21).

299 'Only such freedom (…) is able to defend modern man from the terror of history – a freedom, that is, which has its source and finds its guaranty and support in God. Every other modern freedom (…) is powerless to justify history; and this, for every man who is sincere with himself, is equivalent to the terror of history' (Eliade 1959, 161).

300 Eliade names as examples the nations of the Baltic countries, the Balkans, or colonial territories, claiming that they were all marked by the 'fatality of history' (Eliade 1959, 152). In this context particularly interesting is Nietzsche's opinion that, '[w]e Germans are Hegelians even had there been no Hegel' (FW-357, Nietzsche 2001, 218).

nature gave birth to the supranatural position and also led to attempts to revive the unhistorical approach (as evidenced by the rehabilitation of the idea of the cyclicality in history and sociology, particularly visible in the work of Spengler, Toynbee and Sorokin, see Eliade 1959).

One of the strongest modern phenomena which expresses its own kind of unhistorical consciousness is *scientism*. The religious explanations for the contingent nature of the world are often opposed to scientific ones. Whilst scientific accounts tend to undermine the question of the contingency of the world by trivialising the issue, Christian religion lends it strength through teaching on salvation, as Robert Spaemann argues (Spaemann 2009). Even though scientism arose in opposition to historicism, opposing the 'progress of History' with the 'progress of science' as Husserl notes (Husserl 1992 (trans. A. Shaw), 17), both of them stemmed from the same root. Both lines of thought are, as Kołakowski notes, the descendants of the Enlightenment which had dethroned God the Creator, giving sense to human existence and affairs but deriving different consequences from the 'death of God' (Kołakowski 2005). Historicism places History in God's place as the judge of human existence, seeking within it the true sense of existence. Scientism substitutes God with the predictable Nature and its immutable laws thus giving the illusion of certainty. As Shestov summarises:

> Science does not state, it judges. It does not reflect truth, it creates it according to the autonomous laws which it has itself created. In other words, science is life set before the tribunal of reason (Shestov 1932, 32).

Secularisation depends to a large extent on the separation of science from religion; this had already been explored by Grotius, who wrote that 'even God cannot cause two times two not to make four' (Grotius in Arendt 1961, 70). It was connected with the discovery of immanent sense in nature, which occasionally led to natural laws being treated as a form of dogma. This was opposed by Dostoevsky, who wrote about the insolence of 'two plus two equals four' (Dostoyevsky 2006, 39), and Nietzsche, who felt that the laws of nature were only interpretations, as we have already seen.

Nietzsche regards all three types of consciousness as *prejudices* and values them depending on the extent to which they foster life or restrain it. Historicity as an occidental prejudice can make that humanity never stagnates but constantly moves forward – it desires the future which brings radical change and sees the sense of existence being revealed in the historical process (HL-1). Unhistorical consciousness, however, which Nietzsche sees as a more primal and fundamental ability of experiencing, fosters life and narrows the historical horizon to the extent necessary to permit freedom of action. Thanks to this, 'the historical people' may act and think in an unhistorical manner without being aware of the fact. Nietzsche uses here the analogy of a person in love, whose horizons are so narrowed that one cannot see the world beyond the beloved (or the idea of them) and thus feels their existence even more strongly and is willing to devote more to them than others. In other words, Nietzsche regards the historical and the unhistorical as of equal importance for the health of an individual, a nation and a culture (HL-1). He also considers the unhistorical and suprahistorical positions as *poisonous,* mistakenly used as remedies for the sickness of historical excess that humankind was suffering from at his time (HL-10). Nietzsche does not want to reject historical consciousness, but rather to make it serve life instead of knowledge. History in the service of life must stand in the service of unhistorical power (HL-1).

The problem, however, lies in the fact that there is a radical dissonance between historical and unhistorical consciousness which cannot be overcome. Nietzsche highlights this impasse, citing in the publication mentioned above the idea of the eternal return of the same proposed by Pythagoreans (HL-2). They believed that with an identical alignment of stars determining human actions, everything on earth that had already happened would happen again down to the most minute detail and that this would happen for eternity due to the appearance of the same causes and effects. In this mechanistic view of the universe, the earth appears as a stage production in which Columbus discovers America time and time again, Brutus betrays Caesar, and Nietzsche, one should add, busts into tears at the sight of the suffering of a horse in Turin. The determinism of the Pythagoreans was irreconcilable with historical consciousness. If the historical consciousness does not accept that the world is created and given sense by God anymore then the only alternative to a mechanistic determinism would be the idea of the world as the result of 'a dice-game of chance and the future' (*Würfelspiele der Zukunft und des Zufalls*) which rules out the eternal return of the same (HL-2).[301] When Nietzsche discovered his own 'abysmal thought' about the eternal recurrence seven years after writing *Untimely Mediations*, the abovementioned contradiction between historical consciousness (the will to create – to form what is new) and the unhistorical (life deprived of the will) had not disappeared (Löwith 1987). Nietzsche attempts to bridge the gap between them with the idea of love.

301 Heraclitus CXXV, 'The fairest order in the world is a heap of random sweepings.' (Kahn 2001, 85).

2. The myth of the eternal recurrence and the Dionysian formula of existence: *amor fati*

The now and the past on earth (…) that is what is most unbearable to *me*. (…)
A seer, a willer, a creator, a future himself and a bridge to the future – and alas, at the same time a cripple at this bridge: all that is Zarathustra. (…)
And all my creating and striving amounts to this, that I create and piece together into one, what is now fragment and riddle and grisly accident.
And how could I bear to be a human being if mankind were not also creator and solver of riddles and redeemer of accident?
To redeem those who are the past and to recreate all 'it was' into 'thus I willed it!' – only that would I call redemption!
Will – thus the liberator and joy bringer is called; (…) the will itself is still a prisoner.
Willing liberates, but what is that called, which claps even the liberator in chains?
'It was': thus is called the will's gnashing of teeth and loneliest misery. Impotent against that which has been – it is an angry spectator of everything past.
The will cannot will backward; that it cannot break time and time's greed – that is the will's loneliest misery. (…)
This, yes this alone is *revenge* itself: the will's unwillingness toward time and time's 'it was.' (…)
And now cloud upon cloud rolled in over the spirit, until at last madness preached: 'Everything passes away, therefore everything deserves to pass away!
And this itself is justice, this law of time that it must devour its own children' – thus preached madness.
'All things are ordained ethically according to justice and punishment. Alas, where is redemption from the flux of things and from the punishment called existence?' Thus preached madness. (…)
'No deed can be annihilated; how could it be undone through punishment? This, this is what is eternal about the punishment called existence, that existence must also eternally be deed and guilt again!
Unless the will were to finally redeem itself and willing became not willing – '; but my brothers, you know this fable song of madness!
Away from these fable songs I steered you when I taught you: 'The will is a creator.'
All 'it was' is a fragment, a riddle, a grisly accident – until the creating will says to it: 'But I will it thus! I shall will it thus! (…)
Has the will already become its own redeemer and joy bringer? Has it unlearned the spirit of revenge and all gnashing of teeth?
And who taught it reconciliation with time, and what is higher than any reconciliation?
That will which is the will to power must will something higher than any reconciliation (Za-II-*Erloesung*, Nietzsche 2006a, 110–112).

A spirit like this who has *become free* stands in the middle of the world with a cheerful and trusting fatalism in the *belief* that only the individual is reprehensible, that everything is redeemed and affirmed in the whole – *he does not negate any more*… But a belief like this is the highest of all possible beliefs: I have christened it with the name *Dionysus* (GD-*Streizuege*-49, Nietzsche 2005b, 222–223).

Nietzsche expressed his admiration for the unhistorical consciousness of the Greeks most clearly in *The Birth of Tragedy*, highlighting the importance of the Dionysian mysteries for the development of culture (GT-23).[302] The triumph of the Apollonian spirit over the Dionysian one was interwoven with the irreversible process of the growing individualisation of a human being (GT-10) – a separation of the time-rooted individual from nature and social world which became even more pronounced by Christianity giving the people the gift of free will. The myth of the eternal recurrence can be seen as an attempt to restore unhistorical consciousness, from which the historical consciousness of a human beings could draw its vital juices. It is an expression of the challenge posed by the 'death of God' to everyone who 'still believes in the contemporary gospel of progress, a secularised form of Christian eschatology' as Löwith puts it (Löwith 1987 (trans. A. Shaw), 416–417), seeing Nietzsche as a representative of neo-paganism who desperately tried to 'translate Man back into nature' (Löwith 1957, 222; JGB-230; FW-109).[303] The neo-paganism of Nietzsche did not rest on a desire to restore paganism but rather the creation of a new form of paganism based around the belief in the *Übermensch*. One may better understand this thought by comparing the human nature to a palimpsest, where each subsequent layer contains the former.

It is worth to consider here the role that myths played in antiquity. They primarily served to express, through images and symbols, things which escaped expression in linguistic terms. They did not have an instructional character (the moral aspects were secondary or did not appear in them at all) but rather sought to visualise certain events and behaviours together with their consequences, serving to foster self-reflection and knowledge of the self, having the ability to 'illuminate the fate and reveal the nature of the man' (Snell 1953, 318). In this manner 'the

---

302 '[L]ike art, the state also plunged into this current of timelessness in order to find respite there from the burden and greed of the moment. And a people – or, for that matter, a human being – only has value to the extent that it is able to put the stamp of the eternal on its experiences; for in doing so it sheds, one might say, its worldliness and reveals its unconscious, inner conviction that time is relative and that the true meaning of life is metaphysical. The opposite of this occurs when a people begins to understand itself historically and to demolish the metaphysical buttresses surrounding it; this is usually accompanied by a decided growth in worldliness and a break with the unconscious metaphysics of its previous existence, with all the ethical consequences this entails' (Nietzsche 2007b, 110).

303 A similar dream was expressed by Hölderlin, who wrote that humans fall from Nature like rotten fruits from a tree, and hoped, '[o] tree of life, that I may grow green again' (Hölderlin 1990, 133).

Greeks discovered the human intellect – by reading it into the myths' (Snell 1953, 206), as Snell discerned, writing further:

> [Myth] differs from empirical reality in that it furnishes, along with the facts, also their deeper meaning. The later enlightenment argued that the meaning which emerges from an event is a matter of human interpretation; but in [the myth] this meaning asserts itself as a valid, a divine component of the tale (Snell 1953, 207).

Myths arose from the same need for a deep structure for reality as metaphysics. When some philosophers, such as Empedocles, moved from poetry to philosophy their shift in thinking led to the development of a rational, logical process of explaining of the world which was opposed to the mythical manner of thinking and which in time extinguished it.[304] This in turn led to the creation of science. Nietzsche valued the mythical and religious depiction above the philosophical and scientific ones because the first two were able to engage a human being in its entirety, simultaneously giving people transformational power – in them, the spirit is to be found. Furthermore, the mythic and religious accounts give a feeling of a general sense to things, not a fragmented truth uncovered by reason. In turn, for Nietzsche the mythic account has priority over the religious one since it is beyond moral, it is joyful, free and serves life to the fullest.

Many of the German poets which Nietzsche had been brought up on, such as Friedrich Schlegel for instance, argued for the necessity of creating a new mythology in order to renew European culture (Calasso 2002). In his first phase of activity, Nietzsche perhaps thought in a similar manner, believing in the rebirth of the spirit in music and also in the vitality of the Dionysian mythical consciousness

---

304 Nietzsche regarded Socratic philosophy as the reason for the rejection of the myth and weakening of the spirit, '[w]ithout myth, however, all cultures lose their healthy, creative, natural energy; only a horizon surrounded by myths encloses and unifies a cultural movement. (…) Now place beside this type of mythical culture abstract man, without guidance from myth, abstract education, abstract morality, abstract law, the abstract state; consider the rule-less wandering of artistic fantasy, unbridled by an indigenous myth; think of a culture which has no secure and sacred place of origin and which is condemned to exhaust every possibility and to seek meagre nourishment from all other cultures; that is the present, the result of Socratism's determination to destroy myth. Now mythless man stands there, surrounded by every past there has ever been, eternally hungry, scraping and digging in a search for roots, even if he has to dig for them in the most distant antiquities. The enormous historical need of dissatisfied modern culture, the accumulation of countless other cultures, the consuming desire for knowledge – what does all this point to, if not to the loss of myth, the loss of a mythical home, a mythical, maternal womb?' (GT-23, Nietzsche 2007b, 108–109).

in art. However, in his later works he discarded this dream, accepting that both the mythical and the religious consciousness were *dead* in his era (MAI-248).[305] Nietzsche used myths in a functional manner and his goal was a radical break with the metaphysics of the time. It is hard not to agree with Heidegger who claims that Nietzsche wanted to express something which was unimaginable (the eternal recurrence) leading Western metaphysics which had developed from questions about the beginning (*arche*) and the end (the ultimate goal) of existence, to an end (Heidegger 1967, 427). The idea of the eternal recurrence and the will to power led to an intellectual *cul de sac* 'toward which has moped the whole tradition of Western thought, but the beginning of which and the destiny of which was the asking by the Greeks about the being of beings: the metaphysical question' as Gadamer sums up (Gadamer 2003, 127). Cioran, accurately summarises this writing that 'a civilisation begins by myth and ends in doubt (...) it turns against itself, (...) it *organizes* its metaphysical shipwreck' (Cioran 1970, 76). Nietzsche, who so sorely felt the decadence and nihilism which beset European culture, wanted to give it the impetus needed for its rebirth, to return it once again to its origins and the 'infancy of God' (NF-1885,2[130]), destroying the foundations of the existing metaphysics in the process.[306]

The myth of the eternal recurrence utilised by Nietzsche reveals the above-mentioned aporia between the radical modern will to create and the atemporality of eternal recurrence which seems to annul the will. In historical consciousness, the will is powerless with regards to the past, as we can read above, but it does have the ability to shape the future. From this asymmetry between will and time arises the notion of guilt and punishment – contained by the fact that one cannot turn back time, the will bestows upon us feelings of guilt and the desire for punishment for what has not been done. If we accept that everything which has happened did so an infinite number of times and will do so again in the future, then the will becomes just as powerless towards the future as it is towards the past. The way out of the 'punishment for existence' (as introduced with the theodicy of Anaximander discussed earlier) seems to lie in the Stoic position whereby willing changes into not willing and leads in turn to the disappearance of will. Nietzsche

305 '[W]e *cannot* go back to the old, we *have* burned our boats; all that remains is to be bold, regardless of what may result. – Let us simply *step forward*, let us simply move on!' (Nietzsche 2000, 169).

306 This metaphysical conception recalls the fabric of Penelope, 'humanity will have to begin weaving its tapestry all over again after having, like Penelope, destroyed it by night. But who can guarantee us that it will always find the strength for this once again?' (MAI-251, Nietzsche 2000, 172).

describes such a passive attitude as 'the fable song of madness', against which he announces his will to power. The disappearance of will is equated with the disappearance of life; the will to power is thus the active will, creative and growing powerfully, the highest level of which is love. This kind of will may not negate itself and thus its salvation from the slavery of time lies in the *complete affirmation of what has been and what will be.*

Since the will, as I have written, is for Nietzsche neither a means for making decisions nor the ability to initiate things and events but rather a battle of our drives, it means that our will for the future (the thought that we have an influence on it) is just an useful illusion which allows us to create. A similar useful illusion is the will of the past – recreating the 'it was' into 'thus I willed it' which frees us from feelings of revenge and pangs of conscience. The feelings directed towards the past, which we cannot change, have a reactive character, poisoning one in the process and leading to a loss in their powers. Revenge is understood here metaphysically as a negative spirit, as a lack of will towards 'what was' which leaves one with a sense of defeat (Heidegger 1967). The term redemption (*Erlösung*) applies to freeing from the 'punishment of existence' understood in the moral sense (the consciousness of evil both inflicted and suffered and which cannot later be undone), as well as from the fear of death. The will of the eternal recurrence is the highest reconciliation of the self, universe, time and our own necessity – all becoming becomes innocent when it ceases to be an expression of an obligation or will but simply exists for itself.

In *Untimely Meditations*, Nietzsche writes that everyone, if asked if they would like to relive the last ten or twenty years, would respond 'No!', albeit for different reasons (HL-1). Those people with a clear historical consciousness would be reluctant towards the idea of reliving the past since they hope that the future will bring something radically better. Those with a suprahistorical consciousness, and thus reluctant to face the future, would claim that nothing is to be gained from such a move since the entire existence can be reduced to a moment. Nietzsche rejects both approaches as reactionary towards time and proposes a positive affirmation of both the past and the future. A test of our self-love is the question of whether we want ourselves entirely – the desire to not only repeat the last twenty years but the desire to eternally repeat all the years of our lives. Particularly appropriate seems here Nietzsche's analogy between human life and a work of art which we want to experience repeatedly and entirely (NF-1881,11[165]). In his opinion, human life should be led in a way so that *each* of its parts would be desired repeatedly. To love oneself completely, as Cioran notes, 'is to want to lose nothing of what one is' (Cioran 1970, 139) and thus to love everything which has happened to us and not to want to take anything that had happened back (NF-1888,25[7]). Nietzsche underscores the fact that a lack of desire to accept our own existence stems from a faulty distinction between a person and a person's fate, which he termed Turkish fatalism (MAII,WS-61). Any attempt to fight one's fate is purely illusory since even in this battle, one is fulfilling one's destiny. Paraphrasing Kafka, one may say that in our struggle with life we should always side with life.[307]

The challenge of the eternal recurrence of the self may only be met by free spirits and higher people (the model for him is Goethe), full of internal riches and powerful enough to bear themselves and always joyfully respond to one's fate with a 'yes!' (EH-*Klug*-10). Such a conception of humanity is termed the Dionysian and its formula of existence revolves around *amor fati* (NF-1888,16[32]), the love of one's fate and an expression of love towards our own necessity (FW-276; NF-1881,15[20]). Nietzsche uncovers in this formulation the highest degree of internal development (which is connected with the third spiritual change discussed in the fourth chapter). Nietzsche's love is similar to Christian love in that it has a transformative character – it is the power to change a person and his or her world, to create them anew and embodies the existential *metanoia* (the equivalent of the Christian conversion, which leads to a change in the way the world is perceived).[308] Nietzsche terms *amor fati* to be his morality (NF-1881,15[20]), the final love (NF-1881,16[22]), the innermost nature (EH-WA-4), a formula for human greatness (EH-*Klug*-10).[309] Morality assumes affirming some aspects of existence in accordance with the herd mentality and negating or altering those aspects which are not in accordance with the spirit of the majority; higher people assume a Dionysian aspect of existence which is individual and beyond morality (NF-1888,16[32]).

The desire for delight comes naturally and easily to people but Nietzsche challenges us to do something much harder, to desire both pleasure and pain since

307 I refer to the famous quote by Kafka, 'Im Kampf zwischen dir und der Welt sekundiere der Welt' (Kafka 1970, 52).

308 *Metanoia* from the Greek *meta* (beyond – in this context in the sense of a 'change' or 'transformation') and *noein* (to think) from *nous* (mind) has a pre-Christian significance and relates to changes in thought or the spiritual transformations; in the Greek translation of the New Testament it attains an additional meaning: the rejection of sin and inner transformation, that is atonement and repentance (Mt 3,2). The Latin counterpart of *metanoia* is *conversio* (conversion), signifying a change in direction and rooted in the idea of complete change, of being 'born again' or a 'return to the source'; the phenomenon of conversion featured in antiquity in political, philosophical and religious contexts (Hadot 1999).

309 'My formula for human greatness is *amor fati*: that you do not want anything to be different, not forwards, not backwards, not for all eternity' (Nietzsche 2005b, 99).

they are indelibly marked in our fates. It is not enough to bear the weight of one's necessity, but also love it (EH-*Klug*-10), and this is what takes the greatest courage. Nietzsche's anthropodicy takes on its full meaning and significance in light of the doctrine of *amor fati*. Here we are concerned with the anthropodicy which is beyond the moral and whose fundamental question is the problem of the meaning of suffering, which the author of *The Genealogy of Morality* considers (GM-II-7; GM-III-15).

There are many strategies for dealing with suffering which mainly stem from seeking out its causes or the target of the suffering in order to understand it. Explaining suffering by finding its causes does not sooth suffering – in fact, the opposite is often true. Suffering may be soothed by punishing the person who inflicted the suffering, an example being the instinctive striking of inanimate objects which have caused us pain, like hitting the cupboard that we have just hit our head on, even though the cupboard cannot feel it or have meant to do so. When one is powerless to do anything about the cause of one's pain, one tends to punish the culprit in mind, holding the culprit morally responsible and, which is a symptom of the *ressentiment* discussed earlier. Revenge in every form is reactive and as such impoverishes the spirit. Another equally popular strategy for dealing with pain is teleological – seeking the purpose of pain (looking forward and not back). As Williams notes, the teleological sense of suffering may only help when it serves the objectives of the sufferer or when it has the right relationship with the objective which is an authority for the sufferer (Williams 2006). For Nietzsche, suffering and powerlessness are the main reasons why people created God and the idea of afterlife (Za-I-*Hinterweltler*; Za-II-*Priester*). In early religions, God is seen as cruel, rejoicing in the suffering of people (GM-II-7), whilst in Christianity, God does not want people to suffer; human suffering is not seen as something sensible in itself but rather a part of life which has sense as a whole. 'The extreme greatness of Christianity lies in the fact that it does not seek a supernatural remedy for suffering but a supernatural use for it', as Weil pointed out (Weil 2002, 81).

The complete innocence of existence hinges on the rejection of the thought that one should atone with suffering for one's sins. The crucifixion of Jesus for the salvation of humankind is a guiltless sacrifice which is intended to sanctify human existence; Nietzsche opposed the Crucified with Dionysus, whose vision of the world was holy (*selig*) enough to justify even the most terrible suffering (NF-1888,14[89]). The difference between the Christian and the tragic visions is not about the suffering itself but rather about its significance; from the Christian perspective, for Nietzsche, even the happiest of souls need to be sanctified by the suffering of Jesus, which is a damning indictment of being. The tragic person, however, is strong enough to love one's own pain. To do so, you need to delve into your own deepest pain (Za-III-*Wanderer*). In pain, Zarathustra uncovers the greatest depths of humankind (FW-*Vorrede*-3; Za-III-*Tanzlied*-3; Za-IV-*Nachtwandler*-7).[310] One may conquer pain, as Zarathustra argues, by affirming the eternal recurrence of life with all its pain and suffering (Za-III-*Seligkeit*), when we say 'yes' to life's pleasures and 'yes' to the pain (Za-IV-*Nachtwandler*-10). *Amor fati* should not be mistaken in Nietzsche's philosophy for an ambivalence towards suffering; it is not passive fatalism but rather a 'tragic gay science' (Shestov 1969, 212), which the creative power to will of higher people uses to overcome human being. It is 'an ability to see one's own life as a mysterious necessity of fate', as Buczyńska-Garewicz notes (Buczyńska-Garewicz 2010 (trans. A. Shaw), 184).

3. Subjectivity and the experience of time

A human beings as a being thrown into time, as Cioran writes, suffers from an excess of will and a shortage of existence and is thus 'that which is not' in contrast to God who 'is that which is' (Cioran 1970, 41; cf. Ex 3,14). In assuming the 'death of God', Nietzsche faces the problem of experiencing the self as an enduring 'I' in time, which can by accurately illustrated by the following fable of Kafka:

> He has two antagonists: the first presses him from behind, from the origin. The second blocks the road ahead. He gives battle to both. To be sure, the first supports him in his fight with the second (…) and in the same way the second supports him in his fight with the first (…). But it is only theoretically so. For it is not only the two antagonists who are there, but he himself as well, and who really knows his intentions? His dream, though, is that some time in an unguarded moment (…) he will jump out of the lighting line and be promoted, on account of his experience in lighting, to the position of empire over his antagonists in their fight with each other (Kafka in Arendt 1961, 7).[311]

Nietzsche emphasises that in order to have the power to live and act, one needs both the power of memory and the ability to forget (HL-1). Without the power to forget, the life of people would be impossible – if human beings were to remember every moment of the becoming of the world then all of them would dissipate in

---

310 Dostoevsky wrote in a similar vein that suffering is the source of consciousness and thus one may also take pleasure from it, as I have discussed in the fourth chapter. It is undoubtedly Greek tragedy that we have to thank for the discovery that suffering may be the deepest form of knowledge – a way of experiencing oneself and one's own existence.

311 The story by Kafka is entitled *ER* [*HE*] and was published in *Aufzeichnungen aus dem Jahre 1920*, I quote after Arendt, in translation from the German by W. and E. Muir with some correction made by Arendt.

the process of becoming and they would cease to believe in their own existence.[312] A human being deprived of the ability to remember, 'chained to the wheel of the moment', is something animal-like, could become happy being free of time but unable to create something new, which is only possible in time.

In order to understand this problem better, it is worth considering the two basic experiences of time identified by Ingarden (Ingarden 1983). The first type of experience is the consciousness of the passing of time which is seen as something derivative with respect to our consciousness, having no significant impact on our identity, which seems in turn to be something enduring and representing the foundation of our fleeting existence. Time is thus understood as being like rain, flowing over us as if we were statues of bronze. On the basis of this experience it is possible to bend one's past and future to one's will. Such an experience of the subject is immune to the idea of the cyclical nature of time, as indicated by Bertrand Russell:

> The hypothesis that history is cyclic can be expressed as follows: form the group of all qualities contemporaneous with a given quality; in certain cases the whole of this group precedes itself. Or: in these cases, every group of simultaneous qualities, however large, precedes itself. Such an hypothesis cannot be regarded as logically impossible so long as we say that only qualities occur. To make it impossible, we should have to suppose a momentary subject of qualities, and to hold that this subject owes its identity, not to its character, but to its space-time position (Russell 2005, 102).

The second, very different, experience of time is one in which it reveals its destructive force, where it has the power to change us as well as the world around us. In this experience our 'I' is constituted by experience which has a temporal character. We grasp, as Ingarden writes, 'the fragility of all actual being' and 'we discover the possibility of non-existence', which fills us with awe (Ingarden 1983, 38). The 'I', melting in time, becomes an illusion that it is necessary for survival. In this experience of constant transformation, time itself becomes destroyed if

312 The problem of a man who remembers too much as a result of a brain defect which grants him perfect recall is presented in the story by Jorge Luisa Borges entitled *Fuenes the Memorious* (Borges 1964). The author gives him the ironic title of 'precursor of the superman' and 'a vernacular and rustic Zarathustra'; his memory is like a rubbish bin, he remembers all details, he sees all changes and with difficulty is able to recognise himself in the mirror. He is incapable of abstraction and generalisations – he cannot understand that the term 'dog' may be used to describe different dogs but is also unable to derive the notion of 'dog' from one seen at a particular moment in time; as Borges argues, Fuenes was unable to think since 'to think is to forget differences, generalize, make abstractions' (Borges 1964, 66).

we accept that the past and the future cease to exist as they meet in the present, that they go from nothingness to nothingness. St Augustine devoted considerable attention to this issue.[313] Here the problem of the subjectivisation of time appears, in which time is dependent upon consciousness. It is also connected with the difficulty of grasping the nature of the world and our own unity. As a result, in Neo-Platonism and medieval philosophy there arose 'an intuition that existence in itself is never able to identify with itself, it is not what it is and this is due to its temporal nature' which in turn leads to the assumption of the existence of a timeless, self-identifying Being (God), in relation to whom a human being retains its unity and the world endures (Kołakowski 1988). People have had an 'obsession with the real' since time immemorial, desiring the certainty that there is a timeless, whole truth and which may only be satisfied by the Absolute (Kołakowski 1988; Eliade 1959).

A fundamental problem confronted by Nietzsche after the 'death of God' was how to answer the question of how to assuage this desire for reality and maintain the sense of *unity of the self as a whole* whilst experiencing the constant becoming and transformations it entailed. The feeling of unity is an essential condition of becoming (Buczyńska-Garewicz 2010).[314] When the limits of our 'I' are placed in time and fixed by our consciousness as a unitary whole, the transcendence of our lives becomes possible wherein we constantly transcend the present in both directions – the past and the future. The 'fragmentation' of 'colour-splattered ones' was for him the characteristic trait of the 'last men', who did not feel unity stemming from God, nature or collective identity but rather sank into nihilism and decadence (see Colli 1994; Buczyńska-Garewicz 2010).[315] Nietzsche needed the

313 In Book 11 of his *Confessions* one may read, '[t]ake the two tenses, past and future. How can they "be" when the past is not now and present and the future is not yet present? (…) If then, in order to be time at all, the present is so made that it passes into the past, how can we say that this present also "is"? The cause of its being is that it will cease to be. So indeed we cannot truly say that time exists except in the sense that it tends towards non-existence' (Augustine 1998, 584–585).

314 A similar idea, albeit rooted in a completely different axiological perspective, can be found in Ingarden, who also saw the unified identity of man, built in relation to time, as indispensable for development, for acting and accepting responsibility, 'I am a power which magnifies itself, develops, and outgrows itself – if it is able to collect itself rather than to become dispersed in tiny moments of suffering or submission to pleasure' (Ingarden 1983, 51).

315 The vision of a human being struck with awe by this passing, who constantly seeks to kill time but in doing so harms oneself (falling into time) is brilliantly expressed by Ingarden (Ingarden 1983).

idea of the eternal recurrence in order to root the illusionary 'I' in life itself and not in the metaphysical world. This was to be a guarantee of this, ungraspable in time, entirety which 'can manifest itself as the sheer continuity of the I-am, an enduring presence in the midst of the world's ever-changing transitoriness', as Arendt puts it (Arendt 1981b, 211). This was to teach humans to think *cosmically* or to go beyond the 'I' (egoism) without going in the direction of 'you' (altruism), just beyond any sense of 'me' and 'you' (NF-1881,11[7]). In other words, the idea was to be able to look at everything from beyond the human perspective (NF-1881,11[141]).

The beyond human timeless perspective, which may be seen as the view from eternity (*sub specie aeterni*), was accessible to the Ancient Greeks thanks to their myths (GT-23). This same perspective, when adopted by philosophers, led to the killing of reality – grasping something which is becoming leads to reducing it to beings and thus to its petrification (GD-*Vernunft*-1). Nietzsche often uses the verb 'believe' in relation to the idea of the eternal recurrence, where 'believe' means 'to maintain that something is true' (*für-wahr-halten*); it is also the first intellectual action, 'saying yes' to words which translated into images develop into notions (NF-1884,25[168]). If we understand as 'true' the idea of 'enduring in time' then we uncover the notion of the eternal recurrence as an expression of the heroic will to endure complete becoming, which Nietzsche regards as the highest justice, the function of the will to power (NF-1884,26[149]).

The question then arises as to whether the idea of the eternal recurrence is not an attempt to reduce the process of becoming into being, closing it in a circle. It would then be a form of pantheism, with God identified as a vicious circle (*circulus vitiosus deus*), in which being obtains the greatest importance (JGB-56), and becomes a 'ring of rings' (Za-III-*Siegel*). In his considerations of the essence of religion, Nietzsche himself asks the question of whether the desire to return oneself and the world is not a *cry directed to God* which exists through the existence of the world and in which he is contained (JGB-56). For Heidegger, Nietzsche did not rule out the possibility of the existence of God beyond good and evil, with the 'death of God' only being meant in a moral sense (NF-1886,5[71]).[316] I think, however, that the form of the question used by Nietzsche in his deliberation of this problem indicates that it was more of a thought experiment in which he wanted

316 Heidegger recalled an example from the life of Nietzsche in his high school days, when he admitted to having tried to find the fixed point of being and attempted to fix it in its entirety (Heidegger 1991a). Nietzsche himself admitted that his idea of eternal recurrence contained more in itself than all religions (NF-1881,11[159]); he added that this idea should be a religion for the freest spirits, joyful and haughty (NF-1881,11[339]).

to show the limits of his own thought. In his opinion, the intellectual greatness to which he aspired required overcoming the longing for eternity and the absolute, and this was possible only through loving their opposites, that which endures the least – constant change and the temporal nature of existence (NF-1880,7[212]).

Rejecting the Faustian opposition between eternity (that which does not pass) and change (that which passes), Nietzsche proposes a synthesis of the two which is affirmed by constant becoming and change. He remains a true disciple of Heraclitus, who rejected unity in permanent being and rather favoured the doctrine of the unity of opposites as revealed in the process of constant change (Jaeger 1948).[317] In other words, '[e]ternal recurrence is the most constant permanentizing of the unstable' as Heidegger sums up (Heidegger 1991b, vol. 3, 212).

Nietzsche understands the highest function of the will to power as being the ability 'to imprint the character of being' (*des Seins*) upon becoming (*dem Werden*) – the myth of eternal recurrence became the 'apogee of considerations', since in its most extreme form it brings the world of becoming to the world of being (NF-1886,7[54], Nietzsche 2006b, 138). On the basis of his conception, becoming may not stem from either being or nothingness (NF-1888,14[188]; cf. FW-109). He recognises that the world exists without a beginning or an end, constantly becoming and changing, even though it never started to become and it will never stop. This world lives 'in itself', it is its own becoming and change, it is reminiscent of a snake devouring its tail. For Nietzsche, it is particularly tempting to experience his individual existence in the same manner as he experienced the existence of the universe – as a self-turning wheel (Za-I-*Schaffender*). His thought seems therefore close to the confession of Hölderlin:

> ...I feel a life in me which no god created and no mortal begot. I believe that our existence is from ourselves and that it is only of our own free pleasure that we are so intimately connected with all that is (Hölderlin 1990, 117).

4. The Riddle of Zarathustra

The metaphor of the eternal recurrence belongs to those metaphors which one cannot express in non-metaphorical language. One metaphor leads to another: a ring, a circle, a wheel, a ball, a snake, a hourglass, a whirlwind, a gateway; there are also plays on opposites: weight – lightness, gnashing of teeth – laughing, dread – delight, sickness – health, entry – exit, summit – abyss etc. It is the main

317 'We represent perfection in mutability; we divide the great harmonies of joy into changing melodies', as Hölderlin points out (Hölderlin 1990, 123).

motif of *Thus Spoke Zarathustra.*[318] Its fullest expression can be found in the tale entitled *On the Vision and the Riddle*:

> 'Stop, dwarf!' I said. 'I – or you! But I am the stronger of us two – you do not know my abysmal thought [*meinen abgründlichen Gedanken*]! *That* – you could not bear!' (…)
> 'See this gateway, dwarf!' I continued. 'It has two faces. Two paths come together here; no one has yet walked them to the end.
> This long lane back: it lasts an eternity. And that long lane outward – that is another eternity.
> They contradict each other, these paths; they blatantly offend each other – and here at this gateway is where they come together. The name of the gateway is inscribed at the top: 'Moment' [*Augenblick*].
> But whoever were to walk one of them further – and ever further and ever on: do you believe, dwarf, that these paths contradict each other eternally?' –
> 'All that is straight lies,' murmured the dwarf contemptuously. 'All truth is crooked, time itself is a circle.'
> 'You spirit of gravity!' I said, angrily. 'Do not make it too easy on yourself! Or I shall leave you crouching here where you crouch, lamefoot – and I bore you *this high*!
> See this moment!' I continued. 'From this gateway Moment a long eternal lane stretches *backward*: behind us lies an eternity.
> Must not whatever *can* already have passed this way before? Must not whatever *can* happen, already have happened, been done, passed by before?
> And if everything has already been here before, what do you think of this moment, dwarf? Must this gateway too not already – have been here?
> And are not all things firmly knotted together in such a way that this moment draws after it *all* things to come? Therefore – itself as well?
> For, whatever *can* run, even in this long lane *outward* – *must* run it once more! –
> And this slow spider that creeps in the moonlight, and this moonlight itself, and I and you in the gateway whispering together, whispering of eternal things – must not all of us have been here before?
> – And return and run in that other lane, outward, before us, in this long, eerie lane – must we not return eternally? –' (…)
> And truly, I saw something the like of which I had never seen before. A young shepherd I saw; writhing, choking, twitching, his face distorted, with a thick black snake hanging from his mouth.
> Had I ever seen so much nausea and pale dread in one face? Surely he must have fallen asleep? Then the snake crawled into his throat – where it bit down firmly.

318 The most important parables which feature the idea of the eternal recurrence are: *On Redemption* (part II), *On the Vision and the Riddle* (part III); *The Convalescent* (part III); the culmination of these considerations appears in the form of the hymn of praise in the parable which was originally intended to close the whole book and entitled *The Seven Seals (Or the Yes and Amen Song)* (part III).

> My hand tore at the snake and tore – in vain! It could not tear the snake from his throat. Then it cried out of me: 'Bite down! Bite down!
> Bite off the head! Bite down!' – Thus it cried out of me, my dread, my hatred, my nausea, my pity, all my good and bad cried out of me with one shout. –
> You bold ones around me! You searchers, researchers and whoever among you ever shipped out with cunning sails onto unexplored seas! You riddle-happy ones!
> Now guess me this riddle that I saw back then, now interpret me this vision of the loneliest one!
> For it was a vision and a foreseeing: *what* did I see then as a parable? (…)
> – Meanwhile the shepherd bit down as my shout advised him; he bit with a good bite! Far away he spat the head of the snake – and he leaped to his feet. –
> No longer shepherd, no longer human – a transformed, illuminated, *laughing* being!
> Never yet on earth had I heard a human being laugh as *he* laughed!
> Oh my brothers, I heard a laughter that was no human laughter – and now a thirst gnaws at me, a longing that will never be still. (Za-III-*Gesicht*-2, Nietzsche 2006a, 125–127).

The parable of the conversation between Zarathustra and the dwarf at the gateway as well as that of the shepherd with a snake in his throat are both full of symbolism and have been widely commented upon (see Heidegger 1991a; Löwith 1997). Zarathustra, sailing on board a ship, tells the sailors who love danger (symbolising the 'free spirits') a riddle of his own. As suggested by the author, instead of trying to solve (*lösen*) the riddle, it is better to release it (*erlösen*), just as one releases monsters so they can be transformed into 'heavenly children' (Za-II-*Erhabene*). The problems can be solved but each solution is its own defeat. The riddle (*Rätsel*), on the other hand, is guessed (*raten, rathen* – which also means to advise, to counsel), and the answer is also a mystery, with a new riddle moving the problem to a higher level (cf. Calasso 1994; Heidegger 1991a).[319] Nietzsche teaching on the eternal recurrence through Zarathustra, resembles a Delphic oracle who 'neither declares, nor conceals, but gives a sign' (Heraclitus XXXIII in Kahn 2001, 43). It is in accordance with his assumption that truly deep thinker arouses in us feelings and emotions (WA-*Brief*-6)[320] thus stirring us towards independent thought.

The confrontation with the dwarf takes place in front of a gate bearing the name *Augenblick*, which may be translated as 'moment' and literally means 'in a twinkling of an eye'. This metaphor, with its reference to sight, is helpful in understanding the problem of time. When we look, we never see the individual elements which comprise the picture but we see the picture as a whole immediately, just as

319 As Heidegger puts it, '[b]ut the teacher knows that what he teaches remains a vision and an enigma' (Heidegger 1967, 435).

320 '"Anyone who knocks us over is strong; anyone who lifts us up is divine; anyone who gives us vague presentiments is profound."' (Nietzsche 2005b, 243).

we do not experience time in particular moments but as a certain continuity. The gate-moment is a point to which two opposing paths run to, one leading to the past and the other to the future. The dwarf claims that time is a circle and thus the two paths which lead to eternity do not collide but rather join together, becoming one path. The response of the dwarf is reminiscent of the pessimistic philosophy of Schopenhauer, whose suprahistorical position negating time Nietzsche wants to overcome.[321] Zarathustra thus leaves the dwarf where they met – beneath the gate, on the threshold of a moment.[322] It is no accident that the dwarf is called lamefoot, devil or spirit of gravity who poisons us within, falsifying our image and hindering our development (Za-III-*Geist*). Just like the demon from fragment 342 of *The Gay Science* who brings news of the 'greatest weight', he is a counterpart of Silenus who was pursued by Midas in order to learn the truth of existence. When the king finally caught him, he learnt something that would be better to not know: that human life is meaningless and full of suffering and thus it would be better if he had never existed (GT-3), as it was discussed in the third chapter.

The spirit of gravity warns Zarathustra that he will die from his thoughts, most probably from his 'abysmal thought' about the eternal recurrence since he has gone too far not to have to fall. Here the image of the abyss emerges (Ger. *Abgrund*), that is the existential situation in which one finds oneself when the deconstruction of metaphysics has gone so far that it has surpassed any point of support. Zarathustra is sick from staring into its depths (Za-III-*Gesicht*-1; JGB-146), but he does not want to treat his ailment with pessimism and the abdication of will, which the dwarf seems to advocate. He also rejects the comforting old song of the cyclical nature of time which he hears from his animals (Za-III-*Gensende*-2).[323] He

321 Both the idea of the will to power and the eternal recurrence were inspired by the philosophy of Schopenhauer and, at the same time, were in opposition to it. Instead of Schopenhauer's negation of will, Nietzsche proposes an affirmation of it and, at the same time, an affirmation of becoming instead of the terrible thought of the 'eternal moment'. Whilst Schopenhauer's pessimistic philosophy of the negation of life owes much to the rooting of Hindu ideas in European philosophy, Nietzsche's affirmative revelations owe much to Chinese thought, as Albert Schweitzer suggests. Taken to extremes, both philosophies lead to the absurd since 'the ethical consists neither of life-negation nor of life-affirmation, but is a mysterious combination of the two' (Schweitzer 1987, 249).

322 The eternal present is the Devil's time as Cioran writes, it turns round and round, means sterility and impotence (Cioran 1970).

323 'Everything goes, everything comes back; the wheel of being rolls eternally. Everything dies, everything blossoms again, the year of being runs eternally. Everything breaks, everything is joined anew; the same house of being builds itself eternally. Everything parts, everything greets itself again; the ring of being remains loyal to itself eternally.

laughs at their words which are, for him, 'illusory bridges between things eternally separated' (*Schein-Brücken zwischen Ewig-Geschiedenem*).

Within it there is a reference to a sphere whose centre is everywhere, a famous claim ascribed to Empedocles and often featured in medieval works in order to explain the unity of being (Jaeger 1948). This metaphor is also utilised by Pascal, in considering the problem of a man who 'suspended between two gulfs of the infinity and the void', being 'a mid-point between nothing and everything (…), [is] incapable of seeing the nothingness from where he came, and the infinite in which he is covered', and therefore finds appearances satisfying (Pascal 1999, 230, 67). 'The whole of the visible world is merely an imperceptible speck in nature's ample bosom, no idea comes near to it'; this infinity is called by him an ' infinite sphere, whose centre is everywhere and its circumference nowhere' (Pascal 1999, 230, 66).[324]

Zarathustra experiences this suspension between two infinities but it is not seen as providing a concept of the unity of being, which is associated with a lack of movement, but rather unity in mutability, as it was already mentioned. In the three following stories which conclude the third part, Zarathustra responds to the old lullaby of the animals with his own hymns which come from his newly furnished soul. They are: *On Great Longing*, where he talks with his spirit, *The Other Dance Song*, which is a love song to life and *The Seven Seals (Or the Yes and Amen Song)*, in which he expresses his love for eternity, desiring the eternal recurrence.

The exact teaching on the eternal recurrence which is envisaged by Zarathustra and a riddle for the free spirits is not to be found in the words of the dwarf or of the animals but in the parable of Zarathustra's about the shepherd with a snake in his throat. The metaphor of the shepherd may be seen as an ironic allusion to the Gospels which present Jesus as a shepherd (Mk 6,34; Mk 14,26; J 10,1–21; Mt 26,31). One may also read a connection to Arcadia, as described by Virgil, in which spiritual shepherds live and write poetry.[325] The symbolism of the snake is equally rich – it is a symbol of wisdom (as one of Zarathustra's animals) and also the Christian symbol of sin, or the pagan symbol of rebirth and change (because

---

In every Instant being begins; around every Here rolls the ball There. The middle is everywhere. Crooked is the path of eternity' (Nietzsche 2006a, 175).

324 This idea of an infinite sphere was frequently used in relation to God during the Middle Ages as a metaphor for his perfect unity.

325 For a Classical philologist like Nietzsche, the world of symbols was certainly important in which 'the currents of myth and empirical reality flow one into another', creating 'this half-way land' which 'is neither mythical nor empirical', as Snell writes (Snell 1953, 283).

of its ability to change its skin). Zarathustra admits that he had been the same shepherd himself and that the monster (Ger. *Unthier*) which choked him was knowledge and humankind (Za-III-*Genesende*-2). Zarathustra admits that the thing that terrifies him most about the eternal recurrence is the eternal return of the small human beings alongside the great. He regards a human beings as a synthesis of non-animal and super-animal (NF-1887,9[154]); his liberation from his disgust towards humanity gives him the awareness that desiring what is 'best' in humans is actually longing for what is the worst. Small humans are indispensable in order for great ones to arise and that which is the worst is the greatest source of strength for the greatest creators. The shepherd frees himself from choking on the snake by biting off its head, which changes him and restores him to joy. The severed head of the snake may also symbolise the moment, as Nietzsche observes in his notes (NF-1888,14[188]). By adopting the idea of the circular nature of time, the road to infinity (forward or back) ceases to have significance and the head and the tail of the snake may be confused with one another. Biting off and spitting out the head may symbolise rejecting the desire for eternity contained in the moment as a symbol of perfect and complete being.

The 'abysmal thought' appears here as the highest challenge which may only be met by higher people, the over-rich souls whose love and joy for life is so great that they will be in a position to love even the greatest suffering and despair in life. It is a Dionysian thought, one which is being experienced, as Heidegger notes (Heidegger 1967).[326] In Cioran's words, one may regard the idea of the eternal recurrence as 'a deceiver on a metaphysical level' (Cioran 1970, 176), which was knowingly set in motion by Nietzsche in order to allow humans to overcome their temporal nature. In the parable of *The Slow Death* at the end of the first part, before Zarathustra leaves his friends and listeners for the first time, he throws them a golden ball, calling on them to play the 'holy game' which requires touching the ball and, at the same time, passing it on so that no one holds it in their hands (cf. Lewis 2009).[327] The ball thrown by Zarathustra is his teaching which is intended

326 It obviously causes pain when Zarathustra begins to think about the eternal recurrence (*züchtigt damit*, NF-1883,10[47]).

327 This calls to mind the verses of an untitled poem by Rainer Maria Rilke, a fragment of which Hans-Georg Gadamer used as a motto for his *opus magnum* on hermeneutics (the work entitled *Truth and Method,* Gadamer 1986):

> Catch only what you've thrown yourself, all is
> mere skill and little gain;
> but when you're suddenly the catcher of a ball
> thrown by an eternal partner

to awaken feelings and move its listeners but which must be defeated in order to proceed down the path ahead.

In the Preface to the second edition of *The Gay Science*, which was added after all of the parts of *Thus Spoke Zarathustra* had been completed, Nietzsche warned that the book was an announcement of 'something utterly wicked and mischievous', which could be summarized as '*incipit parodia*' (FW-*Vorrede*-1, Nietzsche 2001, 4). If *Thus Spoke Zarathustra* is a parody of the Gospels, then the idea of the eternal recurrence is a parody of the myth, which may be indicated by the 'inhuman laughter' of the shepherd in the relevant parable of Zarathustra. Through laughter he tried to go beyond himself (Za-IV-*Mensch*-20) and it was through laughter, instead of anger, that he taught to kill (Za-IV-*Eselfest*-1). Nietzsche, as Gadamer notes, was:

> [A] self-conscious parodist. The text of Zarathustra is a long sequence of manifold parodies. Parody is what we understand as a mode of speech that takes up some prior formulations and then transforms them, often in unusual directions, often to distort them ironically. In any case parodist speech does not speak directly but relies on playing around the sense of prior formulation (Gadamer 2003, 126).

It is wrong to identify Nietzsche with Zarathustra, the hero of his dramatized work. Gadamer, in his close hermeneutic reading of the work, shows that it is a drama which tells of the *failure* of Zarathustra as a teacher of the eternal recurrence and the *Übermensch*, as shown by the narration and dialogues of Zarathustra with himself and his animals (Gadamer 2003). We learn through these dialogues that Zarathustra was not ripe for his fruits (Za-II-*Stunde*); that he suffered a collapse as a result of the teaching he announced (Za-III-*Genesende*); that he lacked sufficient faith in his life and that he fundamentally did not love himself enough (Za-III-*Tanzlied*-2); that his wisdom told him to stop talking and to start singing (Za-III-*Siegel*-7). Song seems to be the most appropriate medium for communicating the teachings of Zarathustra, when we take into account Carnap's famous remark that metaphysics chose the wrong form of expression and that instead of philosophical tracts philosophers should be writing poems and symphonies (Copleston 1975).[328] The fourth part, which Nietzsche had originally not planned and which came about somewhat later (it was published privately, only for a narrow circle of the initiated), is the culmina-

---

with accurate and measured swing
towards you, to your center, in an arch
from the great bridgebuilding of God:
why catching then becomes a power –
not yours, a world's (Rilke in Gadamer 2013, v).

328 On the other hand, without poetry there would never be philosophers (Hölderlin 1990). On the significance of song in Nietzsche's philosophy see Jaspers 1979.

tion of the disaster of Zarathustra – the teacher who had undergone the last temptation which was 'pity for the higher men' (Za-IV-*Zeichen*) only to discover that the 'higher men' were not his companions, that they did not completely understand him and rather wanted to use him to create their own religion (Za-IV-*Eselfest*). The failure of Zarathustra seems to indicate that the Promethean atheism of the will to power has only a destructive force and leads to idolatry of the will.[329] We can also read how Zarathustra speaks differently to his listeners and in yet another manner to himself (Za-II-*Erloesung*), which allows to make the conclusion that not everything about the eternal recurrence has been revealed.

It should therefore be borne in mind that the teachings of Zarathustra on the eternal recurrence should not be taken literally. They seem to be correctly interpreted by the protagonists of the work by Stanisław Brzozowski – a group of tuberculosis patients who, gathered together by accident in a southern sanatorium at the beginning of the 20th century, engage in philosophical discussions, as their insight becomes particularly sharpened by the closeness of death:

> I'm talking about the eternal recurrence. Taken as a metaphysical idea, existential, is strangely infertile; in this sense, it is even unseemly to Nietzsche's philosophy since his whole philosophy rules out any such metaphysics. It seems that this idea had a strong psychological influence on Nietzsche's thought and with its aid he was able to rid his work of every vestige of transcendentalism, of all kinds of explanation beyond existence, of justifications, of coming to any final judgements, of any kind of eschatology. (…) No such explanation will ever be: because everything will end and everything will be the same and in spite of this I want there to be a powerful and beautiful life, to be there a human.
> Can I endure this idea about an eternal, absurd recurrence and still want to live, despite it all? This is the thunderclap with which this thought, this idea of eternal recurrence, crashed Zarathustra. Here a human being just must love oneself, a human being, and life with its pain and pleasures, with everything, the whole life as it is… (Brzozowski 2012 (trans. A. Shaw), 43–44).

As Frederick Copleston summarises:

> The eternal recurrence involves the conclusion that there is no given meaning or 'sense' in the Universe. It cannot explain itself and it cannot *ex hypothesi* be explained by anything outside itself: it is a fact which we must accept, renouncing all hope of explanation (Copleston 1975, 208–209).

---

329 Perhaps Nietzsche sensed the same disaster in his own work which does not disqualify him as a philosopher since 'a modern philosopher who has never experienced the feeling of being a charlatan is such a shallow mind that his work is probably not worth reading' (Kołakowski 1988, 1).

Nietzsche does not find a sense which would replace God, he does not seek solace nor does he fall into despair, he simply and heroically stands and confronts the greatest existential fear, taking it to the extreme. This fear is well captured by the words of Macbeth:

> ...Life's but a walking Shadow, a poor player,
> That struts and frets his hour upon the stage,
> And then is heard no more. It is a tale
> Told by an Idiot, full of sound and fury
> Signifying nothing... (Shakespeare 1999, 229).

In Nietzsche's understanding, the meaningless 'tale of the idiot' does not pass forever, but, what is worse, it endures, eternalised by the will to power.[330] Since the world is completely contingent, which should not be trivialized, he proposes to strengthen this thought, by making the contingent world eternally returning in its contingency. The notion of contingency signifies that everything that exists will pass. Nietzsche adds to this that it will not only come to pass once but will do so eternally. Repeatability becomes the mark of necessity (Calasso 1994). In this respect Nietzsche writes that the idea of eternal recurrence, which assumes the nothingness ('senselessness') of the universe as something eternal to be the most extreme form of nihilism (NF-1886,5[71](6)). In Nietzsche, European nihilism obtained its full consciousness, as Camus notes, it is, however, hard to find in him its conqueror at the same time (Camus 1980; cf. Copleston 1975).

IV. The mystical interpretation of the eternal recurrence

At the end of these considerations it is worth to mention that the above parable has been named the 'vision of the loneliest one' (Za-III-*Gesicht*); the formerly discussed thought was also described as stolen into our 'loneliest loneliness' (FW-341). These terms show the personal character of the 'abysmal thought', which leads to the last interpretation of the eternal recurrence that I would like to present. In order to introduce it, it is worth to return to the moment when the thought of the eternal recurrence in its mature form came to Nietzsche – everything came from a revelation (*Offenbarung*), which he experienced during a trip to the lake of Silvaplana, next to the cliffs of Surlej during his stay in the Alps, in August 1881. He was staying in Sils Maria in Upper Engadine, where he often spent his summers and the event was recorded in both his notes and poems:

330 '"Was *that* – life?" I want to say to death. "Well then! One More Time!"' (Za-IV-*Nachtwandler*-1, Nietzsche 2006a, 258).

The basic idea of the work, *the thought of eternal return [der Ewige-Wiederkunfts-Gedanke]*, the highest possible formulation of affirmation –, belongs to August of the year 1881: it was thrown onto paper with the title '6,000 feet beyond people and time'. That day I went through the woods to the lake of Silvaplana; I stopped near Surlei by a huge, pyramidal boulder. That is where this thought came to me. (EH-ZA-1, Nietzsche 2005b, 123).

Sils-Maria

There sat I, waiting, waiting, – yet for naught,
transcending good and evil, sometimes caught
in light, sometimes caught in shadow, all game,
all sea, all midday, all time without aim.
At once then, my friend! One turned into Two –
– and Zarathustra strode into my view… (FW-*Lieder*-13, Nietzsche 2001, 258).

Rattling with diction and dice I outwit the solemn waiting ones; my will and purpose shall elude all these fierce watchers.

To prevent anyone from looking down into my ground and ultimate will, I invented my long bright silence (Za-III-*Oelberg*, Nietzsche 2006a, 139).

By 'revelation' Nietzsche understands an experience known to poets which stemmed from a deeply disturbing thought which continues to haunt us with remarkable clarity (EH-ZA-3).[331] The inspiration which struck Nietzsche concerned the image-figure that is the idea of the eternal recurrence. He did not just think of it but experienced it too, feeling its full cruelty and power which as a result transformed him. Comparing this experience of eternity with the mystical revelation seems justified (Za-IV-*Mittags*). As Buczyńska-Garewicz writes:

[T]he thought of the eternal recurrence is thus a mystical one, as is the intoxication of the midday; it is not theoretical knowledge of the world as much as an intuitive insight into life as a whole (Buczyńska-Garewicz 2013 (trans. A. Shaw), 117).

This recalls the idea of personal illumination in the sense of St Augustine, but with the fundamental difference being that Nietzsche did not feel the presence of God but rather something which would be the opposite of God – a closed, self-

331 'The idea of revelation in the sense of something suddenly becoming *visible* and audible with unspeakable assurance and subtlety, something that throws you down and leaves you deeply shaken – this simply describes the facts of the case. (…) [A] thought lights up in a flash, with necessity, without hesitation as to its form (…). All of this is involuntary to the highest degree, but takes place as if in a storm of feelings of freedom, of unrestricted activity, of power, of divinity… The most remarkable thing is the involuntary nature of the image, the metaphor; you do not know what an image, a metaphor, is any more, everything offers itself up as the closest, simplest, most fitting expression. (…) This is *my* experience of inspiration' (Nietzsche 2005b, 126–127).

sustaining world in which everything, in the tiniest of details, recurs eternally. He frequently emphasised how much this idea had shocked him and that it was for him the most terrifying (NF-1883,20[2]), the most abysmal (*abgründlicher*) thought (EH-*Weise*-3; Za-III-*Gesicht*-2) which he told his friends about only in a whisper (Overbeck 2008). The thought struck him with its necessity and clarity, remaining a mystery to all his friends. Nietzsche criticizes the approach of most philosophers who tried to reduce all the problems of the world to a single problem which could be solved like a Gordian knot (M-547). They approached the world as if it had been purposefully made for people to decode it, as if it had secret, hidden meanings which philosophers could uncover on their way to knowledge.

Nietzsche writes that for him philosophy is a form of confession (JGB-6) and at the same time concealing the most closely guarded truths, creating masks which cover the face (JGB-289). He regards his own thoughts as independent powers which have to be faced (MAI-351). Already in *Untimely Mediations* he highlights the problem of the temporal nature of a human being as one which unsettles him greatly (HL-*Vorrede*). He believes that expressing this nagging doubt in public is a way of avenging oneself upon it. He also adds that these feelings (whose shadows are thoughts FW-179) should be described in a botanical fashion by researching the soil from which they sprang.

The thought of the eternal recurrence thus tells us what the philosopher himself wanted to tell us about his internal fears and worries. If the practice of philosophy is a matter of temperament and if every philosopher, as Murdoch writes, uses it to erect 'a barrier, special to one's own personal fears' (Murdoch 2014, 71), then it means that Nietzsche was most frightened by the necessity for change and the contingent nature of humanity which, in the face of the loss of God, were deprived of a beginning, an end and any sense. He undoubtedly suffered and wanted to awaken a new bliss in himself what Hölderlin described in the following words:

> [A] new bliss rises in the heart when it perseveres and suffers through the midnight of anguish, and that like nightingale voices in the dark, the world's song of life first sounds divinely for us in deep affliction (Hölderlin 1990, 131).

Whether he succeeded or not, we will never know. We only know that in the face of his fears he tried to reach the essence of himself and in his depths he found the idea of *self-redemption*, as he himself records in his last notes (NF-1888,25[7]). It should be stressed that this is not a universal idea for the redemption for humanity but rather the thought that Nietzsche wanted to save himself from himself. Nietzsche through 'a methodical fall into the abyss', as Cioran puts it, 'has reached a deliverance, but a deliverance without salvation, prelude to the integral experience of vacuity' (Cioran 1970, 101 and 86). The discovery of the paradoxical idea of existence as the simultaneous admiration and affirmation of the senselessness of the universe is its own kind of faith which is preceded by despair and resignation; it is a faith in religious means albeit without God (cf. Kierkegaard 1983).

Taking into account the interpretative clues left by the author himself, one may indulge in the thesis that the thought of the eternal recurrence is a *personal thought-feeling of Nietzsche*. It would mean that he thought of it not to convince anyone else or to explain anything but rather to free himself of it. A careful reader of Zarathustra knows that the 'creator' follows his own way down which no other may follow. Thus, one should come to the conclusion that Nietzsche's thought was only his own personal, mystical revelation and not a universal metaphysical or cosmological truth. It is a unique thought which flows from the deepest depths of the philosopher, from his loneliness and his abyss. A bottomless abyss terrifies as it offers no point of support. On the other hand it is the deepest depth because it has no limits. In one of his earliest notebooks Nietzsche cites Hölderlin, '[t]hose who've thought most deeply love what's most alive' (NF-1873,29[202]).[332] If Nietzsche was driven by the message in these words then one may venture the notion that he reached into his own depths in order to love his life.

Nietzsche contemplated his abyss for so long that he became terrified with it finding monsters lurking in the depths of his soul (JGB-146).[333] When considering the internal monsters of Nietzsche, the thought springs to mind that his philosophical idea of the affirmation of life stands in stark contrast to his sickly life, full of suffering. In this respect, Shestov suggests that Nietzsche was 'a martyr in spite of himself', who 'would always say "Yes" with his lips but say "No" inwardly' and be proud of this (Shestov 1969, 245; cf. MAI-73). His love for life was in contrast to *ressentiment* since in his formulation, *amor fati* meant love for our pleasures as well as our pain; that which he admired and that which he despised. He termed this 'personal necessity' or 'personal providence' (FW-277), where even that which he fought against he regarded as necessary, including Christianity or German nationalism (NF-1888,25[7]).

A study of the notes and quotes of Nietzsche is too little to experience the thought of the eternal recurrence in the manner in which the author did in that summer of 1881. He himself repeats that '[y]ou will not have an ear for something

332 From a poem by Hölderlin entitled *Socrates and Alcibiades* (Hölderlin 2008, 33). The verse in original: *Wer das Tiefste gedacht, liebt das Lebendigste.*

333 'Whoever fights with monsters should see to it that he does not become one himself. And when you stare for a long time into an abyss [*Abgrund*], the abyss [*Abgrund*] stares back into you' (Nietzsche 2002, 69).

until experience has given you some headway into it' (EH-*Buecher*-1, Nietzsche 2005b, 101). Franz Kafka puts this particularly poetically in a letter to Oskar Pollak:

> We are as forlorn as children lost in the woods. When you stand in front of me and look at me, what do you know of the griefs that are in me and what do I know of yours. And if I were to cast myself down before you and weep and tell you, what more would you know about me than you know about Hell when someone tells you it is hot and dreadful? For that reason alone we human beings ought to stand before one another as reverently, as reflectively, as lovingly, as we would before the entrance to Hell (Kafka in Karl 1991, 98).[334]

Following the advice of Kafka, it would be necessary to show the greatest respect for Nietzsche's deepest thought whilst accepting that it will never be completely understood. Each interpretation of a thought stemming from internal depths of the philosopher will always be to a certain extent not fair enough to its author, as Colli aptly noted (Colli 1994).

Peregrination through these Nietzschean depths remind of Pushkin's anecdote about the depression of Chancellor Potemkin (Benjamin 1981). Since no one in the government was able to get him to sign important documents as he had locked himself in the Chancellor's chamber, the young, confident functionary Shuvalkin decided to do something about it. Attempting the impossible, he took the documents to Potemkin's office and left a few moments later with the signed act. However, when he presented them to the council members, consternation ensued as it transpired that on every document there was only a signature, written with the shaking hand of the Chancellor, which read – *Shuvalkin, Shuvalkin, Shuvalkin...*

334 A letter of Franz Kafka to Oskar Pollak of November 8, 1903 (Kafka 1958, 27).

Endings: Philosophical Don Juanism

Unsatiated like a flame
My glowing ember squanders me.
Light to all on which I seize,
Ashen everything I leave:
Flame am I most certainly!
Friedrich Nietzsche[335]

In one of his works Karl Jaspers distinguishes between three basic sources of philosophy: 1) *wonder* (that the world exists, that there exists something more than nothing); 2) *doubt* (in the idea that the world is at it appears to be); 3) *awareness of our own vulnerability and helplessness* (resulting from our experiences of the suffering, ending, conflict, accidental and temporary nature of existence) (Jaspers 1954). In the opinion of the philosopher, wonder gave birth to ontology, with being providing the entry point for philosophical considerations; doubt gave rise to epistemology, with consciousness (the thinking self) providing the impetus; while experience of human vulnerability introduced existential philosophy. The latter is a call for adopting an individual perspective on one's own existence and finds its rich expression in literature, with the best examples being the works of Franz Kafka, Fyodor Dostoyevsky and Albert Camus. The philosophy of Nietzsche, which was a radical attempt to overcome the traditional ontology and epistemology, draws its nourishing waters from the third source.

Dionysus is the key to the philosophy of Nietzsche, who began his philosophical career with an academic publication devoted to the myth of Dionysus (which enjoyed a lukewarm reception) and ended it by sending his professors and friends cards which, in the grip of madness, he had signed with the name Dionysus. It is not difficult to understand precisely why Nietzsche selected Dionysus as the patron of his new philosophy of becoming. Dionysus was 'the Lord of the Souls', uniting in himself the reality of man and god, constantly changing form; a god of contrasts and contradictions who contained within himself both ecstasy and horror, wildness and blessing, complete presence and distance, creation and destruction, vitality and death (Otto 1965). He was a crazed god whose madness reflecting the absurd nature of existence was passed on to humans. The fullness of life and the violence of death were present in Dionysus simultaneously; at the

---

335 From a poem entitled *Ecce Homo* in *'Joke, Cunning, and Revenge' Prelude in German Rhymes* included in *The Gay Science* (FW-*Vorspiel*-62, Nietzsche 2001, 23).

moments of the greatest vitality (love, procreation, birth), Dionysus experienced unavoidable suffering which is intertwined in the circle of existence with the pleasure of life. Even though Dionysus did not belong to the gods of Olympus, his cult has tremendous importance for any understanding of the Ancient Greek spirit, as Walter Otto emphasised (Otto 1965). In his opinion, it is deeply incorrect to look down upon the culture of antiquity and regard the Dionysian mysteries as a product of primitive, archaic belief – the Greeks knew more than us: thanks to Dionysia, they had looked into the depths of being, in birth they saw death and in creation, destruction. The Great Dionysia – festival founded in Athens by Pisistratus – lasted for six days, during which dithyrambs were sung, people danced and fell into an ecstatic madness, which was meant to allow Greeks to experience complete unity with the great oneness of creation (GT-5). Instead of experiencing the eternity of the individual life, the ancient cult colliding the Dionysian power of nature with the Apollonian delusion of individuals gave a feeling of *eternal vitality* which aroused the deepest creative forces in the human soul (MAII-VM-408).[336]

During the Dionysia, comedy and tragedy competitions were held. Tragedy was only regarded as good by Athenians when it contained a Dionysian element (Kerényi 1997). This did not mean that the content of the drama had to be connected to the myth of Dionysus but rather that it stimulated something which was regarded as the essence of tragedy – the feeling of terror that helped to cleanse and relieve the audience of suffering (*katharsis*). Tragedy destroyed the rationally constructed order, it disturbed the cohesive image of the world, allowed to understand 'the shadowy nothingness of human strength and human happiness' (Jaeger 1946, 284). In tragedies one was able to experience the fact that the man who 'has mastered the mysteries of language' and who 'has tamed, and made rational' a 'thought, which moves faster than the wind' (Sophocles 2012, 18), remains powerless when confronted with the absurdity and terror of existence. The Apollonian Greek might then feel that 'his entire existence, with all its beauty and moderation, rested on a hidden ground of suffering and knowledge which was exposed to his gaze once more by the Dionysian' (GT-4, Nietzsche 2007b, 27). Athenians did not only experience tragedy on the aesthetic level but also on the physical (GT-7), not only as silent witnesses to the events described but as their participants (GT-15).[337]

---

336 '[I]t is a matter of *eternal liveliness*: for what do "*eternal life*" and life in general matter!' (Nietzsche 2013, 144).

337 'Alas! The magic of these struggles is such, that he who sees them must also take part in them!', as Nietzsche points out (Nietzsche 2007b, 75).

Tragedy, as noted by Jaeger, is 'the highest manifestation of a type of humanity for which art, religion, and philosophy still form an indissoluble unity' (Jaeger 1946, 246). Nietzsche certainly wanted to see a similar mentality reborn, regarding it as an alternative to Christianity which could prevent the paralysing will of nihilism. He did not seek eternal salvation in philosophy, art or religion but rather an eternal desire which could feed the deepest longings of his soul and allow him to love life to its fullest extent and in accordance with the saying of Zarathustra: '"You will, you covet [*begehrst*], you love, and only therefore do you *praise* life!"' (Za-II-*Tanzlied,* Nietzsche 2006b, 84). The paradox of this desire, which one may call the desire for infinity, depends on the fact that the joy of existence contains within itself the pain of change (GT-17), as well as the consciousness of the absurdity of existence (Za-II-*Tanzlied*).[338] Shestov thus aptly describes the philosophy of Nietzsche as the philosophy of tragedy (Shestov 1969), which is unable to meet the ambition of reviving the Greek spirit and thus is transformed into a parody.

Nietzsche initially sought this revival of the highest passions of the soul in the music of Wagner, which made him tremble in both fear and delight. 'Yearning! Yearning! Dying, to yearn; for yearning not to die' – cries the hero of Wagner's opera *Tristan und Isolde* (GT-21, Nietzsche 2007b, 101), which Nietzsche regarded as a great metaphysical work, 'philosophizing in sound' (WB-8). He admired this metaphysical love for its amoral character (NF-1875,11[5]), that it represents the sublime impulse of madness to oppose the tyranny of social norms. He never found anyone 'as dangerously fascinating, with as weird and sweet an infinity' as Tristan, what led him to the conclusion that '[t]he world is an impoverished place for anyone who was never sick enough for this "hellish voluptuousness"' (EH-*Klug*-6, Nietzsche 2005b, 94), in which they experience suffering that 'pertains to the essence of things' (WB-8, Nietzsche 2007c, 231). Love-passion is the equivalent of the Dionysian ecstasy in which one goes beyond oneself. Nietzsche warned that metaphysics was turning against life (NF-1875,12[29]), and that its heroes were dead inside their living bodies (WB-8), since their desire for love had become a desire for suffering and death. For this reason they may not be imitated, as is the case with all philosophical passions rooted in metaphysics:

> Every entity which absorbs the passion of Werter, Tasso, Tristan or Isolde cries to us: be a man and do not imitate me! The same is true of those with philosophical passions

338 'Why? Wherefore? Whereby? Whither? Where? How? Is it not folly to continue living?' – these questions come to Zarathustra when the evening and sadness emerge in him after he had explored life and wisdom (Nietzsche 2006a, 85).

who prize the greatest individual power through knowledge of alchemists and Platonists alike (NF-1880,4[307], Nietzsche 1999 (trans. A. Shaw), vol. 9, 177).

Disillusioned with Wagner, Nietzsche wanted to sever himself from German idealism and its Platonic roots without falling into the pessimism of Schopenhauer. The philosophy of the future expounded by him was intended to allow one to look into the Dionysian abyss with the help of Apollonian images and thus he used the myth of the eternal recurrence and the idea of the *Übermensch*. This philosophy was 'inverted Platonism' (NF-1870,7[156]), that is the love of beautiful appearances stemming from the creative will to power. The eternally unsatisfied longing which was termed *eros* in antiquity was to be the keystone of Nietzsche's philosophy, appearing in the figures of Don Juan, Dionysus and Ariadne. Replacing Tristan with Don Juan in the context of philosophical passions is quite a considerable shift and it is worth examining in more depth.

In accordance with the famous thesis of Denis de Rougemont, passionate love in Western culture is based on two opposing myths – the myth of Tristan and the myth of Don Juan (De Rougemont 1968; De Rougemont 1963) – which, not coincidentally, attained their ultimate form of expression in opera (the first in Wagner, the second in Mozart). Tristan and Isolde are examples of an ideal love which is forbidden and unfulfilled. Their passion requires distance and feeds itself on obstacles (if there are none, their love creates them itself) – the object of desire is unattainable and thus the desire for the other (or rather for the idea of the other) increases (FW-60).[339] The myth of Don Juan developed in the Enlightenment in opposition to the chivalric idea of love as well as the hypocrisy of bourgeois morality. Instead of ideal love, it presents carnal love – although in this case it is also a passion of the mind and not just a pure, base instinct. The eternally unquenchable desire of Don Juan is not directed at a particular, concrete object but towards all objects in general, which he desires to possess only to discard them later. This great seducer scorns and despises all those who allow themselves to be

339 'Not yet to be dead, but no longer alive? As a spiritlike, silent, watching, gliding, hovering intermediate being? As though I were that ship that moves over the dark sea with its white sails like an enormous butterfly! Yes! To move *over* existence! That's it! That would be it! (…) When a man stands in the midst of *his own* noise (…) he is also likely to see gliding past him silent, magical creatures whose happiness and seclusion he yearns for – *women*. He almost believes that his better self lives there amongst the women: in these quiet regions even the loudest surf turns into deathly silence and life itself into a dream about life. (…) The magic and the most powerful effect of women is, to speak the language of the philosophers, action at a distance, *actio in distans*: but that requires, first and foremost – *distance*!' (Nietzsche 2001, 71).

possessed by him. He is a fraud, incapable of loving. Despite the fact that both myths remain in opposition to one another, the image of the passions described in them joins them together in a number of key attributes. In both cases, passion is an expression of both joy and pain since they both concern unhappy love which is an expression of the deepest internal suffering and in which humans made their animal instincts divine (JGB-229).[340] This passion confers a kind of a 'nobility of the soul', giving the illusion of freedom and fulfilment whilst, in reality, being a form of exalted narcissism (Ortega y Gasset 1989; De Rougemont 1968). The highest joy in both of these egotistical desires is eternal desire and not the desire to quench or assuage this longing, which in turn leads to the deepest self-torment being a form of delight (Nietzsche gave this its fullest expression in one of his dithyrambs, DD-*Ariadne;* Za-IV-*Zauberer*-1).[341] Furthermore, each of these passions is born from a desire to overthrow the existing order and may not co-exist with it (it requires the breaking of promises or loyalties); it needs to relate to a system of values which it is opposed to since it is from this opposition that it has sprung and from which it draws its strength. In this respect, both types of passion lead to self-destruction, since by destroying the system of values they oppose, they also destroy themselves; they are merely a masked desire for death.

Nietzsche assigned 'free spirits' – the philosophers of the future – the role of discoverers and experimenters whose skill would depend on their ability to uncover the basis of human habits and challenge their certainties (NF-1885,40[50]). The philosopher was to be a sceptic, a kind of fanatic of mistrust, a seducer and a fraud, who warned others about himself (MAII,WS-213). Nietzsche gives the definition of seducers to great philosophers, as well as Zarathustra (NF-1883,13[4], Za-IV-*Wissenschaft*, EH-*Vorrede*-4), and brings down philosophy to the art of

340 '[A]lmost everything we call "higher culture" is based on the spiritualization and deepening of *cruelty*. The "wild animal" has not been killed off at all; it is alive and well, it has just – become divine. Cruelty is what constitutes the painful sensuality of tragedy. And what pleases us in so-called tragic pity as well as in everything sublime, up to the highest and most delicate of metaphysical tremblings, derives its sweetness exclusively from the intervening component of cruelty. (…) But there is abundant, overabundant pleasure in your own suffering too, in making yourself suffer' (Nietzsche 2002, 120–121).

341 Ariadne cries to Dionysus who tortured her:

> Oh come back,
> My unknown god! My pain! My last –
> happiness! (Nietzsche 2006a, 206).

The inspiration for this motive of the songs, Nietzsche owed to Lou von Salomé, with whom he was unhappily in love (EH-ZA-1).

seduction (FW-99; JGB-205) and the Don Juanism of knowledge (M-327). Philosophical Don Juanism rested on the idea that the philosopher did not desire truth, goodness and beauty (Za-IV-*Schwermuth*),[342] but an eternal delusion which would allow him to perpetually maintain the burning heat of desire (Za-II-*Nachtlied*; Za-IV-*Nachtwandlerlied*). As de Rougemont summarises, 'Nietzsche pursues the obscure and obsessive image of a Truth that will not surrender but possess him forever, worthy at least of his true passion!' (De Rougemont 1963, 106)

In every aspect of knowledge there is 'that dangerous thrill of *self*-directed cruelty', which can drive the discoverer towards knowledge, even against himself (JGB-229, Nietzsche 2002, 119). The Don Juan of knowledge which Nietzsche refers to wants to desire eternally, even if it would lead humanity to its demise:

> Restless discovering and divining has such an attraction for us, and has grown as indispensable to us as is to the lover his unrequited love, which he would at no price relinquish for a state of indifference – perhaps, indeed, we too are *unrequited* lovers! Knowledge has in us been transformed into a passion which shrinks at no sacrifice and at bottom fears nothing but its own extinction (…). Perhaps mankind will even perish of this passion of knowledge! – even this thought has no power over us! (…) And finally: if mankind does not perish of a *passion* it will perish of a *weakness*: which do you prefer? This is the main question. Do we desire for mankind an end in fire and light or one in the sand? (M-429, Nietzsche 2005a, 184).

Don Juanism is not dangerous in the sexual sphere but above all in the sphere of values and spirituality. The extreme nature of Nietzsche's attack on the metaphysical-moral structure of the world rests, as de Lubac accurately points out, on the fact that it is not just an intellectual, historical or metaphysical attack – it is *a spiritual attack (*De Lubac 1998). The paradoxical nature of Nietzsche's

---

342 Old Magician mocks Zarathustra in the following words:

> 'The wooer of *truth*? You?' (…)
> 'No! Mere fool!'
> A beast, a cunning, preying, creeping beast
> That must lie,
> That must knowingly, willingly lie (…)
> …the wooer of truth?
> No! Mere fool! Mere poet!
> Merely speaking colorfully,
> From fools' masks shouting colorfully,
> Climbing around on lying word bridges,
> On colorful rainbows,
> Between false skies
> And false earths' (Nietzsche 2006a, 242–243).

philosophy lies in the fact that through undermining the foundations of Western spirituality it leads to its self-destruction:

> Nietzsche sets up values which destroy the old rules, but which are valid only because of the rules and insofar as they are felt to violate them. Should he succeed in imposing them, they would lose their meaning, since the system that measured them would no longer exist (De Rougemont 1963, 106–107).

The Nietzschean philosophical venture is reminiscent in a certain sense of his own view of Greek philosophers who he admired for their ability to charge into the abyss:

> [T]he Greeks are chariot-drivers who hold the reins of our culture, and every other culture, in their hands, yet the chariot and the horses are almost always made of too-puny stuff and unequal to the glory of their drivers, who then regard it as a joke to drive such a vehicle into the abyss – and then jump across it themselves with the leap of Achilles (GT-15, Nietzsche 2007b, 72).

Perhaps Nietzsche's intention was similar and he regarded it as a joke that his philosophical attack might hasten humanity into the abyss, only to cross it with his own leap of Achilles. Yet he himself was perhaps more reminiscent of Heracles, whom the gods punished with madness which led him to kill his children.

Nietzsche, whom Zweig called 'the pirate in the sea of German philosophy' (Zweig 2012), certainly had the power to seduce. Following in his footsteps, however, leads into the wilderness (seduce, therefore, means to deceive, to take out into the field, to lead to the side, cf. Quignard 2006). Perhaps Gombrowicz was right when he wrote that we have to accept the message of Nietzsche, and 'what's more, we have to extract everything we can from it — all conceivable depth and wealth. Yet, we cannot believe it' (Gombrowicz 2012, 230). The writer does not doubt the avenues of thought or the intuitions of philosophers such as Nietzsche, but he rejects their philosophy because of its results, which human existence cannot come to terms with or assimilate in any way. He summarises it with the words worthy of a true student of Zarathustra, '[w]e will not untie our Gordian knots with our intellect. We will cut through them with our own lives' (Gombrowicz 2012, 231). The philosophy of Nietzsche seems to be the kind of thought that one has to experience first in order to have the power to overcome it and this is ultimately no easy task.[343]

---

343 'My propositions serve as elucidations in the following way: anyone who understands me eventually recognizes them as nonsensical, when he has used them – as steps – to climb up beyond them. (He must, so to speak, throw away the ladder after he has climbed up it.) He must transcend these propositions, and then he will see the world aright', as Wittgenstein claims (Wittgenstein 2002, 6.54, 89).

References

Nietzsche's Works

Nietzsche, Friedrich. 1911a. Philosophy During the Tragic Age of the Greeks. In *The Complete Works of Friedrich Nietzsche. Vol. Two Early Greek Philosophy,* ed. O. Levy, trans. M. A. Mügge, 71–170. New York: The Macmillan Company.

Nietzsche, Friedrich. 1911b. On Truth and Falsity in Their Ultramoral Sense. In *The Complete Works of Friedrich Nietzsche. Vol. Two Early Greek Philosophy,* ed. O. Levy, trans. M. A. Mügge, 171–192. New York: The Macmillan Company.

Nietzsche, Friedrich. 1996. *Selected Letters of Friedrich Nietzsche.* Ed. and trans. Ch. Middleton. Indianapolis, Cambridge: Hackett Publishing Company.

Nietzsche, Friedrich. 1999. *Sämtliche Werke. Kritische Studienausgabe in 15 Einzelbänden.* Ed. G. Colli, and M. Montinari. München, Berlin, and New York: Walter de Gruyter.

Nietzsche, Friedrich. 2000. *Human, All Too Human I.* Trans. G. Handwerk. The Complete Works of Friedrich Nietzsche, vol. 2. Stanford: Stanford University Press.

Nietzsche, Friedrich. 2001. *The Gay Science. With a Prelude in German Rhymes and an Appendix of Songs.* Ed. B. Williams, trans. H. Nauckhoff, poems trans. by A. del Caro. Cambridge: Cambridge University Press.

Nietzsche, Friedrich. 2002. *Beyond Good and Evil. Prelude to a Philosophy of the Future.* Ed. R-P Horstmann, and J. Norman, trans. J. Norman. Cambridge: Cambridge University Press.

Nietzsche, Friedrich. 2005a. *Daybreak. Thoughts on the prejudices of morality.* Ed. M. Clark, and B. Leiter, trans. R.J. Hollingdale. Cambridge: Cambridge University Press.

Nietzsche, Friedrich. 2005b. *The Anti-Christ, Ecce Homo, Twilight of the Idols, and Other Writings.* Ed. A. Ridley, and J. Norman, trans. J. Norman. Cambridge: Cambridge University Press.

Nietzsche, Friedrich. 2006a. *Thus Spoke Zarathustra. A Book for All and None.* Ed. A. del Caro, and R. B. Pippin, trans. A. del Caro. Cambridge: Cambridge University Press.

Nietzsche, Friedrich. 2006b. *Writings from the Late Notebooks.* Ed. R. Bittner, trans. K. Sturge. Cambridge: Cambridge University Press.

Nietzsche, Friedrich. 2007a. *On The Genealogy of Morality.* Ed. K. Ansell-Pearson, trans. C. Diethe. Cambridge: Cambridge University Press.

Nietzsche, Friedrich. 2007b. *The Birth of Tragedy and Other Writings*. Ed. R. Geuss, and R. Speirs, trans. R. Speirs. Cambridge: Cambridge University Press.

Nietzsche, Friedrich. 2007c. *Untimely Meditations*. Ed. D. Breazeale, trans. R.J. Hollingdale. Cambridge: Cambridge University Press.

Nietzsche, Friedrich. 2009. *Digital critical edition of the complete works and letters*. Based on the critical text by G. Colli, and M. Montinari. Berlin, New York: de Gruyter 1967-. Ed. P D'Iorio. http://www.nietzschesource.org/texts/eKGWB.

Nietzsche, Friedrich. 2012a. *Nietzsche's Notebook of 1887–1888*. Trans. D.D. Ferrer. https://archive.org/details/NietzschesNotebookOf1887-1888.ByFredrickNietzsche1844-1900_650.

Nietzsche, Friedrich 2012b. *Nietzsche's Last Notebook 1888*. Trans. D.D. Ferrer. https://archive.org/details/NietzschesNotebookOf1887-1888.ByFredrickNietzsche1844-1900.

Nietzsche, Friedrich. 2013. *Human, All Too Human II and Unpublished Fragments from the Period of Human, All Too Human (Spring 1878-Fall 1879)*. Trans. G. Handwerk. The Complete Works of Friedrich Nietzsche, vol. 4. Stanford: Stanford University Press.

Literature

Acampora, Christa Davis. 2006. Naturalism and Nietzsche's Moral Psychology. In *A Companion to Nietzsche*, ed. K. Ansell-Pearson, 314–334. Oxford: Blackwell Publishing.

Acquinas, St Thomas. 1981. *Summa Theologica*. Benziger Bros. edition, 1947. Trans. Fathers of the English Dominican Province, digital version. http://www.ccel.org/ccel/aquinas/summa.html.

Ansell-Pearson, Keith (ed.). 2006. *A Companion to Nietzsche*. Oxford: Blackwell Publishing.

Arendt, Hannah. 1961. *Between Past and Future. Six Exercises in Political Thought*. New York: The Viking Press.

Arendt, Hannah. 1981a. *Thinking. The Life of the Mind. The Groundbreaking Investigation On How We Think*. Vol. 1. One-Volume Edition. San Diego, New York, and London: A Harvest Book.

Arendt, Hannah. 1981b. *Willing. The Life of the Mind. The Groundbreaking Investigation On How We Think*. Vol. 2. One-Volume Edition. San Diego, New York, and London: A Harvest Book.

Arendt, Hannah. 1990. *On Revolution*. London: Penguin Books.

Arendt, Hannah. 1998. *The Human Condition*. Chicago and London: The University of Chicago Press.

Arendt, Hannah. 2003. *Responsibility and Judgment*. Ed. and trans. J. Kohn. New York: Shocken Books.

Aristotle. 2000. *Nicomachean Ethics*. Ed. and trans. R. Crisp. Cambridge: Cambridge University Press.

Audi, Robert. 2013. The Nature of Normativity and the Project of Naturalizing the Normative. In *The Many Faces of Normativity*, ed. J. Stelmach, B. Brożek, M. Hohol, 15-50. Krakow: Copernicus Center Press.

Augustine, St. 1998. *The Confessions*. Trans. H. Chadwick. Oxford World's Classics, ebook version. Oxford and New York: Oxford University Press.

Augustine, St. 2000. *The City of God*. Trans. M. Dods, ebook version. New York: The Modern Library.

Augustine, St. 2003. *On the Trinity*. Ed. G.B. Matthews, trans. S. McKenna. Cambridge: Cambridge University Press.

Augustine, St. 2010. *On the Free Choice of the Will, On Grace and Free Choice, and Other Writings*. Ed. and trans. P. King. Cambridge: Cambridge University Press.

Aurelius, Marcus. 2006. *Meditations*. Trans. M. Hammond. London: Penguin Books.

Badiou, Alain. 2003. *Saint Paul. The Foundations of Universalism*. Trans. R. Brassier. Stanford: Stanford University Press.

Balke, Freidrich. 2005. From a Biopolitical Point of View: Nietzsche's Philosophy of Crime. In *Nietzsche and Legal Theory. Half-Written Laws*, ed. P. Goodrich, M. Valverde, 49–66. New York: Routledge.

Barry, Brian M. 1989. *A Treatise on Social Justice: Theories of Justice*. Vol. 1. London: Harvester-Wheatsheaf.

Benedict XVI. 2006. *Deus Caritas Est – God is love*. Encyclical Letter. http://w2.vatican.va/content/benedict-xvi/en/encyclicals/documents/hf_ben-xvi_enc_20051225_deus-caritas-est.html.

Benjamin, Walter. 1981. *Benjamin über Kafka. Texte, Briefzeugnisse, Aufzeichnungen*. Ed. H. Schweppenhäuser. Boulder: Suhrkamp.

Bergson, Henri. 1963. *The Two Sources of Morality and Religion and Morality*. Trans. R.A. Audry, and C. Brereton. Notre Dame: University of Notre Dame Press.

Berlin, Isaiah. 1969. *Four Essays on Liberty*. Oxford and New York: Oxford University Press.

Bonhoeffer, Dieter. 1959. *Prisoner for God. Letters and papers from prison*. Ed. E. Bethege, trans. R.H. Fuller. New York: The Macmillan Company.

Borges, Jorge Luis. 1964. *Labyrinths. Selected Stories & Other Writings*. Ed. D.A. Yates, and J.E. Irby. New York: An New Directions Book.

Brandt, Richard B. 1964. The Concepts of Obligation and Duty. *Mind, New Series*, 73(291): 374–393.

Brzozowski, Stanisław. 2012. *Fryderyk Nietzsche*. Ebook version. Virtualo.

Buczyńska-Garewicz, Hanna. 2010. *Człowiek wobec losu [Man Toward Fate]*. Kraków: Universitas.

Buczyńska-Garewicz, Hanna. 2013. *Czytanie Nietzschego [Reading Nietzsche]*. Kraków: Universitas.

Calasso, Roberto. 1994. *The Marriage of Cadmus and Harmony*. Trans. T. Parks, ebook version. New York: Vintage Books.

Calasso, Roberto. 2002. *Literature and the Gods*. Trans. T. Parks, ebook version. New York: Vintage Books.

Camus, Albert. 1980. Nietzsche und Nihilismus. In *Nietzsche*, ed. J. Salaquarda, trans. from French into German J. Streller, 63–77. Darmstadt: Wissenschaftliche Buchgesellschaft.

Cioran, Emil. 1970. *The Fall into Time*. Trans. R. Howard. Chicago: Quadrangle Books.

Clark, Maudemarie. 1990. *Nietzsche on Truth and Philosophy*. New York: Cambridge University Press.

Clark, Maudemarie. 1999. Nietzsche's Antidemocratic Rhetoric. *The Southern Journal of Philosophy*, 37: 119–141.

Colli, Giorgio. 1994. *Po Nietzschem [Dopo Nietzsche]*. Trans. from Italian into Polish S. Kasprzysiak. Kraków: Oficyna Literacka.

Copleston, Frederick. 1975. *Friedrich Nietzsche. Philosopher of Culture*. London: Search Press.

Cox, Christoph. 1999. *Nietzsche: Naturalism and Interpretation*. Berkeley: University of California Press.

Danto, Arthur. 1965. *Nietzsche as Philosopher*. New York: Macmillan.

Deleuze, Gilles. 2002. *Nietzsche and Philosophy*. Trans. H. Tomlison. London and New York: Continuum.

De Lubac, Henri. 1998. *The Drama of Atheist Humanism*. San Francisco: Ignatius Press.

De Rougemont, Denis. 1963. *Love Declared. Essays on the Myths of Love*. Trans. R. Howard. New York: Pantheon Books.

De Rougemont, Denis. 1968. *Miłość a świat kultury zachodniej [Love in the Western World]*. Trans. from French into Polish L. Eustachiewicz. Warszawa: Instytut Wydawniczy Pax.

De Rougemont, Denis. 1992. *Udział diabła [The Devil's Share]*. Trans. from French into Polish A. Frybes. Warszawa: Wydawnictwo Wodnika.

Derrida, Jaques. 1981. *Spurs: Nietzsche's Styles*. Trans. B. Harlow. Chicago: The University of Chicago Press.

Dilthey, Wilhelm. 1996. *Hermeneutics and the Study of History, Selected Works, vol. IV*. Ed. and trans. R.A. Makkreel, and F. Rodi. Princeton and New Jersey: Princeton University Press.

Dollinger, Hermann (ed.). 1948. Der *Briefwechsel zwischen Schiller und Goethe*. Stuttgart: Alfred Kröner Verlag.

Dostoyevsky, Fyodor. 1992. *The Brother Karamazov*. Trans. R. Pevear and L. Volokhonsky. New York: Vintage Classic.

Dostoyevsky, Fyodor. 1999. *Devils*. Trans. M.R. Katz. Oxford: Oxford University Press.

Dostoyevsky, Fyodor. 2006. *Notes from Underground*. Trans. C. Garnett. San Diego: Websters Thesausrus Edition.

Dostoyevsky, Fyodor. 2011. *The Idiot*. Trans. E. Martin, ebook version. Public Domain.

Dworkin, Ronald. 2013. *Religion Without God*. Cambridge: Harvard University Press.

Eckhart. 2009. *The Complete Mystical Works of Meister Eckhart*. Ed. and trans. M.O'C. Walshe. New York: The Crossroad Publishing Company.

Eliade Miracea. 1959. *Cosmos and History. The Myth of the Eternal Return*. Trans. W.R. Trask. New York: Harper Torchbooks.

Elias, Norbert. 2013. *The Civilizing Process. Sociogenetic and Psychogenetic Investigations*. Trans. E. Jephcott. Oxford: Blackwell Publishing.

Feinberg, Joel. 1966. Duties, Rights, and Claims. *American Philosophical Quarterly* 3(2): 137–144.

Feinberg, Joel. 1968. Collective Responsibility. *The Journal of Philosophy*, 65(21): 674–688.

Feinberg, Joel. 1970. Justice and Personal Desert. In *Doing and Deserving. Essays in the Theory of Responsibility*, 55–94. Princeton: Princeton University Press.

Filek, Jacek. 2003. *Filozofia odpowiedzialności XX wieku [The Philosophy of Responsibility of the 20. Century]*. Kraków: Znak.

Filek, Jacek (ed.). 2004. *Filozofia odpowiedzialności XX wieku. Teksty źródłowe [The Philosophy of Responsibility of the 20. Century. Source Materials]*. Kraków: Wydawnictwo Uniwersytetu Jagiellońskiego.

Foucault, Michel. 1977. Nietzsche, Genealogy, History. In *Language, Counter-Memory, Practice: Selected Essays and Interviews*, ed. D.F. Bouchard, 139–164. Ithaca: Cornell University Press.

Foucault, Michel. 1991. *Discipline and Punish. The Birth of the Prison*. Trans. A. Sheridan. New York: Vintage Books.

Frankfurt, Harry G. 1969. Altenrate Possibilities and Moral Responsibility. *The Journal of Philosophy*, 66(23): 829–839.

Frankfurt, Harry G. 1971. Freedom of the Will and the Concpet of the Person. *Journal of Philosophy*, 68(1): 5–25.

Fromm, Erich. 2001. *The Fear of Freedom*. London and New York: Routledge.

Fukuyama, Francis. 1989. The End of History. *The National Interest*, Summer: 3–18.

Gadamer, Hans Georg. 1983. Text und Interpretation. *In Gesammelte Werke, Bd. 2: Hermeneutik: Wahrheit und Methode,* 330–360. Tübingen: J.C.B. Mohr (Paul Siebeck).

Gadamer, Hans Georg. 2003. The Drama of Zarathustra. In *Nietzsche. Critical Assessments,* vol. I, ed. D.W. Conway, and P.S. Groff, trans. Z. Adamczewski, 124–137. New York, London: Routledge.

Gadamer, Hans Georg. 2013. *Truth and Method*. Trans. J. Weinsheimer, D.G. Marshall. London, New Delhi, New York and Sydney: Bloomsbury.

Gauthier, David P. 1963. *Practical Reasoning. The Structure and Foundations of Prudential and Moral Arguments and Their Exemplification in Discourse*. Oxford: Clarendon Press.

Goethe, Johann Wolfgang. 1972. *Faust*. Erster und zweiter Teil. Wiesbaden and Berlin: Reclam.

Goethe, Johann Wolfgang. 2003. *Faust*. Parts I and II. Trans. A. S. Kline, digital version. Poetry in Translation.

Gombrowicz, Witold. 2012. *Diary*. Trans. L. Vallee. New Haven and London: Yale University Press.

Goodrich, Peter, Valverde, Mariana. (eds.). 2005. *Nietzsche and Legal Theory. Half-Written Laws*. New York: Routledge.

Grimm, Jacob and Wilhelm. 1971. *Deutsches Wörterbuch*. 16 Bde. in 32 Teilbänden. Leipzig, http://woerterbuchnetz.de/cgi-bin/WBNetz/wbgui_py?sigle=DWB.

Gschwend, Lukas. 1999. *Nietzsche und Kriminalwissenschaften*. Zürich: Schulthess.

Hadot, Pierre. 1999. *Philosophy as a Way of Life. Spiritual Exercises from Socrates to Foucault*. Ed. A.I. Davidson, trans. M. Chase. Cambridge: Blackwell Publishing.

Harper, Kyle. 2013. *From Shame to Sin: The Christian Transformation of Sexual Morality in Late Antiquity.* Cambridge: Harvard University Press. Harvard University Press.

Hart, Herbert L.A. 1955. Are There Any Natural Rights? *The Philosophical Review*, 64(2): 175–191.

Hart, Herbert L.A. 1984. *Essays in Jurisprudence and Philosophy.* Oxford: Clarendon Press.

Hart, Herbert L.A. 1994. *The Concept of Law*. Oxford: Clarendon Press.

Hart, Herbert L.A. 2008. *Punishment and Responsibility.* Oxford: Oxford University Press.

Hartmann, Nicolai. 2007a. *Ethics. Moral Phenomena.* Vol. I. Trans. S. Coit. London and New York: Routledge.

Hartmann, Nicolai. 2007b. *Ethics. Moral Phenomena*. Vol. II. Trans. S. Coit. London and New York: Routledge.

Havel, Vaclav. 1985. *The Power of the Powerless*. Trans. P. Wilson, http://vaclavhavel.cz/showtrans.php?cat=clanky&val=72_aj_clanky.html&typ=HTML.

Hegel, Georg Wilhelm Friedrich. 1991. *Science of Logic*. Trans. A.V. Miller. Buffalo: Prometheus Books.

Heidegger, Martin. 1967. Who is Nietzsche's Zarathustra? *Review of Metaphysic*, 20(3): 411–431.

Heidegger, Martin. 1968. *What is Called Thinking?* Trans. F.D. Wieck and J. G. Gray. New York, Evanston and London: Harper & Row, Publishers.

Heidegger, Martin. 1977. *Sein und Zeit*. Gesamtausgabe, I. Abteilung: Veröffentlichte Schriften 1914–1970, Band 2. Frankfurt am Main: Vittorio Klostermann.

Heidegger, Martin. 1991a. *Nietzsche, Vol. I and II: The will to Power as Art, The Eternal Recurrence of the Same*. Ed. and trans. D.F. Krell. San Francisco: Harper.

Heidegger, Martin. 1991b. *Nietzsche, Vol. III and IV: The will to Power as Knowledge and as Metaphysics, Nihilism*. Ed. and trans. D.F. Krell. San Francisco: Harper.

Heidegger, Martin. 1998. *Pathmarks*. Ed. W. McNeill. Cambridge: Cambridge University Press.

Heidegger, Martin. 2002. *Off the Beaten Track*. Ed. and trans. J. Young, K. Haynes. Cambridge: Cambridge University Press.

Heidegger, Martin. 2004. *Letters 1925–1975. Hannah Arendt and Martin Heidegger*. Ed. U. Ludz, trans. A. Shields. London: Harcourt.

Heine, Heinrich. 1835. *Zur Geschichte der Religion und Philosophie in Deutschland*. Band II, http://gutenberg.spiegel.de/buch/378/1.

Hölderlin, Friedrich. 1921. *Sämtliche Werke und Briefe in fünf Bänden*. Band 4. Ed. F. Zinkernagel. Leibzig: Infel Verlag.

Hölderlin, Friedrich. 1990. *Hyperion and Selected Poems*. Ed. and trans. E.L. Santner. New York: Continuum.

Hölderlin, Friedrich. 2008. *Odes and Elegies*. Trans. N. Hoff. Middletown: Wesleyan University Press.

Holmes, Oliver Wendell Jr. 2009. *The Path of the Law*. Waiheke Island: The Floating Press.

Homer. 2007. *The Iliad*. Trans. I. Johnston. Arlington: Richer Resources Publications.

Hoy, David C. 1994. Nietzsche, Hume, and the Genealogical Method. In *Nietzsche, Genealogy, Morality. Essays on Nietzsche's Genealogy of Morals*, ed. R. Schacht, 251–268. Berkeley: University of California Press.

Huizinga, Johan. 1980. *Homo Ludens. A Study of the Play-Element in Culture*. London: Routledge & Kegan Paul.

Hume, David. 1960. *A Treatise of Human Nature*. Oxford: Clarendon Press.

Hume, David. 2002. *Dialogues Concerning Natural Religion*. Ebook version. Project Gutenberg.

Hume, David. 2010. *An Enquiry Concerning the Principles of Morals*. Ebook version. Project Gutenberg.

Husserl, Edmund. 1992. *Filozofia jako nauka ścisła [Philosophie als strenge Wissenschaft]*. Trans. from German into Polish W. Galewicz. Warszawa: Aletheia.

Ingarden, Roman. 1983. Man and Time. In *Man and Value*, trans. A. Szylewicz, 33–52. München and Wien: Philosophia Verlag.

Jaeger, Werner. 1946. *Paideia: The Ideals of Greek Culture*. Vol. 1. Trans. G. Highet. Oxford: Basil Blackwell.

Jaeger, Werner. 1948. *The Theology of the Early Greek Philosophers*. Trans. E.S. Robinson. Oxford: Clarendon Press.

Janaway, Christopher. 2006. Naturalism and Genealogy. In *A Companion to Nietzsche*, ed. K. Ansell-Pearson, 337–352. Oxford: Blackwell Publishing.

Janaway, Christopher, and Robertson, Simon (ed.). 2012. *Nietzsche, Naturalism, Normativity*. Oxford: Oxford University Press.

Janion, Maria. 2001. *Żyjąc tracimy życie. Niepokojące tematy egzystencji [In Living, We Die. Perplaxing Topics of Existence]*. Warszawa: WAB.

Jaspers, Karl. 1954. *Way to Wisdom. An Introduction to Philosophy*. New Haven and London: Yale University Press.

Jaspers, Karl. 1955. *Reason and Existenz. Five Lectures*. Trans. W. Earle. Noonday Paperbacks.

Jaspers, Karl. 1961. *Nietzsche and Christianity*. Trans. E.B. Ashton. A Gateway edition. Chicago: Regnery.

Jaspers, Karl. 1979. *Nietzsche. An Introduction to the Understanding of His Philosophical Activity*. Trans. Ch.F. Wallraff, and F. J. Schmitz. A Gateway edition. South Bend: Regnery.

Jean Paul.1992. Speech of the Dead Christ down from the Universe That There is No God. In *Jean Paul: A Reader*, ed. T. Casey, trans. E. Casey, 182. Baltimore: John Hopkins University Press.

John Paul II. 1980. *Dives in Misericordia, On the Mercy of God*. Encyclical Letter, http://www.thedivinemercy.org/message/johnpaul/encyclical.php.

Johnson, Dirk R. 2010. *Nietzsche's Anti-Darwinism*. Cambridge: Cambridge University Press.

Kafka, Franz. 1958. *Briefe*, 1902–1924. Ed. M. Brod. New York: Schocken.

Kafka, Franz. 1970. *Betrachtungen über Sünde, Leid, Hoffnung und den wahren Weg*. Frankfurt am Main: Suhrkamp Verlag. Projekt Gutenberg, http://gutenberg.spiegel.de/buch/franz-kafka-aphorismen-166/1.

Kafka, Franz. 2014. *The Trial*. Trans. D. Wyllie, ebook version. The University of Adelaide.

Kafka, Franz. 2017. *An Imperial Message*. Trans. I. Johnston. Kafka-Online 2007–2017, http://www.kafka-online.info/an-imperial-message.html.

Kahn, Charles H. 2001. *The Art and Thought of Heraclitus*. An edition of the fragments with translation and commentary. Cambridge: Cambridge University Press.

Kant, Immanuel. 1887. *The Philosophy of Law. An Exposition of the Fundamental Principles of Jurisprudence as the Science of Right*. Trans. W. Hastie. Edinburg: T. & T. Clark.

Kant, Immanuel. 1999. On the Common Saying: 'This May Be True in Theory, But It Does Not Apply in Practice'. In *Political Writings*, ed. H. Reiss, trans. H.B. Nisbet, 61–92. New York: Cambridge University Press.

Kant, Immanuel. 2000. *Critique of Pure Reason*. Ed. and trans. P. Guyer, and A. W. Wood. Cambridge: Cambridge University Press.

Kant, Immanuel. 2002a. *Critique of Practical Reason*. Trans. W.S. Pluhar. Cambridge: Hackett Publishing Company.

Kant, Immanuel. 2002b. *Groundwork for the Metaphysics of Morals*. Trans. A.W. Wood. New Haven and London: Yale University Press.

Karl, Frederick R. 1991. *Franz Kafka, Representative Man*. New York: Ticknor & Fields.

Kaufmann, Walter. 1968. *Philosopher, Psychologist, Antichrist*. Princeton: Princeton University Press.

Kaufmann, Walter. 1975. *Without Guilt and Justice. From Decidophobia to Autonomy*. New York: Delta Book.

Kerényi, Károly. 1971. *Der höhere Standpunkt. Zum Humanismus des integrale Menschen*. München: List Verlag.

Kerényi, Károly. 1997. *Dionizos. Archetyp życia niezniszczalnego [Dionysos. Urbild des unzerstörbaren Lebens*]. Trans. from German into Polish I. Kania. Kraków: Wydawnictwo Baran i Suszczyński.

Kierkegaard, Søren. 1944. *Training in Christianity.* Trans. W. Lowrie. Princeton: Princeton University Press.

Kierkegaard, Søren. 1983. *Fear and Trembling. Repetition.* Ed. and trans. H.V. and E.H. Hong. Princeton: Princeton University Press.

Kołakowski, Leszek. 1963. The Priest and the Jester. In *The Modern Polish Mind. An Anthology*, ed. M. Szczepańska Kuncewiczowa, 301–326. New York: Little Brown.

Kołakowski, Leszek. 1988. *Metaphysical Horror*. Oxford: Basil Blackwell.

Kołakowski, Leszek. 1995. *God Owes Us Nothing. A Brief Remark on Pascal's Religion and on The Spirit of Jansenism*. Chicago and London: The University of Chicago Press.

Kołakowski, Leszek. 2001. *Religion: If There Is No God*. South Bend: Saint Augustine Press.

Kołakowski, Leszek. 2005. The Demise of the Historical Man. In *My Correct Views on Everything*, ed. Z. Janowski, 216–226. South Bend: Saint Augustine's Press.

Korsgaard, Christine M. 1989. Personal Identity and the Unity of Agency: A Kantian Response to Parfit. *Philosophy & Public Affairs* 1989, 18(2): 101–132.

Korsgaard, Christine M. 1992. *The Sources of Normativity*. The Tanner Lectures on Human Values, delivered at Clare Hall, Cambridge University, November 16 and 17, 1992, http://tannerlectures.utah.edu/_documents/a-to-z/k/korsgaard94.pdf.

Krasiński, Zygmunt. 1875. *The Undivine Comedy and Other Poems.* Trans. M. Walker Cook. Philadelphia: J.P. Lippincott.

Lakoff, Georg, Johnson, Mark. 2003. *Metaphors we Live By.* London: The University of Chicago Press.

Leiter, Brian. 1994. Perspectivism in Nietzsche's Genealogy of Morals. In *Nietzsche, Genealogy, Morality. Essays on Nietzsche's 'Genealogy of Morals'*, ed. R. Schacht, 334–357. Berkley: University of California Press.

Leiter, Brian. 2002. *Nietzsche on Morality*. London: Routledge.

Leopardi, Giacomo. 2013. *Zibaldone.* Ed. M. Caesar, trans. K. Baldwin, R. Dixon, D. Gibbons, A. Goldstein, G. Slowey, M. Thom, and P. Williams, ebook version. New York: Farrar, Straus and Giroux.

Leśmian, Bolesław. 2000. *Magic and Glory of Twentieth Century Polish Poetry*. Trans. J. Langer, vol I, London.

Levi, Primo. 2015. *The Drowned and the Saved.* In *The Complete Works of Primo Levi*, trans. M.F. Moore, ebook version. Liveright.

Lewis, Clive Staples. 2001. *Mere Christianity.* Ebook version. San Francisco: HarperCollins.

Lewis, Clive Staples. 2009. *The Problem of Pain*. Ebook version. San Francisco: HarperCollins.

Linarelli, John. 2008. Nietzsche in Law's Cathedral: Beyond Reason and Postmodernism. In *Nietzsche and Law*, ed. F.J. Mootz III, P. Goodrich, 413–448. London: Ashgate.

Löwith, Karl. 1957. *Meaning in History. The Theological Implications of the Philosophy of History*. Chicago: The University of Chicago Press.

Löwith, Karl. 1969. *Von Hegel zu Nietzsche. Der revolutionäre Bruch im Denken des neunzehnten Jahrhunderts.* Frankfurt: Fisher Verlag.

Löwith, Karl. 1987. *Nietzsche*. Sämtliche Schriften. Band 6. Stuttgart: Metzler.

Löwith, Karl. 1997. *Nietzsche's Philosophy of the Eternal Recurrence of the Same*. Trans. J.H. Lomax. Berkley, London: University of California Press.

MacIntyre, Alasdair. 1994. Genealogies and Subversions. In *Nietzsche, Genealogy, Morality. Essays on Nietzsche's Genealogy of Morals*, ed. R. Schacht, 284–305. Berkeley: University of California Press.

MacIntyre, Alasdair. 2007. *After Virtue. A Study in Moral Theory*. Notre Dame: Notre Dame University Press.

Magnus, Bernd 1978. *Nietzsche's Existential Imperative*. Bloomington: Indiana University Press.

Mann, Thomas. 1959. Nietzsche's Philosophy in the Light of Recent History. In *Last Essays*, trans. R. and C. Winston, 141–177. New York: Knopf.

Mauthner, Fritz. 1923. *Wörterbuch der Philosophie. Neue Beiträge zu einer Kritik der Sprache*. Band 3. Leipzig: Meiner.

McDowell, John. 2002. Two Sorts of Naturalism. In *Mind, Value, and Reality*, 167–197. Cambridge, MA and London: Harvard University Press.

Merriam-Webster, An Encyclopedia Britannica Company. 2016. http://www.merriam-webster.com/dictionary/dignity.

Miciński, Tadeusz. 2000. *W mroku gwiazd [In the Darkness of Stars]*. Gdańsk: Tower Press.

Mill, John Stuart. 1871. *Utilitarianism*. London: Longmans, Green, Reader, and Dyer.

Milton, John. 2005. *Paradise Lost*. Ed. P. Pullman. Oxford: Oxford University Press.

Miłosz, Czesław. 1996. *Poezje wybrane. Selected Poems*. Trans. D. Brooks et al. Warszawa: Wydawnictwo Literackie.

Mootz, Francis J. III, Goodrich P. (eds.). 2008. *Nietzsche and Law*. London: Ashgate.

Mrożek, Sławomir. 1982. *Małe listy [Small Letters]*. Kraków: Wydawnictwo Literackie.

Murdoch, Iris. 1992. *Metaphysics as a Guide to Morals*. New York: Penguin Books.

Murdoch, Iris. 2014. *The Sovereignty of Good*. London and New York: Routledge.

Nussbaum, Martha. 1999. *Sex & Social Justice*. New York and Oxford: Oxford University Press.

Oppermann, Jan P. 2003. Anaximander's Rhythm and the Question of Justice. *Law and Critique* 14: 45–69.

Ortega y Gasset, Jose. 1950. *The Revolt of the Masses*. New York: New American Library.

Ortega y Gasset, Jose. 1989. *Szkice o miłości [Estudios sobre el Amor]*. Trans. from Spanish into Polish K. Kamyszew. Warszawa: Czytelnik.

Ossowska, Maria. 2004. *Podstawy nauki o moralności [The Foundations of the Studies of Morality]*. Vol. 1. Warszawa: DeAgostini.

Otto, Walter F. 1965. *Dionysus. Myth and Cult*. Trans. R.B. Palmer. Bloomington and London: Indiana University Press.

Overbeck, Franz. 2008. *Nietzsche. Zapiski przyjaciela [Souvernirs sur Nietzsche]*. Trans. into Polish T. Zatorski. Gdańsk: Słowo/ obraz terytoria.

Ovid. 2004. *Metamorphoses*. Trans. D.A. Raeburn. London: Penguin Classics.

Pascal, Blaise. 1999. *Pensees and Other Writings*. Trans. H. Levi. Oxford: Oxford University Press.

Pasley, Malcolm (ed.). 1978. *Nietzsche: Imagery and Thought*. Berkeley: University of California Press.

Petersen, Jens. 2008. *Nietzsches Genialität der Gerechtigkeit*. Berlin: De Gruyter.

Petrażycki, Leon. 2002. *O pobudkach postępowania i o istocie moralności i prawa [On the Motives of Action and the Essence of Morality and Law]*. Warszawa: Oficyna Naukowa.

Picht, Georg. 2004. Pojęcie odpowiedzialności [*Begriff der Verantwortung*]. In *Filozofia odpowiedzialności XX wieku. Teksty źródłowe [The Philosophy of Responsibility of the 20. Century. Source Materials]*, ed. J. Filek, trans. from German into Polish K. Michalski, 137–156. Kraków: Wydawnictwo Uniwersytetu Jagiellońskiego.

Pico della Mirandola, Giovanni. 2012. *Oration on the Dignity of Man. A New Translation and Commentary*. Eds. F. Borghosi, M. Papio, M. Rive. Cambridge: Cambridge University Press.

Plato. 1980. *The Symposium*. In *The Symposium and the Phaedo*. Ed. and trans. R. Larson. Wheeling: Harlan Davidson.

Plato. 1998. *Phaedrus*. In *Gorgias and Phaedrus, Rhetoric, Philosophy and Politics*. Trans. J. H. Nichols Jr. Ithaca and London: Cornell University Press.

Plato. 2002. *Protagoras*. Trans. C.C.W. Taylor. Oxford: Clarendon Press.

Plato. 2004. *Republic*. Trans. C.D.C. Reeve. Cambridge: Hackett Publishing Company.

Plato. 2008. *Timaeus*. In *Timaeus and Critias*. Trans. R. Waterfield. Oxford: Oxford University Press.

Przybylski, Ryszard. 1993. *Słowo i milczenie bohatera Polaków: Studium o 'Dziadach' [Word and Silence of a Polish Hero: The Studies on 'Dziady']*. Warszawa.

Quignard, Pascal. 2006. *Życie sekretne* [*Via secréte*]. Trans. from French into Polish K. Rutkowski. Warszawa: Vesper.

Railton, Peter. 2003. Normative Force and Normative Freedom: Hume and Kant, but Not Hume Versus Kant. In *Facts and Values. Essays Toward a Morality of Consequence*, 322–352. Cambridge: Cambridge University Press.

Ratzinger, Joseph. 2004. *Introduction to Christianity*. Trans. J.R. Foster, ebook version. San Francisco: Communio Books, Ignatianum Press.

Ratzinger, Joseph. 2008. *Jesus of Nazareth From the Baptism in the Jordan to the Transfiguration*. Trans. by A.J. Walker, ebook version. New York: Ignatianum Press.

Ratzsch, Del. 2013. Teleological Arguments for God's Existence. In *The Stanford Encyclopedia of Philosophy* (Summer 2013 Edition), ed. Edward N. Zalta, <http://plato.stanford.edu/archives/sum2013/entries/teleological-arguments/>.

Rawls, John. 1993. *Political Liberalism*. New York: Columbia University Press.

Rawls, John. 1999. *A Theory of Justice*. Cambridge: Harvard University Press.

Richardson, John. 2004. *Nietzsche's New Darwinism*. Oxford: Oxford University Press.

Ricœur, Paul. 1974. *The Conflict of Interpretations. Essays in Hermeneutics*. Evanston: Northerstern University Press.

Rilke, Reiner Maria. 2017. *The Duino Elegies*. Trans. A.S. Kline. Poetry in Translation, http://www.poetryintranslation.com/PITBR/German/Rilke.htm#anchor_Toc509812217.

Ross, Alf. 1957. TÛ-TÛ. *Harvard Law Review*, 70(5): 812–825.

Różewicz, Tadeusz. 2008. *Poezje wybrane. Selected poems*. Trans. A. Czerniawski. Warszawa: Wydawnictwo Literackie.

Rückert, Friedrich. 2017. *Die Weisheit des Brahmanen*. Berlin: Verlag der Contumax.

Russell, Bertrand. 2005. *An Inquiry into Meaning and Truth*. London and New York: Routledge.

Safranski, Rüdiger. 2007. *Romantik: Eine deutsche Affäre*. München: Carl Hanser Verlag.

Salaquarda, Jörg. (ed.). 1980. *Nietzsche*. Darmstadt: Wissenschaftliche Buchgesellschaft.

Scanlon, Thomas M. 2000. *What We Owe to Each Other*. Cambridge: Harvard University Press.

Schacht, Richard (ed.). 1983. *Nietzsche*. London: Routledge.

Schacht, Richard (ed.). 1994. *Nietzsche, Genealogy, Morality. Essays on Nietzsche's 'Genealogy of Morals'*. Berkley: University of California Press.

Scheffler, Samuel. 2008. *Boundaries and Allegiances. Problems of Justice and Responsibility in Liberal Thought*. New York: Oxford University Press.

Scheler, Max. 1985. *Formalism in Ethics*. Trans. M.S. Frings, R. Funk. Evanston: Northwestern University Press.

Scheler, Max. 1991. *Die Stellung des Menschen im Kosmos*. Bonn: Bouvier Verlag.

Scheler, Max. 1994. *Ressentiment*. Ed. A. Tallon. Milwaukee: Marquette University Press.

Scheler, Max. 1998. *Ordo amoris* w znaczeniu opisowym i normatywnym [*Ordo amoris*]. *Kwartalnik filozoficzny*, trans. From German into Polish W. Czapliński, XXVI(4): 123–158.

Schelling, Friedrich Wilhelm Joseph. 2000. *The Ages of the World*. Trans. J.M. Wirth. New York: State of New York Press.

Schiller, Friedrich. 1879. Die Braut von Messina. In *Schillers Sämmtliche Werke*. Stuttgart 1879, http://gutenberg.spiegel.de/buch/3316/7.

Schopenhauer, Arthur. 1958. *The World as Will and Representation*. Vol. 2. Trans. E.F.J. Payne. New York: Dover Publications.

Schopenhauer, Arthur. 2010. *The World as Will and Representation*. Vol. 1. Ed. and trans. J. Norman, A. Welchman, and Ch. Janaway. Cambridge: Cambridge University Press.

Schrift, Alan D. 1990. *Nietzsche and the Question of Interpretation. Between Hermeneutics and Deconstruction*. New York and London: Routledge.

Schwartländer, Johannes. 2004. Odpowiedzialność jako podstawowe pojęcie [*Verantwortung*]. In *Filozofia odpowiedzialności XX wieku. Teksty źródłowe [The Philosophy of Responsibility of the 20. Century. Source Materials]*, ed. J. Filek, trans. from German into Polish J. Filek, 173–186. Kraków: Wydawnictwo Uniwersytetu Jagiellońskiego.

Schweitzer, Albert. 1987. *The Philosophy of Civilization*. Trans. C.T. Campion. New York: Prometheus Books.

Scientific American. 1884. 5. April: 218, https://archive.org/stream/scientific-american-1884-04-05/scientific-american-v50-n14-1884-04-05#page/n11/mode/2up.

Searle, John R. 2010. *Making the Social World. The Structure of Human Civilization*. Oxford: Oxford University Press.

Sedgwick, Peter R. 2013. *Nietzsche's Justice: Naturalism in Search of an Ethics*. McGill-Queen's Studies in the History of Religion. Montreal: McGill-Queen's University Press.

Sedlacek, Tomas. 2011. *Economics of Good and Evil. The Quest for Economic Meaning from Gilgamesh to Wall Street*. Oxford: Oxford University Press.

Shakespeare, William. 1965. *The Tragedy of King Lear*. In *Five Plays,* ed. A.S. Downer. New York: Holt, Rinehart and Winston, Inc.

Shakespeare, William. 1999. *Macbeth*. Ed. A.R. Braunmuller. Cambridge: Cambridge University Press.

Shakespeare, William. 2008. *Richard III*. Ed. B. Raffel. New Haven and London: Yale University Press.

Shaw, George Bernard. 2003. *Man and Superman*. A Comedy and a Philosophy by George Bernard Shaw. A Penn State Electronic Classics Series Publication. Pennsylvania: The Pennsylvania State University.

Shestov, Lev. 1932. *In Job's Balances: On the Sources of the Eternal Truths*. Trans. C. Coventry, and C.A. Macartney. London: J.M. Dent and Sons limited.

Shestov, Lev. 1969. *Dostoyevsky, Tolstoy, and Nietzsche*. Trans. B. Martin. Ohio: Ohio University Press.

Shklar, Judith N. 1990. *The Faces of Injustice*. New Haven and London: Yale University Press.

Simmel, Georg. 2009. *Sociology. Inquire into the Construction of Social Forms*. Vol. 1 Trans. A.J. Blasi, A.K. Jacobs, and M. Kanjirathinkal. Leiden and Boston: Brill.

Simmel, Georg. 2010. *The View of Life. Four Metaphysical Essays with Journal Aphorisms*. Trans. J.A.Y. Andrews, D.N. Levine. Chicago and London: The University of Chicago Press.

Snell, Bruno. 1953. *The Discovery of the Mind. The Greek Origins of European Thought*. Cambridge: Harvard University Press.

Solomon, Robert C. 2003. *Living with Nietzsche. What the Great 'Immoralist' Has to Teach Us*. Oxford: Oxford University Press.

Soniewicka, Marta. 2017. The Origins of the Normative Concept of Human Dignity and Its Legal Applications. In *Normschaffung*, Krakauer-Augbsurger Rechtsstudien, ed. J. Stelmach, R. Schmidt, P. Hellwege, M. Soniewicka, 263–281. Warszawa: Wolters Kluwer.

Sophocles. 2012. *Antigone*. Trans. D. Taylor. London: Methuen Drama/ Bloomsbury Publishing.

Spaemann, Robert. 2009. *Odwieczna pogłoska. Pytanie o Boga i złudzenie nowożytności [Das unsterbliche Gerücht. Die Frage nach Gott und ide Täuschung der Moderne]*. Trans. from German into Polish J. Marecki. Warszawa: Oficyna Naukowa.

Stelmach, Jerzy, Brożek, Bartosz. 2011. *Methods of Legal Reasoning*. Dordrecht: Springer.

Stelmach, Jerzy, Brożek, Bartosz, Hohol, Mateusz (eds.). 2013. *The Many Faces of Normativity*. Kraków: Copernicus Center Press.

Stolleis, Michael. 2004. *Das Auge der Gerechtigkeit. Geschichte einer Metapher*. München: Verlag C.H. Beck.

Stöltzner, Michael. 2012. Taking Eternal Recurrence Scientific: A Comparative Study of Oskar Becker, Felix Hausdorff, and Abel Rey. In *Nietzsches Wissenschaftsphilosophie,* ed. H. Heit, G. Abel, M. Brusotti, 353–366. Berlin and Boston: De Gruyter.

Stróżewski, Władysław. 2013. Axiological Structure of Human Being. In *Existence, Sense and Values. Essays in Metaphysics and Phenomenology*, ed. S.T. Kołodziejczyk, 257–272. Frankfurt am Main: Peter Lang Edition.

Taubes, Jacob. 1993. *Die Politische Theologie des Paulus*. München: Wilhelm Fink Verlag.

Taylor, Charles. 2001. *Sources of The Self. The Making of the Modern Identity*. Cambridge: Harvard University Press.

Thucydides. 2009. *The Peloponnesian War*. Trans. M. Hammond. Oxford: Oxford University Press.

Vaas, Rüdiger. 2012. 'Ewig rollt das Rad des Seins': Der 'Ewige-Wiederkunfts-Gedanke' und seine Aktualität in der modernen physikalischen Kosmologie. In *Nietzsches Wissenschaftsphilosophie*, ed. H. Heit, G. Abel, M. Brusotti, 371–390. Berlin and Boston: De Gruyter.

Valverde, Mariana. 2005. Pain, Memory, and the Creation of the Liberal Legal Subject: Nietzsche on the Criminal Law. In *Nietzsche and Legal Theory. Half-Written Laws*, ed. P. Goodrich, M. Valverde, 67–88. New York: Routledge.

Voegelin, Eric. 1975. *From Enlightenment to Revolution*. Ed. J.H. Hallowell. Durham: Duke University Press.

Von Hayek, Friedrich August. 1978. *The Constitution of Liberty*. Chicago: The University Press of Chicago.

Waldron, Jeremy. 2009. *Dignity, Rank, and Rights*. The Tanner Lectures on Human Values. Delivered at University of California, Berkley, April 21–23, 2009, http://tannerlectures.utah.edu/_documents/a-to-z/w/Waldron_09.pdf.

Warnock, Mary. 1978. Nietzsche's Conception of Truth. In *Nietzsche: Imagery and Thought*, ed. M. Pasley, 33–63. Berkeley: University of California Press.

Weber, Max 1978. *Economy and Society. An Outline of the Interpretive Sociology*. Ed. and trans. G. Roth and C. Wittich. Berkeley: University of California Press.

Weil, Simone. 2002. *Gravity and Grace*. Trans. E. Crawford, and M. von der Ruhr. London and New York: Routledge.

Wellhausen, Julius. 2001. *Prolegomena zur Geschichte Israels*. Berlin: de Gruyter.

Williams, Bernard. 1973. *Problems of the Self*. Cambridge: Cambridge University Press.

Williams, Bernard. 2006. Nietzsche. In *The Sense of the Past. Essays in the History of Philosophy*, ed. M. Burnyeat, 299–337. Princeton and Oxford: Princeton University Press.

Wittgenstein, Ludwig. 1965. Wittgenstein's Lecture on Ethics. In *The Philosophical Review*, LXXIV: 3–12.

Wittgenstein, Ludwig. 1998. *Notebooks 1914–1916*. Ed. G.H. von Wright, and G.E.M. Anscombe, trans. G.E.M. Anscombe. Oxford: Basil Blackwell.

Wittgenstein, Ludwig. 1999. *Philosophical Investigations*. Trans. G.E.M. Anscombe. Oxford: Blackwell Publishing.

Wittgenstein, Ludwig. 2002. *Tractatus Logico-Philosophicus.* Trans. D.F. Pears, and B.F. McGuinness. London and New York: Routledge.

Wojtyła, Karol. 2000. *Osoba i czyn oraz inne studia antropologiczne [Person and Act and Other Anthropological Studies].* Ed. T. Styczeń, W. Chudy, J. W. Gałkowski, A. Rodziński, A. Szostek. Lublin: Wydawnictwo Towarzystwa Naukowego Katolickiego Uniwersytetu Lubelskiego.

Wojtyła, Karol. 2006. *Wykłady lubelskie [Lublinian Lectures].* Lublin: Wydawnictwo Towarzystwa Naukowego Katolickiego Uniwersytetu Lubelskiego.

Yovel, Jonathan. 2005. Gay Science as Law: an Outline for a Nietzschean Jurisprudence. In *Nietzsche and Legal Theory. Half-Written Laws*, ed. P. Goodrich, M. Valverde, 23–48. New York: Routledge.

Zweig, Stefan. 2012. *The Struggle with the Daemon: Hölderlin, Kleist, and Nietzsche.* Trans. E. and C. Paul, ebook version. London: Pushkin Press.

DIA-LOGOS
Schriften zu Philosophie und Sozialwissenschaften
Studies in Philosophy and Social Sciences

Herausgegeben von
Edited by
Tadeusz Buksiński & Piotr W. Juchacz

"*Dia-Logos. Studies in Philosophy and Social Sciences* is a peer-reviewed book series publishing valuable monographs and edited volumes on various aspects of philosophy and social sciences. The series is intended to be an interdisciplinary forum of deliberation according to our firm belief that challenges of the contemporary world require common and multilevel research. The *Dia-Logos* series does not represent a single ideology or school of thought, but it is open to different trends and various styles of reflection, trying to understand better the contemporary world. We invite the submission of manuscripts of monographs and edited volumes from academic philosophers and social scientists."

Bd. / Vol. 1 Piotr W. Juchacz / Roman Kozłowski (Hrsg.): Freiheit und Verantwortung. Moral, Recht und Politik. 2002.

Bd. / Vol. 2 Norbert Leśniewski / Ewa Nowak-Juchacz (Hrsg.): Die Zeit Heideggers. 2002.

Bd. / Vol. 3 Marek Kwiek (ed.): The University, Globalization, Central Europe. 2003.

Bd. / Vol. 4 Ewa Czerwińska-Schupp (Hrsg.): Philosophie an der Schwelle des 21. Jahrhunderts. Geschichte der Philosophie, Philosophische Anthropologie, Ethik, Wissenschaftstheorie, Politische Philosophie. 2003.

Bd. / Vol. 5 Danuta Sobczyńska / Pawel Zeidler / Ewa Zielonacka-Lis (eds.): Chemistry in the Philosophical Melting Pot. 2004.

Bd. / Vol. 6 Marek Kwiek: Intellectuals, Power, and Knowledge. Studies in the Philosophy of Culture and Education. 2004.

Bd. / Vol. 7 Marek Kwiek: The University and the State. A Study into Global Transformations. 2006.

Bd. / Vol. 8 Andrzej Przylebski (Hrsg.): Das Erbe Gadamers. 2006.

Bd. / Vol. 9 Ewa Czerwińska-Schupp (ed.): Values and Norms in the Age of Globalization. 2007.

Bd. / Vol. 10 Tadeusz Buksiński (ed.): Democracy in Western and Post-Communist Countries. Twenty Years after the Fall of Communism. 2009.

Bd. / Vol. 11 Marek Zirk-Sadowski / Mariusz Golecki / Bartosz Wojciechowski (eds.): Multicentrism as an Emerging Paradigm in Legal Theory. 2009.

Bd. / Vol. 12 Bartosz Wojciechowski: Philosophical Approach to the Interculturality of Criminal Law. 2010.

Bd. / Vol. 13 Marek Nowak / Michał Nowosielski (eds.): (Post)transformational Migration. Inequalities, Welfare State, and Horizontal Mobility. 2011.

Bd. / Vol. 14 Tadeusz Buksiński (ed.): Religions in the Public Spheres. 2011.

Bd. / Vol. 15 Bartosz Wojciechowski / Piotr W. Juchacz / Karolina M. Cern (eds.): Legal Rules, Moral Norms and Democratic Principles. 2013.

Bd. / Vol. 16 Ewa Nowak / Dawn E. Schrader / Boris Zizek (eds.): Educating Competencies for Democracy. 2013.

Bd. / Vol. 17 Tadeusz Buksiński (ed.): Identities and Modernizations. 2013.

Bd. / Vol. 18 Karolina M. Cern: The Counterfactual Yardstick. Normativity, Self-Constitutionalisation and the Public Sphere. 2014.

Bd. / Vol. 19 Vito Breda / Lidia Rodak (eds.). Diverse Narratives of Legal Objectivity. An Interdisciplinary Perspective. 2016.

Bd. / Vol. 20 Marek Woszczek: Platonic Wholes and Quantum Ontology. Translated by Katarzyna Kretkowska. 2015.

Bd./Vol. 21 Roman Hauser / Marek Zirk-Sadowski / Bartosz Wojciechowski (eds.): The Common European Constitutional Culture. Its Sources, Limits and Identity. 2016.

Bd./Vol. 22 Aigerim Raimzhanova: Hard, Soft, and Smart Power – Education as a Power Resource. 2017.

Bd./Vol. 23 Roberto Franzini Tibaldeo / Graziano Lingua (eds.): Philosophy and Community Practices. 2017.

Bd./Vol. 24 Marta Soniewicka: After God – The Normative Power of the Will from the Nietzschean Perspective. 2017.

www.peterlang.com